W9-AMP-375

THE ENGLISH DICTIONARY
FROM CAWDREY TO JOHNSON
1604-1755

THE
English Dictionary
FROM CAWDREY
TO JOHNSON
1604-1755

BY

DE WITT T. STARNES
UNIVERSITY OF TEXAS

AND

GERTRUDE E. NOYES
CONNECTICUT COLLEGE

CHAPEL HILL · 1946
THE UNIVERSITY OF NORTH CAROLINA PRESS

FOREWORD

ABOUT TEN YEARS AGO THE AUTHORS OF *The English Dictionary from Cawdrey to Johnson (1604-1755)* became interested, each independently of the other, in investigating the beginnings and the development of English lexicography. Having each published an essay on the subject and having discovered a common objective, they decided that, in the study of so large and complicated a body of materials, it would be wise economy to pool their efforts. The result is this book, the worth of which we leave others to judge.

The method is historical. Questions of philology and etymology have been discussed only in so far as they contribute to the history of the English dictionary in the seventeenth and the first half of the eighteenth centuries. Of the dictionaries, expositors, and glossographies which were printed between 1604 and 1755, the authors give, within the stated limitations, as full, specific, and accurate information as they have been able to ascertain. The qualifications of dictionary-makers for the tasks which they set for themselves, their expressed aims (as far as possible in the language of the compilers themselves), their sources, their methods of compilation, the interrelationships of the various texts, the relation of English dictionaries to contemporary bilingual dictionaries, the readers for whom each work is intended, the vogue and usefulness of the various dictionaries—these are among the more important topics treated in this book. The authors thus provide a complete history, as far as information is available, of each dictionary in its numerous ramifications, and trace the slow and uncertain growth toward a definitive and authoritative dictionary of the English language.

v

The need for such a book is fairly obvious: no comprehensive and analytical study of the development of the English dictionary has hitherto been made. To say so is not to disparage the pioneer work of Henry B. Wheatley, Sir James A. H. Murray, Dr. Percy W. Long, Mr. M. M. Mathews, Professor Arthur G. Kennedy, Mr. Ernest Weekley, and others (see Bibliography and Notes, *passim*). To the work of these scholars, the authors are admittedly indebted. Valuable as their work is, however, it must be stated that no one of these attempted or even aimed to give an exhaustive account of the growth of English lexicography. They prepared the way for later students. The present volume carries on the work so well begun, and, we think, supplies a need which our predecessors in the field foresaw.

While the title of our book indicates that the account extends from Cawdrey to Johnson (1604-1755), we wish to make clear that we do not here include a study of Johnson's *Dictionary*. To treat adequately Johnson's relations to his predecessors, to analyze and evaluate his work, to discuss the abridgments and revisions, and to consider, even in a limited way, the criticism and controversy arising from each revision or Johnsonian offshoot would be to extend this study almost twofold. It seemed wise therefore in the present work to restrict our treatment to the English dictionary before Johnson.

In the division of labor, Mr. Starnes is responsible for the chapters covering the period from 1604 to 1700, and Miss Noyes for the remaining chapters of the text proper. For the Appendices, Mr. Starnes wrote the essay on medieval and Renaissance vocabularies, and Miss Noyes that on cant lexicography. The Bibliography and the Census of English dictionaries in American libraries are the joint work of the authors. It must be added that this book was planned in collaboration and that the aims and methods were freely discussed and agreed upon before the first chapter was written. The author of the first half of the text owes much to the author of the second half; and there has been mutual criticism and suggestion, resulting, the authors think, in a better book than either might have achieved working alone.

Acknowledgments of indebtedness to other writers on English lexicography are made, as far as recognized, at the appropriate places in the text. To their own articles previously published on aspects of English dictionaries, the authors owe a general, sometimes a specific debt. Miss Noyes has made routine use of her essays in *Publications of the Modern Language Association, Notes and Queries,* and *Modern Language Notes,* and is grateful to the editor of *Studies in Philology* for permission to reprint her article on cant lexicography (Appendix II). For permission to use, in much revised form, matter from two of his articles, Mr. Starnes is indebted to the University of Texas *Studies in English.* (For data on all articles here referred to, see Appendix III, Bibliography.)

The authors have, of necessity, ranged widely in gathering materials for this study. Mr. Starnes has worked at the Huntington, the Folger, the Library of Congress, the Rare Book Collection of the University of Texas, the British Museum, and the Bodleian. While Miss Noyes has had much assistance from the above libraries as well as from the New York Public, the University of Chicago, the University of Illinois, Stanford University, and the Newberry libraries, she has worked mainly in the Harvard, Yale, Connecticut College, Boston Public, and Bodleian libraries. In all of these libraries the authors have experienced unfailing courtesy and helpfulness from librarians and assistants.

For generous assistance in the compilation of the census of English dictionaries in American libraries, the authors wish to express their gratitude to Mr. George A. Schwegmann, Jr., Director of Union Catalogs, Library of Congress, and to Miss Julia Harris, Reference Librarian of the University of Texas.

D. T. S.

G. E. N.

CONTENTS

THE ENGLISH DICTIONARY
FROM CAWDREY TO JOHNSON
1604-1755

A

Table Alphabeticall, con-
teyning and teaching the true
writing, and vnderstanding of hard
vsuall English wordes, borrowed from
the Hebrew, Greeke, Latine,
or French. &c.

With the interpretation thereof by
plaine English words, gathered for the benefit &
helpe of Ladies, Gentlewomen, or any other
vnskilfull persons.

Whereby they may the more easilie
and better vnderstand many hard English
wordes, vvhich they shall heare or read in
Scriptures, Sermons, or elswhere, and also
be made able to vse the same aptly
themselues.

Legere, et non intelligere, neglegere est.
As good not read, as not to vnderstand.

AT LONDON,
Printed by I. R. for Edmund Wea-
ner, & are to be sold at his shop at the great
North doore of Paules Church.
1 6 0 4.

Title-page of Robert Cawdrey's *A Table Alphabeticall*. Small octavo.
The first edition of the first English dictionary.

To the Reader.

of place, and applying them to diuers matters, without all diſcretion.

If thou be deſirous (gentle Reader) rightly and readily to vnderſtand, and to profit
by this Table, and ſuch like, then thou muſt
learne the Alphabet, to wit, the order of the
Letters as they ſtand, perfecſly without
booke, and where euery Letter ſtandeth: as
(b) neere the beginning, (n) about the mid-
deſt, and (t) toward the end. Nowe if the
word, which thou art deſirous to finde, begin with (a) then looke in the beginning of
this Table, but if with (v) looke towards
the end. Againe, if thy word beginne with
(ca) looke in the beginning of the letter (c)
but if with (cu) then looke toward the end
of that letter. And ſo of all the reſt. &c.

And further vnderſtand, that whereas all
ſuch words as are deriued & drawne frō the
Greek, are noted with theſe letter, (g). And
the French are marked thus (§) but ſuch
words as are deriued from the latin, haue no
marke at all.

A Table Alphabeticall,

contayning and teaching the true
writing, and vnderſtanding of hard
vſuall Engliſh words. &c.

(∵)

(k) ſtandeth for a kind of.
(g. or gr.) ſtandeth for Greeke.
The French words haue this (§) before them.

A

§ **A** Bandon, caſt away, oꝛ yǽlde vp, to
leaue, oꝛ foꝛſake.

Abaſh, bluſh.

abba, father.

§ abbeſſe, abbateſſe, Miſtris of a Nunne-
rie, comfoꝛters of others.

§ abbettors, counſelloꝛs.

aberration, a going a ſtray, oꝛ wandering.

abbreuiat, ⎱ to ſhoꝛten, oꝛ make
§ abbridge, ⎰ ſhoꝛt.

§ abbut, to lie vnto, oꝛ boꝛder vpon, as one
lands end méets with another.

abecedarie, the oꝛder of the Letters, oꝛ hee
that vſeth them.

aberration, a going aſtray, oꝛ wandering.

§ abet, to maintaine.

B.   § abdi-

An opening in Cawdrey's *A Table Alphabeticall* (1604).

AN ENGLISH EXPOSITOUR,

Or Compleat

DICTIONARY:

TEACHING

The Interpretation of the hardest words, and most usefull terms of Art, used in our Language.

First set forth by *J. B.* D^r of Physick.

Ἔργον γ' ἐδὲν ὄνειδ Θ.

And now the Sixth time Revised, Corrected, and very much augmented with several Additions, *viz.*

A new and copious Supply of Words.

An *Index* directing to the hard Words, by prefixing the common Words before them in an Alphabetical Order.

A brief *Nomenclator*, containing the Names of the most renowned Persons among the Antients, whether Gods and Goddesses (so reputed) Heroes, or Inventours of profitable Arts, Sciences and Faculties.

With divers memorable things out of ancient *History, Poetry, Philosophy,* and *Geography.*

By a Lover of the Arts.

CAMBRIDGE,

Printed by *John Hayes*, Printer to the University, and are to be sold by *G. Sawbridge* at the Bible on Ludgate-hill, *London*, 1680.

Title-page of the sixth edition of John Bullokar's
English Expositor. Small octavo.

THE
SECOND PART
OF
The English Translator.

AB

TO Abate or take away. *Deduct, Deduce.*

Abominable, *Sacrilegious, Detestable.*

to abound, *Exuperate.*

to abound overmuch, *Super-abound.*

too great abundance, *Superfluity, prostuence, uberty, confluence.*

unlawfull Absence from ones place or charge, *Non-residency.*

he which is absent from his charge, *Nonresident.*

which offereth Abuse, *Abusive.*

Accent in tune, *Tone, Symphony.*

Accent in words, *Euphony.*

AC

to accompany one, *Associate.*

dishonestly to accompany a woman, *Constuprate.*

accomplishment, *Peraction.*

to accompt, *Computate.*

an accompt, *Computation.*

to cast an accompt or reckon, *Calculate.*

a casting of accompt, *Calculation.*

evenneffe of accompt, *Pariation.*

to accuse, *Appeach.*

a false accuser, *Sycophant.*

falsly to accuse one, *Calumniate.*

a false accusation, *Calumniation, delation, calumny, category.*

Acknow-

AD

Acknowledgement, *Agnition.*

Acknowledging, *Recognizance.*

to acknowledge, *Agnize.*

to acquit one, *Retaliate, Assoyl.*

a verbal acquaintance, *Accepulation.*

two hundred acres of Land, *Hide of Land.*

to enter an Action against one, *Commence.*

Activity, *Gnavity, Strenuity, Dexterity.*

done with activity or wantonly, *Gesticulated.*

Acts of Princes, *Gests.*

to adde, *Insert.*

any thing added, *Additament, Insertation, Addition.*

Adjoyning, *Adjacent.*

the chief advantage or place, *Prerogative, Priority.*

an Adversary to Christ, *Antichrist.*

the bearing of adversities patiently, *Magnanimity, Fortitude.*

Advisement, *Deliberation.*

Affinity by marriage, *Epigamy.*

to affirm, *Astipulate, Avouch.*

AG

which affirmeth, *Affirmative.*

to affirm with earnestnesse, *Protest.*

an earnest affirming, *Protestation.*

an affirming, *Asseveration, Assertion.*

Afraid, *Agast.*

Afrighted, *Appal'd.*

Again, *Eften.*

to do again, *Iterate, Reiterate.*

a doing again, *Reiteration, Iteration.*

of one Age, *Coetanes.*

Agreeablenesse or congruence, *Omology.*

Agreeable, *Congruent, correspondent, consonant.*

to agree, *Concur, cohere, condog, condescend.*

to agree in one, *Sympathize.*

an agreement in one, *Unanimity.*

an agreement, *Correspondency, Astipulation, concordancy, coherence, congruity.*

to make an agreement, *Mediate, compromise.*

an agreement made for two, *Mediation.*

which maketh an agreement, *Mediatour.*

an

An opening at the beginning of the Second Part of Henry Cockeram's *English Dictionarie*, ninth edition (1650). Small octavo.

THE THIRD PART, TREA-TING OF GODS AND GOD-
desses, Men and Women, Boyes and Maids, Giants and Devils, Birds and Beasts, Monsters and Serpents, Wells and Rivers, Herbs, Stones, Trees, Dogs, Fishes, and the like.

Of Beasts.

Armadillo, a Beast in India, like unto a young Pig, covered over with small shels, like unto Armour, it lives like a Mole in the ground.

Baboon, A Beast like an Ape, but far bigger.

Beaver, A very hot Beast of nature, living much in the water, his stones are much used in Physick, and of great esteem, but not so much esteemed as his skin.

Bore of Pannonia, the cruellest of all Bores.

Buffe, A very fierce beast, much like unto a Bull, having a very long mane.

Chamelion, the least of all Beasts, which breeds Egges or spawn, it changeth it self into any colour that it sits on, except white and red: therefore unconstant men are sometimes called Chamelions; it is said, it only lives by the ayr.

Crocodile, A Beast hatched of an Eg, yet some of them grow to a great bignesse, as ten, twentie, or thirty foot in length, it hath cruell teeth, and a scaly back, with very sharp claws on his feet; if it see a man afraid of him, it will eagerly pursue him, but on the contrary, if he be assaulted, he will shun him. Having eaten the body of a man, it will weep over the head, but in fine eat the head also; thence came the Proverb, She shed Crocodile tears, *viz.* fained tears.

T   *Ermynes*,

The first page of the Third Part of Henry Cockeram's
English Dictionarie, ninth edition (1650).

a mend

GLOSSOGRAPHIA:

OR A

DICTIONARY,

Interpreting all such

Hard Words,

Whether *Hebrew, Greek, Latin,*
Italian, Spanish, French, Teutonick,
Belgick, British or *Saxon;* as are now used in
our refined *English Tongue.*

Also the Terms of *Divinity, Law, Phy-*
sick, Mathematicks, Heraldry, Anatomy, War,
Musick, Architecture; and of several other *Arts*
and *Sciences* Explicated.

With *Etymologies, Definitions,* and
Historical Observations on the same.

Very useful for all such as desire to
understand what they read.

By *T. B.* of the *Inner-Temple,* Barrester.

LONDON:

Printed by *Tho. Newcomb,* and are to be sold by *Hum-*
phrey Moseley, at the Prince's Arms in *St. Pauls*
Church-yard, and *George Sawbridge* at the Bible
on *Ludgate-hil.* 1656.

Title-page of the first edition of Thomas Blount's *Glossographia*. Octavo.

Illacerable (*illacerabilis*) that cannot be torn or rent in pieces.

Illachrymation (*illachrymatio*) a weeping or bewailing.

Illaqueate (*illaqueo*) to bind, snare or entangle.

Illatebration (*illatebratio*) a hiding, or seeking of corners.

Illation (*illatio*) an inference, conclusion, a reason or allegation that inforceth; a bringing in of a matter.

Illatration (*illatratio*) a barking against one.

Illecebrous (*illecebrosus*) that enticeth or allureth.

Illegitimate (*illegitimus*) unlawful, base-born, bastard.

Illepid (*illepidus*) without delectation or Grace, unpleasant.

Illicitous } (*illicitus*) un-
Illicite } lawful, without warrant.

Illigation (*illigatio*) an inwrapping or intangling.

Illimitable, that cannot be limited or bounded.

Illogical, not logical, not according to the rules of Logick.

Illucidate (*illucido*) to enlighten or give light, to cleer, or explicate cleerly.

Illuminous (*illuminosus*) without light.

Illusion (*illusio*) a mocking or scorning.

Illusory (from *Illusor*, a mocker) that mocketh or scorneth.

Illutible (*illutibilis*) that cannot be purged from filth.

Imbargo or **Embargo** (Span.) a stop or stay; an usual word among our Merchants, when their ships or Merchandizes are arrested upon any occasion.

Imbecillity (*imbecillitas*) weakness, feebleness. And some use the word *imbecillated* for weakened or enfeebled.

Imbellick (*imbellis*) unaccustomed to war, nothing manly, cowardly, *Feltham*.

Imber days, or **Imber weeks** (*quatuor tempora*) which weeks are four in the yeer, and anciently, Wednesday, Friday and Saturday in each fasted, according to these old Verses,

Post cineres, Pentec. post crucem, postque Luciam,
Mercurii, Veneris, Sabatho, jejunia sient.

That is, the next Wednesday after *Cineres* or *Ash-wednesday*, after Pentecost, i. *Whitsunday*, after holy-Rood-day, or the Exaltation of the Cross; and the next Wednesday after St. *Lucies* day in December. See Ember.

Imbibe (*imbibo*) to receive in, to drink in.

Imbibition (from *imbibo*) a drinking or receiving in.

Imbossement. See *Embossement*.

Imbossed

A page from Blount's *Glossographia* (1656).

Engraved title-page of Edward Phillips' *The New World of English Words*. Small folio.

THE
NEW WORLD
OF
ENGLISH WORDS:
Or, a General
DICTIONARY:

Containing the Interpretations of such hard words as are derived from other Languages; whether *Hebrew, Arabick, Syriack, Greek, Latin, Italian, French, Spanish, British, Dutch, Saxon,* &c. their Etymologies and perfect Definitions:

Together with

All those Terms that relate to the Arts and Sciences; whether *Theologie, Philosophy, Logick, Rhetorick, Grammer, Ethicks, Law, Natural History, Magick, Physick, Chirurgery, Anatomy, Chimistry, Botanicks, Mathematicks, Arithmetick, Geometry, Astronomy, Astrology, Chiromancy, Physiognomy, Navigation, Fortification, Dialling, Surveying, Musick, Perspective, Architecture, Heraldry, Curiosities, Mechanicks, Staticks, Merchandize, Jewelling, Painting, Graving, Husbandry, Horsemanship, Hawking, Hunting, Fishing,* &c.

To which are added

The significations of Proper Names, Mythology, and Poetical Fictions, Historical Relations, Geographical Descriptions of most Countries and Cities of the World; especially of these three Nations wherein their chiefest Antiquities, Battles, and other most Memorable Passages are mentioned; as also all other Subjects that are useful, and appertain to our English Language.

A Work very necessary for Strangers, as well as our own Countrymen, for all Persons that would rightly understand what they discourse, write, or read.

Collected and published by E. P.

For the greater honour of those Learned Gentlemen and Artists that have been assistant in the most Practical Sciences, their Names are affixed in the next Page.

Dedit Deus his quoque finem. Virgil.

London, Printed by *E. Tyler*, for *Nath. Brooke* at the Sign of the Angel in Cornhill, 1658.

Title-page of Edward Phillips' *The New World of English Words.*

THE
NEW WORLD
OF
WORDS:
OR,
𝕺niverſal 𝕰ngliſh 𝕯ictionary.

CONTAINING

An Account of the Original or Proper Senſe, and Various Significations of all Hard WORDS derived from other Languages, *viz. Hebrew, Arabick,
Syriack, Greek, Latin, Italian, French, Spaniſh, Britiſh, Saxon, Daniſh, Dutch,* &c.
as now made uſe of in our *Engliſh* Tongue.

Together with

A Brief and Plain Explication of all Terms relating to any of the
Arts and Sciences, either Liberal or Mechanical, *viz. Grammar, Rhetorick,
Logick, Theology, Law, Metaphyſicks, Ethicks, Natural Philoſophy, Phyſick, Sur-
gery, Anatomy, Chymiſtry, Pharmacy, Botanicks, Arithmetick, Geometry, Aſtronomy,
Aſtrology, Coſmography, Geography, Hydrography, Navigation, Architecture, Forti-
fication, Dialling, Surveying, Gauging, Opticks. Catoptricks, Dioptricks, Perſpective,
Muſick, Mechanicks, Staticks, Chiromancy, Phyſiognomy, Heraldry, Merchandize,
Maritime* and *Military Affairs, Agriculture, Gardening, Handicrafts, Jewelling,
Painting, Carving, Engraving, Confectionery, Cookery, Horſemanſhip, Hawking,
Hunting, Fowling, Fiſhing,* &c,

To which is Added,

The Interpretation of Proper Names of Men and Women, that derive their
Original from the above-mention'd Ancient and Modern Tongues, with thoſe
of Writs and Proceſſes at Law: Alſo the *Greek* and *Latin* Names of divers ſorts
of *Animals, Plants, Metals, Minerals,* &c. and ſeveral other remarkable Matters
more particularly expreſs'd in the *Preface.*

Compiled by EDWARD PHILLIPS, *Gent.*

The **Sixth Edition**, Reviſed, Corrected, and Improved; with the Addition of
near Twenty Thouſand Words, from the beſt Authors, Domeſtick and Foreign,
that treat of the ſeveral Subjects:

By J. K. Philobibl.

*A Work very neceſſary for Strangers, as well as our own Country-men, in order to the
right underſtanding of what they Speak, Write, or Read.*

Labor improbus omnia vincit. HOR.

LONDON:

Printed for **J. Phillips**, at the *King's-Arms* in *S. Paul's Church-Yard*; **H. Rhodes**,
at the *Star*, the Corner of *Bride-Lane*, in *Fleet-ſtreet*; and **J. Taylor**, at the
Ship in *S. Paul's Church-Yard.* MDCCVI.

Title-page of Edward Phillips' *The New World of Words*,
revised and augmented by John Kersey. Folio.

Cho: Miller.

An. Univerſal Etymological
Engliſh Dictionary:

COMPREHENDING

The Derivations of the Generality of Words in the *Engliſh* Tongue, either Antient or Modern, from the Antient *Britiſh*, *Saxon*, *Daniſh*, *Norman* and Modern *French*, *Teutonic*, *Dutch*, *Spaniſh*, *Italian*, *Latin*, *Greek*, and *Hebrew* Languages, each in their Proper Characters.

AND ALSO

A Brief and clear Explication of all difficult Words derived from any of the aforeſaid Languages; and Terms of Art relating to Anatomy, Botany, Phyſick, Pharmacy, Surgery, Chymiſtry, Philoſophy, Divinity, Mathematicks, Grammar, Logick, Rhetorick, Muſick, Heraldry, Maritime Affairs, Military Diſcipline, Horſemanſhip, Hunting, Hawking, Fowling, Fiſhing, Gardening, Husbandry, Handicrafts, Confectionary, Carving, Cookery, *&c.*

Together with

A Large Collection and Explication of Words and Phraſes uſ'd in our Antient Statutes, Charters, Writs, Old Records, and Proceſſes at Law; and the Etymology and Interpretation of the Proper Names of Men, Women, and Remarkable Places in *Great Britain:* Alſo the Dialects of our different Counties.

Containing many Thouſand Words more than either *Harris*, *Philips*, *Kerſey*, or any *Engliſh* Dictionary before Extant.

To *which is Added* a Collection of our moſt Common Proverbs, with their Explication and Illuſtration.

The wholeWORK compil'd and Methodically digeſted, as well for the Entertainment of the Curious, as the Information of the Ignorant, and for the Benefit of young Students, Artificers, Tradeſmen and Foreigners who are deſirous thorowly to underſtand what they Speak, Read, or Write.

By N. BAILEY, Φιλολόγ☉.

LONDON:

Printed for E. BELL, J. DARBY, A. BETTESWORTH, F. FAYRAM, J. PEMBERTON, J. HOOKE, C. RIVINGTON, F. CLAY, J. BATLEY, and E. SYMON. 1721.

Title-page of Nathan Bailey's *An Universal Etymological Dictionary*. Octavo.

faging upon a walk or trot, his far fore-leg croffes or over-laps the other fore-leg every time or motion, F.

CHE'VALRY [of *chevalier*, F.] knighthood

CHEVA'NTIA [Old Law] a loan of money upon credit.

CHEVAL }
CHEVAUX DE FRIZE }
[Mil. Aff.] a fort of turn-pikes, being fpars of wood, about 10 or 12 foot long, and a foot diameter cut into 6 faces, and bored through ; each hole is arm'd with a fhort fpike, fhod with iron at each end about an inch diameter, 6 foot long and 6 inches diftant one from another ; fo that it points out every way, and is ufed in ftopping fmall overtures or open places, or placed in breaches, alfo as a defence againft horfe.

CHEVR'LLE [in *Heraldry*] fignifies ftreaming, *i. e.* a ftream of light darting from a comet or blazing ftar, vulgarly called the Beard, according to the figure annexed.

CHEVRETTE [in *Mil. Aff.*] an engine for raifing guns or mortars into their carriages ; it is made of 2 pieces of wood about 4 foot long, ftanding upright upon a third which is fquare ; they are about a foot afunder and parallel, being pierced with holes exactly oppofite to one another, with a bolt of iron, which being put thro' thefe holes, higher or lower at pleafure, with ferves, with a handfpike, which takes its poife over this bolt, to raife the gun or mortar.

CHEVELRU'RES [with *French Botan.*] the fibres or ftrings of trees or plants.

CHE'VERIL Leather, a fort of foft tender leather, made of the fkin of wild goats.

CHEVERI'LLUS [Old Law] a young cock or cockling.

CHE'VILS [in a *Ship*] fmall pieces of timber nailed on the infide of it to faften the ropes called fheets or tacks.

CHE'VIN [*chevefne*, F.] the Chub fifh.

CHEVISA'NCE [of *chevir* or *vifier a chef*, F.] a bargain or contract ; alfo an unlawful contract in point of ufury, or a compofition between debtor and creditor, F. L. Term.

CHEVITIÆ }
CHEVISÆ }
[Old Law Records] heads of ploughed lands.

CHE'VRON }
CHE'VERON }
[in *Heraldry*] is an ordinary formed of a twofold line, fpire-wife or pyramidical, the foundation being in the dexter and finifter bafe-points of the efcutcheon, and the acute point of the fpire near to the top of the efcutcheon, as in the figure annexed.

This ordinary refembles a pair of barge-couples or rafters, fuch as carpenters fet on the highest part of a houfe for fupporting the roof, and betokens the achieving fome bufinefs of moment, or furnifhing fome chargeable or memorable work. Some fay it reprefents *Protection*, others fay *Conftancy*; fome the fpurs of knights, others the head-dress of prieftefses, &c.

Per CHEVRON [in *Heraldry*] or *Party per Chevron*, is when the field is divided only by two fingle lines, rifing from the two bafe-points and meeting in a point above, as the Chevron does.

CHE'VRON *abaifs'd* [*Heraldry*] is when its point does not approach the head of the chief, nor reach farther than the middle of the coat.

CHE'VRON *broke*, is when one branch is feparated into two pieces.

CHE'VRON *cloven*, is when the upper point is taken off fo that the two pieces only touch at one of the angles.

CHE'VRON *couched*, is when the point is turned downwards on one fide of the efcutcheon.

CHEVRON *divided*, is when the branches are of feveral metals, or when metal is oppofed to colour.

CHEVRON *inverted*, is when the point is towards the point of the coat, and its branches towards the chief.

CHEVRON *mutilated*, is when it does not touch the extremes of the coat.

CHE'VRONED [in *Heraldry*] is when it is filled with an equal number of Chevrons.

Counter-CHEVRONED [in *Heraldry*] is when a Chevron is fo divided, that colour is oppofed to metal.

CHEVRONE'L [in *Heraldry*] is the diminutive of Chevron, and as fuch contains only one half of the Chevron, as in the figure annexed.

CHEVRONNE'E }
CHEVRONNY'S }
fignifies the parting of the fhield feveral times Chevron-wife, as in the figure above.

'To CHEW [ceopian, *Sax.* kamen, *Teut.*] to grind or break the food between the teeth.

CHEW'ING Balls [with *Farriers*] certain balls compofed of feveral forts of drugs, to be chewed by horfes for the recovery of loft appetite.

CHIA'VE [in *Mufick Books*] is a cliff, a term or character of Mufick, *Ital.*

CHIAU's, an officer of the *Turkifh* court, who does the duty of an ufher ; and alfo an ambaffadour to foreign courts.

CHI'BOL, a fmall fort of onion.

CHICA'NE }
CHICA'NRY }
[of *cicum* the fkin of a pomegranate, according to *menage*; whence the *Spaniards* derive their *chico*, little, flender: chicane, being converfant about trifling things] in *Law* it is an abufe of judiciary proceedings, either with defign to delay the caufe, or to impofe on the judge or the contrary party, a wrangling, crafty manner of pleading a caufe with tricks, quirks and fetches, the perplexing or fplitting a caufe, pettifogging, F.

CHICA'NE }
CHICA'NERY }
[in the *Schools*] is ufed to import vain fophifms, fubtleties and diftinctions, with defign to obfcure truth and protract difputes.

To CHICA'NE [*chicaner*, F.] to perplex or puzzle a caufe ; to ufe quirks, tricks or fetches.

CHICHAR [לגד, *Heb.*] a talent of filver worth 375 pound, of gold 4500.

CHI'CHLINGS, the pulfe called everlafting peas.

A CHICK }
A CHI'CKEN }
[cicen, *Sax.* kicken, *Du.*] the young of a hen.

To CHIDE [cican, *Sax.*] to rebuke or taunt at ; alfo to brawl or brangle.

A CHIDER [cideſte, *Sax.*] a reprehender, a rebuker.

CHIEF [*chef*, F.] firft, principal, foveraign.

Lands held in CHIEF. See *Capite*.

CHIEF [in *Mil. Affairs*] a commander in chief, a general.

CHI'DING [of cican, *Sax.*] rebuke, &c.

A CHIEF [in *Heraldry*, *chef*, F.] is an honourable ordinary, and that which takes up the upper part of the efcutcheon, and reprefents a man's head, and the ornaments us'd on it both by ancients and moderns.

The *Chief*, as all other honourable ordinaries do, muft take up juft one third part of the efcutcheon, efpecially if they be alone in the fhield ; but if there be more of them they muft be leffened in proportion to their number, and the fame, when they are canton'd, attended and bordered upon fome other figures.

In CHIEF, fignifies any thing born in the chief part or top of the efcutcheon.

A CHIEF *Chevron'd*, *bended* or *paled*, is when it has a *Chevron*, *Pale* or *Bend* contiguous to it, and of the fame colour with itfelf.

A CHIEF *fupported*, is when the two thirds at the top are of the colour of the field, and that at bottom of a different colour.

CHIE'FLY [of *chef*, F.] principally.

CHIE'FTAIN, a captain or general.

CHIE'GO [among the *Barbadians*] a fmall infect that gets into the feet, and is very troublefome.

CHIE'RE [with *Florifts*] the *leucoium luteum*, or wall-flower.

CHIE'SE [in *Mufick Books*] is a mark fet to mufick to diftinguifh that defigned for churches, from that which is defigned for chambers or private conforts, as *fonata di chiefa*, is a fonata for the chapel, *Ital.*

CHI'LBLAIN [of *chill* and *blain*] a fort of fwelling occafioned by cold.

A CHILD [cild, *Sax.*] a fon or daughter.

CHI'LDHOOD [cild-had, *Sax.*] the ftate of a child.

CHILDERMASS-*day* [of cild, a child, and mæſſ, *Sax.* the mafs] a feaft obferved on the 28th of *December*, in commemoration of the children of *Bethlehem*, murthered by *Herod*.

CHI'LDING, bringing forth children, child-bearing.

CHILDING [with *Botanifts*] a term ufed of plants, when their offspring exceeds the number of their ordinary kind, as childing daifies, &c.

CHI'LDINGNESS [cild, *Sax.* a child] the frequent bearing children.

CHI'LDISH [cildiſc, *Sax.*] like a child, imprudent, filly.

CHI'LDISHNESS [cildiſcneſ, *Sax.*] fimplicity, unexperiencednefs.

CHI'LDWIT [*Sax.* Law Term] a power to take a fine of one's bond woman, that has been gotten with child without

Lingua Britannica Reformata:

Or, A NEW
ENGLISH DICTIONARY,

Under the Following TITLES,

VIZ.

I. UNIVERSAL; Containing a Definition and Explication of all the Words now used in the English Tongue, in every *Art*, *Science*, *Faculty*, or *Trade*.

II. ETYMOLOGICAL; Exhibiting and Explaining the true Etymon or Original of Words from their respective Mother-Tongues, the *Latin*, *Greek*, *Hebrew*, and *Saxon*; and their Idioms, the *French*, *Italian*, *Spanish*, *German*, *Dutch*, &c.

III. ORTHOGRAPHICAL; Teaching the True and Rational Method of Writing Words, according to the Usage of the most Approved Modern Authors.

IV. ORTHOEPICAL; Directing the True Pronunciation of Words by Single and Double Accents; and by Indicating the Number of Syllables in Words where they are doubtful, by a Numerical Figure.

V. DIACRITICAL; Enumerating the Various Significations of Words in a Proper Order, *viz.* Etymological, Common, Figurative, Poetical, Humorous, Technical, &c. in a Manner not before attempted.

VI. PHILOLOGICAL; Explaining all the Words and Terms, according to the Modern Improvements in the Various Philological Sciences, *viz.* Grammar, Rhetoric, Logic, Metaphysics, Mythology, Theology, Ethics, &c.

VII. MATHEMATICAL; Not only Explaining all Words in *Arithmetic*, *Algebra*, *Logarithms*, *Fluxions*, *Geometry*, *Conics*, *Dialling*, *Navigation*, &c. according to the Modern *Newtonian Mathesis*; but the Terms of Art are illustrated by Proper Examples, and Copper-Plate Figures.

VIII. PHILOSOPHICAL; Explaining all Words and Terms in *Astronomy*, *Geography*, *Optics*, *Hydrostatics*, *Acoustics*, *Mechanics*, *Perspective*, &c. according to the latest Discoveries and Improvements in this Part of Literature.

To which is prefix'd,

An INTRODUCTION,

CONTAINING

A Physico-Grammatical ESSAY

On the Propriety and Rationale of the ENGLISH TONGUE, deduced from a General IDEA of the Nature and Necessity of SPEECH, for HUMAN SOCIETY; a Particular View of the Genius and Usage of the Original *MOTHER TONGUES*, the HEBREW, GREEK, LATIN, and TEUTONIC; with their respective *IDIOMS*, the ITALIAN, FRENCH, SPANISH, SAXON, and GERMAN, so far as they have Relation to the *English* Tongue, and have contributed to its Composition.

By *BENJ. MARTIN.*

LONDON:

Printed for J. HODGES, at the Looking-glass, facing St. Magnus's Church, London-Bridge; S. AUSTEN, in Newgate-street; J. NEWBERY, in St. Paul's Church-Yard; J. WARD, in Little-Britain; R. RAIKES, at Gloucester; J. LEAKE, and W. FREDERICK, at Bath; and B. COLLINS, at Salisbury. MDCCXLIX. [Price Six Shillings.]

Title-page of Benjamin Martin's *Lingua Britannica Reformata*, first edition. Octavo.

A

DICTIONARY

OF THE

ENGLISH LANGUAGE:

IN WHICH

The WORDS are deduced from their ORIGINALS,

AND

ILLUSTRATED in their DIFFERENT SIGNIFICATIONS

BY

EXAMPLES from the beſt WRITERS.

TO WHICH ARE PREFIXED,

A HISTORY of the LANGUAGE,

AND

An ENGLISH GRAMMAR.

By SAMUEL JOHNSON, A.M.

IN TWO VOLUMES.

VOL. I.

Cum tabulis animum cenſoris ſumet honeſti :
Audebit quæcunque parum ſplendoris habebunt,
Et ſine pondere erunt, et honore indigna ferentur,
Verba movere loco ; quamvis invita recedant,
Et verſentur adhuc intra penetralia Veſtæ :
Obſcurata diu populo bonus eruet, atque
Proferet in lucem ſpecioſa vocabula rerum,
Quæ priſcis memorata Catonibus atque Cethegis,
Nunc ſitus informis premit et deſerta vetuſtas.　　Hor.

LONDON,
Printed by W. STRAHAN,
For J. and P. KNAPTON; T. and T. LONGMAN; C. HITCH and L. HAWES;
A. MILLAR; and R. and J. DODSLEY.
MDCCLV.

Title-page of the first edition of Samuel Johnson's *Dictionary of the English Language*. Folio.

A NEW

UNIVERSAL ETYMÓLOGICAL

ENGLISH DICTIONARY:

Containing not only

EXPLANATIONS of the WORDS

IN THE

ENGLISH LANGUAGE;

And the Different SENSES in which they are ufed;

WITH

AUTHORITIES from the BEST WRITERS, to fupport thofe which appear Doubtful;

BUT ALSO THEIR

ETYMOLOGIES

FROM THE

ANCIENT and MODERN LANGUAGES:

AND

ACCENTS directing to their Proper PRONUNCIATION;

Shewing both the

ORTHOGRAPHY and ORTHOEPIA of the *ENGLISH* TONGUE.

ALSO,

Full and Accurate EXPLANATIONS of the various TERMS made ufe of in the feveral
ARTS, SCIENCES, MANUFACTURES, and TRADES.

Illuftrated with COPPER-PLATES.

Originally compiled by *N. BAILEY.*

Affifted in the Mathematical Part by *G. GORDON*; in the Botanical by *P. MILLER*; and in the
Etymological, &c. by *T. LEDIARD*, Gent. Profeffor of the Modern Languages in *Lower Germany.*

And now Re-publifhed with many CORRECTIONS, ADDITIONS, and LITERATE IMPROVEMENTS,
by Different HANDS.

The Etymology of all TERMS mentioned as derived from the *Greek, Hebrew, Arabic,* and other *Afiatic* LANGUAGES,
being Revifed and Corrected

By *JOSEPH NICOL SCOTT*, M. D.

LONDON:

Printed for T. OSBORNE and J. SHIPTON; J. HODGES; R. BALDWIN;
W. JOHNSTON, and J. WARD.

MDCCLV.

Title-page of the Scott-Bailey *A New Universal Etymological
English Dictionary*, first edition. Folio.

THE

COMPLETE

Englifh Dictionary,

Explaining moſt of thoſe

HARD WORDS,

Which are found in the

BEST *ENGLISH* WRITERS.

By a Lover of *Good Engliſh* and
Common Senſe.

John Wesley

N. B. The AUTHOR aſſures you, he thinks this is the
beſt *Englifh* DICTIONARY in the World.

The SECOND EDITION, with ADDITIONS.

BRISTOL:
Printed by WILLIAM PINE;
And Sold by the BOOKSELLERS of *London, Briſtol, &c.*

M.DCC.LXIV.

Title-page of John Wesley's *Complete English Dictionary,*
second edition. Duodecimo.

Chapter I

THE MEDIEVAL AND RENAISSANCE HERITAGE

OF THE ENGLISH DICTIONARY

IN 1604 ROBERT CAWDREY PUBLISHED A SMALL VOLUME ENTITLED *A Table Alphabeticall.* This was the first English dictionary. It contained about 2,500 hard words with brief definitions, some of them scarcely more than synonyms. At this date Shakespeare had already written two-thirds of his plays and was engaged in the composition of his great tragedies, which were to bring enduring fame. Though the great dramatist is reckoned to have had at his command some 15,000 words, it would be hard to establish any connection between his vocabulary and Cawdrey's little English dictionary. Yet Shakespeare and his fellow-dramatists and poets were not without the resources which result from the systematic listing and defining of words through a long period of time—that is, not without dictionaries.

To understand what the heritage of the Elizabethans was with respect to wordbooks and to a tradition in dictionary-making, we need to survey briefly the history of such work. From the Anglo-Saxon period through the Middle Ages, there were interlinear English glosses in Latin or French texts, such as Alexander Neckham's *De Nominibus Utensilium (ca.* 1200) and Latin-English vocabularies [1] and nominales, designed for schoolboys studying a foreign language and useful to them and to older people in getting a better grasp of their native English. This tradition is continued at the end of the fifteenth century and in the early sixteenth in the *Vulgaria* and *Vocabula* of the English schoolmasters: John Stanbridge, William Horman, and Robert Whittinton. The tradition persists during the second half of the sixteenth century in the manuals for teaching foreign languages, such as Claudius Hollyband's *The Frenche Schoole-maister* (1573), an English-French manual; John

Florio's *Firste Fruites* (1578), English-Italian; and William Stepney's *The Spanish Schoolemaster* (1591), English-Spanish. Finally, the influence of the vocabulary tradition is exhibited in John Withals' English-Latin *A Shorte Dictionarie for Yonge Begynners*, first printed in 1553 and frequently thereafter until 1634.

More significant in the history of English lexicography than the glosses, the vocabularies, or the manuals for teaching foreign languages are the numerous bilingual and multilingual dictionaries in which the English vocabulary is prominent. And of special importance among these are the English-Latin and Latin-English dictionaries.[2] The earliest known English-Latin dictionary is the *Promptorium Parvulorum, sive Clericorum* (*ca.* 1440),[3] a storehouse for young boys, especially those preparing for the ministry. This text has about 12,000 English entries with their Latin equivalents. Some forty years later was compiled another English-Latin text called *Catholicon Anglicum* (1483).[4] Though there are in this text only 8,000 English entries, it has a larger number of Latin synonyms than its predecessor, the *Parvulorum*. This type of English-Latin dictionary persists in the sixteenth century in Richard Huloet's *Abcedarium Anglo-Latinum* (1552), Withals' *Shorte Dictionarie* (1553), John Baret's *Alvearie* (1573),[5] and John Rider's *Bibliotheca Scholastica* (1589).

Two of the texts mentioned above show the characteristic organization of the early vocabularies. The first part of Stanbridge's *Vulgaria*, for example, is similar in arrangement to the interlinear gloss. The Latin words with the English gloss in small type above the line run thus across the page:

a lytell bronde	spercle	bronde	cole	idem	asshes
Facula,	sintilla,	fax,	pruna,	carbo,	cinisque,
wood	stycke	andyron	chyppe	tonges	
Lignum,	ligniculum,	ipopirgium,	assula,	forceps,	
bellous	fyreforke	idem	chyppes		
Follis,	furcilla,	rotabulum,	quisquillieque . . .		

Another type of arrangement is represented by the *Abcedarium* of Huloet and the small *Dictionarie* of Withals. As the latter book had continuous vogue through the century, we may regard it as representative. In it the glosses, not yet in alphabetical order, are arranged in columns with the Latin equivalents following. Withals' aim was to help boys in speaking and writing Latin. The list of words and phrases covers in general the whole range of the world and of common human activity. Prominence is given to the English language by placing English words and phrases before the Latin in groups of words centered in a general concept or idea. Under *Building*, for example, the author lists the English and Latin words for various kinds of houses as well as for related groups, such as those concerned with the carpenter and his tools. Under *Water* (*Aqua*) appear, first, words and phrases associated with the general idea; and then a subheading, "The Sea and all that belongeth to it." Here are found the names of fishes of the sea and of ships and their parts and so on through a long list until we reach another group of words under the heading, "The Earth with that which belongeth to it."

The entries below illustrate the method of Withals.

A Ship with other water vessels, etc.
  A ship, *Navis, rates*
  He that maketh the ship, *Naupegus,* gi
  The keale or bottome of a ship, *Carina,* ae
  Hardie shippes, *Audaces carinae*
  The keale of a ship pitched, *Uncta carina*
  The fore part, *Prora,* ae
  A great ship, *Trieris,* ris
  The snoute afore, *Rostrum navis*
  The hinder part of a ship, *Puppis,* pis

   .   .   .   .

  The Starne, *Clavus,* vi
  The balast or lastage of the ship, *Saburra,* ae
  The hatches, *Pergulae*

   .   .   .   .   .

This method suggests a principle of grouping words which might have been successfully used in compiling English dictionaries. By the end of the sixteenth century, however, the alphabetical order of listing words had been established in Latin-English dictionaries. And this principle was adopted by the makers of English dictionaries.

The earliest known Latin-English dictionary has the title, *Medulla Grammatice,* or *Grammatices* (*ca.* 1460). Although this book exists in a large number of manuscripts,[6] it has never been printed. In 1500, Wynkyn de Worde printed a Latin-English dictionary with the title [*H*]*Ortus Vocabulorum*. The author's explanation of the title may be translated thus:

Not unworthily called the garden of words, for just as in gardens are found abundance of flowers, of herbs, and of fruits with which our bodies are strengthened and our spirits refreshed, so in this book are diverse words accommodated to beginners desirous of the pleasures of learning. With these words they may furnish the mind, adorn their speech, and finally, if the Fates permit, grow into very learned men. . . .

The [*H*]*Ortus* was popular through the first quarter of the sixteenth century. With the progress of the new learning and with the introduction of new words, however, the need of a new dictionary was felt. This need Sir Thomas Elyot endeavored to supply with his *Dictionary* (1538), termed in subsequent issues and augmentations *Bibliotheca Eliotae, Elyot's Library*. New editions appeared in 1542(?) and 1545, and in 1548 with considerable augmentation by the Reverend Thomas Cooper. Other editions of the augmented volume were printed in 1552 and 1559. Thereafter the *Bibliotheca* was absorbed by the larger compilation of Cooper, *Thesaurus Linguae Romanae et Britannicae* (1565). Four editions of this work appeared by 1584; and in 1588(?) Thomas Thomas' *Dictionarium Linguae Latinae et Anglicanae*, to some extent an abridgment of Cooper's *Thesaurus*, began its career—a career that lasted far into the seventeenth century. The importance of the Elyot-Cooper dictionaries to this study is in the emphasis placed upon the English idiom in the definitions of Latin words and especially in the translations of Latin illustrative phrases and sentences. In the preface to the *Bibliotheca* (1548) and to the *Thesaurus* (1565) Cooper explains at length the trouble he went to in getting proper English equivalents for the Latin. Examination of his texts serves to substantiate the compiler's claims. The significance of these texts is further emphasized by the fact that the English lexicographers of the seventeenth century frequently looked to the Cooper and the Thomas in framing definitions for "hard" English words.

Other bilingual, or semi-English, dictionaries in the sixteenth century are those concerned with English and the modern foreign languages.

John Palsgrave's *Lesclarcissement de la langue françoyse* (1530) combines features of a grammar, a manual for teaching French, and a
French-English vocabulary. Claudius Hollyband compiled, besides the
manual already referred to, *A Dictionarie French and English* (1593);
and Randle Cotgrave published a more famous work, *A Dictionarie of
the French and English Tongues* (1611). In 1567 William Thomas
compiled an Italian-English dictionary; and this was followed after
many years by the "resolute" John Florio's *Worlde of Wordes*, another
Italian-English dictionary (1598)—a book with a wealth of Elizabethan
idioms, colloquialisms, and even slang, known in all probability to
Shakespeare, Jonson, and other authors. A Spanish-English dictionary
was published in 1591 by Richard Percyvall, and augmented eight years
later by John Minsheu.

It is obvious from this survey that by 1600 a tradition in dictionary-
making, in which English always occupied an important place, had been
established; and that Shakespeare and his fellow-poets and dramatists
had greater linguistic resources than we are wont to think.[7] Considering
the verbal equipment of the Elizabethan writers, we might infer that
there are distinct advantages in learning the vernacular through the
study of bilingual or multilingual dictionaries. Finally, we may say
that all this activity in lexicography was excellent preparation for the
development of the English dictionary.

There were also, from Caxton's day through the next century, other
influences pointing to the emergence and development of the English
dictionary. One of these was the growth of interest in the vernacular,
observable earlier in Italy and France and manifest in various discussions
in England throughout the sixteenth century. This interest in the development of the English vocabulary and of the native literature was
greatly augmented by the revival of interest in the history and literature
of antiquity, by religious controversy, by the emergence of a new national
spirit during the reign of the Tudor sovereigns, and by the establishment
of the printing press in Westminster. Though Caxton, as a good businessman, undoubtedly sought to earn a livelihood from the printing press,
he was no less concerned to improve knowledge and raise the level of
culture among his countrymen. For the glory of England, therefore,
he occupied himself in printing works of English authors, such as Chaucer and Malory, and in translating into the vernacular the writings in

foreign languages. In him the national spirit was manifest. Through him is early expressed the keen interest in the English vocabulary—an interest which persists through the subsequent century. As his prologues and prefaces show, Caxton was seeking the correct answers to such questions as what, if any, particular dialect he should employ, and what words he should use to make the printed books intelligible to the greatest number of readers.

Caxton's concern for the English vocabulary as well as the practical difficulties of the first English printer are interestingly expressed in his *Prologue* to the *Eneydos* (1490). Though this *Prologue* is too long to quote in full, the illustrative story of the eggs may be recorded.

And that common English that is spoken in one shire varieth from another, insomuch that in my days happened that certain merchants were in a ship in Thames for to have sailed over the sea into Zealand, and for lack of wind they tarried at Foreland, and went to land for to refresh them. And one of them named Sheffield, a mercer, came into a house and asked for meat, and especially he asked after eggs; and the goodwife answered that she could speak no French, and the merchant was angry, for he also could speak no French, but would have had eggs, and she understood him not. And then at last another said, that he would have "eyren"; then the goodwife said that she understood him well. Lo, what should a man in these days now write, eggs or eyren? [8]

This interest in the English vocabulary and idiom was destined to increase with the great activity in translations—including the Scripture—from foreign languages, and with the growing tendency of English writers to employ the native language. Prominent among those who, in the first half of the sixteenth century, chose the vernacular as a medium of serious writing were Sir Thomas Elyot, Thomas Wilson, and Roger Ascham. Among these men discussions as to the English vocabulary took fairly definite form. Elyot thought that, though English should be used as a medium for disseminating information and giving currency to new ideas, the native vocabulary was inadequate to the demands made upon it. Accordingly, he borrowed and coined words freely and introduced them into *The Governour, The Castel of Helth,* and other writings; and he defended himself for doing so. [9]

As a tribute to Elyot's work and as a typical expression of concern for the language and the vernacular literature, we wish here to quote from one of the less familiar authors of the period, Richard Sherry. In the dedicatory epistle to his *A Treatise of Schemes and Tropes* (1550), Sherry writes:

Good cause haue we therefore to gyue thankes unto certayne godlye and well learned men, whych by their greate studye enrychynge our tongue both wyth matter and wordes, haue endeuoured to make it so copyous and plentyfull that therein it maye compare wyth anye other whiche so euer is the best. It is not unknowen that oure language for the barbarousnes and lacke of elo-quence hathe bene complayned of, and yet not trewely, for anye defaut in the toungue it selfe, but rather for slackenes of our coūtrimen, whiche haue alwayes set lyght by searchyng out the elegance and proper speaches that be ful many in it: as plainly doth appere not only by the most excellent monu-mentes of our aūciēt forewriters, Gower, Chawcer and Lydgate, but also by the famous workes of many other later: inespeciall of ᵗ ryght worshipful knyght syr Thomas Eliot, which first in hys dictionarye as it were generallye searchinge oute the copye of oure language in all kynde of wordes and phrases, after that setting abrode goodlye monumentes of hys wytte, lernynge and industrye, aswell in historycall knowledge, as of eyther the Philosophies, hathe herebi declared the plentyfulnes of our mother toūge, loue toward hys country, hys tyme not spent in vanitye and tryfles. What shuld I speake of that ornamente Syr Thomas Wyat? which beside most excellente gyftes bothe of fortune and bodye, so flouryshed in the eloquence of hys natiue tongue, that as he passed therin those wyth whome he lyued, so was he lykelye to haue bene equal wyth anye other before hym, had not enuious death to hastely beriued us of thys iewel:... Manye other there be yet lyuynge whose excellente wrytynges do testifye wyth us to be wordes apte and mete elogantly to declare oure myndes in al kindes of Sciences: and that, what sentence soeuer we conceiue, the same to haue Englyshe oracion natural, and holpē by art, wherby it may most eloquētly be uttered. . . .

Here is the national note expressive of pride in the English language and literature—if not yet quite sure of its excellence—and paying respects to Sir Thomas Elyot, the maker of a dictionary, the borrower and coiner of words. Elyot was obviously only one of many writers who took great license in introducing new words and reviving old ones. The result was that by the middle of the century such scholars as Sir John Cheke and Thomas Wilson had become alarmed for the fate of the English language and protested against the linguistic innovations. They objected to the use of archaisms and what they called "inkhornisms," holding that the English language, always borrowing and never paying back, was in a fair way to become bankrupt. The English language should be kept pure. More of the native words—the simple Anglo-Saxon words—should be employed; and words of foreign origin should be rejected. Only thus could the Queen's English preserve its integrity. This opinion was shared by other writers, and in some instances there were definite attempts to practice their theory.[10]

The point of interest for this study is, however, that the utterances of Cheke and Wilson show not only the continued concern for the English vocabulary but mark also a clear-cut division of opinion between the purists and the innovators. For example, George Pettie, later, definitely took issue with Cheke, defending the practice of free borrowing and adaptation. Spenser's extensive use of archaisms and dialect forms, and "E. K.'s" defense of the practice, are well known. The controversy is continued in the seventeenth century in Richard Verstegan's *The Restitution of Decayed Intelligence* (1605), in the *Glossographia* of Blount, and in the prefaces to the dictionaries of Phillips and Coles. Though a wholesome restraining influence, the protests of the purists did not serve, fortunately, to stop extensive borrowing and free coinage. The result was, of course, an increase in the number of "hard" words—those of foreign origin which offered difficulty to the reader.

What to do with the ever-increasing number of hard words, especially those derived from the Latin and Greek languages, presented a problem to purists and innovators alike. The purists, led by the classical scholar, Sir John Cheke, urged the avoidance of the foreign-derived words and a freer use of simple English words from the Anglo-Saxon. Before the end of the sixteenth century, however, it must have been obvious to both parties of the linguistic controversy that Cheke's proposal, even if carried out, was no solution to the problem. There was, however, precedent for a remedy. From the Anglo-Saxon period to the Renaissance, teachers had faced similar problems and had made glosses and bilingual vocabularies to make clear the meaning of hard words. Why not, following this precedent, compile a hard-word dictionary? Toward such a solution the discussions of the English vocabulary in the sixteenth century seemed to lead.

The long tradition in compiling bilingual and multilingual dictionaries and manuals and the keen interest during the Renaissance in the nature and the growth of the English vocabulary were factors in the genesis of the English dictionary. Another factor was the influx of new words through commercial, social, and literary relations with foreign countries, through the glut of translations, through the dictionaries of foreign languages, and through the tendency to free borrowing and coinage. Among the words thus introduced there were many unfamiliar even to fairly literate people. It was, then, almost necessary to compile lists of such words. And it was natural that the compilers should adopt a system already established and should profit by definitions given in reputable bilingual dictionaries. As the Latin-English were the most elaborate and best developed of such lexicons, these, as we shall see, exercised considerable influence on the English dictionaries.

In the last quarter of the sixteenth century another potent influence in the beginnings of the English dictionary was the pedagogical works and schoolbooks. It may be recalled that during the Middle Ages and in the early sixteenth century schoolmasters compiled bilingual vocabularies and nominales, and even small bilingual dictionaries to be used in teaching. The growth of interest in the English language and the English vocabulary led schoolmasters in the last decades of the century to consider the possibility of compiling an English dictionary. The earlier teachers had established the precedent of bilingual vocabularies. With this precedent and with the renewed interest in the English vocabulary, it was but a step to the making of English vocabularies and small dictionaries. The transition may be seen in the work of the schoolmasters: William Bullokar, Richard Mulcaster, and Edmund Coote.

These men, all teachers, had occasion to come more definitely to grips with the problems of spelling, pronunciation, and meanings of English words than did scholars and printers who wrote in general terms about the English language. William Bullokar was the pioneer among them. In 1580 he published *Bullokars Booke at large, for the Amendment of Orthographie for English speech.* On the title-page he refers to the purpose of his book as "the easie, speedie, and perfect reading and writing of English ... by the which Amendment the same Authour hath also framed a ruled Grammar, to be imprinted heere after for the same speech, to no small commoditie of the English Nation, not only to come to easie, speedie and perfect use of our owne language, but also to their easie, speedie, and readie entrance into the secretes of other Languages."

In the verse Prolog the author refers to the necessity of an English dictionary:

> A like consent in Dictionary (to
> Grammar ioind hereto)
> Will cause that Inglish speech shall
> be, the perfectest I know.

And six years later in his *Bref Grammar for English* (1586), he expresses his intention, never carried through, of compiling a dictionary:

> Your good acceptance of thaez painz,
> wil cause me to set hand,
> too perfecting a Dictionary,
> the third strength of this band.

A book on orthography, a grammar, and an English dictionary Bullokar regarded as essential to the study of the English language.

Two years after Bullokar's book on orthography, appeared Richard Mulcaster's *Elementarie* (1582).[11] In tones characteristic of earlier tributes to the native language, Mulcaster emphasizes the worth of the English language and advocates a wider use of it.

> But why not all in *English*, a tung of it self both depe in conceit, & frank in deliuerie? I do not think that anie language, be it whatsoeuer, is better able to vtter all argumēts, either with more pith, or greater planesse, then our *English* tung is, if the *English* vtterer be as skilfull in the matter, which he is to vtter: as the foren vtterer is.[12]

Mulcaster goes farther, however, than merely defending or praising the English language. He is interested in making available to students the instruments by which they may become more skillful in the use of their native tongue. One of these, which he himself does not undertake to compile, is an English dictionary. In the margin of the *Elementarie* are the words: "A perfit English dictionarie wished for." [13] And in the text proper he writes:

> It were a thing verie praiseworthie in my opinion, and no lesse profitable then praise worthie, if som one well learned and as laborious a man, wold gather all the words which we vse in our *English* tung, whether naturall or incorporate, out of all professions, as well learned as not, into one dictionarie, and besides the right writing, which is incident to the Alphabete, wold open

vnto vs therein, both their naturall force, and their proper vse: that by his honest trauell we might be as able to iudge of our own tung, which we haue by rote, as we ar of others, which we learn by rule. The want whereof, is the onelie cause why, that verie manie men, being excellentlie well learned in foren speche, can hardlie discern what theie haue at home, still shooting fair, but oft missing far, hard censors ouer other, ill executors themselues.[14]

Citing precedents for dictionary-making in various other countries, ancient and modern, and even for dictionaries of single authors, as of Boccaccio in Italian, Mulcaster concludes that, if English wits would do so much for their tongue, "we should then know what we both write and speak: we should then discern the depth of their conceits, which either coined our own words, or incorporated the foren. Whereas at this daie: we be skillfull abrode and ignorant at home, wondring at others not waing our own." [15] Then under the heading of "The Generall Table" Mulcaster inserts a list of about 8,000 English words—words without definitions but such words as should be defined in a dictionary.

In 1594 was published the *Grammatica Anglicana* by "P. Gr." or Paul Graves, according to Otto Funke, editor of a recent edition of this work.[16] The *Grammatica* contains besides the treatise on grammar a *Dictionariolum*, a vocabulary of English words with their Latin equivalents, and a *Vocabula* with words and phrases from Chaucer and their equivalents in Elizabethan English. This work is in the tradition of Bullokar and Mulcaster, and is another example of the interest which English schoolmasters were taking in the grammar and vocabulary.

Nearer to the English dictionary proper is *The English Schoole Master* (1596) by Edmund Coote. This work exemplifies a twofold tradition in the period. Its title and in part its contents imitate the foreign-language manuals, such as Hollyband's *The Frenche Schoolemaister* (1573), Florio's *Firste Fruites* (1578), and Stepney's *The Spanish Schoolemaster* (1591). In these manuals the foreign language and the English are printed in parallel columns. They contain instructions in the grammar of the foreign language concerned, dialogues of London life, prayers, graces, a catechism, and at the end a bilingual vocabulary of various words in common use. Coote's *English Schoole-Master* has a similar organization—the grammar, the catechism, the prayers, and the vocabulary. But Coote, like Bullokar and Mulcaster, is concerned solely with the English language and grammar; and his vocabulary is an English list of hard words together with simple definitions. He thus in a measure combines the two traditions, and in adding definitions goes beyond either. His vocabulary approximates, in fact, a brief dictionary. And in Coote's *English Schoole-Master* we have the immediate predecessor of the first English dictionary—*A Table Alphabeticall* by Robert Cawdrey.

In the chapters which follow we shall trace the growth of the English dictionary from Cawdrey to Johnson. We shall endeavor to explain the purposes of English lexicographers, to consider their qualifications for their task, to describe the audiences for whom the dictionaries were compiled, the sources of information, the relationship of English dictionaries to Latin-English and English-Latin lexicons, the interrelationships of the English dictionaries, and the development of the various departments of lexicography. In short, we shall attempt to give a systematic historical account of the evolution of the English dictionary during the first one hundred and fifty years of its existence.

Chapter II

ROBERT CAWDREY's *A Table Alphabeticall* (1604)

WE HAVE SCANTY INFORMATION ON THE LIFE OF ROBERT Cawdrey. We know, however, that he, like Mulcaster and Coote, was a schoolmaster. In the dedicatories to his *Treasurie or Storehouse of Similies* (1600) and *A Table Alphabeticall* (1604) he refers to the time when "I taught the Grammer schoole at Okeham in the County of Rutland" and when Sir James Harington was his "scholler (and now my singuler benefactor)." He states further that the *Table* is a work "long ago for the most part gathered by me, but lately augmented by my sonne Thomas, who now is Schoolemaster in London."

A Table Alphabeticall, a small octavo volume, bears the following inscription on the title-page:

A Table Alphabeticall, conteyning and teaching the true writing, and understanding of hard usuall English wordes, borrowed from the Hebrew, Greeke, Latine, or French. &c.

With the interpretation thereof by plaine English words, gathered for the benefit & helpe of Ladies, Gentlewomen, or any other unskilfull persons.

Whereby they may the more easilie and better understand many hard English wordes, which they shall heare or read in Scriptures, Sermons, or elswhere, and also be made able to use the same aptly themselves. . . .

At London, . . . 1604.[1]

A comparison of *A Table Alphabeticall* with Coote's *The English Schoole-Master* shows that the latter work was the immediate inspiration of Cawdrey.[2] He begins to borrow phrases even in his title-page. Compare the following from the title-pages of the two texts:

13

COOTE, 1596

... And further also, teacheth a direct course, how any unskilfull person may easily both understand any hard English words, which they shal in the Scriptures, Sermons, or elsewhere heare or reade: and also be made able to use the same aptly themselves.

I have set downe a Table contayning and teaching the true writing and understanding of any hard English word, borrowed from the Greeke, Latine, or French, and how to knowe the one from the other, with the interpretation thereof by a plaine English word ("The Schoole-master his Profession," Sig. A 2v).

CAWDREY, 1604

... gathered for the benefit & helpe of Ladies, Gentlewomen, or any other unskilfull persons. Whereby they may the more easilie and better understand many hard English wordes, which they shall heare or read in Scriptures, Sermons, or elswhere, and also be made able to use the same aptly themselves.

A Table Alphabeticall, conteyning and teaching the true writing, and understanding of hard usuall English wordes, borrowed from the Hebrew, Greeke, Latine, or French. &c. With the interpretation thereof by plaine English words.

In his Dedicatorie Cawdrey repeats a part of what he had borrowed on his title-page and concludes with another passage from Coote's brief address, "The Schoole-master his Profession."

COOTE

... whereby Children shall be prepared for the understanding of thousands of Latine words before they enter the Grammar Schoole; which also will bring much delight and iudgement to others. Therefore if thou understandest not any word in this booke, not before expounded, seeke the Table.

CAWDREY

And Children heereby may be prepared for the understanding of a great number of Latine words: which also will bring much delight & iudgement to others, by the use of this little worke....

If, following Coote's suggestion, we turn to the *Table* in his text, we find certain instructions how to use it. In Cawdrey are almost verbatim directions for the use of *The Table Alphabeticall*. Coote's Table contains about 1,500 words, the more common undefined and the others defined often by a single synonym. Unquestionably, Cawdrey made use of this list and, in some cases, was satisfied with the simple definitions of Coote, as in the following instances:

COOTE	CAWDREY
Magistrate governour.	*Magistrate*, governour.
Magician using witch-craft.	*Magitian*, (g) one using witchcraft.
Magnificence sumptuousness.	*Magnificence*, sumptuousnes.
Maladie disease.	*Maladie*, disease.
Male-contented discontented.	*Malecontent*, discontented.
Maranatha accursed.	*Maranatha*, (g) accursed.
Mart faire.	*Marte*, a faire.
Mechanicall g. handy-craft.	{ *Mechanicall*, (g) { *Mechanick*, handie craft.
Mutation change.	*Mutation*, change.
Myrrhe k of sweet gumme.	*Myrrhe*, (g) sweet gumme.
Mysticall that hath a mysterie in it.	*Mysticall*, (g) that hath a misterie in it.

It is to be remembered, however, that Cawdrey had in his *Table* nearly twice as many words as were in Coote's and that half the number of definitions which Cawdrey borrowed from his predecessor he expanded by information from other sources. Though Cawdrey received from Coote's *English Schoole-Master* his initial impulse to compile a dictionary, adopted his method, and borrowed about 90 per cent of Coote's words and definitions, he derived much matter from other sources. Cawdrey was not, in other words, a man of one book. He evinces familiarity, for example, with Wilson's *Arte of Rhetorique*, especially the discussion of the English vocabulary. A part of this, indeed, Cawdrey incorporates in his "To the Reader." [8] He shares at least in the general Renaissance interest in the vernacular.

A second definite source of *A Table Alphabeticall* is Thomas' Latin-English dictionary (1588?). Thomas and his predecessors, Cooper and Elyot, had established a precedent in dictionary-making and had taken special pains to render Latin terms into current English phraseology. In Thomas, then, Cawdrey would find the original forms of "hard English words" together with their definitions. To Thomas, Cawdrey turned for many of his words and definitions, as the following parallels show:

THOMAS, 1596 edition	CAWDREY, 1604
Hectice, ... An Hecticke fever, inflaming the heart and soundest or substantiallest part of the bodie.	*Hecticke,* inflaming the heart and soundest part of the bodie.
Hemisphaerium, ... Halfe the compasse of the visible heaven....	*Hemisphere,* halfe the compasse of heaven, that we see.
Homonymia, ... When divers things are signified by one word.	*Homonimie,* When divers things are signified by one word.
Horizon, ... A circle dividing the halfe sphere of the firmament from the other halfe which we doe not see.	*Horizon,* ... A circle, dividing the halfe of the firmament, from the other halfe which we see not.
Incendo, ... To inflame: to set fire on a thing: to burne: to incense, ... to stirre up ... to make verie angrie, to vexe, moove, or chafe: ...	*Incend,* kindle, burne, vexe or chafe, to incense, to stirre up, or set on fire, or to anger.
Neotericus, ... One of late time.	*Neotericke,* One of late time.
Obnubilo, ... To make darke with cloudes, ...	*Obnubilate,* to make darke.
Palinodia, ... A recantation, ... an unsaying of that one hath spoken or written.	*Palinodie,* a recanting or unsaying of anything.
Pervicacia, ... Obstinacie, headinesse, stiffeneckednesse: ...	*Pervicacie,* obstinacie, stifneckednes.

The list need not be increased; the fact is that more than 40 per cent of Cawdrey's words together with the definitions come directly from Thomas' dictionary. Furthermore, 50 per cent of the definitions which Cawdrey borrows from Coote he supplements generously by matter from Thomas. In other words, Cawdrey's *Table* has many composite definitions deriving from both Coote and Thomas. Compare the following:

COOTE, 1596	THOMAS, 1596 Edition	CAWDREY, 1604
Adulterate counterfeit.	*Adultero,* ... To counterfeite or forge, to corrupt: ...	*Adulterate,* to counterfeit or corrupt.

COOTE, 1596	THOMAS, 1596 Edition	CAWDREY, 1604
Aggravate make grievous.	*Aggravo,*...To make heavie: also to aggravate, to make more grievous:...	*Aggravate*, make more grievous, and more heavie.
Alacrity cheerefulnesse.	*Alacritas,* . . . Cheereful-nesse, livelinesse, cour-age,...	*Alacritie*, cheerefulnes, livelines.
Apocrypha g. not of au-thority.	*Apocryphus,* . . . A thing hid, the originall or au-thoritie whereof is not knowne.	*Apocrypha* (g), not of authoritie, a thing hidden, whose origi-nall is not knowne.
Capitall deadly or great.	*Capitalis,*...Mortall, dead-ly, worthy death: worthie shame, infamie, grievous punishment:...	*Capitall*, deadly or great, or worthy of shame, and punishment.
Castigation chastisement.	*Castigatio,*...A chastising, correcting, or blaming.	*Castigation*, chastisement, blaming, correction.
Celebrate make famous.	*Celebro,*...to doe solemn-ely and honourably,... to commend and praise greatly:...to make fa-mous.... to honour and worshippe, ...	*Celebrate*, holy, make fa-mous, to publish, to commend, to keepe solemlie.
Circumspect heedy.	*Circunspectus,* . . . Wise, p r u d e n t, circumspect, which advisedly consider-eth what hee ought or what hee hath to doe....	*Circumspect*, h e e d i e , quick of sight, wise, and dooing matters advisedly.
Deduct take out.	*Deduco,*...to drawe out: ...to abate, deduct, or diminish of a summe:...	*Deduct*, to take or drawe out, abate or diminish.

An analysis of the entries under nine letters—*I, L, M, N, O, P, R, S, T*—in Cawdrey and a comparison with the entries under the same letters in Thomas and Coote give interesting and, we think, valid conclusions regarding the relationship of the three texts. This involves the study of about 1,200 words in Cawdrey's list and enables us to under-stand more definitely the relation of *A Table Alphabeticall* to its sources.

The analysis shows, with respect to entries under the nine letters of the alphabet, that Cawdrey absorbs 87 per cent of Coote's word list and that this amount from Coote constitutes 40 per cent of the total in Cawdrey's *Table*. Of this 40 per cent, half the number of definitions are also from Coote; the other half are from Coote, generously supplemented by words and phrases from Thomas. The analysis shows further that 43 per cent of Cawdrey's word list together with the definitions derives from Thomas. This percentage plus the augmentations of Coote's definitions via Thomas indicates, as far as word list and definitions are concerned, a heavier indebtedness to Thomas than to Coote. It should be added that Cawdrey takes 17 to 18 per cent of his word list and definitions from sources other than Coote and Thomas.

On the basis of a study of the three texts—Thomas, Coote, and Cawdrey—we may reconstruct Cawdrey's procedure. The idea of an English dictionary may have come from Mulcaster, but this was emphasized by the work of Coote. From Coote, Cawdrey got much of his introductory matter and, we think, the original word list with the one-word or one-phrase definitions. Later, Robert Cawdrey, or more probably his son Thomas, used the Latin-English dictionary of Thomas Thomas to supplement the simple definitions from Coote and to increase the word list together with new definitions. That this was the procedure is evidenced by the fact that, in the composite definitions, the part from Coote is almost always placed first. Then follow the words and phrases from Thomas. That Coote's *English Schoole-Master* should have been the inspiration and the basis of the original form of the Cawdrey but that Thomas' Latin-English dictionary finally should have furnished a larger proportion of words and definitions seems quite logical when we consider the relative size of the two texts.

In choosing words to define, it is obvious that Cawdrey did not attempt to be inclusive. He, like Coote in the *Schoole-Master*, chose what he regarded as the more difficult words—hard words; and, like Coote, he gave often only a single synonym or phrase as an equivalent. Occasionally, however, he went beyond Coote in supplying additional synonyms and brief explanations, approximating adequate definitions. To the illustrations already used, we may add the following as characteristic of Cawdrey:

Barke, small ship.
Barnacle, (k) bird.
Barrester, one allowed to give counsell, or to plede.
Barreter, a contentious person, quarreler, or fighter.
Barter, to bargaine, or change.
Baud, whore.
Bavin, a faggot, or kid.
Bashfull, blush, or shamefast.

.   .   .   .

Hipocrite, (g) such a one as in his outward apparrell, countenance and
   behaviour, pretendeth to be another man, then he is indeede, or a
   deceiver.
Importunate, requiring earnestly, without beeing satisfied, till the request
   be obteyned.
Incorporate, to graft one thing into the bodie of another, to make one bodie
   or substance.

Though *A Table Alphabeticall* went through four editions—1st,
1604, 2nd, date unknown, 3rd, 1613, 4th, 1617—and though the title-
page of the 1613 edition employs the phrase "much inlarged," the
augmentation was negligible. Nor were there any important changes
in the edition of 1617, except in the title. This reads, *A Table Alphabeticall, or the English Expositor.* The subtitle was borrowed from a
rival publication by Dr. John Bullokar, which had been printed in 1616.

Chapter III

JOHN BULLOKAR's *An English Expositor* (1616)

FROM THE MEAGER RECORDS CONCERNING BULLOKAR, WE LEARN
that he lived from about 1580 to 1641; that he was a doctor
of physic, residing at Chichester in 1616; that in 1618 he published a life of Christ in six-line stanzas; that he compiled
his *English Expositor* "at the request of a worthy gentleman whose
love prevailed much with him"; and that he kept it some years before
publishing. In 1616, Bullokar's, the second English dictionary to be
printed, appeared with the title-page phrased as follows:

An English Expositor: Teaching the Interpretation of the hardest words
used in our Language.
With Sundry Explications, Descriptions, and Discourses.
By I. B. Doctor of Physicke. . . .
London, Printed by Iohn Legatt. 1616.

This title-page together with Bullokar's "To the Courteous Reader"
constitutes the compiler's own description of his book. "To the Courteous Reader" runs, in part, thus:

Yet this I will say . . . that in my younger yeares it hath cost mee some
observation, reading, study, and charge; which you may easily beleeve, considering the great store of strange words, our speech doth borrow, not only
from the Latine, and Greeke, (and from the ancient Hebrew) but also from
forraine vulgar languages round about us: beside sundry olde words now
growne out of use, and divers termes of art, proper to the learned in Logicke,
Philosophy, Law, Physicke, Astronomie, etc., yea and Divinitie it selfe, best
knowen to the several professors there of. And herein I hope such learned
will deeme no wrong offered to themselves or dishonour to Learning, in that

I open the signification of such words, to the capacitie of the ignorant, whereby they may conceive and use them as well as those which have bestowed long study in the languages, for considering it is familiar among best writers to usurpe strange words (and sometimes necessary by reason our speech is not sufficiently furnished with apt terms to express all meanings) I suppose withall their desire is that they should be understood; which I (knowing that *bonum quo communius eo melius*) have endeavoured by this Booke, though not exquisitely, yet (I trust) in some reasonable measure to performe....

An English Expositor thus described is another small octavo volume but has almost twice as many entries as Cawdrey's *A Table*. Like Cawdrey, Bullokar, in "To the Courteous Reader," seems to show familiarity with the traditional discussion of the English vocabulary. Bullokar, however, seems more sympathetic than Cawdrey to the custom English writers have of usurping "strange words" from foreign languages; and Bullokar emphasizes more than his predecessor the necessity of giving special attention to hard words of foreign origin and to "olde words growne out of use." Thus *The Expositor* even more than *A Table* is a dictionary of "hard" words, and, as such, temporarily establishes the hard-word type of dictionary.

Bullokar's definitions are often more detailed and generally more satisfactory than those of Cawdrey, though the doctor of Chichester sometimes extends unduly his definitions, inserting from his medical lore or pseudo-science all sorts of curious information on animals, herbs, stones, and what not. He often cites authorities, as Avicenna, Galen, Pliny, for an assertion; he marks obsolete terms and cautions against their use.

In Bullokar's reference to "olde words now growne out of use, and divers termes of art, proper to the learned in Logicke, Philosophy, Law, Physicke, Astronomie," there is an extension in the scope of the dictionary. For such an extension, Bullokar had precedent in the Latin-English dictionaries of Cooper and Thomas. These compilers had made similar claims and had exemplified them. But Bullokar goes even farther; he frequently specifies in his definition to what profession or special field of knowledge a term belongs. He is thus the first compiler of an English dictionary to indicate the department in which a term applies. Examples of Bullokar's practice are evident in the following entries:

Endorsed. A terme of Herauldrie, when two beastes are painted with their backs turned to each other.

Enthymeme. A terme of Logick. It signifieth an imperfect syllogisme. . . .

Epicycle. A terme used in Astronomy. It signifieth a lesser circle, whose center or middle part is in the circumference of a greater circle. . . .

Essoine. A terme in the common Law, when a man cannot well appeare at a day appointed in court, and is therefore allowed by the Court to bee absent without penaltie.

To Thomas, Bullokar owes more than the precedent of placing terms in their field; he adapts or borrows outright many definitions from Thomas' Latin-English dictionary. Compare, for example, the following:

THOMAS, 1606 Edition	BULLOKAR, 1616
Alacritas, . . . Cheerefulnes, livelinesse, courage, readines. . . .	*Alacritie.* Cheerefulnesse; courage, quicknesse.
Anathema, . . . A gift or offering which is hanged up in the Church: a man which in times past was given to the devill: excommunication, execration. . .	*Anathema.* Any thing hanged up in a Church, as an offering to God: sometime it signifieth excommunication; or a man excommunicated and delivered to the power of the divell.
Catalogus, . . . A rehearsall in wordes, or table in writing of the number of things, a roll, a bill, a scroll, a catalogue: also a register of proper names.	*Catalogue.* A roll, a bill, a register of names or other things.
Labyrinthus, . . . A labyrinth or place full of intricate windings and turnings, made in such wise, that whosoever came into it could not get out againe without a very perfect guide, or without a threed directing him. . . .	*Labyrinth.* An intricate building or place made with so many turnings and windings that whosoever went into it could not get out without a perfect guide.
Rumino, . . . To chew the cudde as neate doe: also to call to remembrance and consider with ones selfe, to study and thinke upon matters.	*Ruminate.* To chew over againe as beasts doe, that chew the cud: wherfore it is often taken to studie and thinke much of a matter.

Bullokar borrowed freely from Thomas; he also contracted a debt to Cawdrey's *A Table Alphabeticall,* as a comparison of the following entries will show:

CAWDREY, 1604	BULLOKAR, 1616
Aggravate, make more grievous, and more heavie.	*Aggravate*. To make any thing in words more grievous, heavier, or worse than it is.
Allude, to speake one thing that hath resemblance and respect to another.	*Allude*. To speake any thing which hath resemblance, or privelie is directed to touch another matter.
Apocrypha, not of authoritie, a thing hidden, whose originall is not knowne.	*Apocrypha*. That which is hidden and not knowne. Doubtfull.
Delineate, to drawe the proportion of anything.	*Delineate*. To draw the first proportion of a thing.
Enhaunce, to lift up, or make greater.	*Enhaunce*. To advance or make greater.
Faction, devision of people into sundry parts and opinions.	*Faction*. A section or division into sundry opinions.
Gargarise, to wash the mouth, and throate within, by stirring some liquor up and downe in the mouth.	*Gargarize*. To wash or scoure the mouth with any Physicall liquor.
Intricate, inwrapped, doubtfull, hard to be knowne.	*Intricate*. Wrapped, intangled, hard to bee understood.

That Cawdrey's *Table* and Thomas' *Dictionarium* served as a basis for Bullokar's *Expositor*, the illustrations, which could be multiplied, show clearly. Naturally, the greater debt is to the Latin-English, as this is by far the larger work.

It should be noted, also, that many words defined by Cawdrey are omitted from the *Expositor*. Some of these are: *Agglutinate, Antecessor, Artifice, Blattering, Discerne, Gibbocitie, Imperated, Madefie, Obnubilate, Perfricate, Pervicacie*. Since the *Expositor* contained a much larger number of words, it is evident that it included very many other words not in the *Table Alphabeticall*.

Bullokar died in 1641, the year in which the third edition [1] of the *Expositor* was printed. There had been no revision [2] of the text during the author's lifetime. Though the title-page of the 1656 edition has the words, "Newly Revised, Corrected, and with the addition of above a thousand words enlarged . . . by W. S.," there are, in fact, few actual additions to the entries or few changes of any kind, except minor ones in spelling and in arrangement of words.

It was with the significant revision in 1663, by "A Lover of the Arts," that the real vogue of the *Expositor* began. Thereafter, it was printed at least eleven times by 1731, the date of the last edition. The title-page of the revised edition of 1663 suggests concisely the changes and augmentations.

An English Expositour, or Compleat Dictionary: Teaching the Interpretation of the hardest words, and most useful terms of Art used in our Language.

First set forth by J. B. Dr. of Physick. And now the fourth time Revised, Corrected, and very much augmented with several Additions, viz. A new and copious supply of Words. An Index directing to the hard Words, by prefixing the common Words before them in an Alphabetical Order. A brief Nomenclator, containing the Names of the most renowned Persons among the Ancients, whether Gods & Goddesses (so reputed), Heroes, or Inventours of profitable Arts, Sciences and Faculties. With divers memorable things out of ancient History, Poetry, Philosophy, and Geography....

By a Lover of the Arts. Cambridge.... 1663.

As the title-page announces, the word list of the earlier Bullokar is greatly augmented; and two large new sections, the Index and the Nomenclator, are added. These new features [3] "owe their inception and much of their actual content" to a rival publication, *The English Dictionarie*,[4] compiled by Henry Cockeram and first published in 1623. Earlier editions of Cockeram's *Dictionarie* owed much, as we shall see, to Bullokar's *Expositor*. In 1663, then, the reviser and publisher of the *Expositor* adopted the plan and borrowed some of the materials of the competitive and indebted Cockeram—feeling doubtless that this procedure was not only justifiable but a sort of poetic justice.

In the revised *Expositor* of 1663, the number of entries, or word list, was expanded by free borrowing from Cockeram. In the first pages of the revised text, to the point *Adr-* in the alphabet, thirty-three words come directly from Cockeram's *Dictionarie;* [5] and, though there is some difference in the phrasing of definitions, the interpretations of terms are the same. The *Index Anglico-Latinus* of the revised *Expositor* corresponds roughly to Part II of Cockeram,[6] and the *Nomenclator* to Part III. The increased popularity of the *Expositor* after 1663 was probably due to the change in organization and to the intelligent adaptation of features of Cockeram's *Dictionarie*.

The final revision of the Bullokar was made by R. Browne in 1707 at the suggestion of the booksellers, A. and J. Churchill. Browne, author of a spelling book, *The English School Reform'd,* undertook the revision in order to promote the joint sale of the new *Expositor* and the spelling book for use in schools. Every English school could thus "be furnished with two very useful and necessary Companions, at a very easy charge; and that is, That for spelling and this for Explaining of the English Tongue." Browne's augmentation was in Part I, where he increased the total number of words by adding mainly to the rhetorical terms and Biblical items. Parts II and III are substantially unchanged. The revised edition was successful enough to prolong the life of the Bullokar for four issues, or until 1731.

Chapter IV

HENRY COCKERAM's *The English Dictionarie* (1623)

THOUGH THE VOLUMES OF CAWDREY AND BULLOKAR ARE IN reality small English dictionaries, they were not so called. It remained for Henry Cockeram, in 1623, to be the first to employ as title the term, "English Dictionarie." The title-page of Cockeram's small octavo volume reads:

The English Dictionarie: or, An Interpreter of hard English Words.

Enabling as well Ladies and Gentlewomen, young Schollers, Clarkes, Merchants, as also Strangers of any Nation, to the understanding of the more difficult authors already printed in our Language, and the more speedy attaining of an elegant perfection of the English tongue, both in reading, speaking and writing.

Being a Collection of the choicest words contained in the *Table Alphabeticall* and *English Expositor*, and of some thousand of words never published by any heretofore.

By H. C. Gent. London, ... 1623.

This title-page is from an issue of the 1623 edition of Cockeram printed and sold by Edmund Weaver. In the same year another issue was printed for Nathaniel Butter.[1] The principal difference between the latter issue and that printed for Weaver is the omission from Butter's title-page of the reference to the *Table Alphabeticall* and the *English Expositor*—a reference which had been in effect an acknowledgment of indebtedness to these texts. It seems likely that Weaver as printer of the *Table Alphabeticall* may have insisted on Cockeram's acknowledgment of his debt to Cawdrey. Butter, of course, would have had no such reason. By the second edition of the *English Dictionarie*, in 1626, Cockeram's work and Bullokar's may have supplanted Cawdrey's *Table* so that Weaver no longer thought it necessary to protect the latter's interests. At any rate, the names of Cawdrey and Bullokar are not mentioned on the title-pages of subsequent editions of Cockeram. What then appears to be a candid acknowledgment of indebtedness to his predecessors redounds but little to Cockeram's credit; for his indebtedness, large at the beginning, as we shall see presently, continued to increase in subsequent editions. Before tracing his debt to his predecessors, however, let us notice the author's address, or "Premonition," as he calls it, to his readers. This presents the purpose and organization of his book.

At the beginning Cockeram states that "what any before me in this kinde have begun, I have not onely fully finished, but thoroughly perfected." The truth of this assertion we may judge later. The author then explains the order of his text.

First the method is plaine and easie, being alphabeticall, by which the capacity of the meanest may soon be inlightened. The first Booke hath the choicest words themselves now in use, wherewith our language is inriched and become so copious, to which words the common sense is annexed. The second Booke containes the vulgar words, which whensoever any desirous of a more curious explanation by a more refined and elegant speech shall looke into, he shall there receive the exact and ample word to expresse the same: Wherein by the way let me pray thee to observe that I have also inserted (as occasion served) even the *mocke-words* which are ridiculously used in our language, that those who desire a generality of knowledge may not bee ignorant of the sense, even of the *fustian termes,* used by too many who study rather to bee heard speake, than to understand themselves. The last Booke is a recitall of severall persons, Gods and Goddesses, Giants and Devils, Monsters and Serpents, Birds and Beasts, Rivers, Fishes, Herbs, Stones, Trees, and the like, to the intent that the diligent learner may not pretend the defect of any helpe which may informe his discourse or practice. I might insist upon the generall use of this worke, especially for Ladies and Gentlewomen, Clarkes, Merchants, young Schollers, Strangers, Travellers, and all such as desire to know the plenty of the English. . . .

The mention of "Ladies and Gentlewomen" in the concluding lines of this "Premonition" almost echoes the language of Cawdrey on the title-page of the *Table* (cf. p. 13). Yet Cockeram, as his title-page affirms, is, like Cawdrey and Bullokar, still in the hard-word tradition of dictionary-making. Many of the hard words are of foreign origin, especially Latin. No indication is given, however, as to the source of a word or as to the department to which it belongs, though a number are obviously law terms. Definitions are generally very brief, consisting, as in Cawdrey's *Table*, of simple words or phrases which are the synonyms of the hard words. There are some exceptions. A few words, as *Feofment, Predicament, Tribune, Zone*—all of which are from Bullokar—occupy a half column or more. Strange words, words which one suspects were never seen in English writing, and familiar words with definitions unconsciously humorous in phrasing are not unusual in Cockeram. Some of these are:

> *Commotrix.* A maid that makes ready and unready her Mistris.
> *Cotabulate.* To planch.
> *Glacitate.* To cry like a gander.
> *Mathematicean.* One that is skilled in Augurie, Geometrie, and Astronomie.
> *Parentate.* To celebrate ones parents funerals.
> *Phylologie.* Love of much babling.

More characteristic of the definitions in the first part of this dictionary are the following consecutive entries:

> *Finite.* Which hath an end.
> *Firme.* Strong, sound.
> *Firmitie.* Strength.
> *Fissure.* A chincke or cleft.
> *Fistulate.* To ramme or beat downe stones.
> *Fixe.* To fasten.
> *Fixed.* Fastened.
> *Flagellate.* To whip or scourge.
> *Flagitate.* Earnestly to importune.
> *Flagitious.* Wicked, lewd.
> *Flagrant.* Burning.
> *Flammigerate.* To cast out flames.

By the division of his work into three "Bookes"—especially by the addition of the third book concerned with "Gods & Goddesses" and miscellaneous topics—Cockeram seeks to extend the range of appeal. He is in this third book following the precedent of contemporary Latin-English dictionaries. And this extension resulted in his having almost as many entries as Cawdrey and Bullokar together.

To these compilers, Cockeram was, however, greatly indebted, especially in his first book. Correspondences to Cawdrey may be seen in the following words and definitions which do not appear in Bullokar:

CAWDREY, 1604	COCKERAM, 1623
Agglutinate, to ioyne together.	*Agglutinate*. To ioyne or glue together.
Concinnate, made fit, finely apparalled.	*Concinnate*. To make fit.
Gibbocitie, crookednes.	*Gibbocitie*. Crookednesse.
Hallucinate, to deceive or blind.	*Hallucinate*. To deceive.
Madefie, dip, make wet.	*Madefie*. To make wet.
Neotericke, one of late time.	*Neotericke*. One of late time.
Periclitation, ieopardie, or hazarding.	*Periclitation*. Ieopardie, hazard.

Though Cockeram borrowed occasionally from Cawdrey, especially words not in the *Expositor*, his indebtedness to Bullokar was far greater. Out of 50 words with their definitions chosen at random from various letters of the alphabet in Bullokar, Cockeram takes over the entries, wholly or largely, of 35. Other parallel sections chosen at random reveal that, in 18 words of Bullokar and 16 of Cockeram, 10 words are identical, 9 definitions are equivalent, and 8 practically verbatim.[2] The following entries will indicate, further, the nature of Cockeram's borrowings:

BULLOKAR, 1616	COCKERAM, 1623
Benign. Friendly, gentle, favourable, courteous, kinde.	*Benigne*. Gentle, favourable.
Bigamie. The marriage of two wives; not both together but severally after the death of the first. . . .	*Bigamie*. The Marriage of two wives.
Briggandine. A coat of defence.	*Brigandine*. A coat of defence.
Catarrh. A distillation of humours out of the head into the mouth and throat. . . .	*Catarrhe*. A distillation of watrie humours out of the head.
Censor. A grave officer having authority to control and correct manners.	*Censor*. A grave officer having power to correct matters.
Centre. The point in the midst of a round circle or the inward middle part of a globe. Wherfore the Earth is called the Center of the World, because it is in the midst therof.	*Center*. The point in the midst of a round circle, and therefore the earth is called the center of the world because it is in the middest thereof.

BULLOKAR, 1616	COCKERAM, 1623
Circumlocution. A long circumstance, a speaking of many words where few may suffice.	*Circumlocution.* A speaking of many words.
Computation. An account or reckoning; a numbering.	*Computation.* An account.
Cypher. A circle in Arithmetick like the letter O; which of it selfe is of no value, but increaseth the value of other Figures after which it is joyned.	*Cypher.* A circle in Arithmetick, like the letter (O).
Degenerate. To turn out of kinde, to turn worse.	*Degenerate.* To turne out of kind.

As the parallel entries listed above show, Cockeram in the first edition of his *Dictionarie* (1623) was heavily indebted to Bullokar. But the indebtedness did not stop there. It should be recalled that, excepting slight changes in spelling, Bullokar's book remained the same through the 1656 edition. Cockeram, on the other hand, enlarged many of his definitions between his first (1623) and his seventh (1642) editions. For the expansions he continued to draw from Bullokar.[3]

BULLOKAR, 1616 and 1641	COCKERAM, 1623	COCKERAM, 1642
Abbettour. Hee that counselleth or comforteth another to doe any evill.	*Abbettour.* Which counselleth one to doe evill.	*Abbettour,* Which counselleth, or comforteth one to doe evill.
Abbot. A spirituall Lord over a religious house of Monkes.	*Abbot.* A spirituall Lord.	*Abbott,* A spiritual Lord over a religious house of Monkes.
Abisse. A bottomlesse pit, any deepnesse so great that it cannot be sounded.	*Abisse.* A bottomlesse pit.	*Abysse,* A bottomlesse pit, or gulfe, any deepnesse so great that it cannot bee sounded.
Ablepsie. Want of sight, blindnesse, unadvisednesse.	*Ablepsie.* Blindnesse, want of sight.	*Ablepsie,* Blindnesse, want of sight, unadvisednesse.
Abridge. To shorten, to cut off, to gather onely the principall points.	*Abridge.* To shorten.	*Abridge,* To shorten, to cut off, to gather onely the principall points.

BULLOKAR, 1616 and 1641	COCKERAM, 1623	COCKERAM, 1642
Adoption. The choosing and making one to bee as his sonne to him.	*Adoption.* The chusing of one to be his sonne.	*Adoption,* The chusing and making of one to be as his sonne to him.
Annuitie. A yearely payment of money to one, not in way of rent, but upon some other occasion.	*Annuitie.* Yeerely payment of money to one.	*Annuitie,* Yearely payment of money to one, not in way of rent, but otherwise.

Although there is ample evidence of Cockeram's continual borrowing from Bullokar, it must not be supposed that the compiler of the *Dictionarie* accepted all that he found in the *Expositor*. Many terms he rejected outright; others he simplified or abridged. And Cockeram added many words even in the first part of his first edition from sources other than Cawdrey or Bullokar. For many entries and definitions of words—words which one suspects were rarely or never used in the author's own day—Cockeram obviously consulted contemporary Latin-English dictionaries. One needs only to glance at the entries on almost any page to see the Latinisms. Under the letter *N*, for example, are 80 entries: of these probably 40 are from Bullokar; 33 are directly or indirectly from Thomas' Latin-English dictionary.

THOMAS, 1606 Edition	COCKERAM, 1623
Natatio, . . . A swimming.	*Natation.* A swimming.
Naufragium, . . . Wracke on the sea, losse, detriment, shipwracke.	*Naufrage.* Shipwracke.
Naumachia, . . . A warre or battell by Sea. . . .	*Naumachie.* A battell or fight at sea.
Naustibulum, . . . A hive like a shippe, or a haven for shippes.	*Naustible.* A Port or Haven for ships.
Naxia, . . . A kinde of whetstone in the ile of Cyprus	*Nax.* A kinde of Whetstone.
Necessitudo, . . . Neede, necessitie: kinne, alliance.	*Necessitude.* Kinne, alliance in bloud.
Necyomantia, . . . Necromancie, divination by calling of spirits.	*Necyomantie.* Divination by calling up damned spirits.
Neogamus, . . . Newly married, a bridegroome.	*Neogamus.* A Bridegroome.

Thomas, 1606 Edition	Cockeram, 1623
Neoptolemus, . . . A young or new souldier.	*Neoptolimus.* A new souldier.
Neuricus, . . . That hath the goute or griefe in the sinewes.	*Neuricall.* Gowtie.
Nexilis, . . . That may be knit or tyed. . . .	*Nexible.* Which may bee knit.
Nictatio, . . . A winking or twinckling with the eyes.	*Nictation.* The twinckling of the eye.
Nidulor, . . . To build or make a nest.	*Nidulate.* To build a nest.
Nixurio, . . . To endeavour or attempt a thing.	*Nixuriate.* To indevour, to attempt.

Though the percentage of words and definitions derived from Thomas' Latin-English dictionary may not be relatively so large in other letters of the alphabet as in the *N* of Cockeram, the indebtedness throughout the first part is fairly large and fairly obvious. For the student of lexicography the first part of the Cockeram, the sources of which we have just considered, is most important. The second and third parts of the early editions, however, require consideration.

It will be remembered that in his second book or division Cockeram had listed "vulgar" words together with their more "refined or elegant" equivalents. His list was based upon entries found in Rider's *Bibliotheca Scholastica,* or the later revisions (1606, 1612, 1617) of this book by Francis Holyoke. The lists below will show where Cockeram found his "vulgar" and his "refined" terms.

Rider, 1589; Rider-Holyoke, 1617		Cockeram, 1623	
To Charge, or burden	Onero	*To charge,*	Onerate
So charged	Oneratus		
Chargeable or burdenous	Onerosus	*Chargeable,*	Onerous
To charme, or enchaunt		*To Charme,*	Incantate
	Incanto, excanto		
A Charme or enchauntement	Incantatio	*A Charme,*	Incantation
Chaste	Castus, continens	*Chaste,*	Continent
Chastitie	Castitas, . . . continentia	*Chastitie,*	Continencie
To Chastise	Castigo	*to Chastise,*	Castigate
Chiefe, or principall	Primus	*the Cheefe,*	Prime
Cheapnes	Vilitas	*Cheapnesse,*	Vility
Cheese made of mares milke	Hippace	*a Cheese made of Mares milke,*	
			Hippace

RIDER, 1589; RIDER-HOLYOKE, 1617		COCKERAM, 1623	
To Cherish	Foveo	*to Cherish,*	Foster
To Chide, or rebuke	Iurgo, objurgo	*to Chide,*	Objurgate
A Chiding	Objurgatio	*Chidings,*	Rixations, Objurgations
To bee great with Childe	Gravidor	*to be with Childe,*	Gravidate
The childe in the mothers wombe before it have perfect shape		*the Childe in the wombe ere it have received any perfect shape,*	Embryon
	Embrio, . . . Embryon		
Great with childe	Gravida, pregnans	*a being great with Childe,*	
			Pregnation, Gravidation
Childishness	Pueritia, puerilitas	*Childishness,*	Puerility
Chill with colds	Algidus	*Chill with cold,*	Algide

To extend this list is needless. It is obvious that Cockeram found most, if not all, of his so-called "vulgar" words in the English-Latin section of the Rider-Holyoke dictionary; and the "more refined and elegant" terms represent Cockeram's attempt to Anglicize Rider's Latin equivalents of the English. This process is significant in thus introducing a great many Latin words into the English vocabulary. Some of these were already current; others were not. Though many of the Anglicized Latin words thus introduced did not catch on, some remained a permanent part of the English vocabulary.

The third book of Cockeram's *Dictionarie*, as it was before the revision of 1670, was also much indebted to the English-Latin part of the Rider-Holyoke dictionary. Besides the proper names of gods and men and odd lore on these, Cockeram had in this section items on birds, fishes, herbs, stones, etc. It is on the latter topics that he draws most obviously from the Rider-Holyoke. Compare, for example, in the two dictionaries the items: under Hawks, *Short-winged Hawkes, Long-winged Hawkes;* under Fishes and Herbs, *Psycotrophi, Cephalus, Ærica, Musculus, Ophiusta, Mycophonos, Vlex, Achimedis, Anacampseras;* under Stones and Trees, *Amanis cornu, Amphitane, Androdamas, Dendritis, Onyx, Gemites, Sycamore.*[4]

Though such miscellaneous lore on men and gods and beasts as appears in the third part of the *Dictionarie* was common in the larger Latin-English dictionaries, Cockeram was the first to introduce it into English lexicography. His innovation, an encyclopedic feature, extends the scope and usefulness of the dictionary. Through its use the reader may identify ancient men and women, the more common mythological allusions, as well as the pseudo-scientific references to birds and beasts. Many of the entries are entertaining as well as instructive. Note, for example, the following:

Chamelion, the least of all Beasts, which breeds Egges or spawn, it changeth it self into any colour that it sits on, except white and red: therefore unconstant men are sometimes called Chamelions; it is said, it only lives by ayr.

Gagulus Icterus, a Bird, whom if any one behold that hath the Yellow-Jaundies, immediately they become whole, and the Bird dieth.

Hiena, a subtil Beast like a Wolf, having a mane and hair on his body, counterfeiting the voice of a man; in the night it will call shepherds out of their houses, and kill them; he is sometime male, and sometime female.

Lizard, A little Beast much like the Evet, but without poison, breeding in Italy and other Countreyes: the dung of this Beast is good to take away the spots in the eye, and cleareth the sight, and the head thereof being bruised and laid to, draweth out thorns, or any thing sticking in the flesh.

Scolopendra, a Fish which feeling himself taken with the hook, casteth out his bowels, and then having loosed the hook, swalloweth them again.

Cockeram's innovation definitely anticipates certain features, such as the brief biographies, common to most English dictionaries of the present day.

From 1642 through 1658—that is, from the seventh through the eleventh editions—few changes except in spelling were made in the Cockeram dictionaries. In the meantime, Bullokar's *Expositor,* the rival dictionary, had been revised in 1663, and reorganized into a threefold dictionary after the manner of Cockeram's. The reviser had augmented Bullokar's word list by borrowing from Cockeram.[5] In 1670 appeared the twelfth and last known edition of Cockeram's *Dictionarie.* This edition, extensively revised, incorporated the new features of the rival *Expositor.* Even the wording of the new title-page indicates the reviser's competitive spirit. It begins: "The English Dictionary; or an EXPOSITOR of Hard English Words, Newly Refined. . . ." "S.C.," the reviser, then explains that the whole dictionary has been cast into a new form and method. The major changes in organization are: (1) the introduction, after each letter of the alphabet in the first part, of law terms and definitions; (2) the omission of the second list, the "vulgar" words with "choice equivalents"; and (3) the extensive revision of the third part, which now becomes the second part.

The new hard-word list differs considerably from that in the last edition (1658) of Cockeram. Though many words are omitted, many more are added so that the total number is increased by about 2,000. Definitions are shortened and clarified. The law terms, which are introduced in this first part of the 1670 Cockeram and which had long been a feature of Bullokar, Blount, and other dictionaries, were derived ultimately, if not directly, from Rastell's *Termes de la Ley*.

The proper names, formerly the third part of the dictionary, now form the second part with the list and the items considerably altered. The new heading runs: "Table of the Proper Names of Gods, Goddesses, Men, Women, Giants, Birds, Beasts, Serpents, Rivers, etc." These are arranged alphabetically and are generally more compact and explicit than in earlier issues.[6]

The introduction of geographical terms and English place names is in keeping with the precedent in the Latin-English dictionaries of the sixteenth and seventeenth centuries and Charles Stephanus' *Dictionarium Historicum, Geographicum, Poeticum*.

To conclude the study of Cockeram's work, we may state that, in making a threefold division of his dictionary, the compiler extends the range of interest and appeal far beyond that of Cawdrey and Bullokar and introduces more entries than both his predecessors have. Cockeram's plan of organization was adopted, in 1663, by the revisers of Bullokar's *Expositor*. Though without sound linguistic knowledge, Cockeram attempts to distinguish among choice words of current usage, vulgar words, and refined and elegant terms. In thus drawing attention to the desirability of discriminating between words, the compiler, by implication, anticipates the idea of a standard of good usage. In the third book, Cockeram introduces for the first time into the English dictionary the biographical sketch and miscellaneous information—an encyclopedic feature destined to be adopted by most lexicographers of the present day.

Precedent for this custom Cockeram found in the Latin-English dictionaries of the sixteenth and seventeenth centuries—in Cooper, Thomas, Rider-Holyoke. The chief observation, indeed, to be made about Cockeram's *Dictionarie* is its close relationship to the bilingual Latin-

English and English-Latin dictionaries current in his day. These determine Cockeram's organization, much of his word list and definitions, the biographical and miscellaneous matter, and, of course, the introduction into English of many Latin words. His English *Dictionarie* thus follows the long tradition of the Latin-English and English-Latin dictionaries.

Chapter V

THOMAS BLOUNT's *Glossographia* (1656)

THOUGH THE DICTIONARIES OF BULLOKAR AND COCKERAM continued to be published at regular intervals, no new English dictionary was compiled between 1623 and 1656. In the latter year Thomas Blount first published his *Glossographia*. Blount (1618-1679), a barrister of the Inner Temple and a Roman Catholic, published, besides the dictionary, the *Academie of Eloquence* (1654),[1] *A Law Dictionary* (1670), *Fragmenta Antiquitatis, Ancient Tenures of Land* (1679), and other works. The title-page of the *Glossographia*, an octavo volume, runs:

Glossographia: or a Dictionary, Interpreting all such Hard Words, Whether Hebrew, Greek, Latin, Italian, Spanish, French, Teutonick, Belgick, British or Saxon; as are now used in our refined English Tongue.

Also the Terms of Divinity, Law, Physick, Mathematicks, Heraldry, Anatomy, War, Musick, Architecture; and of several other Arts and Sciences Explicated.

With Etymologies, Definitions, and Historical Observations on the same. Very useful for all such as desire to understand what they read.

By T. B. of the Inner-Temple, Barrester. London. ... 1656.

Despite the competition from the dictionaries already in circulation and from that of Edward Phillips published in 1658, Blount's *Glossographia* enjoyed a fair degree of popularity. Editions appeared as follows: 1st, 1656; 2nd, 1661; 3rd, 1670; 4th, 1674; 5th, 1681. On the title-page of the second edition the author states that "above Five hundred choice Words are added." As the size of the pages and the printer's signatures remain the same, we must infer either many substitutions or an overestimate of the number of new entries. The latter inference seems

37

nearer the truth. In the third edition of 1670 "many additions" are claimed; and there is an expansion of ten leaves, or about 400 words. The fourth and fifth editions show practically no further augmentations of the *Glossographia*.

As the title-page shows, the *Glossographia* is more ambitious than preceding works of the kind. The borrowed words or hard words that Blount proposes to interpret include those derived from a large number of foreign languages, ancient and modern. Though for this extension Blount found suggestions in Bullokar, he was doubtless influenced by the polyglot lexicon of Minsheu, an authority cited in "To the Reader" and in the text proper. Blount intends his text to be useful not only to "the more-knowing women and less-knowing men" and the unlearned, as in the earlier dictionaries, but to the "best of Schollers" and to "all such as desire to understand what they read."

The genesis and purposes of the work the author explains at length in his "To the Reader." He writes that, though he had a "reasonable knowledge in the Latine and French Tongues . . . and a smattering both of Greek and other Languages," yet he often found himself "gravelled in English Books." He cites some of the words of foreign origin which he had encountered in reading French, Turkish, and Roman history, and books of divinity. Not only did words in his reading "gravell" him; but so did many of the terms he heard spoken by tradesmen, shopkeepers, cooks, and others.[2] Thinking he was not alone in his ignorance of such terms, Blount wished to compile a book that would be useful to himself as well as to others in understanding the language.

What Blount writes about strange words found in his reading and others heard among London tradesmen reveals a sensitive ear and an awareness of words—prerequisites for a lexicographer. The address throughout shows a better understanding of the nature of language and of some of the problems of the lexicographer than is exhibited by his predecessors in the field. His theory, however, is more commendable than his practice. An analysis of the *Glossographia* and its sources seems to indicate that Blount did not know how best to supply the need he perceived or, for some reason, was unwilling to take the trouble to do so. He professes to have "done little with my own Pencil" and makes a blanket acknowledgment of indebtedness to Scapula, Minsheu, Cotgrave,

Rider, Florio, Thomasius, Davies, Cowell, and others. Though there is slight indebtedness to most of these, the general list appears to be a means of concealing his chief obligations. To Thomas' *Dictionarium* and to Francis Holyoke's *Dictionarium Etymologicum*, the latter partially concealed by the name "Rider," [3] Blount owed his greatest debt. Before giving the details of Blount's obligation to these Latin-English sources, we shall notice briefly his minor debts to Bullokar and other compilers.

Though Bullokar is not mentioned in the general list of authorities in Blount's address to the reader, he is cited, from time to time, in the text proper. But Blount in his first edition by no means gives credit for all of his borrowings from Bullokar. In subsequent editions Blount even omits many of the acknowledgments he had made to his predecessor in the first. Compare the following, from the first editions of Bullokar and Blount:

Bullokar, 1616

Audience. An hearing, or hearkning: sometime it signifieth an assembly of people hearkening to something spoken.

Axiom. A Maxim, or Proposition, or short sentence generally allowed to be true; as in saying—*The whole is greater then a part....*

Azymes. A solemnity of seven days among the Jews, in which it was not lawful to eat leavened bread: the Pasche or Easter of the Jews.

Eccho. A rebounding, or sounding back of any noise, or voice in a wood, valley, or hollow place. Poets feign that the Eccho was a Nymph so called, which being rejected of one, whom she loved, pined away for sorrow in the woods, where her voice still remaineth answering the outcries of all complaints.

Blount, 1656

Audience ... the sence of hearing, listning; sometime it signifies an assembly of people hearkening to something spoken. ...

Axiome ... A maxim or general ground in any Art: a Proposition or short Sentence generally allowed to be true, as in saying *The whole is greater then its part.*

Azymes ... was a solemnity of seven days among the Jews, in which it was not lawful to eat leavened bread; the Pasche or Easter of the Jews. *Bull.*

Eccho or Echo ... a resounding or giving again of any noyse, or voyce in a Wood, Valley, or Hollow place. Poets feign that this Eccho was a Nymph so called, who being rejected by one whom she loved, pined away for sorrow in the Woods, where her voyce still remains answering the outcries of all complaints.

Further illustrations of Blount's indebtedness to Bullokar may be found in these entries: *Alabaster, Allegory, Allelujah, Aloesuccotrina, Antiperistasis, Architect, Arke, Arteries, Aspect, Astronomie, Attired, Balme, Bissextile, Bitumen, Boras, Burnish.* Eleven of these borrowings Blount acknowledged in the first edition, but very few of them in the second and subsequent editions.[4]

In 1667 Blount edited John Rastell's *Terms of the Law* (*Les Termes de la Ley*), the famous dictionary of law terms in French and English. As Blount himself was a lawyer and as every lawyer knew this famous book, it is not strange that Blount should have used it in compiling the *Glossographia.* Although Blount got information from other law treatises, such as Cowell's *Interpreter,* he drew freely from Rastell, as did later compilers. Space forbids further quotation of definitions; but definitions of the following terms are typical of those which Blount borrows from Rastell's *Terms of the Law:*

Baston, Bilinguis, Borrow English, Conders, Confiscate, Conjuration, Coraage, Cornage, Coverture, Court-baron, Cranage, Courtilage, Dammage-fesant.[5]

Blount's borrowing from Bullokar, Cowell, and Rastell is quite overshadowed by his greater debt to two Latin-English dictionaries: Thomas Thomas' *Dictionarium Linguae Latinae et Anglicanae* and Francis Holyoke's *Dictionarium Etymologicum.* These two closely related texts —Holyoke had borrowed freely from Thomas—Blount must have kept open before him in compiling the *Glossographia.* He followed first one, then the other, sometimes making a composite definition by borrowing phrases from each. The parallel entries below, from Blount and his sources, illustrate the nature of their relationships.

THOMAS, 1632 Edition	HOLYOKE, 1639 Edition	BLOUNT, 1656
Adaequo, . . . To make even, plaine, or alike: to advance himselfe that he may be like or equall to another.	*Adaequo* . . . To make even, equall, or plaine, to make like, to match, to attaine.	*Adequate* (adaequo) make even, plain or level, to advance himself, that he may be even with or like to another.
Adulatio, . . . Properly the fawning of a dogge: flatterie.	*Adulatio* . . . flattery, fawning	*Adulation* (adulatio) properly the fawning of a dog, flattery.

THOMAS, 1632 Edition	HOLYOKE, 1639 Edition	BLOUNT, 1656
Adumbratio, . . . A shadowing or bare pourtraying of a thing: also an imitation or expressing of another thing, somewhat to the likenes and nature of the same.	*Adumbratio* . . . A shadowing, a likenesse or resembling, a portraying, also an imitation.	*Adumbration* (adumbratio) a shadowing or bare portraying of a thing; also an imitation or expressing of another thing somewhat to the likeness and nature of the same.
Aduncus, . . . C r o o k e d downewards, hooked.	*Aduncus* . . . Hooked, crooked, writhen.	*Aduncous* (a d u n c u s) crooked. *A d u n q u e* downwards, hooked.
Acrimonia, . . . Sharpnesse that biteth the tongue and pearceth the head . . . also sharpnesse in speaking our mind; livelines, quicknes of wit.	*Acrimonia* . . . Sowrenesse or sharpnesse; vehemence in speech, livelinesse of minde, quicknesse of wit.	*Acrimony* (acrimonia) sharpness, sourness.
Aculeatus, . . . That pricketh or stingeth, biting, taunting, spitefull.	*Aculeatus* . . . that hath a sting, or pricke, biting, vexing.	*Aculeate* (aculeatus) that hath a sting or pricke, biting, vexing. *Bac.*
Acumino, . . . To sharpen.	*Acumino* . . . To make sharp-edged, to whet.	*Acuminate* (acumino) to make sharp-edged or pointed.
Acupictor, . . . A n e m - broiderer.	*Acupictor* . . . A n e m - broiderer, one that worketh needle work.	*Acupictor* (Latine) an Embroiderer, or any one that works with a Needle.
Adonai, hebr. Lord.	*Adonai,* nomen Dei apud Heb. . . . A Lord or Sustainer, our great Lord.	*Adonai* (Hebr.) a Lord or sustainer, the Jews use this as an ordinary name of God.
Advigilo, . . . To watch, to take good heede, to take paines, to use diligence.	*Advigilo* . . . To watch diligently, to apply, to give himself earnestly unto.	*Advigilate* (advigilo) to watch diligently.
Adamo, . . . to love foolishly or wantonly: to desire fervently.	*A d a m o* . . . to l o v e deerely or tenderly, foolishly to love, fervently to desire.	*Adamate* (adamo) to love dearly, to love foolishly or wantonly; to desire fervently.

THOMAS, 1632 Edition	HOLYOKE, 1639 Edition	BLOUNT, 1656
Adeptio, . . . Obtaining, acquisition, or getting.	*Adeptio* . . . An attaining, a getting, an enjoying.	*Adeption* (adeptio) an obtaining, a getting or enjoying. *Adeption* (adeptio) an obtaining, acquisition, or getting.[6]
Adoxia, . . . Slander, ignominy, infamy.	*Adoxia* . . . Ignominy, shame, reproach or slander, dishonour.	*Adoxy* (adoxia) ignominy, shame, slander, infamy.
Advesperascit, . . . It waxeth night, it draweth to the evening.	*Advesperascit* . . . It groweth towards evening.	*Advesperate* (advesperascit) it waxeth or grows toward night.

A comparative study of the entries above shows that Blount derives the first four from Thomas, the next six from Holyoke, and the final four from both Thomas and Holyoke—the last four, that is, are composites. This is the characteristic procedure of Blount. An examination of 77 consecutive entries, from *Acrimony* to *Adustion* in the *Glossographia,* for example, shows 27 to derive from Bullokar, Cowell, and elsewhere; and 50 entries, or almost 65 per cent, together with their definitions, to come from the Latin-English dictionaries of Thomas and Holyoke. Specifically 12 are from Thomas, 23 from Holyoke, 9 from either, 6 from both.

As further evidence of Blount's borrowing, consider the entries under the letter *A* in the *Glossographia.* Of 924 entries under the first letter of the alphabet, 627, or about 68 per cent, derive, partly or wholly, from Thomas and Holyoke. Thus the percentage of Latin-derived words for all entries under *A* is slightly higher than that in the list from *Acrimony* to *Adustion,* and about 10 per cent above the average for the whole text. In short, a careful estimate, letter by letter, of the borrowings in the *Glossographia* indicates that 58 per cent of Blount's entries derive, partly or wholly, from the Latin-English dictionaries of Thomas and Holyoke.[7]

What is the significance of this amazing performance? In the first place this is another illustration of the close dependence of seventeenth-century English dictionaries on Latin-English dictionaries of this period, a tendency already noted in the work of Cawdrey and Cockeram. In the second place Blount's extensive borrowing from the Latin-English dictionaries and his practice of Anglicizing Latin words is an excellent example of the way Latin became a part of the English vocabulary. Though some of the words thus brought in by Blount were already in use and though others which he introduced did not become established, many must have remained as a part of the English vocabulary.

Again Blount's free adaptation of Latin words from Thomas and Holyoke raises a question as to his procedure in including words from contemporary writers. Many words, for example, which Blount designates as from Bacon (*Bac.*) or Browne (*Vulg. Er.*) derive, in fact, directly from the Latin-English dictionaries. Apparently, Blount first introduced the word from the Latin and then, having discovered that it was used by one of the writers mentioned, he so designated. This procedure is quite different from that suggested in Blount's address to the reader. There he states that he has included many words from such authors as Lord Bacon, Dr. Browne, and Sir Kenelm Digby and has added the authors' names "that I might not be thought to be the innovator of them." In the light of Blount's practice, we must regard his statement as a defense against anticipated criticism of his numerous innovations.

It is interesting to discover, on the other hand, that a large number of unusual words from the Latin dictionaries not assigned by Blount to any writers were actually employed by contemporary authors. Walter Charleton, for example, published in 1651 his translation of *Epicurus His Morals*. In this book are more than fifty of the Anglo-Latin words [8] found in Blount. As the *Glossographia* was not printed until 1656, this could not have been Charleton's source. Nor was Charleton the source of Blount, for Blount's definitions are from Holyoke's Latin-English dictionary. In a similar way, there are numerous correspondences between the *Glossographia* and Sir Thomas Browne's *Pseudodoxia Epidemica, or Enquiries into Vulgar and Common Errors*. Of thirty words [9] collected from the *Vulgar Errors*, twenty are in the *Glossographia* without designation as to source; ten are in the same book but assigned to "Dr. B." or "*Vulg. Er.*" But Blount's definitions of the thirty derive from the Latin-English dictionaries of Thomas and Holyoke. Two conclusions may be drawn: (1) Blount first found his words and definitions in the Latin-English dictionaries and then, occasionally, supplied the names of authors in whose writing the words appeared; (2) Charleton, Browne, and others may have acquired the words from Blount's source —the Latin-English dictionaries. As one of the declared purposes of Blount was to enable the reader to understand what he found in English books, his dictionary seems partially to have served this end. Its publication at fairly regular intervals for a period of twenty-five years indicates that it was a useful book in its day.

Blount borrows definitions so freely and from such a variety of sources that it is doubtful whether any series of consecutive entries can be regarded as absolutely characteristic. In length the definitions run from a single phrase to a short expository essay of a column or more in his text. As a rule he indicates the foreign language from which a term is derived, the department to which it belongs, and, occasionally, an English writer by whom it is used. Among the terms requiring the expository essay are: *Artery, Assize, Augury, Babel, Divination,* and *Salique Law.* As nearly typical as any of the shorter definitions are the entries from *Depositum* to *Depudicate:*

Depositum (Lat.) a pledge or gage, that which is committed of trust to be kept, also a wager or stake.

Depredation (depraedatio) a robbing or spoiling, a preying upon.

Deprave (depravo) to corrupt, make crooked, to wrest.

Deprecation (deprecatio) a praying for pardon, and putting away by prayer.

Depredable (depredabilis) that may be robbed or spoiled. *Bac*[*on*].

Deprehend (deprehendo) to take at unawares, to take in the very act.

Depression (depressio) a pressing or weighing down.

Depretiate (depretio) to make the price less, to make cheaper.

Depromption (depromptio) a drawing or bringing forth.

Depudicate (depudico) to deflowre, to violate.

Some of the definitions in the *Glossographia* amuse by their phrasing or by their fanciful etymology, as:

Hony-Moon, applied to those married persons that love well at first, and decline in affection afterwards; it is hony now, but it will change as the moon. *Min.*

Tomboy, (a girle or wench that leaps up and down like a boy) comes from the Saxon *tumbe,* to dance, *tumbod,* danced; hence also comes the word *tumbling,* still in use.

Ventriloquist (*ventriloquus*) one that has an evil spirit speaking in his belly, or one that by use and practice can speak as it were out of his belly, not moving his lips.

It is not easy to evaluate Blount's work as a lexicographer. In some respects, he was better equipped than his predecessors. He had more leisure for study, he read more widely, he seemed better to understand the nature of language, he was more generous with respect to the introduction of new words—in fact, he recorded a great number seldom or never used, and he made certain innovations, which we shall discuss presently. Though he shows some progress, yet he depended too little on reading actual documents and recording words therefrom and too much on Latin-English dictionaries. Despite his shortcomings, certain items should be placed on the credit side of the ledger for Blount.

He continued, for example, the commendable practice of Bullokar, in placing a term in the department to which it belongs. A few illustrative entries, chosen at random, are: *Degree, Dispauper, Dodecatamerie, Drapery, Embost, Empanel, Encheson, Enthymeme, Epicycle.*

Blount, more than his predecessors, if we can judge from his "To the Reader," seems to have thought of language as a living, growing organism changing from year to year. This idea is explicit in his statement of the difficulties of the lexicographer. He had feared that his "labor would find no end, since our English tongue daily changes habit." (We may venture to suggest that the compiler's awareness of the difficulty of his task may have induced too great dependence on the Latin-English dictionaries.) Blount offers no protest against change; he saw change as inevitable. He realized the work involved in compiling a satisfactory dictionary and the necessity of frequent revision.

It is a question how much credit should be given Blount for the practice of introducing new words. He introduced a great many, not always with discrimination. His stout defense of his practice, in the address to the reader, may well be an attempt to justify a *fait accompli* inadvertently through his wide borrowing. Whatever the motive is, the defense is worthy of note. The objection that the use of newly-coined words is subject to censure is, Blount writes, "confuted by our best modern Authors, who have both infinitely inriched and enobled our Language, by admitting and naturalizing thousands of foreign words. . . . A few years have rendered them familiar even to vulgar capacities."

Such words, he informs us, appear in the works of Lord Bacon, Mr. Montagu, Sir Kenelm Digby, Sir Henry Wotton, Dr. Browne, and others. Words from these authors, Blount tells us, he has entered, adding the authors' names "that I might not be thought to be the innovator of them." In the light of the egregious number of neologisms Blount takes from Thomas and Holyoke, his statement is specious. Theoretically, however, Blount makes a good case for new words, concluding with the wise observation that one's "genius" and the character of the subject will determine the applicability of a word. In his address, Blount seems to have been cognizant of the traditional discussion of the English vocabulary and aligns himself with the liberal-minded who approve new words.

Blount is the first lexicographer of a purely English dictionary to attempt etymology of words. He indicates his aim on the title-page; and in his "To the Reader," he writes, "To some words I have added Etymologies, to others Historical observations, as they occurred, and this but *ex obliquo*." In case of a term derived from a foreign language, the compiler usually inserts in parentheses the foreign word or a letter indicating the language from which the word is derived. In some cases, as Blount himself states, he attempts to explain the origin of the word. Examples of his etymologizing may be seen under the entries: *Arthur, Druids, Shrew, Tumbrell, Turbant, Turneament, Vatican.* The proper name *Arthur*, for example, Blount explains as "a British word composed of *Arth*, which signifies a Bear, and *grw*, which signifies a man (*Vir*). So *Arthur, quasi* a man that for his strength and terror may be called a *Bear*." Of *Druids*, Blount writes, "They took their name from Δρυς, an *Oake*, because they held nothing more holy than an Oak . . . or because they were wont to exercise their superstition in Oaken groves. . . ." A *Shrew* is "a kind of Field-Mouse, which if he go over a beasts back, will make him lame in the Chine; and if he bite, the beast swells to the heart, and dyes. *Ges<ner>*. From hence came our English phrase, *I beshrew thee*, when we wish ill; and we call a curst woman, a *Shrew*."

However fanciful such etymologies may be, Blount deserves credit for having introduced the principle into the English dictionary proper. In bilingual and polyglot lexicons prior to the publication of the *Glossographia*, the author found ample precedent. Cooper, Thomas,

Francis Holyoke in their Latin-English dictionaries, and Minsheu in his polyglot *Guide into Tongues* (1617) all attempted etymology,[10] as they conceived it. In this element of technique as in hundreds of the definitions the *Glossographia* exemplifies once again the influence of bilingual lexicography, particularly Latin-English, on the development of the English dictionary. And this influence continues to the time of Samuel Johnson.

To Blount belongs the credit for being the first English lexicographer to cite the authorities he had consulted. He thus shows recognition of the task involved in his work and points the way to his successors in the field. He writes:

> To compile and compleat a Work of this nature and importance, would necessarily require an Encyclopedic of knowledge, and the concurrence of many learned Heads; yet that I may a little secure the Reader from a just apprehension of my disability for so great an undertaking, I profess to have done little with my own Pencil; but have extracted the quintessence of Scapula, Minsheu, Cotgrave, Rider, Florio, Thomasius, Dasipodius, and Hexam's Dutch, Dr. Davies Welsh Dictionary, Cowel's Interpreter and other able Authors for so much as tended to my purpose.

Though the *Glossographia* is more comprehensive generally than the earlier English dictionaries, it does not attempt to be all-inclusive. The author omits "poetical stories," except a few necessary to explain such terms as "Pandora's box," "tantalize," etc. For items of this kind, the reader is referred to a Latin dictionary Englished by Mr. Ross.[11] Likewise, "old Saxon words" have in great measure been excluded. These will be treated, the reader is informed, in an excellent dictionary, shortly expected, by the "learned Mr. Somner." [12]

Chapter VI

EDWARD PHILLIPS'

The New World of English Words (1658)

IN 1658, TWO YEARS AFTER THE PUBLICATION OF BLOUNT'S *Glosso-graphia*, Edward Phillips published a small folio entitled *The New World of English Words*. Phillips, the nephew of John Milton, was in youth instructed by the poet and attended Magdalen Hall, Oxford. He left the University without taking a degree and became a hack-writer in London. He is chiefly remembered for his dictionary. The title-page of this volume runs thus:

The New World of English Words: Or, a General Dictionary: Containing the Interpretations of such hard words as are derived from other Languages; whether Hebrew, Arabick, Syriack, Greek, Latin, Italian, French, Spanish, British, Dutch, &c., their Etymologies and perfect Definitions:

Together with All those Terms that relate to the Arts and Sciences; whether Theologie, Philosophy, Logic, Rhetorick, Grammer, Ethicks, Law, Natural History, Magick, Physick. ... [The author includes thirty-one other subjects in this list.]

To which are added The signification of Proper Names, Mythology, and Poetical Fictions, Historical Relations, Geographical Descriptions of most Countries and Cities of the World. ...

A Work very necessary for Strangers, as well as our own Countreymen, for all Persons that would rightly understand what they discourse, write, or read.

Collected and published by E. P.... London, ...1658.

The New World of English Words [1] contains approximately 11,000 entries. The increase in the number of definitions or entries over those in the *Glossographia* is accounted for, in part, by the inclusion of proper names, and historical and mythological items. The phrasing and content of Phillips' definitions are usually determined by his sources, as may be seen in the illustrations below. Though he frequently condenses the original to advantage, his efforts to compress or change the order of phrasing sometimes result in obscurity, as Blount points out. See the definitions of *Franchise Royal, To Grown,* and *Pathopep,* which are quoted below.

A study of the proper names and the items recorded under them reveals their source to be Charles Stephanus' *Dictionarium Historicum, Geographicum, Poeticum* (1553). This popular work was frequently reissued through the sixteenth and seventeenth centuries. For Latin-English dictionaries from about 1570 on, Stephanus was the chief source of information on proper names historical, mythological, geographical. These bilingual dictionaries, such as Cooper, Thomas, Holyoke, etc., devoted a special section to proper names, and included much of the matter from Stephanus. From the same source directly, or by way of an English translation, Phillips derived his information on proper names. As the practice of thus including names of men and gods, countries and places, was so common in the bilingual lexicons and as it had been used by Cockeram in the third part of his English dictionary long before *The New World of English Words,* it can hardly be regarded as an innovation by Phillips.

Other subordinate sources of Phillips are the small dictionaries of Bullokar and Cockeram. From these he borrowed some definitions. For many law terms, besides those which had appeared in Blount, Phillips turned to Rastell's *Termes de la Ley,* which had originally appeared in 1525 but had been many times reissued, and to Cowell's *The Interpreter* (1607, 1637, etc.).[2] As these law lexicons are themselves closely related, it is not always possible to determine which is Phillips' source. In the case of *Custos brevium, Debets & solet,* and *Defendimus* either Rastell or Cowell could have been the source. In *Departure in spite of the court,* Rastell is the obvious source; in *Declaration* Phillips drew upon both texts. In the entries *Deforsour, Demand, Demesne or Demain, Denizen, Deodand, De Deoneranda, Departer, Detinue,* the source is Cowell. A comparative study of the law terms in the *New World* shows, indeed, that by far the larger number derives from Cowell's *Interpreter.* All told, the law terms borrowed from these two sources and from Blount's *Glossographia* are so great in number that one wonders what Phillips' alleged specialist in the law may have contributed.

Notwithstanding his debts to Stephanus and the law lexicons of Rastell and Cowell, Phillips' chief source was Thomas Blount's *Glossographia*. As the title-page of the *New World* shows, Phillips' claims are very similar to, though more pretentious than, those of his immediate predecessor. Further study of the texts reveals that for his title, much of his "Advertisement to the Reader," and for hundreds of his definitions, Phillips is directly dependent upon Blount. Apparently attempting to conceal his indebtedness, Phillips, in his "Advertisement," seeks to disparage and discredit the work of Blount. His debt to the *Glossographia* is, however, so obvious that he who runs may read. Compare, for example, the following:

BLOUNT, 1656	PHILLIPS, 1658
Capricorn (capricornus) the Goat or one of the 12 signes of the Zodiack, . . . so the Sun (when in Mid-December, he enters the Tropick of Capricorn) ascends our Hemisphere. *Min.*	*Capricorn,* a Goat, also the name of one of the twelve signs of the Zodiack, into which the Sun enters in the midst of Winter.
Caprification (caprificatio) husbanding or dressing wild fig-trees or other Trees.	*Caprification,* (Lat.) a term in Husbandry, the dressing of wild vines or fig-trees.
Capriole (Fr.) a caper in dancing, also the leaping of a horse above ground, called by horsemen the Goats leap.	*Capriole,* (French) a caper in dancing, also a term in Horsemanship, called the Goatleap.
Capstand an Instrument to wind up things of great weight, a Crane. *Bul.*	*Capstand* or *Capstern,* a term in Navigation, being an instrument in a ship to weigh Anchor, a winde-beame or draw-beame.
Capsulary (from capsula) pertaining to a little Coffer, Chest or Casket.	*Capsulary,* (Lat.) belonging to a little chest or coffer.
Captation (captatio) subtility to get favor, a cunning endeavor to get a thing.	*Captation,* (Lat.) an endeavouring to get favor or applause.
Captious (captiosus) full of craft, curious, . . . taking hold of every little occasion to pick quarrels.	*Captious,* (Lat.) apt to take exceptions.

BLOUNT, 1656	PHILLIPS, 1658
Captivate (captivo) to take captive or prisoner.	*Captivate*, (Lat.) to take prisoner: it is also taken in an amorous sense.
Caracol (fr. the Fr.) to cast themselves into a round ring, as souldiers do.	*Caracol*, (French) spoken chiefly for souldiers, to cast themselves into a round ring.
Caravan . . . (Fr. Caravane) a convoy of souldiers for the safety of Merchants that travel by Land.	*Caravan*, (French) a convoy of souldiers for the safety of Merchants that travel by land in the Eastern Countries.

As further illustration of Phillips' indebtedness, compare in the two texts the entries between *Cabula* and *Cardiognostick*. Phillips here has 211 entries including proper names; 156 excluding proper names, for which the source is Charles Stephanus. In the same range of entries, Blount has 148 words. Of these, Phillips appropriates 104; that is, of his 156 entries exclusive of proper names Phillips borrows 104 from Blount. Something like this percentage will obtain for the whole text.

Blount soon learned with anger to what extent Phillips had appropriated the *Glossographia*. He was further vexed by the belief that Phillips was the compiler of a new law dictionary, *Nomothetes*, which Blount supposed to be based on his own law dictionary. In 1673, therefore, Blount published his *A World of Errors Discovered in the New World of Words, or General English Dictionary, and in Nomothetes, or The Interpreter of Law-Words and Terms*, in which he exposed Phillips' wholesale thefts, showing that the pilferer had copied even the errors of the *Glossographia*.[3] In the prefatory address of *A World of Errors*, Blount tells his story so well that the pertinent parts will be quoted.

TO THE READER

Must this then be suffered? A Gentleman for his divertisement writes a Book, and this Book happens to be acceptable to the World, and sell; a Bookseller, not interested in the Copy, instantly employs some Mercenary to jumble up another like Book out of this, with some Alterations and Additions, and give it a new Title; and the first Author's out-done, and his Publisher half undone.

Thus it fared with my *Glossographia*, the fruit of above Twenty years spare hours, first published in 1656. Twelve Moneths had not passed, but there appeared in Print this *New World of Words, or General English Dictionary*, extracted almost wholly out of mine, and taking in its first Edition even a great part of my Preface; onely some words were added and others altered, to make it pass as the Authors legitimate off-spring. In these Additions and Alterations he not seldom erred, yet had not those Errors been continued, with new supplies to a Second and third Impression, so little was I concerned at the particular injury, that these Notes (in great part collected from his first Edition) had never reproached his Theft to the World.

First therefore, this gallant Piece [Phillips' *New World*] faces it with a pompous Frontispiece, wherein are sculped our two famous *Universities*, the Pictures of Sir *Francis Bacon*, Sir *Henry Spelman*, Mr. *Selden*, *Camden*, and others of our most Learned Men of the last Age, with a Scholar of each University in his Formalities. And the Title Page affirms the work *to be very necessary for strangers, as well as our own Countrymen:* As if our Author intended the World should believe his Book to be the *Factotum* of all *Great Britains* learning, and himself the Parent of so immense a Production.

Soon after we find a *Catalogue* prefixed of the names of divers Learned Persons of this Age, *Eminent in or contributory to any of those Arts, Sciences, or faculties contained in the following Work.* Whereby the Author would at least obscurely insinuate, that those Learned Persons had contributed to or assisted him in it, thereby to advance its reputation; but I believe nothing less, having heard some of the chief of them utterly disown both the Author and his Work.

[Blount here cites Dr. Skinner's judgment of the *New World* and its author—an adverse judgment—and then proceeds:] What then will *Strangers* think of it; what our own *Countreymen?* They will say, *Canis festinans caecos parit catulos:* That such a Dictionary cannot be hudled up in Eight or ten Moneths, nor without much industry and care, though the Author be never so learned. . . .

After summarizing Phillips' borrowings and his shortcomings in various fields, Blount gives in alphabetical order a list of 100 specimen entries, with acid comments on the errors. The following are representative:

Bigamy, The marriage of two Wives at the same time, which according to Common Law hinders a man from taking holy orders.

Here our Author speaks some truth, at peradventure: For he that marries two Wives at the same time commits Felony, and the punishment of Felony is Death; which (suppose it be by hanging) may very

well hinder him from taking holy Orders—I find he does not understand the word.

Chace (French) A Warren—

He might as well have said a Bull is an Ox; for *Chace* and *Warren*
(so they are written) differ as much.

Emergent, An Emergent occasion is taken for a business of great consequence.

Well guessed! An *Emergent occasion,* is that which rises unexpectedly
out of some other, and was not foreseen.

Franchise Royal, Is where the King Grants to a person and his heirs to be
quit, or the like.

To be quit, of, God knows what.

Gallon (Spanish) A measure containing two quarts.

Our author had better omitted this word, since every Alewife can
contradict him.

To *Grown,* The Foresters say, a Buck *growneth.*

But what it means you must learn elsewhere; for this is all he says
of the word.

Lungis (French) A tall slim Man, that hath no length to his heighth.

Quasi, A low gross Man that has no thickness to his bulk.

None of a Day, The third quarter of a day, from Noon till Sun-set.

Where then shall we find the other three-quarters?—He should have
said from Noon till the Sun be half-way down.

Pathopep (Greek) An expression of a Passion, in Rhetorick it is a figure
by which the mind.

We are left to guess at the rest; for so he leaves it. And *Pathopep* is
an unknown word of his *New World.*

Quaver, A measure of time in Musick, being the half of a Crotchet, as a
Crotchet the half of a Quaver, a Semiquaver, &c.

What fustian is here? Just so, two is the half of four, and four the
half of two; and *Semi-quaver* is explicated by a dumb '*&c.*'

Blount's statements in this address to the reader are substantiated by
the evidence in the texts, excepting the allegation that Phillips was
employed by an unscrupulous bookseller to compile the *New World
of Words.* And the latter statement seems at least plausible. That
Phillips' dictionary was extracted largely from Blount's *Glossographia,*
that Phillips took part of Blount's Preface, that he made many errors
in his haste, that he had a pompous frontispiece, that he had a catalogue

of the names of eminent persons allegedly contributors to the dictionary
—all these are established facts. The equivocal nature of Phillips'
catalogue may be seen from the headings of his lists. In 1658, Phillips
writes: "The names of those learned Gentlemen and artists, as also
of those Arts and Sciences, to which they contributed their assistance."
Then follows the list of names. In the 1671 edition, the list is somewhat changed and the heading runs: "The Names of the Learned
Persons of this Age, Eminent in, or Contributory to, any of those Arts,
Sciences or Faculties contained in the following Work." When we read
these headings, we are ready to accept Blount's word that some of those
named "utterly" disowned the author and his work. There is no evidence in the text to indicate that specialists did actually make contributions.

Though what we have written thus far has reference to the first
edition (1658) of the *New World*, it is applicable in general to subsequent editions printed during Phillips' lifetime. The second edition
(1662), for example, reveals only minor changes and little or no augmentation, the printer's signatures being the same as in the first. In
the third edition (1671) there is an increase of perhaps 2,000 words,
making a total of 13,000 for the volume. Anthony a Wood [4] states
that Phillips for this edition "did involve most of 'Blount's Law Dictionary' into another edition of the said *New World of Words* which
he was then about to print." Wood then quotes part of a letter sent
to him by Blount, 14 March, 1670, complaining that his *Law Dictionary*
was being surreptitiously transcribed at the press and disguised with a
new title. Wood interprets Blount's reference to mean that Phillips
was thus augmenting the third edition of the *New World*. Blount was
really referring to a new law dictionary, *Nomothetes*, which was being
compiled by Thomas Manley, though Blount seems to have thought by
Phillips. Now the 1671 edition of the *New World* has a good many
definitions of law terms very similar to those in Blount's *Law Dictionary*; but these definitions, many of which had appeared in the 1658
edition of the *New World*, came from Cowell's *Interpreter*, also the
source of Blount. Though the *Nomothetes*, the law dictionary by
Manley, did borrow some definitions from Blount, it borrowed much
more from Cowell. Blount was touchy on the subject; he was measuring
his competitors' corn by his own bushel. The increase in the 1671 *New*

World then was, in the matter of law terms, derived from Cowell; and in certain Biblical items presumably from their natural source.

The fourth edition (1678) of the *New World* presents a slight increase in the main word list and adds two other peculiar lists. The first is termed: "An Appendix of several words necessary to be added to the foregoing Dictionary, with an Amplification or Emendation of others." It is difficult to determine what is the basis of this odd assortment. A few of the words under the letter *E*, for example, are: *Earning, Ecclesiastes, Eftsoones, E.G. (Exempli Gratia), Egrets, Eleutherius, To Embarrass, Embrasures, Enallage, Enceinte, Endemious, Enna, Envoy, Epiphanius, Erasbles.* One of the more interesting remarks accompanies the following entry: "*California,* a very large part of Northern America, uncertain whether Continent or Island." For a part of this list Phillips depended upon Bullokar and Cockeram.

The second miscellaneous list is headed with these words: "A Collection of such affected words from the Latin and Greek, as are either to be used warily, and upon occasion only, or totally to be rejected as Barbarous, and illegally compounded or derived; the most notorious of which last are noted with an Obelisk." The idea of such a collection may have been suggested by Cockeram's twofold list of "vulgar" words and "fustian" terms together with the more "refined and elegant" terms. Cockeram, however, was not the source for the words and definitions. These come directly from Blount's *Glossographia,* probably the 1670 edition. It looks as though Phillips, by thus putting in a black list words chosen from the *Glossographia,* were making a side hit at Blount, who had been attacking Phillips for plagiarism. The following definitions of "barbarous and illegally compounded" words, for example, in the *New World* (1678) correspond almost verbatim to entries in the *Glossographia* of 1670:

Cacography (Greek) ill writing.
Cacologie (Greek) evil communication, a discourse of ill things.
Catoptographicks (Greek) Books treating of that part of perspective called Catoptrica.
Caesariated (Lat.) having a great bush or large locks of hair.
Cephalonomancy (Greek ...) a Divination by the broil'd head of an Asse.
Ceratine, made of wax.
Ceromancie (Hybr.) a Divination by wax put into water.

Chironomer (Greek) an Instructor in certain gestures to be used with the hand in dancing, fencing, or the like.

Cindalism (Gr.) a play used among children, commonly called Dust-point.

Cinerulent (Lat.) full of dust or ashes.

Circumbilivagination, a going round, or in a circular motion.

Circumstantiation (Lat.) a making out by Circumstances.

To *Circumvest* (Lat.) to cloath about.

These and, in fact, Phillips' entire list, except for a few additions from some other source, derive from the 1670 Blount. Other "affected" words and "barbarisms" thus derived are: *Autograph, Bibliography, Cacoponie, Divagation, Euthanasie, Evangelize, Ferocious, Hageographie, Inimical, Misanthrope, Misogynist*—words now approved.

The fifth edition (1696), with another issue in 1700, represents the first thoroughgoing and intelligent revision of the *New World.*[5] As the date of Phillips' death is put at 1696, it seems doubtful whether he was responsible for this revision. At any rate the word list is increased to about 17,000 items, and all are placed in a single vocabulary. The list of curious words in the fourth edition has disappeared; classical names are omitted or the items on these much abbreviated; Chaucerian words are added, as also are many legal, medical, and technical terms. As stated on the title-page, the reviser has drawn new matter from such works as Furetière's *Dictionnaire Universel,* Chauvin's *Lexicon Rationale,* and Ozunam's *Dictionnaire Mathématique.*

To complete the record, we may mention here one subsequent revision of Phillips' *New World*—that by J. Kersey in 1706, which was reprinted in 1720. The Kersey-Phillips text contained about 38,000 words, and was one of the first of the universal dictionaries. But the detailed account of this volume must await our discussion of Kersey.

It is difficult to assess the value of Edward Phillips' efforts as a lexicographer, for he, even more than his predecessors, was dependent upon the work of other compilers. He took freely and without acknowledgment whatever he deemed suited to his purpose. He put to work very few original ideas, though he gave emphasis to some already current. The format of the *New World,* a small folio, is more attractive and dignified than are those of his predecessors. He introduces a greater number of proper names, including place names, and probably more old words. He thus extends the word list. Exemplifying the traditional discussion of the English vocabulary and following the precedent of Davies' Welsh-Latin and Latin-Welsh dictionary (*Antiquae Linguae Britannicae Dictionarium*, 1632) and borrowing from Davies and from Verstegan's *Restitution of Decayed Intelligence* (1605), Phillips writes a Preface concerned with the history of the English language. He gave prominence to the practice of Bullokar and Blount in introducing in the entry a term indicating the department to which a word belonged. His claim of having a corps of specialists—a claim not in fact supported by the evidence—to contribute to his dictionary was an excellent idea, and was brazenly advertised. It remained, however, for later lexicographers to put this idea into practice.

We may say then that the *New World* exemplifies and gives prominence to certain methods already employed but not consistently used, such as giving information about persons and places, consulting specialists in the various fields of knowledge, and indicating the field to which a term belongs. Such was the foundation upon which Kersey was to build a competent dictionary.

Chapter VII

ELISHA COLES'S *An English Dictionary* (1676)

TWO YEARS BEFORE THE FOURTH EDITION OF PHILLIPS' *New World* appeared, Elisha Coles published his octavo *English Dictionary* (1676). We hear of Coles as a teacher of Latin and English in London, 1663, as usher of Merchant Taylors' school, 1677, and a year later as master of Galway school. He published among other items a treatise on shorthand (1674) and, besides his English dictionary, a Latin dictionary in 1677. He died in 1680. He is one of a long list of schoolmasters of the sixteenth and seventeenth centuries who published dictionaries.

Coles is in the tradition of his forebears. He knows them all, we are informed in his "To the Reader," from Dr. Bullokar to Dr. Skinner. And the title-page conveys the conventional purpose. It reads:

An English Dictionary: Explaining The difficult Terms that are used in Divinity, Husbandry, Physick, Phylosophy, Law, Navigation, Mathematicks, and other Arts and Sciences.

Containing Many thousand of Hard Words (and proper names of Places) more than are in any other English Dictionary or Expositor.

Together with The Etymological Derivatives of them from their proper Fountains, whether Hebrew, Greek, Latin, French, or any other Language.

In a Method more Comprehensive, than any that is extant.

By E. Coles, . . . London, . . . 1676.

A comparison of this title-page with that of Phillips in *A New World of English Words* shows that, though Coles is not so sweeping in his claims, he professes the same general purpose, in phrasing suggestive of the original. Each will explain the "hard words" or "difficult terms" derived from foreign languages; each will define terms used in the arts and sciences; each will deal with proper names of places; and each will give the etymological derivations. Both will indicate old words from Chaucer, Gower, etc.; and both will show from what language the terms are derived.

A comparative study of the texts proper proves that Coles's indebtedness did not stop with the title-page and the adoption of Phillips' general plan. Coles took over hundreds of the entries and definitions which he found in *A New World*. That these definitions are from Phillips, not from Bullokar or Blount, a consecutive reading of the dictionaries in question will reveal. Coles and Phillips, for example, have many words in common not in Blount or Bullokar; and, in the case of words running through the series of texts, those in Coles can be shown to be nearer to Phillips than to any other. Evidence supporting these statements is found in the definitions between the entries *Bitumen* and *Boniface*, in the texts referred to.

Within the range indicated, some of the terms with definitions common to Phillips and Coles are these: *Black-book, Blacklow, Blackman Forest, Black-rod, Black-buried, Blandiloquence, Blandishment, Blankers, Blankmanger, Blasco, Blatant, Blateration, Blazon, Blay (Bleak), Blee, Bleach, Blemishes*. The following definitions may be taken as typical:

PHILLIPS, 1671 Edition	COLES, 1676
Cab, An Hebr. measure of 3 pints.	*Cab*, h. three pints.
Cabades, a King of Persia, who succeeded Perozes. . . .	*Cabades*, King of Persia.
Cabala, an Hebrew word, signifying receiving, also a science among the Jews, comprehending the secret wayes of expounding the Law, which were revealed by God to Moses.	*Cabal*,-la, h. (receiving) Jewish tradition; their secret science of expounding divine mysteries; also a secret Council.
Cabalin, fountain, see Hypocrene.	*Cabaline*, [fountain] of the Muses.
Cabbage, of a Deer (a Term in hunting) that part of the head where the horns are planted.	*Cabbage*, that part of the Deers head where the horns are planted.
Cablish (a term used by the writers of forest laws) signifying Brushwood.	*Cablish*, Brush-wood.

PHILLIPS, 1671 Edition	COLES, 1676
Cabos'd, (Span.) a term in Heraldry spoken of the head of any beast . . . cut off close to the shoulder.	*Cabos'd*, Sp. having the head cut off close to the Shoulder.
Cabura, an odoriferous fountain of Mesopotamia, wherein Juno was used to wash.	*Cabura*, a fountain of Mesopotamia where Juno used to wash.
Cacams, Doctors among the Jews.	*Cacams*, Jewish doctors.
Cacafuego, a Spanish word signifying shitefire.	*Cacafuego*, Sp. Shite-fire.
Cacao, the Fruit of an Indian tree so called, the Kernels wherof are somewhat bigger than Almonds. . . .	*Cacao*, an Indian tree, also the fruit, and kernel thereof.
Cachexy, (Greek) a physical term signifying an ill disposition of the body.	*Cachexy*, ill disposition of body.
Cacchination, (Lat.) a loud laughter.	*Cachinnation*, 1. loud Laughter.
Cackrell, a kind of fish.	*Cackrell*, a kind of Fish.
Cacochimie, (Greek) a physical word, signifying ill juice which is caused in the body through bad nutriment or ill digestion.	*Cacochymy*, g. ill juice through bad digestion.

Further confirmation of Coles's dependence on Phillips is seen in the examination of parallel sections of the word lists. On his first page Coles, for example, has 93 words and Phillips, 60 to the corresponding point in the alphabet. In this space Coles has taken over 56 of Phillips' 60 words. For entries in common, Coles's definitions are obviously based on Phillips but are always shortened. Whereas in many cases the definition suffers from too great compression, there is often a gain in clarity. Coles seems to have been especially attracted by the proper names and the legendary material in Phillips. In the section analyzed, for example, Coles borrows every proper name.[1]

Though Coles follows Phillips in the general vocabulary and in the entry of proper names, he departs from the conventional in including canting terms and dialectal words. These appear in the general list in alphabetical order, and are designated by abbreviations explained by Coles in his introduction.[2] Some of the entries run thus:

Craddanly, Lanc. as crossantly, cowardly.
Cowl, E. tub as *coule.*
Crank, E. lusty, jovial, brisk.
Crawly-mawly, Nf. pretty well.
Creem it into his hand. Che. put it in slily and secretly.
Crowse, No. brisk.
Dacker, Li. waver, stagger.
Damber, C. a rascal.
Dazed [bread] Li. dough-baked.
Dell, Doxy, C. a wench.
Deuswins, C. a twopence.
Didder, No. quiver [with cold.]
Dosome [beast] Che. content with nothing, also thriving.
Doundrins, Der. afternoons drinkings.
Easter, No. the back or stock of the chimney.
Eath, Sc. an Oath.
Echen, O. Increase or help.
Ellinge, Ss. solitary, lonely.
Skeer the *Esse.* Che. separate the dead ashes from the embers.

So throughout are inserted the canting terms and dialect words. The canting terms are taken from Richard Head's *The Canting Academy* (1673). Coles borrows most of the words in Head's list and adds little besides. Definitions are brief, sometimes verbatim as in Head; and a few longer definitions show similarity in phrasing. For his dialectal words, Coles found and used the convenient list in John Ray's *Collection of English Words Not Generally Used* (1674).[3]

What with the canting terms, the dialect words, and old words, in addition to the regular vocabulary, Coles extended his word list to about 25,000, or some 8,000 more than the fourth revised edition of Phillips' *New World.* In thus increasing his word list, however, Coles made the error of cutting down many definitions so that too frequently a single word or short phrase has to serve as a definition. This procedure, of course, results in many unsatisfactory definitions. Among those unduly compressed are the following:

Glimmer, fire.
Lesion, a hurting.
Premature, too soon ripe.

Realize, to cause.
Receptacle, a storehouse.
Reduction, a bringing back.
Regular, orderly.
Rupture, a burstness.
Rustick, clownish.
Rotation, a wheeling.

Though a liberal borrower, Coles had some new ideas about dictionary-making—ideas expressed in his "To the Reader" and generally
exemplified in the text proper. He points out, for example, the shortcomings of the earlier compilers, with whose work he claims familiarity.
Most of these, he insists, are themselves in need of an expositor. Words
in their dictionaries are hard to find. He writes:

Suppose you want the meaning of *Belperopis* or *Dulcarnon,* they are not
in the common Herd; where will you look them? In the Law-terms? They
are not there. Sure then they are Proper Names; but they are not there
neither. What's to be done? Why, look till you find, and you will not lose
your labour.

Coles proposes to arrange his entries so that the terms can be easily
found. "Some," he writes, "that pretend to correction [correctness] and
exactness transcribe out of other (hand over head) their very faults
and all." Whether or not this remark was directed at Edward Phillips,
it is entirely applicable, as was shown by Blount in his *World of Errors
Discovered,* etc. (1673).

Finally, many of the definitions found in the work of his predecessors,
he asserts, are absurd. Some of these terms Coles lists, as follows:

Ejaculation, a yelling.
Eviration, a yielding (*i.e.,* a gelding).
Fidicula, a falling vulture.
Iopena, a song of rejoicing.
Lungis, a tall slim man that hath no length to his height.

Such uncritical borrowing and such foolish definitions, Coles himself
will try to avoid.

Furthermore—and here appear, we think, his real contributions—he
will (1) retain and augment the number of "Old Words," that is, "such

as occur in Chaucer, Gower, Pierce Ploughman, and Julian Barnes [Julia Berners?]." This is not a new custom, but new emphasis upon a practice introduced by Bullokar and followed by Phillips. (2) Coles defines many dialect words. "Here," he writes, "is a large addition of many words and phrases that belong to our English Dialects in the several Counties. . . ." Though the custom of collecting dialect words was not new, no one before Coles had deliberately chosen to introduce them into a general dictionary. This may then be regarded as an innovation. (3) Coles enters in his dictionary canting terms. " 'Tis no disparagement," writes Coles, "to understand the Canting Terms. It may chance to save your throat from being cut, or (at least) your Pocket from being pickt." As early as the sixteenth century separate collections of such terms had been made, but Coles is the first consciously to introduce them into an English dictionary proper.[4] He thus increased not only the usefulness but the timeliness of his dictionary, as there was a lively current interest in both cant and dialect. (4) Another practical expedient is the inclusion of market towns of England, and cities and towns on the Continent. (5) Coles extends the technical terms and varies the treatment of proper names, retaining in condensed form the stories associated with classical persons. (6) He often includes groups of related words,[5] whereas his predecessors chose apparently at random the adjective, the noun, or the verb form to represent the group. Coles is therefore receptive to almost every element in the vocabulary except the everyday words—the last to be admitted into the English dictionary.

Coles died in 1680, without ever having revised his dictionary; nor was it revised by anyone else. Notwithstanding, it was reissued at least ten times [6] and retained its popularity for more than fifty years on the market against formidable competition. This long vogue is the strongest testimonial to the general usefulness of Coles's *English Dictionary*.

Chapter VIII

Gazophylacium Anglicanum (1689)

THE NEXT ENGLISH DICTIONARY AFTER COLES AND INDEED the last to be published before the end of the seventeenth century was an anonymous etymological lexicon in octavc format, entitled *Gazophylacium Anglicanum,* or English Treasury (1689). As this dictionary was based upon Stephen Skinner's *Etymologicon Linguae Anglicanae* (1671), a dictionary compiled largely in Latin but concerned with the etymology of English words, and as Skinner's book is in the tradition of etymological dictionaries of the period, and incidentally a borrower from Phillips' *New World,* it is necessary here briefly to sketch in Skinner and the background of the *Gazophylacium.*[1]

The *Etymologicon Linguae Anglicanae* (1671) by Stephen Skinner appears at first to represent a radical departure from the beaten paths of English lexicography. But there was definite foreshadowing of the sort of work that Skinner published. The Latin-English dictionaries of Thomas Cooper and Thomas Thomas had, at the end of the sixteenth century, undertaken to indicate the etymology of many Latin words. Early in the seventeenth century Francis Holyoke had published his *Dictionarium Etymologicum Latinum,* a volume which may well have suggested a title for Skinner's work. In 1617 appeared Minsheu's prodigious *Guide into Tongues,* a polyglot dictionary with the English first and with great emphasis upon etymology.[2] Blount and Phillips had boldly proclaimed on their title-pages that their dictionaries contained etymologies as well as definitions of terms. It matters little, so far as this study is concerned, whether these dictionaries lived up to their claims. The point is that the authors seemed to recognize the importance of the subject, and prepared the way for more solid work.

There was, too, in other ways, preparation for the *Etymologicon*. This is to be seen in the expressed desire of scholars, such as Wilson, Cheke, and their school, to have more of the Anglo-Saxon words used, and in the revival of the study of Anglo-Saxon in the seventeenth century. This revival is marked by accounts of the history of the English or British language, such as those of Camden, of Verstegan, and of Dr. John Davies; [3] and by Verstegan's glossary of Anglo-Saxon words, and William Somner's *Dictionarium Saxonico-Latino-Anglicum* (1659).

In the *Praefatio* Skinner gives an account of the history of the language, which exhibits his knowledge of Phillips' Preface on the same subject. The two authors have common references to Becanus, to Chaucer, to the Cambro-Britannica language, etc. But each reflects, also, independent knowledge of Verstegan, and of Davies' *Praefatio*, entitled "Ubi De Linguae Britannicae Origine, Aliarumque Linguarum ortu & Mutatione." And in the text proper Skinner refers fairly frequently to Minsheu and Verstegan. The upshot of all this is that the *Etymologicon* of Skinner represents not something new under the sun of lexicography, but rather a convergence of influences from Latin-English dictionaries, from the accounts of the native language, and from his predecessors in compiling English dictionaries.

And among his antecedents, Edward Phillips, curiously enough, seems to have contributed most, so far as definitions are concerned. We have mentioned above Skinner's indebtedness to the Preface of *A New World of English Words*. Not until 1855 was the relationship of the *Etymologicon* to the text of Phillips discovered. [4] On February 17 of that year Albert Way pointed out, in *Notes and Queries*, [5] that Skinner referred frequently, in his Latin definitions and comments, to a *Dictionarium Anglicum* of 1658. Way cited a number of entries under which Skinner referred, without mentioning the author's name, to the English dictionary, and inquired what lexicographer Skinner had reference to. On March 3 of the same year S. W. Singer and W. R. Arrowsmith replied, independently, in the same journal, each identifying as the author of the English dictionary in question Edward Phillips, and his *New World of English Words* as one source of Skinner's definitions. (It is noteworthy that Skinner puts his definitions in Latin, so that his borrowings are not so readily detected.) To the borrowings of Skinner noted by Singer, we have been able to add a considerable list, showing that the *Etymologicon* is a wholesale borrower from the *New World*.[6]

Singer further points out that, though Skinner plunders Phillips' dictionary, he is constantly abusive of his unnamed author. The author is asleep; he is miserably ignorant; the definition is a figment of the author's imagination: so run the ungrateful comments of Skinner. One wonders whether, when Phillips read these comments, he remembered his own abuse of Blount, under similar circumstances. The whirligig of time brings in his revenges.

Notwithstanding certain borrowings from Phillips, the organization and the purpose of Skinner's book are altogether different. The author's aim is to explain the etymology of English words in general; definitions are apparently of less importance. Besides the general word list, Skinner has lists of botanical terms, of forensic terms (even the old and obsolete), of words derived from Old English, and of proper names of rivers, cities, men and women, etc.

With this information in mind, we may return to the smaller anonymous etymological dictionary. The title-page of the first edition runs:

Gazophylacium Anglicanum: Containing the Derivation of English Words,...
Proving the Dutch and Saxon to be the prime Fountains....
London,... 1689.

Apparently, the Latin title of this book was not entirely satisfactory. At any rate when an issue appeared two years after the first, the title was English and the title-page ran thus:

A New English Dictionary, Shewing the Etymological Derivation of the English Tongue, in Two Parts.
Part I. Explaining all the common English Words, and shewing their Derivation from the proper Fountains.
Part II. An Etymological Explication of the Proper Names of Men, Women, Rivers, Counties, Cities, Towns, Villages, &c. which were formerly used by the English-Saxons, or are now common amongst Us.
A Work of great Use to the English Reader, who is curious to know the Original of his Mother Tongue.
London,... MDCXCI.

In the Preface the anonymous author professes to have "taken his Pattern" from the studies of Junius, the etymological dictionary of

Skinner, and others. The two classes of words mentioned on the title-page correspond closely to the first and fifth word lists in Skinner. The author indeed simply translates the lists and definitions from Skinner, sometimes condensing or omitting matter from the original. The entries which follow serve to show the relationship of the two texts.

SKINNER, 1671

Dole, Donativum Principis, ab AS. Dal, Divisio, Dael, Belg. *Deel, Deyl,* Teut. *Theil,* Pars, AS. *Daelan,* Belg. *Deelen, Deylen,* Teut. *Theylen,* Distribuere, v. *Deal.*

Doller, à Belg. *Daler,* Teut. *Thaler,* Nummus Argenteus Germanicus, utr. à Belg. *Talen, Betalen,* Teut. *Zablen, Bezablen,* Solvere. Martinius deflectit à Teut. *Thal,* dialecto Germano-Saxonica, *Dal,* Vallis, & ideo dictum putat, quod primum hic nummus in *Joacheims Thal* (i.e.) Valle Joachimica in Saxonica casus fuit, ideoque etiam *Joachimicus* appellatur. Non absurdum etiam esset deducere, ab AS. *Dal,* Divisio, *Dael,* Portio, quia sc. est Aurei seu Ducati dimidium.

Dolphin, sic olim appellatus est Princeps Provinciae Viennensis Allobrogum & nunc Primogenitus Regis Galliae unde & ipsa Provincia nomen fortita est, a Fr. G. *Daulphin* & *Daulphine,* sic dict., a *Delphino* quem hi Principes pro Insigni Gentilitio gestabant.

Dolt, Hebes, Fungus, à Teut. *Doll,* Stolidus, Insanus, Assonat etiam Hisp. *Tonto,* Stupidus, Stultus, sed revera à Lat. *Attonitus,* ortum ducit.

Gazophylacium, 1689

Dole, from the AS *Dal, Dael,* Belg. *Deyl,* Teut. *Theil,* a part, or pittance; these from the Verbs *Daelan, Deylen, Theylen,* to distribute. V. Deal.

Doller, from the Belg. *Daler,* Teut. *Thaler,* a German silver-coin, both from the Belg. *Talen,* Teut. *Zihlen,* to pay. Martinius derives it from the Teut. *Thal,* a Valley; it being first coined in the Valley of Joachim in Saxony.

Dolphin, formerly the title of the Prince of Vienna; now, of the first-born of the French King; from the French G. *Daulphin,* and *Daulphine,* a Dolphin, which those princes carried in their Coat of Arms.

Dolt, from the Teut. *Doll,* imprudent; or from the Lat. *Attonitus,* stupefied.

The author explains his method as follows:

Observe that ... that Word is set next the English, from which I have judged it most likely to be derived; and the Synonymous Words of the other

European Languages follow: which shews, I have left it to the Opinion of the Reader, to draw from which he pleases.

The author's concern with etymology results in hasty and unsatisfactory definitions. In condensing Skinner's explanation, he frequently produces a ludicrous effect.[7]

The Preface has some interesting statements reflecting the then current attitude toward languages. The author writes, for example:

The Confusion of Languages at Babel (for before it, all the then World spoke one and the same Dialect, supposed to be Hebrew) gave Rise to all the several Languages in the Universe; of which the primitive Language of this Nation was one; and, had it not been corrupted, perhaps as good and intelligible as the best; but being so alter'd by the aforesaid Accidents, it has quite lost its primitive Glory, as well as that of the French and other Nations.

What the "aforesaid Accidents" were which caused corruption of the English language, the author explains in another paragraph:

My Native Language, which is so strangely corrupted through Time, that when I look'd an hundred or an hundred and fifty Years only behind me, I could scarce imagine it ever to have been the Language of my Ancestors, or even of the country I was born in, 'tis so chang'd through Commerce, Correspondence, Travellers, and such like Accidents: Much more may you imagine it to be alter'd in a thousand or two thousand Years, by Conquests, Invasions, Transmigrations of the Government: So that...it is brought to what we now find it, even a Composition of most, if not all the Languages of Europe; especially the Belgick or Low-Dutch, Saxon, Teutonic or High-Dutch, Cambro-British or Welsh, French, Spanish, Italian, and Latin; and now and then of the Old and Modern Danish, and Ancient High-Dutch; also of the Greek, Hebrew, Arabick, Chaldee, Syriack and Turckick.

Although theories of the seventeenth century concerning the origin and growth of the English language have been much revised or wholly discarded as the result of subsequent historical study, the anonymous author of the *Gazophylacium* and his immediate forebears deserve more than passing mention for their attempts to find the original of the native English and for their emphasis upon the Germanic element in the vocabulary. They thus point the way to the future development of philology and lexicography.

Chapter IX

j. k.'s *A New English Dictionary* (1702)

THOUGH SMALL AND UNPRETENTIOUS, J. K.'s *New English Dictionary* of 1702 appeared at a critical stage in the evolution of the English dictionary and made a vital contribution. Its preface attacks preceding dictionaries at their most vulnerable points and outlines a new function for an English dictionary; and its text, unlike some of its predecessors, lives up to the professions made in the preface.

The author of this dictionary has never been determined; but the most persistent and plausible suggestion is John Kersey, able lexicographer who revised Edward Phillips' *New World of Words* in 1706 and compiled his own *Dictionarium Anglo-Britannicum* in 1708. This identification has been somewhat half-heartedly questioned on the grounds (1) that in none of the eight editions of the *New English Dictionary* did Kersey acknowledge the work as his, and (2) that the concept and method of lexicography used here differ from those in Kersey's acknowledged works.[1] No other identification has, however, been suggested; and the objections raised are hardly insuperable. The use of name or initials on title-pages is erratic at best in the early dictionaries and even more so in the schoolbooks, with which this work will be shown to have a close affinity.

Indeed, under the circumstances of early eighteenth-century lexicography it seems not unlikely that this work is Kersey's. Kersey, like Nathan Bailey, was a progressive and businesslike lexicographer who in the course of his career experimented with different types of dictionary for different uses and strata of readers.[2] His revision of Phillips, a distinguished universal dictionary, was designed as a reference work for

69

advanced students of literature, science, and the arts; and his *Diction-arium Anglo-Britannicum,* the first abridged dictionary, was suitable for the use of the general reading public. Such a versatile lexicographer may well have begun his career with an equally useful, independent, and forward-looking work in its less ambitious field—the *New English Dictionary,* intended "to instruct Youth, and even adult Persons, who are ignorant of the Learned Languages, in the *Orthography,* or true and most accurate manner of Spelling, Reading and Writing the genuine Words of their own Mother-tongue." [3] It would hardly be surprising if "J. K., Philobibl." (note the initials), as he later styled himself,[4] the author of such impressive works, did not bother to acknowledge his first modest attempt at lexicography.

From our perspective, however, the *New English Dictionary* is seen not only to have been successful in its humble sphere but to have steered the English dictionary into a wiser and more tolerant course. The stress of the title-page on the hitherto neglected common word is conspicuous:

A New English Dictionary: Or, a Compleat Collection Of the Most Proper and Significant Words, Commonly used in the Language; With a Short and Clear Exposition of Difficult Words and Terms of Art.

The whole digested into Alphabetical Order; and chiefly designed for the benefit of Young Scholars, Tradesmen, Artificers, and the Female Sex, who would learn to spell truely; being so fitted to every Capacity, that it may be a continual help to all that want an Instructor.

By. J. K.   London:... 1702.

The importance of this work, then, lies in its introduction into the English dictionary of the bulk of the English language—that is, of the essential words of daily speech, writing, and reading. Cawdrey, almost one hundred years before, had launched the English dictionary on its career somewhat uncertainly with his *Table Alphabeticall* stressing hard usual words but admitting also hard unusual words. His successors, Bullokar and Cockeram, however, yielded more and more to the lure of the unusual until successive editions of their dictionaries vied with each other in their claims to the longest lists of the hardest, oddest, and most specialized words. The "hard" word tradition naturally persisted with the lawyer Blount and the learned Phillips, who dedicated his pretentious work to the sister universities. Coles was open-minded enough to include archaic words, dialect, and even cant but still neglected every-day words. Spelling books and elementary grammars meanwhile had carried lists of ordinary words, though without definitions except for an occasional distinction between easily confused words. If J. K. could not at a single step close the gap between the two traditions and produce a modern dictionary with its tolerant inclusiveness and service to all types of people, he at least called attention to the forgotten words and the forgotten class of readers.

The preface shows the author to be an intelligent critic of his prede-cessors and a vigorous reformer. He disposes of Coles, his immediate predecessor and rival on the market, as follows:

... Mr. *Coles* in his elaborate Work, has inserted several Words purely *Latin*, without any alteration, as *Dimidietas* for an half; *Sufflamen*, for a Trigger, and some hundreds only vary'd with an *English* Termination, which are scarce ever us'd by any ancient or modern Writer, even in a Figurative, Philosophical, or Poetical Sense; ... Besides an innumerable multitude of *Greek, Latin, French, Italian, Spanish, British, Saxon,* and old *English* Words that are often introduc'd even without changing their Original Terminations, and which are never used in *English;* with others that are peculiar to distinct Counties of *England, Scotland,* and *Ireland,* and never us'd or understood any where else. So that a plain Country-man, in looking for a common *English* Word, amidst so vast a Wood of such as are above the reach of his Capacity, must needs lose the sight of it, and be extremely discouraged, if not forc'd to give over the search.... Moreover, in the explaining of *English* Words deriv'd from the *Latin,* he makes no scruple of producing such senses as are only peculiar to the Original; ...

J. K. closes his criticism of Coles with a clear-cut statement of the differ-ence between their purposes and with an announcement of his own design, which is consciously revolutionary. What J. K. proposes is, in fact, the Englishing of the English dictionary in a double sense—by adhering to English vocabulary and usage, and by fitting his work to the needs of more Englishmen.

However, it must be acknowledged, That the Design of this Ingenious Author ... is very different from ours; That apparently being to oblige the Publick, with as large a Collection as possibly could be made, of all sorts of hard and obsolete Words, both domestick and foreign, as well Proper Names, as the Terms of all Arts and Sciences, Poetical Fictions, &c. Whereas, ours is intended only to explain such *English* Words as are genuine, and used by Persons of clear Judgment and good Style; leaving out all those foreign Terms, that in Mr. *Coles's* time were viciously introduc'd into our Language, by those who sought to approve themselves Learned rather by unintelligible Words than by proper Language.

Lastly, it ought to be observ'd, That very few of the genuine and common significant Words of the *English* Tongue are contain'd in either of the two Dictionaries but now cited [Coles and Bullokar], or in any other particular Work of the like nature, hitherto published; ...

... we have taken care to make a Collection of all the most proper and significant *English* Words, that are now commonly us'd either in Speech, or in the familiar way of Writing Letters, &c.; omitting at the same time, such as are obsolete, barbarous, foreign or pecular to the several Counties of *England;* as also many difficult, abstruse and uncouth Terms of Art, as altogether unnecessary, nay even prejudicial to the endeavours of young Beginners, and unlearned Persons, and whereof seldom any use does occur: However, the most useful Terms in all Faculties are briefly explain'd; ...

The *New English Dictionary,* containing about 28,000 words, the majority of which were making their first appearance in an English dictionary, is, as Dr. P. W. Long pointed out, "clearly an outgrowth of the spelling book, and is designed primarily for those who are endeavoring to master the language in an elementary way. It is thus the ancestor of our dictionary for the counting-house and the elementary schools." [5] Obviously in type of readers addressed, stress on orthography, make-up of the word list, and type of definition there are many points in common between J. K.'s work and the current spelling books. We may mention, for example, such books as the following, each of which went through many editions and carried extensive alphabetical tables: N. Strong's *England's Perfect School-Master,* R. Brown's *English School Reform'd,* E. Young's *The Compleat English-Scholar, Cocker's Accomplish'd School-Master,* and J. Hawkins' *English School-Master Compleated.*[6] Possibly J. K. drew up his basic word list from the tables in such school texts and then added related forms and some more difficult words from other sources, notably Coles. While J. K. thus produced a new type of dictionary and an important new storehouse of words, the influence of the spelling books upon the technique of definition was regrettable. Definitions of the least common words usually echo Coles, but these form only a small percentage of the whole.[7] Derivatives, related words, and some very common words are merely listed without explanations. Many of the definitions seem shockingly haphazard; these may, however, be judged charitably as the earliest attempts to explain common words, it being an embarrassing fact in dictionary-making that the easiest words most persistently defy definition. The admission of the common word into the dictionary had come late; its adequate definition was to come much later—if indeed this problem can yet be said to be solved. The following items are representative of the current spellers and of J. K.'s pioneering dictionary:

SPELLING BOOKS	J. K.
Neigh, like a horse	*About*, as about Noon.
Noah's ark	To *sit abroad* upon *eggs*, as a bird does.
Nose, on the face	To *accent* Words.
Oar, of a boat	*Ake*, as, my head akes.
Pens, to write with	*And*, and if, and not.
[the above from Young]	*Any*, anyone, anywhere, &c.
Plot not against the King	An *Apron*, for a Woman, &c.
Pray to God	An *Arm* of a man's body, of a tree, or of
Ruff for the Neck	the sea.
Shoot with a Gun	An *Elephant*, a Beast.
Bury the Dead	A *Goat*, a Beast.
[the above from Brown]	*May*, the most pleasant Month of the Year.

The *New English Dictionary*, as revised by J. K. in 1713, retains its peculiar character but benefits by the author's ripened experience. The vocabulary has become more representative, with ordinary words still predominating but with more unusual ones added. All words are now defined, and the technique of definition has improved. Although the number of items has been reduced to 21,000, there is no doubt that the general usefulness of the work is expanded. The Preface describes the changes as follows:

Now forasmuch as the former Edition of our New *English Dictionary*, has met with a general acceptation, and the Copies have for some time been scarce, we are encouraged to present it again to the Publick in a more accomplish'd Dress; not doubting but the Improvements and Additions will appear very considerable. To that end, many Compound or Double Words, as a *Bird-Cage*, an *Apple-tree*, a *Pigeon-house*, &c. are struck out, as altogether superfluous; since *Bird* and *Cage*, with all the rest may be found separately under their respective Articles. In the room of these, is inserted a great number of proper and emphatical Words, that were wanting in the last Impression. And farther, whereas the Original or Principal Terms were at first only explained, and the others left naked; now every individual Word is Illustrated with a clear and comprehensive Exposition. There are also annexed at the end, three Tables of very good use, *viz.* I. Of Proper Names of Men, especially such as are contained in the *Old* and *New Testaments,* in which is shewed the Etymology, or true Original of them, as they are derived from various Languages. II. Of Proper Names of Women, explained after the same manner. III. Of Nicknames, or *English* Christian names abbreviated or made short.

These tables of names, though featured here and on the new title-page, do not constitute an especially novel or useful development. The list of names covers twelve pages, but only the etymological meanings are given. Such names, often more fully treated, had appeared in school-books and scattered through the word lists in other dictionaries.[8] The improvements in definition will be evident from the following items:

1702 Edition	1713 Edition
A *Gad* of steel.	A *Gad*, a measure of 9 or 10 feet, a small bar of steel.
The *Gaffle* of a cross-bow.	The *Gaffle* or Steel of a cross-bow.
A *Gag*.	A *Gag*, a stopple to hinder one from crying out.
A *Gage*, and to *Gage* (in several senses).	A *Gage*, a rod to measure casks with. To *Gage* or *Gauge*, to measure with a gage.
To *Gaggle* like a goose.	To *Gaggle*, to cry like a goose.
A *Gallop*.	A *Gallop*, the swiftest pace of a horse.

That the author still regards his work as an elementary tool is clear from his recommendation in this edition of the parallel study of "Mr. *John Brightland's* Accurate *Grammar,* with the Arts of Poetry. Rhetorick, Logick, &c. in our Mother-Tongue, in order to compleat his Incomparable Design, to settle an *English Education,* for the proper Advantage of the Youth of *Great Britain.*"[9] J. K.'s success in fulfilling this educational aim is attested by Isaac Watts's recommendation of his work in *The Art of Reading and Writing English* (1720):

> In your younger days especially, take all proper opportunities for writing, and be careful to spell every word true: This may be done by the help of some small *English* dictionary, where the words are put down in the order of the alphabet; and if you doubt of the spelling of any word, write it not without first consulting the dictionary.

> The best dictionary that I know for this purpose, is intitled, A New *English* Dictionary, &c. by *J. K.* The second edition, 1713 in a small octavo.[10]

More impressive, however, is Watts's insistence in 1731 that, despite Bailey's and other fine dictionaries then available, J. K.'s is still the most useful for young scholars and even "for the bulk of mankind."

> I am so far from disapproving that paragraph which you have printed from my little book of reading and writing, that even since the larger Dictionary of Mr. *Bailey* is published, which may be very entertaining and useful to persons of a polite education, yet for the bulk of mankind, this small one of *J. K.* is much more convenient; and I wish it were in the hands of all young persons, to acquaint them better with their mother-tongue.[11]

Although J. K.'s *New English Dictionary* held its popularity for seventy years, it was not again extensively revised and showed only a very occasional addition to the word list.[12]

Chapter X

Cocker's English Dictionary (1704)

Cocker's English Dictionary, 1704, WAS NEITHER PROGRES-
sive nor influential. While unimportant in the development
of the English dictionary, it is, however, an interesting
work with more than its share of complex relationships and
problems. Here we may say that the fine art of borrowing from one's
predecessors reaches its zenith, and the author's own contribution sinks
to a minimum. His contribution, in fact, consists merely in the novel
plan of his dictionary and in the ingenuity with which he blends and
focuses the work of his predecessors.

The title-page of this octavo volume reads:

Cocker's English Dictionary: Interpreting The most refined and difficult
words in Divinity, Philosophy, Law, Physick, Mathematicks, Husbandry,
Mechanicks, &c. With an Exposition of those hard words, which are derived
from other Languages; ...

To which is Added An Historico-Poetical Dictionary, containing the
Proper Names of Men, Women, Rivers, Countries, Cities, Castles, Towns,
Mountains, &c. in England, Scotland and Ireland, &c. And the feigned Stories
of Heathen Gods, with other Poetical Inventions.

Also The Interpretation of the most usual Terms in Military Discipline.

Likewise The Terms which Merchants and others make use of in Trade
and Commerce; And the Coins of most Countries in Europe, and several
Parts of the World. ...

By Edward Cocker, the Late Famous Practitioner in Fair Writing and
Arithmetick.

Perused and Published from the Authors Correct Copy, by John Hawkins.
London, ... 1704.

We must consider first the complicated problem of authorship. The real and posthumous careers of Edward Cocker, supposed author of this dictionary, and of John Hawkins, supposed editor, are enigmatic. Cocker's dates have been established as 1631-1676, and Hawkins was "flourishing" in 1677 and died in 1692.[1] Cocker is credited, among others, with the following miscellaneous and commercially successful works: some twenty-nine copybooks appearing from 1657 to 1676; *Cocker's Arithmetick*, published in 1678 ("Perused and Published by John Hawkins by the Authors correct Copy" two years after the latter's death) and reaching a sixty-fifth edition in 1787; *Cocker's Decimal Arithmetick*, published in 1685 ("Perused and Published by John Hawkins" nine years after the author's death) and reaching a sixth edition in 1729; and *Cocker's English Dictionary*, published in 1704 (twenty-eight years after his death, "Perused and Published from the Authors correct Copy, by John Hawkins," who had himself been dead twelve years) and reaching a third edition in 1724.[2] Cocker appears to have founded his own school near St. George's Church in Southwark to which Hawkins succeeded.[3] Hawkins' best known works were: *Clavis Commercii* (1689) and *The English School-Master Compleated* (ca. 1692).

Cocker's reputation has passed through three phases. He was esteemed in his own day as schoolmaster, engraver, and above all calligrapher. In Evelyn's *Sculptura* (1662), Cocker heads the list of contemporary English calligraphers, who are said to be comparable to the most celebrated French and Italian masters of that art.[4] Pepys praises his work as engraver, finds his company agreeable and his literary taste discriminating, and even asks his advice for failing eyesight.[5]

By the eighteenth century the copybooks are outmoded, but the arithmetics continue in high favor. Edward Hatton in his *New View of London* (1708) reflects the changed attitude toward Cocker when he describes him as "a Person well skilled in all the parts of Arithmetick." [6] Throughout the century, in fact, Cocker was known primarily as a mathematician; and "according to Cocker" became a password in mathematical circles—an ironical situation in the light of subsequent disclosures that Cocker may have had little or no connection with these works.

In the nineteenth century the oddities of Cocker's career and reputation aroused scepticism in A. De Morgan, who declares in his *Arithmetical Books* (1847): "I am perfectly satisfied that *Cocker's Arithmetick* is a forgery of Hawkins, with some assistance, it may be, from Cocker's papers. ...." [7] The calligrapher and the arithmetician had overshadowed the lexicographer all these years; but the last finally came into the limelight, when H. B. Wheatley began his study of early dictionaries. In an article called "Who Was Cocker?" (1884), Wheatley pointed out that Hawkins died several years before the publication of the dictionary and suggested that it was the booksellers rather than Hawkins who were responsible for the apparent forgery of that work.[8] With Cocker's original fame as a calligrapher and growing reputation as a mathematician, Hawkins' own reputation as a mathematician, and their joint output of a whole series of successful texts, the booksellers would have found in this combination of names a rare decoy for the book trade. Wheatley then put the unanswerable question: If the work were a *bona fide* product of Cocker and promised to be such a commercial prize, how can one account for the manuscript's lying unused almost thirty years? Similarly, if the work were the product of Hawkins, how can one account for its lying unused twelve years?

The most recent discussion of the problem is to be found in Sir Ambrose Heal's *English Writing-Masters and Their Copy-Books. 1570-1800*.[9] Sir Ambrose here records the existence of Edward Cocker, Jr. (1658-1723), writing master and scrivener, and comments on the authorship of the dictionary:

Speculation as to the identity of the ghostly editor is not very profitable, but it is perhaps apposite to remember that the *Arithmetick*, the *Decimal Arithmetick*, and the *Dictionary* were all published by a little group of London Bridge booksellers who were, no doubt, agreeable to carrying on the good work. ... It is well within the bounds of probability that the editing of ... the *Dictionary* was due to the filial efforts of Edward Cocker Junior.[10]

Of these alternative theories we should be inclined on internal evidence to favor the first.[11] An examination of the dictionary proves it to be no more than a rather ingenious compilation from other dictionaries. It therefore seems less like a filial devoir than like a piece of hack work designed by enterprising and unscrupulous booksellers to profit by the trade value of Cocker's and Hawkins' names. In any case it is paradoxical to debate the authorship of a work which has no original material.

Let us now examine the plan of the work, which is unusual for a general English dictionary of the period but which may have been suggested by Stephen Skinner's *Etymologicon Linguae Anglicanae,* 1671, with which the compiler of "Cocker's" was undoubtedly familiar. Skinner's work contains five lists, whereas "Cocker's" has four: general ("hard" words), "historico-poetical," military, and commercial. The first two of these are paralleled in Skinner and are conventional features, but the latter two appear here for the first time in a general English dictionary. Their inclusion is justified on the grounds that "in this War-like Age, we often encounter with Military Terms in our Gazzets and other publick news, several of them newly invented, and which few or none have yet taken notice of in Print, and are little understood by many" and that trade is "now . . . extraordinarily improved and enlarged with Foreign Nations, and Merchants [are now] making use of Words in Traffick not commonly apprehended." [12]

Cocker's English Dictionary, containing in all about 22,000 words, is easily traced to its sources. The discourse on the English language which comprises the bulk of the preface and bears Hawkins' signature is condensed from the preface to Edward Phillips' *New World of English Words,* 1658, etc. The list of "hard" words is based on Elisha Coles's *English Dictionary,* published in 1676 and often reprinted without revision. The compiler of "Cocker's" takes over almost all the "hard" words with identical or similar definitions, the borrowing being disguised only by the fact that he omits Coles's many proper names, which he is merely reserving for his second list. Compare the following entries:

Coles, 1701 Edition	"Cocker's," 1704
Faculty, 1. power or ability, also a license or dispensation; also a trade, mystery or profession.	*Faculty,* power, ability, or calling, also a Licence or priviledge, mystery, or profession.
February, the month of	*February,* the Month of Februation, sacrificing, and praying for the dead.
Februation, 1. sacrificing and praying for the souls of the dead.	
Fellon-oun, o. cruel; also an angry blister at the fingers end, &c.	*Fellon,* cruel, also an angry blister at the fingers end.
Fence month, from June the 9th to July the 9th, when Deer begin to fawn, and it is unlawful to hunt in the forest.	*Fence month,* from June the 9th to July the 9th, when Deer begin to fawn, then it is not lawful to hunt in the Forrest.

The second vocabulary, whose full heading is given on the title-page, is a composite product. The compiler of "Cocker's" has taken the majority of his proper names from Coles; these items, which are mainly classical, may be traced back through Phillips to Charles Stephanus' *Dictionarium Historicum, Geographicum, Poeticum* of 1553. The following demonstrate the debt to Coles:

Coles, 1701 Edition	"Cocker's," 1704
Gaal, h. abomination.	*Gaal*, a proper name, *i.e.* Abomination *Heb.*
Gabranterici, Britains inhabiting part of Yorkshire.	*Gabranterici*, Britains inhabiting part of Yorkshire.
Gabriel, h. the strength of God.	*Gabriel*, a proper name, *i.e.* the strength of God.
Gabriosentum, a Frontier Garrison of the Romans, supposed to be where New-Castle and Gates-head now stand.	*Gabrio-centum*, a Frontier Garrison of the *Romans*, supposed to be Gateshead at New-Castle.
Gaddi, a rare Florentine painter who excelled in Mosaic work.	*Gaddo*, a famous Italian Painter in Mosaick work.

Many other items in this list, for the most part Germanic or Celtic, are derived probably from Skinner's *Etymologicon* (1671) or possibly from the anonymous *Gazophylacium Anglicanum* (1689, 1691), which appropriated in translation two of Skinner's word lists. Skinner's authoritative folio seems a more likely source, and had been discussed by Coles in his preface. Also, if the compiler of "Cocker's" had used the little known *Gazophylacium*, it is hardly likely that he would have gone to the trouble of rephrasing the definitions, as he did not do so in his borrowings from Coles's much better known work. Compare the following items:

Skinner, 1671	*Gazophylacium*, 1689	"Cocker's," 1704
Offchurch, in Com. Warw. ab Offa Merciorum Rege Conditore, cujus filius *Fremondus* ibi sepultus est.	*Offchurch*, in Warw. from *Offa*, King of the Mercii, and the Builder thereof, whose Son, Fremund, was there interr'd.	*Offchurch*, in Warwickshire, from Offa, King of the Mercians, who Built it, and whose Son Fremund was Buried there.

The third list, headed "An Explanation of the Terms used in the Art of War," is much shorter. The source here is the dictionary of "l'Art Militaire" which forms the second part of the Sieur de Guillet's *Les Arts de l'Homme d'Epée.* This work appeared in 1670 and underwent sixteen editions before its anonymous translation into English in 1705 as *The Gentleman's Dictionary.* Here the compiler of "Cocker's" is eclectic; he selects certain terms, abridges definitions, and omits the illustrations from French history. Compare the following definitions:

Guillet, 1680 Edition	"Cocker's," 1704
Aide de Camp est un Officier qui s'attache auprés de l'un ou de l'autre des Officiers Généraux, à sçavoir, du Général, du Lieutenant-Général & du Maréchal de Camp, & qui reçoit & porte les Ordres de l'un ou de l'autre, selon les diverses occasions qui s'en peuvent presenter dans un Camp. Quand le Roy est à l'Armée, Sa Majesté choisit des jeunes Hommes de qualité pour porter ses Ordres de part & d'autre, sous le tître d'Aides de Camp du Roy.	*Aide de Camp,* an Officer who upon all occasions receives and carries the Generals, Lieutenant-Generals or Major Generals Orders. When the King is in the Field, young Gentlemen of Quality perform this Office, and are called the Kings *Aides de Camp.*

The work concludes with "An Alphabetical Explanation of the most difficult Terms used in Trade and Merchandize." The source here is the dictionary for commercial terms which appeared for the first time in the second edition (1697) of Edward Hatton's *Merchants Magazine.* Hatton's dictionary comprises about 450 words with detailed explanations. "Cocker's" appropriates about two-thirds of these with definitions verbatim. The table of coins prefixed to "Cocker's" also comes from Hatton.

"Cocker's" was extensively revised before its reappearance in 1715, but there was no further revision for the third and last edition in 1724. The revision takes two forms: "Cocker's" borrows further from Coles, whose dictionary was still holding the market, and introduces certain new features to meet contemporary vogues.

Most prominent of the further capitulations to Coles is the merging of the four vocabularies into one. This at once destroys the most distinctive feature of "Cocker's" and makes more conspicuous than ever before the great similarity between "Cocker's" and Coles's vocabularies.

Coles had vigorously defended his single word list on the basis that the use of more than one word list "supposes things to be known before they are explained." [13] The reviser of "Cocker's" now concedes in his preface, which incidentally still bears Hawkins' name, that "the bringing of all Words whatsoever into one continued Alphabet may be much readier for the finding out what is desired." Other grudging concessions to Coles concern the inclusion of archaic expressions and cant terms:

It is alledged by some Dictionary-makers [Coles's preface], That old obsolete Words may be very necessary for understanding of such ancient Authors as *Chaucer, Gower,* &c. but I am of the Opinion of the Ingenious Mr. *Blount,* who . . . says, 'That he expresly shunned them, as altogether useless, since one in a thousand never heard of their Names, nor ever saw or read their Works.'

It is likewise asserted [Coles's preface], 'That it is no Disparagement to understand the Canting Terms of the Tribe of Gypsies, Cheats and Beggars, because it may chance to save a Man's throat from being cut': As if these Miscreants would be kinder to any one for speaking, or understanding, a little of their Gibberish.

I have therefore inserted some few, but omitted a multitude of both these kinds, . . .

The reviser then appropriates from Coles about seventy-five of the commoner cant words and a larger group of "old words." [14] Lastly, while the original compiler of "Cocker's" had paid no attention to etymology, the reviser indicates the language from which each word is taken, as Coles had done all along.

New features introduced at this time are enumerated on the title-page as: "Historical Remarks upon the Lives and Actions of Emperors, Popes, Kings, . . . both in the former and latter Ages of the World. With Brief Observations upon the Reign of every English Monarch. . . . Also a short View of what is Considerable in every County of England and Wales."

This material no doubt reflects a wave of nationalism resulting from foreign victories, the union with Scotland, the spread of news sheets, the increase in road-building and consequently in travel in all parts of the islands. "Descriptions of Great Britain," road maps and itineraries, lives of the English kings, and formal histories abound as shown by the Term Catalogues for this period. Such is the avid curiosity about things English which the reviser aims to satisfy. An odd feature of this material is the fact that it was apparently introduced as an afterthought, as none of it appears before the letter *H;* this discrepancy is curiously corrected by grouping rulers whose names begin with an earlier initial under *King* and *Queen* and by describing counties whose names begin with an earlier initial under one of their cities.[15] The brief and poorly planned accounts of rulers appear to have been hasty abridgments from such popular sources as G(eorge) L(ivermore)'s *Compendious History of the Monarchs of England,* 1712; William Winstanley's *England's Worthies,* 1660, etc. The items on counties appear to have been derived from Edward and John Chamberlayne's frequently reissued *Angliae Notitia,* with supplementary remarks on local traditions from John Speed's *England, Wales, Scotland, and Ireland Described,* 1666, etc.

With these changes the ghostly reviser of a ghostly author and a ghostly editor lays aside his labors with satisfaction, declaring the work "very Necessary for all Persons, who desire to understand the Affairs of the World, as well as the Language and Transactions of their own Country." [16]

Chapter XI

JOHN KERSEY'S REVISION OF EDWARD PHILLIPS'

The New World of Words (1706)

JOHN KERSEY'S REVISION OF PHILLIPS' *New World of Words* IN 1706 was so thoroughgoing as to produce what must be regarded as a new dictionary.[1] This folio volume was a universal dictionary, so intelligently planned and executed as to constitute a distinguished performance and a worthy forerunner of Johnson. The title-page, oddly enough, retains the earlier pattern,[2] referring only casually to the addition of some 20,000 words:

The New World of Words: Or, Universal English Dictionary. Containing An Account of the Original or Proper Sense, and Various Significations of all Hard Words derived from other Languages, viz....

Together with A Brief and Plain Explication of all Terms relating to any of the Arts and Sciences, either Liberal or Mechanical, viz....

To which is Added, The Interpretation of Proper Names of Men and Women, ... with those of Writs and Processes at Law: Also the Greek and Latin Names of divers sorts of Animals, Plants, Metals, Minerals, &c....

Compiled by Edward Phillips, Gent. The Sixth Edition, Revised, Corrected, and Improved; with the Addition of near Twenty Thousand Words, from the best Authors, Domestick and Foreign, that treat of the several Subjects: By J. K. Philobibl. London:... MDCCVI.

A new and businesslike preface, however, indicates the extent of the revision. Kersey here claims that his collection "made out of the most approved Authors" is "far the largest of any hitherto extant." This claim is readily substantiated, as the Kersey-Phillips vocabulary is estimated at 38,000 words, representing a tremendous increase over the preceding (1700) edition of Phillips with its 17,000 detailed entries and the nearest rival, the 1701 Coles with about 25,000 briefer entries. The nature of the revision is explained as follows:

> The Whole has been carefully Revis'd . . . and it was judg'd expedient to leave out all Abstracts of the Lives of Eminent Persons, Poetical Fictions, Geographical Descriptions . . . in regard that they are already treated of at large, in several particular Dictionaries. In the room of these, are inserted near Twenty Thousand hard Words and Terms in all Arts and Sciences, . . . To which are added many Country-Words, and such as are us'd in our ancient Latin Writers, old Records. . . . Also the *Greek* and *Latin* Names of many sorts of Beasts, Birds, Fishes, Insects, Plants, . . . The Magistrates and Officers of the Grecian and Roman Empires. . . . Besides a summary View of Religious Orders, and other Remarkable Things in England, and our American Plantations; . . .

The most significant change is undoubtedly the abandonment of the "poetical fictions" and the substitution of a whole new scientific and technical vocabulary. Thus at a single stroke the large collection of classical and medieval legends which had been carelessly copied and alternately expanded and abridged for some fifty years was cast out to be replaced by a body of new learning, partly the live result of recent research and partly the most authoritative theories of recent writers. This new material, competently and interestingly treated, came from a fine contemporary work by John Harris, M.A., F.R.S.; published in 1704, this work bore the brief but impressive title:

> Lexicon Technicum: Or, An Universal English Dictionary of Arts and Sciences: Explaining not only the Terms of Art, But the Arts Themselves.

In his scientific items, comprising about half of his total vocabulary, Kersey follows Harris closely, though often abridging a long discussion. Compare the following:

HARRIS, 1704	KERSEY-PHILLIPS, 1706
Abductores, in the general are the same with Abducent Muscles . . . those which serve to open or pull back divers Parts of the Body, as the Arms, Legs, Eyes, Nostrils, Lips, &c. . . . Their Opposites are usually called Adductors or Adducent Muscles.	*Abductores*, or Abducent Muscles (in the general) are all those which serve to open or pull back divers Parts of the Body, as the Arms, Legs, Eyes, Nostrils, Lips, &c. And the Opposites to these are usually termed Aductores, or Adducent Muscles.

Harris, 1704	Kersey-Phillips, 1706
Absorbents, are Medicines that temper and qualifie the Acid Juices in the Body, by imbibing or drinking them up. Thus *Alkali's* are said by some to Absorb Acids.	*Absorbents,* Medicines that temper and qualifie the sharp Juices in the Body, by imbibing or soaking them up. Thus *Alkali's* are said to absorb *Acids.*
Accension, is the enkindling or setting any Body on Fire.	*Accension,* (in Philosophy) the Inkindling, or setting any natural Body on Fire.

Other bodies of words introduced into the 1706 revision—which, though not new to the English dictionary like the scientific vocabulary just discussed, are notably expanded—are legal terms and dialect.

The legal terms came mainly from White Kennett's revision in 1701 of J. Cowell's famous *Interpreter* (1607), as instanced by the following items:

Cowell, 1701 Edition	Kersey-Phillips, 1706
Abarnare, To detect, or discover any secret Crime. *Sax. Abarian,* to uncover, disclose or make bare. . . .	*Abarnare,* an old *Latin* Law-term, signifying to detect or discover any secret Crime; from the *Saxon* word *Abarian,* to make bare, uncover, or disclose.
Abbatis, An *Avener* or Steward of the Stables; the word was sometimes used for a common Hostler, . . .	*Abbatis* (in old Records) an Avener or Steward of the Stables; an Hostler.

The relationship with Cowell is, however, a complex one. Besides adding legal terms from Kennett's recent revision of Cowell, Kersey retained items which earlier editions of Phillips had borrowed from earlier editions of Cowell or indirectly from Cowell through Blount's *Glossographia.* Other legal items, originating in Cowell, came over with the copious borrowing from Harris' *Lexicon.* Thus several streams of borrowing from Cowell converge in the Kersey-Phillips.

The "country-words" (dialectal and agricultural terms) comprise a large selection from John Ray's *Collection of English Words Not Generally Used* (1674, etc.) and virtually the entire *Dictionarium Rusticum* from John Worlidge's *Systema Agriculturae* (1669, etc.). It may be noted here that W. E. A. Axon some time ago made a collection of the dialect words in Bailey's *Universal Etymological English Dictionary* of 1721 for the English Dialect Society [3] and that D. and M. Förster subsequently pointed out that most of these dialect words had already appeared in Kersey's *Dictionarium Anglo-Britannicum* of 1708.[4] The same group of words may, however, be traced one step farther back, for they had first entered the English dictionary with Kersey's revision of Phillips. Coles had indeed included some dialect in his dictionary,[5] but the feature is developed and stressed for the first time in the work we are now studying. The following will serve as examples of these rural and dialectal terms and their treatment:

Karl-Cat, a Word often us'd in *Lincoln-shire*, for a Male or Boar-Cat.

Karle-Hemp, (Country-Word) the latter green Hemp.

Kebbars or *Cullars*, refuse Sheep taken out of the Flock.

Keeve or *Keever*, a kind of Tub or Brewing-Vessel, in which the Ale or Beer works before it is tunn'd.

Kidcrow, (Country-Word) a Place for a sucking Calf to lye in.

Kipe, a Basket made of Osiers, broader at Bottom, and narrow'd by Degrees to the Top, but left open at both Ends; which is used for taking of Fish, particularly at *Otmore* in *Oxford-shire*, where this manner of Fishing is called *Kiping*, and going to *Kipe*.

Knolls, a Word us'd in some Counties for Turnips.

Knots, a delicious sort of small Fowl well known in some Parts of *England*, and so call'd from *Canutus* the *Danish* King, by whom they were highly esteem'd.

The rest of the vocabulary, aside from some miscellaneous items, consists of two bodies of words: the remains of the earlier Phillips (the surviving "hard" words) and a considerable body of ordinary words. Although the first group had served Kersey as a basic word list and constitutes the only continuity between this and former editions of Phillips, it too is disguised. The reason for change here is highly significant. The stock subject discussed in the prefaces of the various dictionaries up to this time has been the content of the vocabulary—its scope and nature; little attention has been paid to the definitions. Kersey, however, as an intelligent lexicographer and reformer, saw the defects of his predecessors in this essential and stressed the need of careful definitions: "As for the individual Terms, care has been taken everywhere to set down their Original and Proper Signification . . . with all possible Perspicuity and Brevity, . . ."[6] Previous definitions had been vague, formless, incomplete, leisurely; perspicuity and brevity were the great desiderata. As Phillips' original definitions had been verbose, Kersey now rewrites many—sometimes merely condensing them but often expanding them to show several senses of a word, the latter an important step forward in the technique of definition.

Phillips, 1696 Edition	Kersey-Phillips, 1706
A *Conclusion*, (*Lat.*) a shutting up or ending of a business. In Logick it is the last of the three Propositions of a *Syllogism*, the first being the *Major*, the second the *Minor*.	*Conclusion*, the end, close, or Issue of a thing; a Consequence or Inference: In *Logick*, the last of the three Propositions of a Syllogism: Also a Term us'd in Law, when a Man by his own Act upon Record, has concluded, or charg'd himself with a Duty, or other thing: It is also taken for the end or latter part of any Declaration, Bar, Replication, &c.
To *Confess*, is the Acknowledgment and Declaration which the People make of their Sins, that they may receive Absolution.	To *Confess*, to acknowledge, own, or allow; to hear the Confession of a Penitent, to declare one's Sins in Order to Absolution.
Consort, (*Lat.*) a Fellow, Companion, or Mate: Also a piece of Musick consisting of three or more parts, which is either Instrumental or Vocal.	*Consort*, a partaker of the same Condition; a Companion, or Mate; the Wife of a Soveraign Prince, or other great Person: Also the Harmony made by several Voices or Musical Instruments; a Musick-meeting.

As to the ordinary words, the Kersey-Phillips has a good many items and definitions in common with J. K.'s *New English Dictionary* of 1702. Either Kersey has borrowed these from the earlier work (his own?), or it is conceivable that a master list served for both these works as well as for Kersey's *Dictionarium Anglo-Britannicum* of 1708. Definitions taken from the 1702 work are often expanded or clarified. Compare the following:

J. K., 1702	Kersey-Phillips, 1706
To *glimmer*, or begin to appear; as, the light does.	To *Glimmer*, to begin to appear by Degrees, as the Light does at Break of Day.
A *Griffin*, a fabulous creature, having the head, wings and feet of an eagle, and the other parts like a lion.	A *Griffin*, a Bird of Prey, like an Eagle, or a fabulous Creature, said to have the Head, Wings and Feet of an Eagle, and the other Parts like a Lion.

J. K., 1702	KERSEY-PHILLIPS, 1706
Groteck, or antick work; rude figures that represent things after an odd and confused manner.	*Grotesks*, or *Grotesk-work* (in *Painting* or *Carving*) Antick Work, certain rude Figures made at the Pleasure of the Artist, which represent Things after an odd and confused manner.
To *guggle*, or make a noise; as a bottle that is emptying.	To *Guggle*, to make a noise like a narrow-mouth'd Bottle that is emptying.
A *Guimad*, a fish peculiar to the River *Dee* and the Lake *Pemble-meer*.	*Guimad*, a Fish peculiar to the River *Dee* in *Cheshire*, and the Lake *Pemble-meer*.

Obviously this work, which was reissued in 1720 without revision, has made great strides forward. Kersey has here rejected confused and outmoded material as well as useless apparatus and inefficient methods. In their stead he has introduced stimulating and important contemporaneous material, has followed up J. K.'s policy of recognizing the ordinary words by sanctioning their admission into the vocabulary of a universal dictionary, and has taken steps toward the evolution of a modern technique of definition. In one respect Kersey is not progressive; about half of his words carry no etymological data, and the others merely have a letter denoting the language from which they are derived. Etymology, then, is a feature that needs development; and progress in this department will be the main claim of Nathan Bailey, the next important lexicographer.

Chapter XII

Glossographia Anglicana Nova (1707)

THE ANONYMOUS *Glossographia Anglicana Nova* OF 1707 IS A
hybrid. Its title and title-page bear so strong a resemblance
to those of Blount's *Glossographia* of 1656 [1] that the
work has often been hastily dismissed as a late edition of
Blount. The close relationship to Blount cannot be denied; but another
and even more important relationship, to be shown below, must also be
recognized.

The title-page reads as follows:

Glossographia Anglicana Nova: Or, A Dictionary, Interpreting Such Hard
Words of whatever Language, as are at present used in the English Tongue,
with their Etymologies, Definitions, &c.

Also, The Terms of Divinity, Law, Physick, Mathematicks, History, Agriculture, Logick, Metaphysicks, Grammar, Poetry, Musick, Heraldry, Architecture, Painting, War, and all other Arts and Sciences are herein explain'd,
from the best Modern Authors, as, Sir Isaac Newton, Dr. Harris, Dr.
Gregory, Mr. Lock, Mr. Evelyn, Mr. Dryden, Mr. Blunt, &c.

Very useful to all those that desire to understand what they read. London,
...1707.

The preface, written under the protective cover of anonymity, is a
frank and personable document. The author first acknowledges with the
casualness of a dilettante that his work is "purposely small, that if it
shou'd not wholly answer the Design with which it was wrote, the Mis-
chief and Inconvenience of it might not be great." It is indeed surprising
at this period to encounter a dictionary containing only about 14,500
entries; these are, however, treated with unusual fullness, and the work
itself is a large octavo of 576 pages.

The author proceeds to weigh his predecessors in the balance and finds them sadly wanting. No fraternal or filial devotion tempers his treatment of Blount:

I have observ'd, that Blunt, Philips, Cole [*sic*], and others, have been favourably receiv'd; I may add, have been in some measure useful to that Rank of Readers to which they address'd themselves. It is true, Blunt offer'd his Service to the Learned World, and generously submitted to the Labour and Drudgery of gleaning the scatter'd Sciences, and ranging the Definitions and Terms of Art each Alphabetically; the Misfortune was, he went a simpling in a Field Twenty Years, as himself confesses, without discovering many new Plants; which had been pardonable in him, had he given us the true Names, Vertues and Qualities of several of the old. Philips, to whose laudable Industry we owe a much more bulky Performance, was no better qualified for paving the Way to any one of the Sciences, having neither Skill, Tools nor Materials: So that Cole, after all, with his few Pretences, has as much real Worth as either of the former, and may make good the part of a Guide to Tradesmen and illiterate Readers, who are suppos'd to seek for the Etymology of every Word that Custom has not familiarly acquainted 'em with.

The purpose of this dictionary is declared to be twofold. Like its predecessors, it was written with the view of "instructing the Ignorant, and calculated . . . for the use of such as are not able to read a good Historian, or any Polite *English* Writer without an Interpreter." Words inserted for this purpose are usually taken with their definitions from the maligned Blount. This rather pedestrian aim is, however, offset by a more distinctive and progressive one:

. . . yet I have chiefly consulted the Advantage of such as are gently advancing to Science; and for want of Opportunities of Learned Helps, have the Misfortune to be their own Conductors, or have not Money sufficient to lay in the necessary Furniture of Learning. These I have chiefly respected, and for the Sake of these it is to be wish'd, that they whose Abilities are greatest, wou'd employ 'em in making Knowledge as easy as may be.

Stress on science is, then, the most formative and forward-looking feature of this dictionary. We have just described the great body of scientific material introduced into the Kersey-Phillips, a work of encyclopedic proportions designed for reference use by the better educated. Whereas Kersey pioneered in introducing scientific terms into the general English dictionary, the author of the *Glossographia Anglicana Nova* attempts further to popularize science and to make such information available in cheaper and handier form. The source of this technical vocabulary and the most conspicuous influence on this work is, as with the Kersey-Phillips, John Harris' fine *Lexicon Technicum* of 1704. This time the relationship is commercial as well as intellectual, for both works were sponsored by the same group of booksellers. The *Glossographia Anglicana Nova* is thus not only an offshoot of the larger Harris enterprise but serves as an advertisement of the other work, a two-volume edition of which was even then in preparation.[2] Whether from advertising zeal or from unusual candor, the author describes in the preface his sources and method of compilation, with his dominant scientific interest and his confidence in Harris always to the fore.

Whilst I was compiling this, the Ingenious Dr. *Harris's Lexicon Technicum* laid before me, to which I am indebted for a considerable Part of this Book. I had likewise recourse to the Lexicographers of less Note, from whom I borrow'd what I thought for my Purpose, and follow'd 'em where I safely might; for I did not think my self oblig'd to stumble after them because I follow'd them: Tho' I frankly own, that bating that Part of the Book which defines Terms of Art in Natural Philosophy, Astronomy, and other Mathematical Sciences [*i.e.*, the part based on Harris], the rest of it may come in for a Share of that Inaccuracy they have been censur'd for. I did not make it my Business so much to mark their Errors in other things as to avoid 'em in these.

In the preface the author incidentally refers to his work as an abridgment; in a limited sense this description is true and accounts for the author's practice of extensive verbatim borrowings, but otherwise it is misleading, because the author is following more than one source. In addition to the heavy debts to Harris and Blount, the author also made considerable use of the Kersey-Phillips *New World of Words* (1706) for miscellaneous items. Probably about the same number of words was taken from Harris and Blount, though the Harris definitions by their length and novelty occupy much more space and stamp the book with its peculiar character. The Kersey-Phillips borrowing, although much smaller, is noticeable. The Harris definitions are almost always and the Kersey-Phillips definitions are often condensed.

Abatement, 1. A *Delf*, which is a Square born in the middle of the Field, thus; and belongs to one that hath revoked his Challenge, or eaten his Words.

2. A *Point Dexter parted Tenn:* due to him that is a *Braggadocio*, or boasts of more than he did, or can do.

3. A *Point in Point Sanguine*, thus; due to him that is Lazy and Sloathful in the Wars.

Abatement, First a *Delf*, which is a Square born in the Middle of the Field, thus; and belongs to one that revokes his Challenge.

II. A *Point Dexter parted Tenn*, due to one that boasts of more than he can do.

III. A *Point in Point Sanguine*, thus; due to one that is Lazy in the Wars.

Abawed, abashed, daunted, a word us'd by the famous *English* Poet, *Geffrey Chaucer*.

Abashed, made ashamed or confounded.

Abassi, a Coin, current in *Persia* and other *Eastern* Countries, worth about two *Spanish* Reals, or 1 *s*. 2 *d*. Sterling.

Abbreuvoir (*Fr.*) a Watering-place: In *Masonry*,
Abbreuvoirs are the spaces between the Stones to put the Mortar in as they are laying.

Abawed, Abashed, Daunted. *Chaucer*.

Abashed, made Ashamed.

Abassi, a Coyn, current in the Eastern Countries, worth about one Shilling and two Pence Sterling.

Abbrevoir, (Fr.) in Masonry, signifies the Spaces between the Stones, where the Mortar is put.

The Blount items, being briefer, are often taken *in toto* [3] but sometimes show condensation as in the following instances:

Abessed, or Abbaised (Fr. *abaissé*) debased, dejected, humbled, bent, or brought down.

Abjuration (*abjuratio*) a forswearing or renouncing by Oath. In our Common Law it is an Oath taken to forsake the Realm for ever.

Abessed, (Fr.) debased, dejected, or brought down.

Abjuration, (Lat.) a Forswearing or Denying upon Oath. In our Common Law, it is an Oath taken to forsake the Kingdom for ever.

The author also takes his lead from Blount in two other respects. He includes etymology but treats it casually; he annotates less than half of his items and, disdaining the original forms conveniently offered by Blount, merely notes the origin as "Lat.," "Gr.," "Fr.," as shown in the examples just quoted. On the other hand, from Blount's slight beginning with two woodcuts, this author goes on to illustrate helpfully his numerous heraldic terms.[4] The *Glossographia Anglicana Nova* is thus the first English dictionary to make any considerable use of woodcuts; the next development in this respect does not appear until 1727, when Nathan Bailey in his *Universal Etymological English Dictionary*, Volume II, illustrates scientific as well as heraldic terms.

The second edition of the *Glossographia Anglicana Nova*, which appeared in 1719, shows no important change. Although the title-page claims above three thousand additional words, we should estimate that only about one thousand miscellaneous items have been added.

Chapter XIII

JOHN KERSEY's *Dictionarium Anglo-Britannicum* (1708)

LTHOUGH JOHN KERSEY's *Dictionarium Anglo-Britannicum* OF
1708 offers no new material, it deserves recognition as the
first abridged dictionary and as a competent solution of the
problems arising in this new type.
The crowded title-page may be reduced as follows:

Dictionarium Anglo-Britannicum: Or, A General English Dictionary,
Comprehending A Brief, but Emphatical and Clear Explication of all sorts of
difficult Words, ... as also, of all Terms relating to Arts and Sciences, both
Liberal and Mechanical, ...
To which is Added, A Large Collection of Words and Phrases, as well
Latin as English, made use of in our Ancient Statutes, ... Besides an Inter-
pretation of the proper Names of Men and Women, ...
The Whole Work Compil'd, and Methodically Digested, for the Benefit
of Young Students, Tradesmen, Artificers, Foreigners, and others, ...
By John Kersey, Philobibl. London, ... 1708.

In the preface the author explains his clear-cut and ambitious design
for his work. He observes that, although many dictionaries are already
available, the larger ones are too inconvenient and expensive for widespread use and the smaller ones are too limited in content and defective
in execution. Kersey's aim for the *Dictionarium Anglo-Britannicum* is,
then, to extend the scope and accuracy so far expected only in the larger
dictionaries to "a portable Volume, which may be had at any easie
Rate." The author rightly claims for his octavo work a more extensive
and varied vocabulary than is "to be met with in any one Single Dictionary of the Lower Class, hitherto Extant." In fact, Kersey's vocabulary,
estimated at 35,000 words, far surpasses that of any preceding diction-

ary with the single exception of the folio Kersey-Phillips, which, amazingly enough considering the difference in physical size, it almost equals. The Kersey-Phillips, it will be recalled, contained about 38,000 words.

The *Dictionarium Anglo-Britannicum* is actually an abridgment of the Kersey-Phillips *New World of Words* of 1706. Although the author does not state this fact, there is no attempt to conceal the affinity between the works, which is obvious upon even the most cursory examination. The same booksellers sponsored both undertakings, the title-pages show certain similarities, and the preface of the *Dictionarium Anglo-Britannicum* carries the following recommendation of the parent work:

But if any are for making a more strict Search into the inmost Recesses of the Imperial Mine, they need only have recourse to the last Edition of *Phillips's Dictionary*, set forth by us, with very large Additions and Improvements, (An. 1706), where they'll find the various sorts of rich Oar amply display'd in their natural Order and Position.

As long ago as 1912, R. H. Thornton described the *Dictionarium Anglo-Britannicum* contemptuously as "little more than a boiling down of Phillips's *World of Words*" and charged that the reduction had resulted in unsatisfactory definitions.[1] The specimens which Thornton offers for his point were, however, unrepresentative, as they dealt with the common words which still eluded definition. H. B. Wheatley also dismissed the *Dictionarium Anglo-Britannicum* briefly as "almost exclusively a Dictionary of hard words." [2] It should be noted, however, that the work has, besides the hard words "to be found in . . . our Noted Writers," a scattering of everyday words such as were introduced in J. K.'s *New English Dictionary* of 1702 and retained in the Kersey-Phillips of 1706, and the enlarged dialectal [3] and legal lists and whole new scientific vocabulary introduced by the 1706 volume. Thus for its size the work is unprecedented in flexibility and usefulness.

A close comparison of the word lists of the 1706 Kersey-Phillips and the 1708 *Dictionarium Anglo-Britannicum* shows that the latter takes over all items except cross references and adds only a few obsolete words or variant forms. Of the first 630 words of the 1706 vocabulary, for example, only the occasional cross references are omitted, and only three obsolete words and four variant forms are added.[4] Except for some ordinary words, where the 1706 definitions were still inferior, all defini-

tions are capably and clearly shortened. Here, as in the preface to his
1706 volume, Kersey professes a special concern for the form and
clarity of his definitions, and promises "a concise, but plain, and familiar
Explication" [5] of his words. Parallel definitions illustrate Kersey's
method of abridgment:

KERSEY-PHILLIPS, 1706	*Dictionarium Anglo-Britannicum*, 1708
Abaddon, (*Heb. i.e.* a Destroyer) one of the Names of Satan or the Devil in the Revelation of St. *John.*	*Abaddon,* (*H.* a Destroyer) one of the Names of Satan or the Devil.
Abdevenam, the Head of the twelfth House in a Scheme or Figure of the Heavens, sometimes so call'd by Astrologers.	*Abdevenam,* (in *Astrol.*) the Head of the Twelfth House, in a Scheme or Figure of the Heavens.
Abdi, (*Heb.* my Servant) the Father of *Kish,* and Grandfather of *Saul* the first King of *Israel.*	*Abdi,* (*H.* my Servant) the Grandfather of King *Saul.*
Abishering, an old Law-word, which properly signifies Forfeiture; a being quit of Amerciaments, Forfeits or Fines, for a Transgression prov'd before any Judge: It is otherwise express'd *Misherising* or *Miskering.*	*Abishering,* (O.L.T.) a being free from Amerciaments, Forfeits or Fines, for any Transgression.

Although the *Dictionarium Anglo-Britannicum* was reissued in 1715
and 1721 and was said to be corrected and enlarged, there is no per-
ceptible increase in the word list.

Chapter XIV

NATHAN BAILEY'S

An Universal Etymological English Dictionary (1721)

THE FIRST DECADE OF THE EIGHTEENTH CENTURY HAD PRO-
duced five new dictionaries, and its lexicography had been
dominated by the activities of John Kersey. With his dictionaries on different levels reissued at intervals, Kersey
evidently satisfied the needs of his time, for no new dictionary appeared
for thirteen years after his *Dictionarium Anglo-Britannicum.*

In 1721 the next important lexicographer, Nathan Bailey, produced
his octavo *Universal Etymological English Dictionary,* most popular of
all dictionaries antedating Johnson. The spotlight of fame which has long
been focused on Johnson and has recently spread to his immediate predecessor, Bailey, has unfortunately thrown Kersey into the shadow. Kersey
was, however, a notable pioneer, rejecting outmoded material and
methods, working toward modern concepts, and in general playing his
role of lexicographer with responsibility and intelligence. He must be
credited with the first universal dictionary; with the first abridged dictionary; with the largest, most useful, and most competently executed
dictionaries produced up to his time. On this secure foundation Bailey
built with enterprise and resourcefulness a whole structure of fine new
dictionaries. These in their turn were to serve as a firm base for Johnson's work.

While Kersey's life was practically unknown, the few facts about
Bailey are rather oddly telescoped in the article in the *Dictionary of
National Biography* as follows: "Of the compiler nothing is known
beyond the fact that he belonged to the seventh-day baptists, being ad-
mitted to membership 6 Nov. 1691, and kept a boarding school at
Stepney, where he died on 27 June 1742." [1] A glance at the bibliography

of Bailey, however, proves him to have been learned and industrious. The following digest indicates the scope of his lexicographical activity; he would appear, indeed, to have been something of a professional lexicographer. The *Dictionarium Rusticum, Urbanicum & Botanicum*, which does not bear Bailey's signature but is usually ascribed to him, was published in 1704 and reached a third edition in 1726; his *Universal Etymological English Dictionary*, published in 1721, reached a thirtieth edition in 1802; the supplementary volume of the *Universal Etymological English Dictionary* underwent seven editions with considerable revision from 1727 to 1776; the *Dictionarium Britannicum* appeared in 1730 and again, greatly enlarged, in 1736; and the *Dictionarium Domesticum* appeared in 1736.[2] Among other works by Bailey may be mentioned his translation of Erasmus' *Colloquies*, his editions of Ovid's *Metamorphoses* and *Tristia*, a spelling book, a grammar, and various Latin exercise books for schoolboys. His busy career closed in 1742, as noted above.

With this general background we turn now to the representative eighteenth-century dictionary, the title-page of which may be abridged:

An Universal Etymological English Dictionary: Comprehending The Derivations of the Generality of Words in the English Tongue, either Antient or Modern, from the Antient British, Saxon, Danish, Norman and Modern French, Teutonic, Dutch, Spanish, Italian, Latin, Greek, and Hebrew Languages, each in their proper Characters.

And Also A Brief and clear Explication of all difficult Words...and Terms of Art relating to Anatomy, Botany, Physick,...

Together with A Large Collection and Explication of Words and Phrases us'd in our Antient Statutes, Charters, Writs, Old Records, and Processes at Law; and the Etymology and Interpretation of the Proper Names of Men, Women, and Remarkable Places in Great Britain: Also the Dialects of our Different Counties.

Containing many Thousand Words more than either Harris, Philips, Kersey, or any English Dictionary before Extant.

To which is Added a Collection of our most Common Proverbs, with their Explication and Illustration.

The whole work compil'd and Methodically digested, as well for the Entertainment of the Curious, as the Information of the Ignorant, and for the Benefit of young Students, Artificers, Tradesmen and Foreigners,...

By N. Bailey, φιλόλογος. London:...1721.

Notable features here are the prominence given to the etymological aspect of the work in both title and title-page, the resemblance to the title-page of Kersey's *Dictionarium Anglo-Britannicum,* the addition of proverbs, and the return to the early seventeenth-century idea that dictionaries may entertain as well as inform.[3] A glance at title-pages and prefaces up to this point reveals that, despite random hopes to the contrary and with the exception of the folio dictionaries, lexicographers still commonly assumed that their works would be used mainly by the little educated. Bailey, however, is making a gesture toward a wider audience and a wider usefulness. As proof of his success in this endeavor, it may be pertinent to recall here the familiar fact that no less a figure than William Pitt, the First Earl of Chatham, found Bailey's dictionary both entertaining and profitable reading.[4]

The introduction offers first a history of the English language of the kind introduced by Phillips but somewhat broader and more detailed. Specimens of "the Saxon Tongue" are given as well as comments by various scholars on the properties and capacities of the English language. The author then comments on his predecessors with unusual courtesy but with annoying vagueness:

It is not my Design to depreciate the Labours of those worthy Authors, whose Writings of this kind have saved me much Pains. I shall only say, as *facile est inventis addere,* in perusing the best Books of this Kind Extant, I have found in them both a Redundancy and Deficiency, the former of which I have omitted, to make room for the latter, having inrich'd it with several 1000 *English* Words and Phrases, in no *English* Dictionary before extant.

A conservative estimate places Bailey's vocabulary at about 40,000 words; thus his bulky octavo of about 950 pages treats more items than even the folio Kersey-Phillips of 1706 with its 38,000 items.

The greater part of the introduction is given over to a discussion of etymology as the peculiar contribution of this dictionary. Sceptical as to the popularity of this material, however, Bailey takes care to point out that it need not encumber anyone who is not interested in such subtleties.

As for the Etymological Part, or those Words from Foreign Languages whence the *English* Words were deriv'd, I think I am the first who has attempted it in *English,* except what Mr. *Blunt* has done in his *Glossography,* which is but a very small Part, and those of a *Latin* Derivation chiefly, besides a small Extract of Dr. *Skinner's Etymologicon.*

However, I shall not enlarge at present on the Usefulness of that Part, supposing that such Persons who understand the Language need no such Information; and as to them which do not, the Etymological Part is separated so distinctly from the Rest, being inclosed within Crotchets, that they may pass it over without any manner of Trouble or Inconvenience.

Bailey then explains the various principles he has followed in presenting the etymology of different parts of speech. He concludes the discussion, however, on a defensive note, warning readers not to be surprised if the etymon sometimes seems far removed from the present word in spelling and meaning. Finally, he admits that most of his etymological data is borrowed and seems thus to disclaim responsibility for the material. It appears, then, that the etymological feature, which had been so long neglected, is developed here not through any special conviction or competence on Bailey's part but as a novelty, an advertising point, and a justification for bringing out a new dictionary. "And besides, very few of the Etymological Words are my own, but I have generally the Suffrage of *Somner, Camden, Verstegan, Spelman, Casaubon,* Dr. *Th. Henshaw, Skinner, Junius, Menagius, Minshew,* and other great Names and approved Etymologists to bear me out."

It may be advisable at this point to take a backward glance at earlier lexicographers and their policies in regard to etymology. The pioneer, Robert Cawdrey, introduced symbols to indicate the languages from which words were derived but was extremely casual in putting his system into practice. Bullokar and Cockeram disregarded etymology, although the omission is understandable as their vocabularies were known to be almost exclusively classical in origin. Blount was the first to give etymology prominence. His usual practice was to give the root word, although sometimes he merely cited the language of origin; on rare occasions he went so far as to analyze the meaning of the root word. Phillips, both in the earlier and in the revised form, showed little interest in this department, noting opposite a few terms the language from which each was supposedly derived. Coles and the later editions of "Cocker" merely used a letter to indicate the language of origin but carried this method out with praiseworthy care and completeness. Both the *Glossographia Anglicana Nova* and Kersey's *Dictionarium Anglo-Britannicum* annotated only a small proportion of their items with the name of the original language.[5]

Bailey's work in this department is, as one might expect at this date, far from definitive; but it is equally far in advance of any predecessor. At his best he offers not only the original language but the root word and not only the immediate but the ultimate sources of the word, as in the following examples:

Circumvent, (*Circonvenir,* F. *Circumventum,* L.)...
Cistern, (*Cisterne,* F. of *Cisterna,* L.)...
Citadel, (*Citadelle,* F. of *Cittadella,* Ital.)...
Cite, (*Citer,* F. of *Citare,* L.)...
Citizen, (*Citoyen,* F. of *Civis,* L.)...

It must be admitted that Bailey does not venture far beyond his etymological authorities, that he sometimes omits etymology altogether, and that he is guilty of perpetuating some of Skinner's unhappiest conjectures.[6] He has, however, established etymology as one of the requisites of any reputable dictionary; and his focus on this feature is to bear fine fruit in his own later dictionaries as well as in those of his successors.[7]

In the make-up of his word list Bailey owes most to Kersey, but he has borrowed widely. It is easy to picture Bailey at work, more or less in the modern manner, surrounded by sources which he constantly compares and each of which he taps for its specialty. For his basic word list, Bailey takes almost every item from Kersey's *Dictionarium Anglo-Britannicum* with identical definitions but with etymologies added from the special etymological sources acknowledged in the introduction; these Kersey items comprise more than two-thirds of Bailey's list. The following parallel items will show the relations of the works as well as further illustrate Bailey's etymological method:

KERSEY, 1708	BAILEY, 1721
Electricity, (in *Philos.*) the Quality that Amber, Jeat, Sealing-Wax, &c. have of drawing all sorts of very light Bodies to them, when rubbed.	*Elect ty,* is the Quality that Amber, Jet, Sealing-wax, &c. has of attracting very light Bodies to them, when the attracting Body is rubbed or chafed.
Elk, a strong swift Beast as high as a Horse, and shap'd like a Hart.	*Elk,* (Elch, *Sax.*) a strong, swift Beast, in Shape like an Hart, and as tall as a Horse.

KERSEY, 1708

BAILEY, 1721

Elysian Fields, a certain Paradise of delightful Meadows, into which the Heathens held that the Souls of Just Men pass'd after Death.

Elysian Fields, a certain Paradice of delightful Groves and Meadows, into which the Heathens held that the Souls of good Men passed after Death.

Ember-Weeks, Four Seasons in the Year more especially set a-part for Prayer and Fasting, and of great Antiquity in the Church, *viz.* the first Week in *Lent,* the Week after *Whitsuntide,* the Week following the 14th Day of *September,* and that following *December* 13th.

Ember-Weeks, are four Seasons in the Year, anciently set apart more particularly for Prayer and Fasting; *viz.* the first Week in *Lent,* the next after *Whitsunday,* the 14th of *September,* and 13th of *December.*

Emerald, (*Sp.*) a precious Stone of a Green Colour: Among Heralds, the Green Colour in the Coats of Noblemen.

Emerald, (*Esmeraude,* F. *Esmeralda,* Span. *Smaragdus,* L. of Σμαϱάγδος, Gr.) a precious Stone.
Emerald, (in *Heraldry*) the green Colour in the Coats of Noblemen.

Enantiosis or *Antenantiosis,* (G.) Contrariety: In *Rhetorick,* a Figure when that is spoken by a contrary, which is intended should be understood, as it were by Affirmation.

Enantiosis, ('Εναντίωδις Gr.) Contrariety; a Rhetorical Figure, when that is spoken by a Contrary, which is intended should be understood, as it were, by Affirmation.

Other borrowings may be briefly indicated. Bailey was apparently not satisfied with the abridged definitions of some specialized terms in the *Dictionarium Anglo-Britannicum* but preferred to use the fuller explanations from the Kersey-Phillips *World of Words* (1706 or 1720 edition); such items had, of course, stemmed from Harris' *Lexicon Technicum* (1704). Many common Anglo-Saxon words were taken from the first list in Skinner's *Etymologicon Linguae Anglicanae* (1671), and English names and place names came from the fifth list in the same source. While the majority of the dialectal and rural terms had already appeared in Kersey,[8] some additional expressions were added from Coles's *English Dictionary,* which was still being reprinted, and from John Ray's popular *Collection of English Words Not Generally Used* (1674, etc.). The scope of the vocabulary is attested by the fact that Bailey even admits a smattering of cant terms, taken from Coles.[9] An occasional definition reverts directly to Blount, Harris, and other sources. Both the variety of the material and the array of sources are impressive.

Of special interest is the treatment of obsolete expressions, which had been a frequent cause of contention among lexicographers.[10] Bailey's policy here, as with cant and dialect, is to be all-inclusive; he therefore takes over a body of such terms from Skinner (fourth list) and Coles. Not content with a general list, however, he also interests himself in obsolete expressions used by the great writers. In the first edition the *Universal Etymological English Dictionary* includes expressions used by Spenser and so designated. Bailey derives his material here from the recent edition of Spenser by John Hughes (1715), which carries a "Glossary Explaining the Old and Obscure Words." [11] Bailey has adopted practically the entire list with the distinctive definitions verbatim. The second edition of the *Universal Etymological English Dictionary* (1724) adds similar expressions found in Chaucer and so designated. Material here shows an acquaintance with the old Speght edition (1598) but is mainly based upon the recent edition by John Urry (1721), carrying a glossary which is thought to have been mainly the work of Timothy Thomas.[12] Finally, the third edition (1726) adds similar expressions used by Shakespeare. These could have been derived from the 1714 edition of Shakespeare's works by Nicholas Rowe but were more probably taken from the current edition by Pope (1725), which had the same glossary.[13] It was mainly from this rich collection of obsolete words that Chatterton constructed his poetic language for his Rowley poems.[14]

Another novel feature of Bailey's work reflecting a personal interest is his introduction of proverbs.[15] While there are only about ninety proverbs in all,[16] and these are hardly conspicuous in a work of this size, they are discussed in lively style and provide the leisurely reader with an occasional fine diversion. Among these are to be found practically all of the proverbs (about fifty) in Oswald Dyke's *English Proverbs with Moral Reflections* (third edition, 1713), with "explications" shortened from Dykes's long-winded and moralizing discussions. Bailey adds equivalents from other languages, ancient and modern, to conform with his supposed linguistic interest. To indicate the nature of this material, we quote one proverb with its complete treatment as derived from Dykes.

Dykes, 1713 Edition	Bailey, 1721
Jack will never make a *Gentleman*. ... In short, every one is not a *Gentleman*, that is *vulgarly* call'd so now-a-days, ...	Jack will never make a Gentleman. This Proverb teaches, that every one will not make a Gentleman, that is *vulgarly*

DYKES, 1713 Edition	BAILEY, 1721
There's more than the bare *Name* requir'd to the making of him what he *ought* to be by *Birth*, *Honour*, and *Merit*. Let a Man get never so much *Money* to buy *Land*, ... he cannot purchase one Grain of GENTILITY with it, but will remain JACK in the Proverb still, without *Vertue*, *Learning*, and *Wisdom*, to enrich the Faculties of his Mind, to *enhance* the glory of his Wealth, and to *ennoble* his Blood. Give this JACK what *Breeding*, what *Education*, what *Preferment* you please, he will discover himself at one Time or another, to be what he *was* from the Beginning, in Point of Behaviour, to be of mean Extract, ungenteel, awkward, ungenerous, a *Gentleman* at second Hand only, or a vainglorious *Upstart*: For *you can never make a silken Purse of a Sow's Ear.*... But to pursue this *Topick* a little more to the Letter of the Latin, *every Wood will not make a MERCURY.*...	called so, now-a-days: There is more than the bare Name required, to the making him what he ought to be by *Birth, Honour* and *Merit*: For let a Man get never so much Money to buy an *Estate*, he cannot purchase one grain of GENTILITY with it, but he will discover himself one Time or other, in Point of Behaviour, to be of a mean Extract, awkward, ungenteel, and ungenerous, a *Gentleman* at Second-hand only, or a vain-glorious *Upstart*: For *you cannot make a silken Purse of a Sow's Ear; Ex quovis ligno Mercurius non fit*, say the *Latins*.

Briefer and more racy are the explanations of proverbs associated with certain localities, such as: "As sure as God's in Gloucestershire," "The Traceys have always the wind in their faces," "As good as George of Green," etc. Such material is drawn from John Ray's *Collection of English Proverbs* (1670, etc.):

RAY, 1670 Edition	BAILEY, 1721
All goeth down Gutter-lane. *Gutter-lane* (the right spelling whereof is *Guthurn-lane*, from him the once owner thereof) is a small Lane (inhabited anciently by gold-beaters) leading out of *Cheap-side*, East of *Foster-lane*. The Proverb is applied to those, who spend all in drunkenness and gluttony, meer belly-gods: *Guttur* being Latine for the throat.	All goes down Gutter-Lane. This Proverb is applied to those who spend all in Drunkenness and Gluttony, mere Belly-Gods, alluding to the *Latin* word *Guttur*, which signifies the Throat.

RAY, 1670 Edition	BAILEY, 1721
As wise as a Man of Gotham (*Nottinghamshire*). It passeth for the Periphrasis of a fool, and an hundred fopperies are feigned and fathered on the Towns folk of *Gotham*, a village in this County.	As wise as a Man of Gotham. This Proverb passes for the Periphrasis of a Fool, and an hundred Fopperies are feigned and father'd on the Townfolk of *Gotham*, a Village in *Nottinghamshire*.

The subsequent history of the *Universal Etymological English Dictionary* is impressive. Its thirty editions burst forth continually with erratic overlappings and irregular numbering up to the year 1802; [17] and the growth of the vocabulary, while not so phenomenal as successive title-pages would lead the credulous to expect, was steady. The 1728 edition, for example, had about 42,500 words, the 1770 edition about 44,000, and the 1783 edition reached about 50,000; later editions did not attempt further expansion.

Early editions, except for the development of obsolete terms already discussed and the indication of accent from 1731 on,[18] showed no particular tendencies in expansion. Miscellaneous material from the erratic supplementary volume (to be discussed next as a separate work) was, however, incorporated at intervals. By the middle of the century the obsolete and dialectal terms were being gradually reduced; and newer expressions, related forms, and the usual odd bits of information were added.[19]

The twenty-fourth edition dated 1782,[20] however, appears with a new preface signed by Edward Harwood, D. D. and was obviously intended to combat the formidable competition with Johnson. This preface, a floridly written affair, exalts the lexicographer as one of "God's creatures . . . by his divine benevolence, originally predestinated to this great and useful end." After disarming his reader by a generous tribute to Johnson, Harwood outdoes himself in praising Bailey and his unsurpassable dictionary. The following passage is of interest as showing the grounds on which Bailey's dictionary claimed superiority to Johnson's and as incidentally implying some criticism of Johnson:

The Character of Bailey's Dictionary hath long been deservedly established, and through a series of many years hath acquired a just reputation, which all the numerous competitors we have lately seen hath not been able to eclipse. . . .

The peculiar and unrivaled Excellence of this Work is the definition and explanation of many hundred technical terms, which belong to respective Sciences, which are not found in other Dictionaries. Particularly are the terms in *Anatomy, Physic, Natural Philosophy,* and the *Mathematics* concisely and familiarly illustrated in this Thesaurus. In short, its principal excellence is, that it is a *Scientific Dictionary,* . . . The Etymological part is written in plain and easy language, the hard and obscure words not rendered harder and obscurer by a studied pomp and ostentation of diction, but everything is treated with perspicuity as well as erudition, Mr. Bailey possessing a happy method of communicating his ideas.

Aside from the militant preface, however, this edition shows little change; and Harwood claims only to have corrected typographical errors and to have added a mere two hundred words.

The twenty-fifth edition of the *Universal Etymological English Dictionary,* appearing in the following year, omits all mention of Harwood, carries an entirely new preface, and boasts an enlargement of two thousand words. The underlying purpose of the revision is, however, obviously the same as in the preceding edition. The editor again tries to offset the growing popularity of Johnson's dictionary by stressing what he regards as the peculiar merits of Bailey's: its "extensive plan," "the perspicuity and conciseness of its definitions," its intelligibility to all along with its special appeal to the learned through etymology, and above all the stress on science and on recent discoveries and developments in all fields.[21] The vocabulary has gained many items; they are, however, miscellaneous in character rather than predominantly scientific as the editor leads us to expect.[22] The *Universal Etymological English Dictionary* carries this preface and word list without further revision to the end of its record-breaking career in 1802. Spanning eighty years, this work may logically be considered the most popular and representative dictionary of the eighteenth century.

Chapter XV

NATHAN BAILEY'S

The Universal Etymological English Dictionary,

VOLUME II (1727)

THE SO-CALLED SECOND VOLUME OF BAILEY'S *Universal Etymological English Dictionary* has long been a puzzle. Issued at irregular intervals without any attempt to parallel issues of the original *Universal Etymological English Dictionary*, it would be more accurately called a supplement than a second volume. Even as a supplement, however, it is erratic, as, especially in the earlier editions, it repeats much material which was already available in the previous volume and actually constitutes a complete work in itself. Another enigmatic feature is that this volume changed so often and so radically in content that it hardly preserves its identity.

In its shifting contents and vague purpose, this octavo work bears all the marks of a bookseller's freak. The *Universal Etymological English Dictionary* was sponsored throughout the twenties by a large group of booksellers including J. Darby, A. Bettesworth, F. Fayram, J. Pemberton, J. Hooke, C. Rivington, F. Clay, J. Batley, E. Symon, and others. The first three editions of the second volume (1727, 1731, and 1737) were, however, published by Thomas Cox, who also published Bailey's folio *Dictionarium Britannicum* in 1730. In bringing out the second volume Cox obviously had a double purpose; besides attracting some of the trade attached to Bailey's name, he was preparing the way for the folio work by demonstrating that the original *Universal Etymological English Dictionary* was not to be regarded as satisfactory or complete. To those who already possessed this work he hoped to sell his supplementary volume, while to others he offered the *Dictionarium Britannicum*. Thus, while the latter work was being more painstakingly compiled, the smaller one was bringing in some profit and also serving as an advertisement for the larger venture. We can only conjecture Bailey's part in all this, but as lion of rival booksellers he was no doubt busily at work and not averse to any additional profit from his labors.

The title-page of the second volume will be given in considerable detail, as Bailey here both outlines and justifies his work:

The Universal Etymological English Dictionary:

In Two Parts:

Containing

I. An additional Collection

  1. Of some thousands of Words not in the former Volume, with their Etymologies and Explications: Also accented, to direct to their proper Pronunciation.

  2. Of a considerable number of Terms of Art in Anatomy, ... and all other Arts and Sciences, together with their Explications, E t y m o l o g i e s and engraven Schemes, where necessary, for the more easy and clear apprehending them.

  3. Of proper Names of Persons and Places in Great Britain, with their Etymologies ...

  4. The Theogony, Theology, and Mythology of the Egyptians, Greeks, Romans, &c. being an Account of their Deities, Solemnities, Religious or Civil, Oracles, Auguries, Hieroglyphicks, &c. necessary to be understood: especially by the Readers of English Poetry.

II. An Orthographical Dictionary, shewing both the Orthography and Orthoepia of the English Tongue, by

  1. Accents placed on each Word, directing to their true Pronunciation.

  2. Asterisms, distinguishing those Words of approv'd Authority from those that are not.

  3. Their various Senses and Significations, in English, and also French and Latin, for the sake of Foreigners, who desire an Acquaintance with the English Tongue.

  4. The Idioms, Phrases, and proverbial Sentences, peculiar to it. ...

Volume II. By N. Bailey, φιλόλογος. London: ... MDCCXXVII

Archbishop Trench's familiar indictment of the lexicographers preceding Johnson seems especially applicable to this volume:

A Dictionary ought to know its own limits, not merely as to what it should include, but also what it should exclude.... Our early lexicographers, ...from failing to recognize any proper limits to their work, from the desire to combine in it as many utilities as possible, present often the strangest medleys in the books which they have produced. These are not Dictionaries of words only, but of persons, places, things; they are gazetteers, mythologies, scientific encyclopedias, and a hundred things more; all, of course, most imperfectly, even according to the standard of knowledge of their own time, and with a selection utterly capricious of what they put in, and what they leave out.[1]

In the preface Bailey describes this work as composed of items he did not have room for in the original *Universal Etymological English Dictionary*, additional material since encountered in the course of wide reading, and many contributions from "Persons of generous and communicative Dispositions." [2] He also stresses the extensive use of cuts, an entertaining as well as an instructive device, in which he had been preceded much earlier by Blount and more recently by the *Glossographia Anglicana Nova* and far surpassed in scale by Harris' *Lexicon Technicum*, which was perhaps his immediate inspiration.[3] Bailey also marks the accentuation of words, a phase which had been totally disregarded by preceding lexicographers but which had been commonly associated with spelling books and grammars. Bailey may have been induced to make this innovation partly as a result of the recent popularity of two works by Thomas Dyche: *A Guide to the English Tongue*, 1709 and *A Dictionary*, 1723, both of which stressed pronunciation as well as spelling.[4] It is probable too that, as the difficult technical vocabulary increased in Bailey's original dictionary, the public clamored for a guide to pronunciation. As to etymology, the only development is Bailey's remark that he has occasionally indicated the origin of a word as "uncertain"—undeniably a step forward in discretion as well as in accuracy.

An analysis of the first word list, the "Additional Collection," reveals surprising variety both in content and in sources. Serving both as base and as filler, many words already in the *Universal Etymological English Dictionary* are included with identical or enlarged definitions, as well as many additional forms of words already in the earlier volume. Some of these additional forms are legitimate and are subsequently admitted to the *Universal Etymological English Dictionary;* others are again obvious padding. Very unusual and "hard" words also reappear as in the earliest dictionaries, which prided themselves on the oddity of their items. The following section, doubtless deriving material from current Latin-English dictionaries, is representative of this retrogressive feature:

Admurmuration, a murmuring at.

Adnascentia (with *Anatomists*) branches which sprout out of the main Stock, as in the Veins or Arteries.

Adnihilated (*adnihilatus,* L.) made void, frustrated.

Adnubilated (*adnubilatus,* L.) darkened or clouded.

Adolable (*adolabilis,* L.)...without Deceit.

Adolescenturiation (of *adolescenturire,* L.) to begin to be, or to play the young Man.

Adonia ('Αδωνια, Gr.) a Solemnity of two Days, celebrated in most Cities of *Greece* in Honour of *Venus,* or to the Memory of *Adonis....*

More interesting are the many long items on specialized terms. For the considerable vocabulary of heraldic terms, the main source was James Coats's *New Dictionary of Heraldry,* 1725. It appears, however, that Bailey was widely read on this subject and that he derived further information and illustrative plates from John Guillim's *Display of Heraldry,* the sixth edition of which in 1724 bore a dictionary; from Le Sieur de la Colombière's *Science Héroïque,* second edition, 1669, which enlarged especially on the significance of colors and animals; and from Sylvanus Morgan's *Sphere of Gentry,* 1661. Numerous long entries on horsemanship and military science were taken verbatim from the first and second parts of the *Gentleman's Dictionary,* adapted from the French of Georges Guillet de St. Georges in 1705. The third and last part of the *Gentleman's Dictionary,* the "Art of Navigation," had been already tapped by Kersey in revising Phillips in 1706; and these items had passed on to Kersey's *Dictionarium Anglo-Britannicum* and thence to the original *Universal Etymological English Dictionary.* Items on mythology were accessible in similar phrasing in so many places that it is hard to specify an exact source. Also, as translator of Ovid and classical scholar of attainments, Bailey would have been capable of composing many such items himself. It is obvious, however, that he had at hand *The Great Historical, Geographical, Genealogical and Poetical Dictionary* compiled by Lewis Morery and revised by Jeremy Collier in 1701-1705, from which various items are condensed. Others were probably derived from the *Dictionarium Sacrum seu Religiosum* attributed to Daniel Defoe (second edition, 1723) and from various other convenient sources.

While the "Additional Collection" is a stable feature of the second volume and gives it what tenuous identity it has, the Orthographical Dictionary, which occupies the latter half of the first edition, appears here for the only time. The first part of the book was intended mainly for the entertainment of the educated and curious; the second part serves various purposes and groups. For the less educated, it indicates accentuation, spelling, meaning, and level of usage,[5] while, by giving equivalents in French and Latin and idiomatic phrases, it may also be of great assistance to "Foreigners who desire an acquaintance with the English Tongue." For this section Bailey doubtless consulted such current English-French and English-Latin dictionaries as A. Boyer's *Royal Dictionary Abridged*, Guy Miège's *Short Dictionary English and French*, E. Coles's *Dictionary English-Latin and Latin-English*, A. Littleton's *Linguae Latinae Liber Dictionarius*, etc.

The second edition (1731) shows considerable rearrangement, described by the author as follows:

Since the Publication of the first Edition of this second Volume, my Business having call'd me to the Perusal of a great Number of Authors treating of all Arts and Sciences, it has given me an Opportunity of collecting a considerable Number of Words not in the two first Volumes in Octavo; whereupon, in order to render this Work as compleat as I possibly can, I have entirely left out the *English, French* and *Latin* Dictionary, design'd chiefly for the Use of Foreigners, to make Room for these additional Improvements. As for those who would have this Work compleat in one Volume, I recommend to them my *Dictionarium Britannicum* in *Folio*, which I hope will give them entire Satisfaction.

Accordingly, the "Additional Collection" is considerably enlarged, the most notable changes being the addition of a good many legal and other terms from the *Dictionarium Britannicum* and the extension of the use of cuts.[6] Besides this expanded vocabulary there is a brief list of the names of persons and places with their etymologies.

In the third edition (1737) the work begins to assume its final form. Bailey now writes in his Preface:

I shall only take this Opportunity to apprise the Reader, that in this third Edition I have struck out several hundred Words that were in the former Edition of a near affinity to those in the first Volume, and therefore may be well enough spared, and have supply'd their Places with other Articles that I presume will be more acceptable.

And for the Satisfaction (but not the Imitation) of the Curious, I have added a Collection of Words, &c. used by the *Canting* Tribe.

This edition is characterized, then, by two developments. The "Additional Collection" undergoes a long needed revision, by which useless and annoying overlappings with the first volume are eliminated; and, as a novel feature meeting a contemporary vogue, a canting vocabulary is introduced.

The main word list has now become a formidable storehouse of specialized and unusual terms—scientific, heraldic, legal, religious, etc. The following section is representative:

Lambdoidal Suture, Lambent Medicines, Lamentine (a fish), *Lamia* (mythological character and sea monster), *Lamiae* ("she devils"), *Perpetual Lamp, Lampadary* or *Lampadaphoria* (officer in the Church of Constantinople), *Lampas* (farriers' term), *Lampasse* (heraldry), *Lampetians* ("a set of heretics"), *Lampay* (eel, with hieroglyphical meaning), *Lamprophori* ("new converts"), *Lancepesade* (military officer), *Lanca* (religious sect among the Chinese), etc.

It will be recalled that a considerable number of cant terms had appeared in the *Universal Etymological English Dictionary* from its first edition on; these were scattered through the main word list, though marked as cant. Bailey now makes a further concession to the surprising current interest in cant by adding a separate vocabulary, consisting of thirty-six pages, under the heading: "A Collection of the Canting Words and Terms, both ancient and modern, used by Beggars, Gypsies, Cheats, House-Breakers, Shop-Lifters, Foot-Pads, Highway-Men, &c." Here Bailey appropriates almost all the words with definitions verbatim or slightly curtailed from the anonymous *New Canting Dictionary* of 1725.[7] The following items will give a notion of this material:

> *Adam Tiler,* the Comerade of a Pick pocket, who receives stollen Goods or Money, and scours off with them. *Tip the coal to Adam Tiler;* i.e. give the Money, Watch, &c. to a running Companion, that the Pick-Pocket may have nothing found upon him, when he is apprehended.
>
> *Ambidexter,* one that goes snacks in Gaming with both Parties; also a Lawyer that takes Fees of Plaintiff and Defendant at once.

Amusers, who were wont to have their Pockets filled with Dirt, which they would throw into the Eyes of People they had a mind to rob, and so run away, while their Comerade, who followed them, under the Notion of pitying the half blinded Person, laid his Hand on whatever came next.

Anglers, alias *Hookers;* petty Thieves, who have a Stick with a Hook at the End, wherewith they pluck Things out of Windows, Grates, &c.

Bing-awast, Get you hence: Begone; haste away; *He Bing'd awast in a Darkmans,* i.e. He Stole away in the Night-time. *Bing we to Rum vile?* i.e. Go we to *London.*

Bit, Robbed, Cheated or Out-Witted. Also Drunk, as *He has bit his Grannum;* He is very Drunk. *Bit the Blow,* performed the Theft, played the Cheat, *You have bit a great Blow;* You have robbed somebody of or to a considerable Value.

Cane upon Abel, a good Stick or Cudgel, well-favouredly laid on a Man's Shoulders.

With this edition both Cox's and Bailey's connections with the work ceased.[8]

After Bailey's death (1742) this odd volume seems to have faltered in its career and to have drifted from bookseller to bookseller. A fourth edition, dated 1756 and printed for T. Waller, bears the new title, *The New Universal Etymological English Dictionary,* and shows a fairly extensive revision.[9] The simplified title-page describes the work as "Corrected, and much improved throughout, by the Addition of Great Variety of Examples, explaining the true Significations of the Words, taken from the best Authors."[10] Another fourth edition—dated 1759, printed for J. Rivington and J. Fletcher, and entitled *The New Universal English Dictionary*—is identical with the 1756 volume except for the title-page, which attributes the improvements to "Mr. Buchanan." The fifth edition, dated 1760 and printed for W. Johnston, is identical in content and retains Mr. Buchanan as editor. Whether Mr. Buchanan was merely late in receiving credit for the revision made in 1756 or whether his name was added as a publisher's lure and he thus profited by some one else's labor, we cannot now determine. The British Museum Catalogue identifies "Mr. Buchanan" plausibly as James Buchanan, author of *Linguae Britannicae vera Pronunciatio: or, A New English Dictionary,* 1757; *An Essay towards establishing a Standard for an*

Elegant and Uniform Pronunciation of the English Language, 1766;
and other works.[11]

The work as it emerged from this revision is a curious hybrid. As
a base it retains the main list as previously carried except for occasional
deletions; but, in conformity with the usual Bailey practice, a new
feature is introduced to fit a contemporary vogue. This time the most
striking lexicographical development was, of course, Johnson's introduction into his *Dictionary* of 1755 of quotations to illustrate his definitions. Here the reviser adopts not only the method but the material of
Johnson.[12] This new material, however, forms only a small part of the
whole; and for the majority of the items, which are highly specialized
and many of which do not appear in Johnson's word list, the reviser
retains Bailey's definitions. It is only a small minority of common words
which carry definitions and quotations from Johnson.[13] The following
are typical entries, taken from Johnson verbatim though usually with
fewer quotations:

> To *Justle* (from *just, jouster,* F.) to encounter, to clash, to rush against
> each other.
>> Not one starry spark,
>> But Gods meet Gods, and *justle* in the dark.
>>> *Lee.*
>
>> Courtiers therefore *justle* for a grant;
>> And, when they break their friendship, plead their want.
>>> *Dryd. Kn. Tale.*
>
>> Murmuring noises rise in ev'ry street;
>> The more remote run stumbling with their fear,
>> And, in the dark, men *justle* as they meet.
>>> *Dryden.*
>
>> When elephant 'gainst elephant did rear
>> His trunk, and castles *justled* in the air,
>> My sword thy way to victory had shown.
>>> *Dryden.*

> *Justly* (from *juste,* F. *justus,* L.) 1. Uprightly, honestly, in a just manner.
>
>> Nothing can *justly* be despised, that cannot *justly* be blamed:
>> where there is no choice, there can be no blame.   *South.*

With ignominy scourg'd in open sight;
Next view the *Tarquin* kings; th'avenging sword
Of Brutus *justly* drawn, and *Rome* restor'd.   *Dryden.*

2. Properly, exactly, accurately.

Their artful hands instruct the lute to sound,
Their feet assist their hands, and *justly* beat the ground.
                                                    Dryden.

The canting vocabulary is retained in this revision.

Although the final editions in 1775 and 1776, printed for William Cavell, are inaccessible, the work appears not to have been further revised.[14]

Chapter XVI

NATHAN BAILEY AND OTHERS,

Dictionarium Britannicum (1730)

FROM THE POPULAR *Universal Etymological English Dictionary* and the erratic second volume, the two works just discussed, Nathan Bailey at last evolved his fine folio dictionary, the *Dictionarium Britannicum*. Far more comprehensive and more competently executed than any predecessor, this work is justly famous in its own right as well as for the important role it later played as working base for Johnson's dictionary. The *Dictionarium Britannicum* is thus the second milestone on the road that leads to Johnson and on to scholarly modern lexicography: the Kersey-Phillips *New World of Words* of 1706 had pioneered as the first folio universal dictionary; now Bailey's *Dictionarium Britannicum* in 1730 made signal advances in scope, etymology, and other lexicographical technique. From these achievements we can look forward easily to the culmination of early English lexicography in 1755 with the two great folios—Johnson's and the Scott-Bailey.

The title-page of the *Dictionarium Britannicum* may be reduced as follows:

Dictionarium Britannicum: Or a more Compleat Universal Etymological English Dictionary than any Extant.

Containing Not only the Words, and their Explications; but their Etymologies...

Also Explaining hard and technical Words, or Terms of Art, in all the Arts, Sciences, and Mysteries following. Together with Accents directing to their proper Pronuntiation, shewing both the Orthography and Orthoepia of the English Tongue....

Illustrated with near Five Hundred Cuts, ...

Likewise A Collection and Explanation of Words and Phrases us'd in our antient Charters, Statutes, Writs, Old Records and Processes at Law.

Also The Theogony, Theology, and Mythology of the Egyptians, Greeks, Romans &c....

To which is added, A Collection of Proper Names of Persons and Places in Great-Britain, with their Etymologies and Explications.

The Whole digested into an Alphabetical Order, not only for the Information of the Ignorant, but the Entertainment of the Curious; and also the Benefit of Artificers, Tradesmen, Young Students and Foreigners....

Collected by several Hands, The Mathematical Part by G. Gordon, the Botanical by P. Miller. The Whole Revis'd and Improv'd, with many thousand Additions, By N. Bailey, φιλόλογος. London:... M,DCC,XXX.

It is indeed surprising and disappointing that such an important work lacks a preface.[1] The title-page makes it clear, however, that this dictionary follows faithfully in the Bailey tradition with such characteristic features as: stress on etymology, indication of accent, extensive use of woodcuts, and the professed purpose of entertaining as well as informing the reader. The appearance of two collaborators on the title-page would seem to be a significant departure; but an investigation of the text leads us to believe that this was mainly a device for investing the work with greater authority, distinction, and novelty.[2]

The *Dictionarium Britannicum* contains in all about 48,000 items or 10,000 more than the Kersey-Phillips. Its main word list can be briefly described as a blending of the most important and interesting items from the *Universal Etymological English Dictionary* and the second volume with a small proportion of new material. Very eccentric and rare words and forms are now pruned; proverbs are eliminated; and proper nouns are roughly divided into two groups in the manner of some modern dictionaries, legendary names being retained in the main list but historical or geographical ones being usually relegated to the table of proper names.

Entries on important words are enlarged with historical or statistical information until they approach the encyclopedic article in character and sometimes in proportions. Consider, for example, the following item, which offers more data as to background and more criticism than was customary in dictionaries of the period:

Gothick Building, a manner of Building brought into Use after those barbarous People, the *Goths* and *Vandals,* made their Irruptions into *Italy;* who demolished the greatest Part of the antient *Roman* Architecture, as also the *Moors* and *Arabs* did the *Grecian;* and instead of these admirable and regular Orders and Modes of Building, introduc'd a licentious and fantastical Mode, wild and chimerical, whose Profiles are incorrect, which, altho' it was sometimes adorn'd with expensive and costly Carvings, but lamentable Imagery, has not that Augustness, Beauty and just Symmetry, which the antient *Greek* and *Roman* Fabricks had: However, it is oftentimes found very strong, and appears rich and pompous, as particularly in several *English* Cathedrals.

Antient Gothick Architecture, is that which the *Goths* brought with them from the *North* in the sixth Century. Those Edifices built after this manner are exceeding massive, heavy and coarse.

Modern Gothick Architecture, is light, delicate and rich to an extreme, full of whimsical and impertinent Ornaments, as *Westminster-Abbey, Coventry-Cross,* &c.

While for such items Bailey still made some use of John Harris' *Lexicon Technicum,* which had been often revised and expanded since its appearance in 1704, the above item and many others show that this source was now generally supplemented or supplanted by a more recent work, Ephraim Chambers' *Cyclopaedia; Or, An Universal Dictionary of Arts and Sciences* of 1728. The following parallel entries show Bailey's indebtedness to Chambers:

CHAMBERS, 1728	BAILEY, 1730
Abbies . . . One third of the best Benefices in England were antiently, by the Pope's Grant, appropriated to Abbies, and other Religious Houses, which, upon their Dissolution under King Henry VIII. became Lay-Fees: 190 such were dissolv'd of between 200 l. and 3500 l. yearly Revenue, which at a Medium amounted to 2853000 l. per Annum.	*Abbies,* anciently one third of the best Benefices in *England,* were by the Pope's Grant appropriated to Abbies, and other religious Houses, which when they were dissolved by K. *Henry* VIII. and became Lay-Fees, there were 190 dissolved, whose Revenues were from 200 to 3500 l. *per Annum,* which at a Medium amounted to 2853000 l. *per Annum.*[3]

Here also for the first time a painstaking attempt is made to build up complete families of words arranged in an orderly fashion with all derived and related expressions. Thus, the explanations of the various forms and uses of the word *Action* extend to almost a page; and *Abstract* introduces the following group:

> *Abstract* ("short Draught"), *Abstract* (with Logicians), *Abstract* (in Philosophy), An *Abstract* Idea, To *Abstract*, *Abstract* Numbers, *Abstracted* (Mathematics), *Abstracted* Nouns (Grammar), *Abstractedly*, *Abstractive*, *Abstraction* (in Philosophy)—a long discussion with examples.

As to the actual extent of the new material, we should estimate that one in eight to ten items is new in the sense that it had not previously appeared in the octavo volumes. Some of these items are technical, but many are merely additional adjective or adverb forms with perfunctory definitions.[4] More significant is the new material added to the brief entries which had appeared in the earlier dictionaries. The following analysis, showing the make-up of the opening definitions, may make Bailey's procedure in compilation clear. In the table, "1" and "2" are used to indicate respectively the *Universal Etymological English Dictionary* of 1721 and the so-called second volume of 1727.

A—1, 2	*Abaptiston*—1
Ab—2	*Abarcy*—2
Abacot—1	*Abare*—2
Abactors—1	*Abarnare*—1
Abacus—1, 2, enlarged	*Abarticulation*—1
Abaddir—2	*Abase* (sea term)—new
Abaft—1	*Abash*—1
Abagion—2	*Abashment*—1
Abalienation—2	*Abatamentum* (law word)—new
Abandon—1	*Abate*—1, 2
Abandum—1	*Abatement*—1, 2
Abanet—1	*Abbots*—1, 2, enlarged

Besides the main vocabulary and the inevitable supplement of "Words that came late or were omitted by accident," there is a sixteen-page "Alphabetical Table of the Names of Persons and Places in Great Britain." This list, surprisingly enough, contains almost as many Biblical as British items; its material was not new but was culled from the *Universal Etymological English Dictionary*.

The second edition appeared in 1736 with "numerous Additions and Improvements" and with a new collaborator in Etymology, "T. Lediard, Gent. Professor of the Modern Languages in Lower Germany."[5] The preface now added is an enlargement of that in the *Universal Etymological English Dictionary* in florid style, which may well be the product of Lediard's pen, and bridges the whole history of language from Babel to its climax in the English tongue. After citing the opinions of various authorities as to the character of the English language, the author finally declares it to be "strong and significant," "copious," "musical and harmonious." It is the "closest, clearest, most chaste and reserv'd in its Diction of all the Modern Languages and also the most just and severe in its Ornaments, and also the honestest, most open and undesigning." Unlike French and Italian, it is "of a masculine Quality" and "has been compar'd to the River *Nile*, in that it preserves a Majesty even in Abundance; . . ."

More helpful is the explicit description of the changes made in this edition and the help the author has received in various departments: [6]

Therefore I shall only observe that I have endeavoured to render the Subject Matter of the Book answerable to those Branches of the Title *Universal* and *Etymological*.

As to the First, I have in this Edition not only my self with great Application endeavoured to inrich it with all the Words that I could find in the Reading of a very large Number of Authors and on very various, if not all Subjects; but have been favoured with the Assistance of some generous Spirits, who have contributed thereto; among which I am oblig'd to Dr. *Martin*, Professor of Botany; Mr. *Philip Miller*; Mr. *Gordon*; but to none more than to the Rev. Mr. *Collier*, Rector of *Langford* near *Sarum*; who has with great Pains and Application voluntarily and generously communicated a very large Collection.

And in Order to render the Work still more compleat, there has been inserted a great Number of *English* Proverbs with their Explications and Use; also the Iconology of the Ancients; shewing after what Manner they painted, engrav'd, carv'd, &c. their Gods, Goddesses; the Passions, Vertues and Vices by them personified; of great Use for Designers, Painters, Carvers, &c.

2. As to the Term *Etymological*, there has been likewise vast Additions made to that Part, by Mr. *Thomas Lediard*, Professor of the modern Languages; by which it will appear, that as the Southern Languages, *Italian, Spanish, Portugueze* and *French* are at least for the greatest Part produc'd from the *Latin* Stock, so the Northern; as, *Dutch, High German, Danish, Swedish, Irish,* &c. are Branches of the *Teutonick, Celtic,* or *Gothic.*

The "vast Additions" in etymology include, besides the new preface with its historical and critical observations, much more minute and comprehensive annotations on individual words. The following items show the range in treatment:

> *Litigate* (*litigare*, L.)
> *Litoral* (*litoralis*, of *litus*, L. the sea shore)
> *Litter* (prob. of *litiére* of *lit*, F. a bed)
> *Little* (*litel*, *lytel* or *lytle*, Sax. *litet* and *liten*, Su. *lidet* or *lille*, Dan. *luttel*, Du. *lut*, L.G.)

The word list is, indeed, greatly expanded; it now includes probably 60,000 words or more.[7] Besides many additional items from the various sciences, Bailey has revived certain features from the octavo works. From the *Universal Etymological English Dictionary* he has reinstated the proverbs, though they are many times multiplied here. Those proverbs which had appeared in the *Universal Etymological English Dictionary* retain their original moralizing explications; but those added in this edition carry brief and often facetious comments, such as:

> *Maidens must be mild and meek*
> *Swift to hear, and slow to speak.*

This us'd to be the advice of mothers to their daughters in former days: but the most seem to be of another mind nowadays, and to think nothing is prettier than to let their *Tongues run before their Wit*.

> *An Old Physician, a Young Lawyer.*

An old Physician is good because of his experience; a young lawyer, because, perhaps, not having great practice, he may be glad to be honest and diligent to recommend himself to the world.

> *No Companion like the Penny.*

For it will procure any.

> *Praise the Sea, but keep on Land.*

I.e. You may admire the sea as much as you will; But the land is much more eligible.

> *Pride goes before,*
> *Shame follows after.*
>   Or,
> *Pride goes before a Fall.*

It generally happens so.

Such isolated proverbs do not, however, give an adequate conception of the extent to which proverbs and other incidental features actually moulded the nature of this edition. The crispness, the clarity, and the accuracy which had been gradually developing in the definitions are here wantonly sacrificed to novelty of presentation. Definitions added or rewritten at this time tend to be leisurely, continuous, essaylike; and the basic and often prosaic meanings are lost among the picturesque derived meanings, legends of varied origins, historical and artistic associations, and shrewd, trite, or facetious advice on the conduct of life. When so much colorful material is incorporated, the more pedestrian tasks of the lexicographer are naturally neglected; and the result is a readable "all-purpose" reference book rather than a fine dictionary. The items given below in their complete form will convey the special nature and tone of the 1736 revision.

Little [etymology quoted above], small.
> By Little and Little the Sea is drain'd.
> F. Goute à Goute (drops by drops) la mer s'égoute.
> A spur to preservation.
>> A Little House well fill'd;
>> A Little Land well rill'd:
>> And a Little Wife well will'd
>> are without dispute three very good things, and so any thing that is good tho' little in quantity.
> Little said soon amended. v. *Amend*.
> Little Strokes fell great Oaks. v. *Stroaks*.

To Live (*libhan* or *leofan*, Sax. *lefwe*, Dan. *lefwa*, Su. *Leben*,
> Du. and L.G. *liben*, H.G.), to enjoy life.
> He Liveth long who Liveth well.
>> Or,
> It is not how long but how well we Live.
> v. Life consists, &c. under *Life*.
> As long Lives a merry heart as a sad.
>> We may very well add, *and longer too*. The meaning however of this proverb is that immoderate sorrow tends to no good end.
> One may Live and learn.
>> Or,
> We are never to old to learn.

Gr. Γηϱόις χω δ'αι εὶ πολλὰ διδασκήμενοδις.

A famous saying of Solon, *Discenti assidue multa senecta venit.*
And well might he say so, for as *Hippocrates* says, *Ars longa, Vita brevis.* These sayings, however, at least the first, is chiefly us'd, as an exclamation when we see something we had never seen.

Live and let Live.

G. Leben und leben lassen. That is, have such a just medium in all your dealings, that you may have a living gain by others, and others the same by you.[8]

Another feature restored from the Bailey octavos is the so-called "Iconology of the Ancients," including much esoteric material which had appeared earlier in the second volume. Here are included legends, historical facts, interpretations, and methods of presenting in the arts or literature gods and goddesses, allegorical figures, animals, etc. Ultimately this material had come from a bewildering array of sources— bestiaries, medieval encyclopedias, heraldic works, emblem literature, saints legends, folk lore, popular superstitions, etc. The entry on the *Lion*, which will be given complete, not only illustrates this "iconology" but shows the improved etymology, the dwarfed basic definition but the extended essaylike discussion, and the free use of proverbs—all characteristic of this edition.

Li̇́on (*lio*, Sax. *leyon*, Su. *lew*, Du. and L.G. *laewe*, H.G.F. *liena*, It. *leon*, Sp. *leam*, Port. of *leo*, L. λεῶν, Gr.), the most courageous and generous of all wild beasts, the emblem of strength and valour.

If the Lion's skin cannot, the Fox's shall.

L. Si leonina Pellis non satis est, assuenda Vulpina.

Gr. 'Αν ἡ λεοντὴ μὴ ὑικητοι, τὸν αλωπεκεὶν πρόσυφον. Erasm.

F. Si la Peau du Lion ne suffit pas, il y faut coudre celle du Renard.

All which signify no more than, what I can't do by force I'll do by cunning. The L. likewise say; *Dolus an Virtus quis in Hoste requirit.*

A *Lion* being looked upon as the king of beasts, is esteemed the most magnanimous, the most generous, the most bold, and the most fierce of all fourfooted beasts; and therefore has been chosen by heralds, to represent the greatest heroes, who have been endued with these qualities.

The *Lion* (*Emblematically*) is used to represent vigilancy; some being of opinion, that he never sleeps. And he also represents command and monarchical dominion: and also the magnanimity of majesty, at once exercising awe and clemency, subduing those that resist, and sparing those that submit.

A *Lion,* with a serpent about his neck, is an emblem of valour joined with conduct.

Lion (in *Blazonry*) in blazoning a lion, their teeth and talons must always be mentioned, they being their own armour, and are in coat armour for the most part made of a different colour from the body of a beast; and therefore speaking of their teeth and talons, you must say they are armed so and so.

A *Lion* (*Hieroglyphically*) wiping out with his tail the impressions of his feet, was a representation of the great creator, covering the marks of his divinity by the works of nature, and hiding his immediate power, by the visible agency of inferiour beings.

Miscellaneous additions in 1736, many of which had appeared in the 1727 or 1731 editions of the second volume, were cant, Eastern terms, variant forms, and oddities of all kinds. The table of proper names, now just doubled, bears the more accurate heading: "Alphabetical Table of Names of Persons and Places in Great Britain and Others mentioned in Sacred Scriptures: The Theology and Mythology of the Ancients, with their Morals and Etymologies."

After this *tour de force* we can sympathize with Bailey as he concludes his Preface with the boast: "I shall only add, that there has been that Pains taken to inrich this Edition with Words and Phrases that I apprehend any Additions to future Editions cannot be very considerable." It has no doubt been apparent from the foregoing discussion, however, that the 1736 edition, though so much larger than the 1730, is inferior to it from the point of view of lexicography. The author has here yielded to the cardinal temptations which have beset lexicographers all along: he has included too many oddities and he has drawn no clear or consistent distinction between the provinces and methods of the dictionary and the encyclopedia. In these respects, however, Bailey was merely of his time, whereas in innumerable other respects he was much in advance of it; furthermore the very features which seem regrettable from a modern point of view may well have conduced most to his enormous contemporary popularity. While the great folio of 1755 was to consist mainly of Bailey's work and rightly to bear his name, it was edited by Joseph Nicol Scott; and the 1736 *Dictionarium Britannicum* was the last triumph which Bailey had the pleasure of seeing before his death in 1742.

Chapter XVII

THOMAS DYCHE AND WILLIAM PARDON'S

A New General English Dictionary (1735)

YCHE AND PARDON'S OCTAVO *New General English Diction-ary* is now remembered mainly as a highly popular con-temporary of Bailey's various dictionaries. Its career ran from 1735 to 1794; and it boasted eighteen editions, sev-eral of which were reprinted.[1] It seems at first incredible that any work could thus hold the market while four well planned and carefully dis-tinguished dictionaries with their various editions and revisions were issuing with modern efficiency and clocklike regularity from the store-house of Bailey. It will be observed, however, that Dyche and Pardon had the shrewdness not to compete directly with Bailey; as the title-page and the introduction will evidence, Dyche and Pardon addressed a neglected audience, minimized or eliminated the departments in which Bailey specialized, and substituted others which were claimed to be superior on practical grounds. Also it should now be obvious that we have arrived at a dictionary-conscious age. The middle and late eighteenth century not only absorbed the innumerable dictionaries of Bailey and Johnson and various other more modest works but abounded in technical dictionaries and even went to the length of affixing a glossary to any work whose language was at all unusual. According to the estab-lished custom in the long chain of lexicographers, Dyche and Pardon derived from Bailey basic material as well as valuable lessons in retain-ing the public favor; they did not, however, appreciate or imitate the finer attainments of Bailey. Yet the *New General English Dictionary* has a pronounced individuality and independent policies; and, like many other inferior works, it made its own contribution to the development of lexicography.

Thomas Dyche, the originator of this work, was a schoolmaster and falls therefore in the line of Cawdrey, Coles, and Bailey—all of whom made important practical contributions to the dictionary. Dyche had a school for a short time in Fetter Lane, London, but was better known in later years when he became the master of the free school at Stratford Bow in Middlesex. He died sometime between 1731 and 1735.[2]

Dyche was the author of several remarkably successful schoolbooks, of which his *Guide to the English Tongue* was the most conspicuous. Published in 1709, it attained a forty-eighth edition in 1774 and was still being printed as late as 1830.[3] While this work is on the general plan of the elementary schoolbooks of the period, the author's keen interest in pronunciation gives it a special character. Whereas other schoolbooks listed words merely according to the number of syllables, Dyche stressed proper pronunciation from the very beginning by listing together words of two syllables accented on the first syllable, words of two syllables accented on the second syllable, etc. He hoped that the child would thus not only avoid a "Vicious Pronunciation" in the many words listed but would also become early aware of the importance of proper pronunciation. So meticulous was Dyche that he "invented" for this work the device of the double accent (") for use in words where a single consonant is pronounced double (as in *cha"pel*, pronounced *chuppel*).[4]

The "Dyche system" having attained considerable repute, Dyche then produced a spelling dictionary called *A Dictionary of all the Words Commonly us'd in the English Tongue; And of the most usual Proper Names; With Accents directing to their true Pronunciation.*[5] This work—which appeared in 1723, reached a third edition in 1731, and a seventh about 1756[6]—was not actually a dictionary, as it contained no definitions but was rather an extension of the *Guide to the English Tongue* offering further assistance in spelling and pronunciation. The Preface suggests several improvements in spelling which have since been more or less generally adopted, such as: reducing the ending in *ck* to *c* in "borrow'd Words," in *ll* to *l*, and in *our* to *or* and dropping final *e* when it is not necessary to lengthen a syllable. This work lists about 21,000 words with the spelling and accentuation which Dyche judged best after a serious study of the principles involved. Other works by Dyche equally painstakingly executed and successful were his *Vocabu-*

larium Latiale, 1708 or 1709, which was reprinted as late as 1806; *The Youth's Guide to the Latin Tongue*, 1716; a translation of the *Fables* of Phaedrus, etc.

About "William Pardon, Gentleman" unfortunately no information is available. The *New General English Dictionary* is, however, so different in character from the earlier Dyche works that we are naturally tempted to visit its eccentricities on the unknown Pardon.

The title-page reads as follows:

A New General English Dictionary; Peculiarly calculated for the Use and Improvement Of such as are unacquainted with the Learned Languages.

Wherein the Difficult Words, and Technical Terms made use of in Anatomy, ... Are not only fully explain'd, but accented on their proper Syllable, to prevent a vicious Pronunciation; and mark'd with Initial Letters, to denote the Part of Speech to which each Word peculiarly belongs.

To which is prefixed, A Compendious English Grammar, ...

Together with A Supplement, Of the Proper Names of the most noted Kingdoms, Provinces, Cities, Towns, Rivers, &c. throughout the known world. As Also Of the most celebrated Emperors, Kings, Queens, Priests, Poets, Philosophers, Generals, &c. ... The Whole Alphabetically digested, and accented ...

Originally begun by the late Reverend Mr. Thomas Dyche, School-Master at Stratford-le-Bow, Author of the Guide to the English Tongue, the Spelling-Dictionary, &c.

And now finished by William Pardon, Gent.

London: ... MDCCXXXV.

The title-page shows, first of all, that Dyche and Pardon have conceded to Bailey his special audience of the educated, the intellectually alert, and the linguistically minded. This work reverts to earlier lexicographical tradition by focusing on a lower level; it addresses the less educated and, specifically, those who have no knowledge of foreign languages and no desire to repair that deficiency. It is also designed for school use:

The Whole is intended for the Information of the Unlearned, and particularly recommended to those Boarding-Schools, where *English* only is taught, as is the Case commonly among the Ladies, by a careful Use whereof I doubt not but the Teachers will soon find the Benefit from the Improvement their Scholars will insensibly make, not only in Orthography, or true Spelling, but in Writing coherently and correctly, the Want whereof is universally complained of among the Fair Sex.[7]

In order to meet the needs of this humbler audience, Dyche and Pardon eliminate the etymology which had been the special province of Bailey and promise more practical aids in its stead:

Derivations and Etymologies are entirely left out: First, because of their Uncertainty, ... secondly, upon account of their Uselessness to those Persons that these Sort of Books are most helpful to, which are commonly such, whose Education, Reading, and Leisure, are bounded within a narrow Compass; and therefore such Helps and Hints, as were judged more universally beneficial, are substituted. ...[8]

The *New General English Dictionary* is often credited with two innovations, both practical in nature: the indication of accent and the introduction of grammar. It should be obvious from the foregoing discussion that the first claim is not accurate. It must be conceded that Dyche quickened the interest of the period in pronunciation through his earlier writings, but accentuation had been marked in several Bailey dictionaries antedating the *New General English Dictionary*. This feature, it will be recalled, had first appeared in Bailey's second volume of 1727 and had thence been transferred to the *Dictionarium Britannicum* in 1730 and to the *Universal Etymological English Dictionary* in the 1731 edition. Yet it is to be remembered not only that Dyche did give the initial impetus to the study of pronunciation but that the stress of the title page and the introduction of the *New General English Dictionary* on pronunciation was largely instrumental in establishing this department as a requisite of an English dictionary.

The only direct and incontestable contribution by Dyche and Pardon is then in the grammatical province. Here too we must moderate our praise by observing that the actual service was in pointing out the desirability of offering such information in a dictionary rather than in demonstrating the ideal treatment. Prefixed to the work is "A Compendious English Grammar," which contrives in the space of nine pages of minute print to discuss the parts of speech, declension, conjugation, and comparison, with examples and paradigms. Here is the remote precedent for many modern dictionaries which carry such a helpful grammatical section. Dyche and Pardon's handling of this material is, however, rather unorthodox. They state, for example, that "A Sentence consists of three Words at least"; and, while they mark every word with a capital letter denoting its part of speech, they allow only four parts on the following reasoning:

... because there are but three Parts that make any Variation in their Terminations, &c. that is: *Nouns Substantives, Nouns Adjectives,* and *Verbs,* the four other Parts, which by the Generality of Grammarians are called *Adverbs, Conjunctions, Prepositions,* and *Interjections,* are here called by one general Name of *Particles;* ...[9]

The "Compendious English Grammar" may also be criticized for its wordiness. The following definition of the noun is typical:

By a *Noun Substantive,* I mean the plain simple Name of any material or ideal Substance or Thing, upon the Pronunciation whereof an Idea is excited in the Mind of the Hearer what Species of Beings or Things are then intended, without Regard to any inherent or accidental Qualities or Modes that may immediately result from, or belong to that particular Creature or Thing then signified; ...[10]

Surely a simpler style would have been more appropriate for a practical work and for uneducated readers.

The vocabulary is unusually small for the period, consisting in the first edition of only about 20,000 words. Its make-up is also surprising, for here as in the grammar Dyche and Pardon seem to combine oddly the practical and the elaborate. Most of the words are extremely rare and difficult; but the explanations, though wordy, are obviously intended to be patient and elementary. The Introduction explains the unusual principle on which the vocabulary was selected:

... a great Number of Words are purposely omitted, purely to make Room for many useful, short, and beneficial Abstracts from large Treatises, upon the Manners and religious Customs of the Ancients, as well Jews as Gentiles; as also the various Sects of Christians, likewise in Philosophy, &c.

While the definitions are often reduced from their encyclopedic sources, they still remain much longer than those in contemporary dictionaries. Hence despite the comparative smallness of the vocabulary the work runs to 823 pages.

Dyche and Pardon's choice of sources is impressive, though too ambitious for a practical and elementary work such as they professed to produce. Not content with Bailey's *Universal Etymological English Dictionary*, which as the most recent successful octavo dictionary would have been their logical working base, they went directly to Bailey's folio *Dictionarium Britannicum*. In other fields also they chose the most recent and authoritative works. The fact that these were usually encyclopedias accounts for much of the character of the *New General English Dictionary*; for, despite the elementary level on which the work was originally designed, both the word list and the explanations have a would-be encyclopedic quality [11] rather than the businesslike tone and intelligently limited treatment of the dictionary.

In adopting the *Dictionarium Britannicum* of 1730 as a base, Dyche and Pardon tend to conserve the oddest items and drop the commonest. Probably two-thirds or more of the Dyche and Pardon vocabulary comes directly from Bailey. Definitions commonly include Bailey's but are verbose; while the average definition is leisurely, many even descend to puerile or gossipy style. Also, as previously noted, Dyche and Pardon sometimes render a difficult word more difficult by their explanation. The following examples allow comparison of the Bailey, and the Dyche and Pardon styles of definition:

BAILEY, 1730	DYCHE AND PARDON, 1735
To Kneel, (...) to stand or bear one self upon the Knees.	*To Kneel* (V.) to stand or bear one's self upon one's Knees as if upon one's Feet, and this is by us esteemed the most humble Posture for Supplicants of all Sorts, and is therefore used in the Church at the Confessions, and in the Petitions likewise in the King's Presence, and in Courts of Judicature upon extraordinary Occasions.
Nail, (...) ... an Iron Pin for fastening or nailing Boards together.	*Nails* (S.) in *Building*, is one of the most necessary instruments used by workmen; they are commonly made of iron, and of as many shapes and sizes as the nature of the business they are applied to requires; they are also used in many other businesses, as by coopers, copper-smiths, &c. but by all of them to fasten their work together, and strengthen it by ren-

BAILEY, 1730

Noctambuld'tion, (...) a walking in the night, or in sleep.

DYCHE AND PARDON, 1735

dering the parts assistant, and adhering to one another.

Noctambuld'tion (S.) a disorder that occasions persons to walk or go about in their sleep, during which time, they will open doors, windows, &c. go upon the ridges of houses and dangerous precipices, commonly without any hurt or inconvenience, unless interrupted by some unpassable place, or the over-officiousness of some person; and this is frequently done without putting on any other cloaths than such as they lie in bed with.

While Bailey supplied both "hard" words and technical terms, many other specialized items were added from Augustin Calmet's *Historical, Critical, Geographical, Chronological, and Etymological Dictionary of the Holy Bible* (Paris, 1720), which had been translated into English in 1732. Entries from this source were usually taken verbatim, though often with abridgment, and were in some cases acknowledged.[12] Scientific and other miscellaneous items were taken from Ephraim Chambers' *Cyclopaedia: Or, An Universal Dictionary of Arts and Sciences,* 1728, which had supplanted John Harris' *Lexicon Technicum.* Chambers' long and detailed articles needed adroit telescoping, as illustrated in the following instances:

CHAMBERS, 1728

Abbess, the superior of an Abbey, or convent of Nuns. The *Abbess* has the same rights and authority over the nuns, that the Abbots regular have over their monks. Her sex, indeed, does not allow her to perform the spiritual functions annexed to the priesthood.

F. Martene, in his treatise on the rights of the church, observes, that some *abbesses* have formerly confessed their nuns. But he adds, that their excessive curiosity carried them such lengths, that there arose a necessity of checking it. . . .

DYCHE AND PARDON, 1735

A'bbess (S.) the governess or superior of an abbey, or convent of nuns; and tho' the sex hinders their performing those spiritual functions appropriated to the priesthood, yet there are instances of some nunneries, where the *abbesses* formerly confess'd their nuns and performed other priestly offices; but their excessive curiosity made it necessary to check and lay it aside.

CHAMBERS, 1728

Alley, in *Gardening,* a straight parallel walk, bordered, or bounded on each hand with trees, shrubs, or the like. The word *alley* is derived from ... *Alleys* are usually laid either with grass or gravel. According to Lord Bacon, ... An *alley* is distinguished from a *path* in this, that in an *alley* there must be always room enough for two persons, at least, to walk a breast; so that it must never be less than five feet in breadth; and there are some who hold, that it ought never to have more than fifteen. *Alleys, counter,* are the little alleys by the sides of the great ones. *Alley, front,* is that which runs straight in the face of a building. *Alley, transverse,* ... *Alley, diagonal,* ... *Alley, sloping,* ... *Alley,* in the *New Husbandry,* ... *Alley,* in ziczac, ... *Alley,* in *Perspective,* is that which is larger at the entrance than at the exit; to give it the greater appearance of length. *Alley of compartiment* is that which separates the squares of a *parterre.*

DYCHE AND PARDON, 1735

A'lley (S.) a narrow street, lane or passage, where, tho' many houses are built, yet carts, coaches and other carriages cannot go thro them; also an even, straight walk in a garden, on each side whereof are planted trees, hedges, shrubs, or low plants, as briars, box-trees, &c. Some make this difference between an *alley* and a *path,* viz. that an *alley* must be wide enough for two people to walk abreast, whereas a *path* is undetermined. In a *Compartment,* it separates the squares in a parterre; in *Perspective,* it is that which is larger at the entrance than at the going out, to make the length seem greater. *Counter Alley,* a little *alley* by the side of a great one. Front *Alley,* a walk that goes from the front of a building, and is planted with trees, commonly called a *vista* or *visto.*[13]

Also an occasional item still stems from the older authorities: Lewis Morery's *Great Historical, Geographical, Genealogical and Poetical Dictionary,* Daniel Defoe's *Dictionarium Sacrum seu Religiosum,* and John Harris' *Lexicon Technicum.*[14]

The *New General English Dictionary* also carries a supplementary list of miscellaneous names; these are unidentified and are intended solely for help in orthography and pronunciation. The list is elaborately introduced as follows:

The Design of the following Catalogue of Names of Persons and Places is, that such Readers as are conversant with English Books only may meet with a large Collection ready made to their Hands, in order to know how to spell them.... And as most of the antient Histories are now translated into *English,* the Names of the principal Actors must of course become familiar to the Readers: so that 'twas judged proper to insert the following

Alphabet, wherein Kings, Emperors, Queens, Priests, Philosophers, Rulers, Judges, &c. are promiscuously set down and mark'd, where the Stress or Tone of the Voice should be, in order to shew the proper Pronuntiation.

There were two revisions of the *New General English Dictionary*, the first of which occurred by 1744 [15] and probably contributed significantly to the continued popularity of the dictionary. Of the three thousand items introduced at this time, a few were technical terms, and a few were "particles"; but the great majority were, as the title-page indicates, "Market Towns in *England* and *Wales*" with "a general Description of the Places, their Situations, Market days, Government, Manufactures, Number of Representatives sent to Parliament, Distance from *London*, both in computed and measured Miles, &c." [16] While Phillips, Coles, and Bailey had carried brief items on shires and towns, the revised version of *Cocker's English Dictionary* (second edition in 1715 and third in 1724) was the only preceding dictionary which had offered any comparable treatment of this material. [17] Here again Pardon chose an authoritative source, the six-volume *Magna Britannia et Hibernia* of Thomas Cox, 1720-1731. This large work is organized by shires and under each shire offers a comprehensive discussion of each town, including geographical features, civil and church history, churches and public buildings, eminent citizens, industries, market and fair days. A single entry will suffice to illustrate Pardon's method of selection from Cox's copious material.

Cox, 1720

Berkshire, . . . A little lower is *Abington*, a handsome well-built Town, . . . The Place is very ancient, remarkable for Devotion even in the Time of the *Britains*; . . . But it had not only its Name, but chief Glory, from the Abbey, which was one of the finest and richest in England. . . . [history of the abbey and famous abbots]

There are two Churches in the Town; the one dedicated to St. *Helena*, and the other to St. *Nicholas*, . . .

The Market-House, built here of late Years, is of most curious Ashler Work-

Dyche and Pardon, 1748 Edition

A'bbingdon or *A'bingdon* or *A'bington* (S.) a handsome, well-built corporation town in *Berkshire*, 46 computed, and 55 measured miles from *London*; was anciently noted for its early embracing the Christian religion, and its fine abbey or monastery, where many great men were bred; there are two churches in the town, *viz.* St. *Helen's* and St. *Nicholas's*; the patronage of the first is in the king, and of the last in the lord keeper; the market-house, which has been built of late years, is of most curious *Ashler* workmanship, and may challenge the pre-emi-

Cox, 1720

manship, which may challenge the Pre-eminence of any in England, being built on lofty Pillars, with a large Hall above, in which the County-Assizes are frequently held.

The Town consists of several Streets, which center in a most spacious Area, where the Market is kept, which is very considerable, especially for Barley. Vast Quantities of Mault are made here, . . .

Abington was made a Free Borough and Corporation by Charter from Queen *Mary* I, . . . By this it is made a Free Borough and Town-Corporate, consisting of a Mayor, two Bailiffs, and nine Alder-men, which twelve were to be called *Principal Burgesses*, who only, and their Successors, shall have Right to chuse one Burgess in Parliament. . . .

The Market-Days are now on *Mondays* and *Fridays*, and the three Fairs are yearly kept on

The 8th of *June*, 25th of *July*, and 30th of *November*. . . .

DYCHE AND PARDON, 1748 Edition

nence of any in *England*, being built on lofty pillars, with a large hall above, in which the county assizes are frequently held. The town consists of several streets, which centre in a most spacious area, where the market is kept, which is very considerable, especially for barley and malt. This town was made a free borough and town corporate, by charter from queen *Mary* I. and consisting of a mayor, two bailiffs, and nine aldermen, which twelve only have the right of chusing the burgess, that represents the corporation in parliament. The market days are Mondays and Fridays, besides which there are three fairs kept annually on the 9th of *June*, 25th of *July*, and 30th of *November*.

In this form Dyche and Pardon's *New General English Dictionary* ran through 1781. The irregular 1794 edition (called "the seventeenth edition, considerably improved"), however, shows extensive revision. The title-page omits all mention of Pardon without, unfortunately, designating the current editor. The work now includes almost 30,000 words or 10,000 more than in its original form; and both word list and definitions have been vigorously overhauled. The addition of other forms of words already present and of other towns may be regarded as routine expansion. The reviser, however, seems to reveal his personal interests when he omits specialized terms from various fields to make way for many entries on birds, fish, plants, minerals, etc. A statistical approach may most easily clarify the nature of the revision. The *K* section, as it was carried from 1744 to 1781, had contained 138 words, of which the present reviser retained 113 and dropped 25; he then proceeded to add 76, at least a third of which were longer entries reflecting a personal interest in natural science. The following such additions are typical:

Kaolin, Kecksy ("name given to hemlock"), *Kelp, Kestrel, Kiddaw, Kidney bean, Kidney wort, Killas* (gray earth), *Killow* (black earth), *Kine, Kincob* (a flower), *Kingfish, Kingfisher, Kingspear* (a plant), *Kipper, Kittiwake, Knapweed, Knotberry, Knotgrass, Kraken, Kupfer.*[18]

The resultant word list, while considerably better balanced than the one it replaced, is still noticeably difficult and specialized. The definitions, most of which have been rewritten, are, however, greatly improved; and the work now loses its encyclopedic aspirations and assumes the character of a dictionary. To illustrate the salutary condensation which the reviser practiced, we cite the following definitions:

1744 Edition	1794 Edition

Ke'rchief or Cover-Cloth (S.), a thin light Garment made of all Sorts of Stuff, sometimes to be tied or thrown round the Neck or Head of a Person, or to wear in the Pocket, to be taken out by the Hand to wipe off the Dust, Sweat, or other Mucus of Nature.

Ke'rchief (S.), a thin light garment to cover the neck or head, any loose cloth used in dress.

Nap (S.), that part of the wool or hair of woollen cloth that rises above the shoot; also a short doze or fit of sleep that a person takes to refresh himself after long sitting up, labour, fatigue, &c.

Nap (S.), down, the shaggy surface of woollen cloth; also slumber, a short sleep.

Na'rrow (A.) any thing that has but a little breadth; also spoken sometimes of a person of a small capacity, who is said to have but a *narrow* or shallow understanding; among *Bowlers,* it is applied to the bias of the bowl when it holds too much; and when a niggardly or covetous wretch who will not allow himself what his fortune is able to supply him with, or when he refuses to assist the distressed in any sort of proportion to what their necessities call for, and his estate will allow, such an one is called a *narrow*-souled fellow.

Na'rrow (A.), not broad, not wide, strait, small, niggardly, covetous, contracted, of confined sentiments, near, close.

To show interesting shifts in points of view, the following definitions may be instanced:

1744 Edition

Latitudind'rians (S.) persons that take too free a liberty in speaking and acting in relation to religious matters.

Pope (S.) the chief or head bishop of the Roman communion, who pretends to have authority over the whole Christian church, under the pretence of being St. *Peter's* successor, as bishop of *Rome*, tho' some have asserted that St. *Peter* never was at *Rome*.

1794 Edition

Latitudind'rian (S.) a person of moderation and charity, with relation to religious matters, who believes there is a latitude in the way to heaven, which may admit people of different persuasions.

Pope (S.) the bishop of Rome, or head of the Roman communion, who is chosen by the cardinals out of their own order; a small bird of the duck kind, usually called puffin; a small river fish, otherwise named the ruff; a game at cards, sometimes termed pope joan.

Finally, to illustrate the change from encyclopedic to dictionary range and style, the following may be compared:

1744 Edition

La'byrinth (S.) a term for the regular disposing of buildings, trees, or walls, with so many windings and turnings that it is difficult to find the way out of it; ancient history furnishes us with four very famous ones, the first . . .; it is now a common thing in a large garden to have a *labyrinth* in one part of it; in *common Speech*, it signifies any difficulty that a person knows not how to extricate himself from; among the *Anatomists*, the second cavity of the internal ear, which is hollowed out of the *os petrosum*, is so called.

Lake (S.) a curious crimson colour for *Painters*; also a large collection of fresh waters that have no open communication with the sea, and are commonly in inland countries, some of which are so large, as to be called seas, as the *Caspian* sea, . . . The other most considerable lakes are . . .

1794 Edition

La'byrinth (S.) a maze, a place formed with so many intricate windings that it is difficult to find the way out; in *Anatomy*, the second cavity of the internal ear, which is hollowed with several windings.

Lake (S.) a large collection of water inclosed in the cavity of some inland place; a small diffusion of water; also a preparation of different substances into a kind of magistery for the use of painters.

some both emit and receive rivers, others
only emit them, others only receive, and
others neither receive nor emit them, but
are formed. . . .

Thus ended the long career of a work marked by an odd combination
of inferior and progressive features. Its basic weakness lay in its failure
to recognize and remain within the confines of the dictionary, and an
equally grave fault was the general verbosity and occasional triviality
of the definitions. Yet Dyche and Pardon not only suited the tastes
of a large public for sixty years but improved the technique of lexicography by the introduction of the grammatical department and by
the continued stress on accentuation, which was to lead eventually to a
more adequate treatment of the difficult subject of pronunciation.

Chapter XVIII

THE IDENTICAL DICTIONARIES OF 1735 (B. N. DEFOE)

1737 (ANONYMOUS), 1739 (J. SPARROW)

AND 1741 (JAMES MANLOVE)

W E OPEN THIS SECTION BY QUOTING IN FULL THE TITLE-pages of the four little known works which I intend to discuss together here and which I shall show to be identical. The title-pages follow in chronological order:

1. A Compleat English Dictionary.
   Containing the True Meaning Of all Words in the English Language:
   Also The Proper Names of all the Kingdoms, Towns, and Cities in the World: Properly Explain'd and Alphabetically Dispos'd.
   Design'd for the Use of Gentlemen, Ladies, Foreigners, Artificers, Tradesmen; and All who desire to Speak or Write English in its present Purity and Perfection.
   By B. N. Defoe, Gent.
   Westminster: Printed for John Brindley,... Olive Payne,... John Jolliffe, ... Alexander Lyon, and Charles Corbett, ... MDCCXXXV.

2. A New English Dictionary,
   Containing a Large and almost Compleat Collection of Useful English Words. Those of no real Use, with which the Larger Works of this sort are generally stuff'd, being intirely omitted.
   Also, The Proper Names of all the Kingdoms, Cities, Towns, Remarkable Persons, &c. &c. &c. in the World.
   Design'd to assist Gentlemen, Ladies, Foreigners, Artificers, Tradesmen, &c. to Speak, Read or Write English in the greatest Purity and Perfection.
   London: Printed for, and sold by Olive Payne,... M.DCC.XXXVII.

3. A New English Dictionary,
   Containing a compleat Collection of useful English Words, those of

no real use, with which the larger works of this Kind are generally stuff'd, being intirely omitted.

Design'd to assist Gentlemen, Ladies, Foreigners, Artificers, Tradesmen, &c. to speak, read or write English in its present purity and perfection, the whole founded intirely upon a new plan, and is the best in its kind ever yet printed.

By J. Sparrow, Gent.   London (O. Payne) 1739[1]

4. A New Dictionary of All Such English Words
(With their Explanation) As are generally made Use of, in Speaking or Writing the English Language with Accuracy and Politeness.
By James Manlove, Philomath.
[Engraving of Virgil]
London: Printed, for J. Wilcox in the Strand. 1741.

We shall next consider the prefatory material, which is notably thin and perfunctory and which—except for the general claim that the work makes an agreeable and inexpensive "Pocket Companion"—makes no statements as to aims, scope, methods, or audience. The 1735 volume carries the following brief preface, here quoted in full:

The Design of the following Sheets is so fully explain'd by the Title Page, that there is but little Occasion for any other Introduction than what that might furnish. A very short Preface may therefore suffice.

The Compiler cannot charge himself with having spared any Pains to render them correct, and so useful, as might justify his Publication of them to the World.

And 'tis hoped, it will not be pleaded to his Disadvantage, that whilst this Work answers all the valuable Purposes that ought to be expected from a Performance of this Nature, 'tis so fitted, as at Pleasure to be made a Pocket Companion; and for a very small Expence to become the Source of Amusement or Instruction Abroad as well as at Home.

The anonymous editor in 1737 (probably the bookseller, O. Payne) evidently recognized the inanity of this preface and omitted it, allowing the word list to follow immediately after the title-page. The 1739 work resumed part or all of the original preface;[2] and the 1741 work again reprinted the original preface with the addition of the following highly hypocritical paragraph:

This being the Author's first Essay of this Sort, he commits it to the Candour of those who will condescend to give it Reception; humbly hoping for the Approbation of the Publick, if upon Perusal it shall be found that he has endeavoured to deserve it.

These four small volumes have occasioned a good deal of confusion, the 1735 volume sometimes being attributed to Daniel Defoe despite the refutation of the title-page and the 1737 volume being often attributed to J. K. or John Kersey because of the identity of the title with that of J. K.'s dictionary. An examination of the 1735, 1737, and 1741 volumes side by side in the Harvard Library, however, soon established the fact that, with the exception of the trivial prefatory matter, they are identical. With this observation should be combined Wheatley's remark that the 1737 and the 1739 volumes, which he had seen, are identical.[3]

It is at once obvious that the issuance of the same work four times variously disguised with new "authors," titles, and preface is to be studied in the light of the booksellers involved. It will have been observed from the title-pages that several booksellers sponsored the original work and that one of them, Olive (or Oliver) Payne reissued it in a new form in 1737 and in a third form in 1739. Evidently the other booksellers concerned in the first volume were content to let the unsuccessful project lapse and allowed the sole rights and the unused stock to devolve upon Payne. O. Payne's career as a bookseller was brief and unfortunate; he was in business only from 1733 to 1739, when he went bankrupt.[4] Payne's two attempts to promote the dictionary reflect both inexperience and desperation. On his withdrawal from business, another bookseller, J. Wilcox, acquired the ownership of the ill-fated work and, with emphatic protestations of "newness," made a final vain attempt to launch it on a career. Being a shrewd and successful businessman,[5] Wilcox then allowed the work to fall into oblivion.

Little is known about the supposed authors of this work in its various forms. B. N. Defoe, whose name appears on the original title-page, may indeed have compiled the work; his function in this case would have been purely editorial, as it will be shown below that the dictionary contains no new material. Defoe was probably little more than a hack writer and is remembered only as one of the editors of *The Thursday's Journal*, later called *The London Journal*, which ran from 1719 to

1738.[6] His name may thus have had some small drawing power at the time when the dictionary first appeared. Payne showed his inexperience in allowing the 1737 work to appear anonymously; such an insignificant work had need of at least an illustrious name to gain it any attention in an age when many established dictionaries and well known lexicographers had large followings. J. Sparrow, whose name appears on the 1739 title-page, was probably even less known than Defoe, as he is remembered only as a translator of miscellaneous French works.[7] We have not been able to find any information about Manlove, the supposed author of the last volume.

It is not difficult to understand why this work failed to arouse public interest. Its authors enjoyed little or no prestige, its titles were nondescript, its prefaces lacked point, and its vocabulary was second-hand. It was a mediocre compilation, and it lacked even the benefit of such shaping of the prefatory apparatus and such advertising as a progressive bookseller could have given it. This was therefore just another dictionary; it did not improve—or, what is worse, even claim to improve—in any respect on its predecessors; and it did not experiment in any new field or with any new method. It merely marked time in a period when lexicography was taking great strides forward and when any intelligent purchaser would require some degree of character and competence in his dictionary.

If the original booksellers had analyzed the work in order to promote its sale more vigorously, as did for example the sellers of Dyche and Pardon, they might perhaps have best aimed at a low level of readers educationally and have focused on the simple, practical, handy, and inexpensive nature of the work. The compiler has, in fact, merely made a small abridgment of Bailey's *Universal Etymological English Dictionary*, containing about 16,000 words. The resultant vocabulary consists of three main classes: rather ordinary words, names of Biblical persons, and names of British shires and towns. While such a word list defies unity and seems odd to the modern, it apparently catered to three distinct needs and interests of the time, since these groups of words had appeared along with other specialized groups in several other dictionaries of the period. The section quoted below illustrates both the method of abridging Bailey's definitions and the make-up of the word list held in common by the four dictionaries under discussion.[8] The compiler of this word list, it will be observed, disregarded etymology, grammar, pronunciation, and usage; he offers definitions and nothing more.

BAILEY, 1733 Edition	THE FOUR DICTIONARIES
Abiah, (...) the Son of *Samuel* the Prophet.	*Abiah*, the Son of *Samuel* the Prophet.
Abiather, (...) the Name of a Son of *Abimilech*.	*Abiathar*, the Name of a Son of *Abimilech*.
Abib, (...) the first Month in the *Jewish* Ecclesiastical Year, which answers commonly to Part of our *March*, and Part of *April*.	*Abib*, the Name of the first Month among the *Jews*, answering to part of our March and April.
To *Abide*, (...) to continue, tarry or stay; to dwell or live in a Place; to suffer or endure.	To *Abide*, to tarry or stay in a Place; to suffer or endure.
Abject, (...) cast away, mean, base, vile. An *Abject*, (...) a Person of no Repute or Esteem.	*Abject*, mean, base, or vile. An *Abject*, a Person of no repute or esteem.
Abjection, (...) abject Condition, low Estate, Meanness, Vileness.	*Abjection*, a low mean condition.
Abiezer, (...) one of King *David's* 30 Champions.	*Abiezer*, one of King *David's* thirty Champions.
Abigail, (...) *Nabal's* Wife, and afterwards King *David's*.	*Abigail*, *Nabal's* Wife, and afterwards King *David's*.
Abimelech, (...) a King of *Gerar*.	*Abimelech*, a King of *Gerar*.
Abingdon, (...) a Town in Berkshire.	*Abingdon*, a Town in Barkshire.
Abishag, (...) a beautiful Young Virgin who cherished K. *David* in his old Age.	*Abishag*, a beautiful Virgin who cherished King *David* in his old Age.

The general make-up of the present work recalls that of J. K.'s *New English Dictionary*, published in 1702, revised in 1713, and reissued as late as 1772. Both feature ordinary words and Biblical names; [9] but the present dictionary adds the geographical feature, which had more recently risen to popularity.[10] Whereas J. K. arrived at his vocabulary by adapting the material of the spelling books and of Coles's practical dictionary, the compiler of this work used a more difficult approach, for he undertook to reduce the copious and complicated vocabulary of Bailey to suit his own purposes. A study of the *L* sections in Bailey's

Universal Etymological English Dictionary and in the word list carried by the four dictionaries illustrates the compiler's procedure as well as the difference in level of learning of the two vocabularies concerned. The compiler consistently omitted terms which Bailey had designated as Chaucerian, Spenserian, Shakespearean, or obsolete (*Laas, Lacert, Laie, Laine, Langoreth,* etc.) and hard words of classical origin, such as *Labefaction* ("a weakening"), *Labrose* ("having a Brink or Brim, or great Lips"), *Laciniated* ("notched"), *Lambdacism* ("a Fault in speaking, when one insists too long upon the Letter *L*"), etc. He also eliminated medical, anatomical, surgical, and chemical items (*Lac Lunae, Lac Sulphuris, Lacteal Fever, Laetificantia, Lagophthalmy, Lapidilium, Lapis Admirabilis, Laqueus,* etc.); legal terms (*Lada, Lafordswick, Lagslite,* etc.); miscellaneous scientific words (*Lapillation,* among the Paracelsians, etc.); military expressions (*Lancepesade, Lancinate,* etc.); sea phrases (*Lagan, Land-to, Laskets,* etc.); heraldic terms (*Langued,* etc.); musical and artistic entries (*Languente, Languido, Lacunar, Larmier,* etc.); hunting jargon (*Laprice,* etc.); proverbs; etc. In short, of Bailey's carefully varied and balanced vocabulary the compiler retained little more than a third and thus obtained a surprisingly simple word list, as may be seen from the following section:

Large, Lark, Lascivious, Lasciviousness, Lash, Lask, Lassitude, Last, A Last, To Last, Lasting, Latch, Latchet, Late, Latest, Latent, Lateron, Lateward, Lath, Lather, Latin, Latinist, Latitude, Latitudinarians, Latten, Lattice, Laud, Laudable, Lavender, Laugh, Laughter, Lavish, Laundress, Laureat, Poet Laureat, Laurel, Law, Law of Arms, Law of Nature, Lawless, Lawn, Lax, Lay, Lay Land, To Lay, Layman, Laystall, Layer, Lazy, etc.[11]

While definitions, following Bailey's, are usually adequate, it is interesting to note that certain classes of words still baffle the lexicographer. The following words, for example, are defined as in Bailey; but the inadequacy of their definitions is more noticeable in a small word list of which familiar words form the bulk.

Bed, to lie or rest upon.[12]
Table, a Piece of Household-Stuff well known.
A *Lark,* a Singing Bird.
To *Laugh,* an Action well known.

As might be expected and as is probably still true, the definitions of animals are least satisfactory. Compare the following:

BAILEY, 1733 Edition	THE FOUR DICTIONARIES
Cat, (...) a domestick Creature which kills *Mice*.[18]	(no item)
Dog, (...) a Quadruped well known.	*Dog*, an Animal well known.
Goat, (...) a Beast.	*Goat*, a Beast.
Elephant, (...) the largest, strongest, and most intelligent of Four-footed Beasts.	*Elephant*, the biggest, strongest, and most intelligent of all four-footed Beasts.

Thus, although using Bailey's competent dictionary as a base, the present dictionary was retrogressive in nature, recalling in general character and in certain limitations J. K.'s earlier work, which had, however, actually filled a need and enjoyed a long career. It will be of interest to compare the present work also with the *Pocket Dictionary* of 1753, which, though anonymous and derivative in material, was carefully planned and focused, and went through several editions. The *Pocket Dictionary* wisely incorporated some of the recently developed methods and trends, and achieved for itself a character and a *raison d'être*—both of which were sadly lacking in the case of the dictionary which made four unsuccessful bids for public favor in 1735, 1737, 1739, and 1741.

Chapter XIX

BENJAMIN MARTIN'S
Lingua Britannica Reformata (1749)

M ARTIN'S *Lingua Britannica Reformata* IS A DICTIONARY with a plan. Preceding dictionaries had seemed to grow without a plan; or, if the author had some scheme in mind, he felt little responsibility for sharing it with his readers. Seventeenth-century lexicographers had usually devoted their prefaces to informal remarks on the considerations which led them to compile a dictionary and on their attitude toward one or two disputed points in dictionary-making. Phillips added a history of the language, Bailey explained systematically his procedure in regard to etymology, and Dyche and Pardon offered their compendious grammar. All these efforts were limited, however; and even Bailey's folio *Dictionarium Britannicum*, undoubtedly the finest dictionary up to 1755, appeared without the grace of a preface. So the dictionaries accumulated, with each writer inheriting a mass of material which he tried to shape according to his own not too clearly defined or justified preferences. From the storehouse of words thus constituted, from the pattern of one or more preceding dictionaries, and from some special interest of the author the new dictionary grew rather than from an impartial consideration of the various departments of lexicography and the ideal methods of handling them.

Martin's work comes at a strategic juncture and marks a change in the concept of a dictionary and of the lexicographer's function. This is, we believe, a significant development which reflects the temper of the times and which had its roots in many remote and more recent happenings. As far back as 1664 the Royal Society included among its activities a committee "for improving the English tongue." [1] The triumphant completion of the *Dictionnaire de l'Académie française* in 1694 made the English uncomfortably aware of their backwardness in the study of their own tongue, and from then on the air was full of schemes for improving the English language and giving it greater prestige. Defoe in 1698 devoted a section of his *Essay on Projects* to Academies, wherein he lauded the French Academy and its great achievement but contended that "the English tongue is a subject not at all less worthy the labour of such a society than the French, and capable of a much greater perfection." He therefore proposed a society

to encourage polite learning, to polish and refine the English tongue, and advance the so much neglected faculty of correct language, to establish purity and propriety of style, and to purge it from all the irregular additions that ignorance and affectation have introduced and all those innovations in speech, if I may call them such, which some dogmatic writers have the confidence to foster upon their native language, as if their authority were sufficient to make their own fancy legitimate.[2]

In 1712 Swift in his *Proposal for Correcting, Improving and Ascertaining the English Tongue* also lamented the corruptions which had crept into the language and insisted that authorities should be appointed to "reform our language" and thereafter "to ascertain and fix [it] for ever."[3] In 1718 appeared the second edition of the *Dictionnaire*, which, because of its revision in alphabetical order, enjoyed even greater popularity than its original form. Meanwhile the relative merits of the English and French languages, the French dictionary, and a possible English counterpart were being avidly discussed in coffee houses, salons, and literary and learned groups in the city and at the universities.

An article by Mary Segar calls attention to the pertinent fact that some plans for a large dictionary were actually drawn up at this time, though for various reasons they failed to materialize.[4] The first of these was Addison's design for making a dictionary with quotations, a design commented upon by Johnson.[5] When Addison became secretary of state, however, he laid this project aside; or perhaps, as Miss Segar suggests, he relinquished it to his friend, Ambrose Philips. The latter's published "Proposals for Printing an English Dictionary" in two folio volumes have been "recently found in a private collection," signed but undated. Philips' plan as there outlined is most ambitious, including orthography, etymology, definitions of all the proper and figurative uses of each word, idioms, proverbial sayings, notes as to usage, etc. Although Addison's and Philips' schemes were never realized, they must have further stimulated the already lively discussion of the universal topic. No doubt Pope's keen interest in the dictionary project also incited public discussion.[6]

Between such elaborate schemes for a great dictionary and the dictionaries which were actually being produced at the time there is a wide gulf. Even Bailey's, the best dictionaries available, had evolved in a short-sighted fashion as improvements on their immediate predecessors rather than as attempts at a perfect dictionary. So it happens that, as late as 1747, Warburton complains bitterly:

[The English tongue is] yet destitute of a Test or Standard to apply to, in cases of doubt or difficulty, ... For we have neither Grammar nor Dictionary, neither Chart nor Compass, to guide us through this wide sea of Words.[7]

In that same year, however, appeared Johnson's *Plan of a Dictionary of the English Language,* a notable document which showed that the problem had at last found its master, one who had the vision, the learning, the common sense, and the tenacity to execute a project comparable to that which had for so long occupied the French Academy. Through his familiarity with the works of his predecessors, Johnson was realistic in outlook; yet he dared to attempt "a dictionary by which the pronunciation of our language may be fixed and its attainment facilitated; by which its purity may be preserved, its use ascertained, and its duration lengthened." [8] Under such a burden of responsibility Johnson formulated a comprehensive and minute plan, discussing selection of the vocabulary, orthography, pronunciation, etymology, syntax, definitions, usage, citations of authorities, etc. We are here reminded of Boswell's comment on Johnson's high aspirations when the latter was said to have compared his work not with those of his predecessors but "with speculative perfection." [9]

While our discussion has apparently taken us far afield, it has actually, we hope, been preparing us for a clearer understanding of Martin's dictionary both in itself and in its role as precursor of Johnson.[10] The expectancy of the time was, however, only one phase of the matter; Martin's own personal predilections played their part in inducing the special character of his dictionary.

Benjamin Martin was an amazingly versatile and busy man, who was at home in science, literature, and philosophy, who won repute both as an inventor and as a popularizer of knowledge, and who fathered countless projects. The article in the *Dictionary of National Biography* characterizes him succinctly as "mathematician, instrument maker, and general compiler." [11] Beginning life as a ploughboy and later teaching at Guildford and Chichester, he became an authority on mathematics and astronomy and "an ardent champion of the Newtonian system." [12] Coming to London, he gained further fame as an inventor and maker of optical and other fine scientific instruments; and finally he was the author of more than thirty works, all of which were broad in scope and many of which attained several volumes. The following may serve to indicate the range of his interests and the nature of his compilations. The *Bibliotheca Technologica or Philological Library of Literary Arts and Sciences*, 1737, is described as "epitomising the current information and ideas of the time under twenty-five headings." The work oddly called *Martin's Magazine* was more accurately described in a sub-title as "A New and Comprehensive System of Philosophy, Natural History, Philology, Mathematical Institutions, and Biographies"; of the fourteen volumes of this work projected, seven were produced between 1755 and 1764. Perhaps the most popular of his works, however, was the *Philosophical Grammar* in four parts: I. Somatology, II. Cosmology, III. Ærology, and IV. Geology, 1735; this attained at least seven editions in English and three editions in French during Martin's lifetime. Lastly, we may mention his final work, appearing in 1782, *The Young Gentleman and Lady's Philosophy*, a dialogue dealing characteristically with the heavens, the earth, the animal, vegetable, and mineral kingdoms. These facts will suffice to show that Martin had scope of vision, skill in organization, and the zeal of the popularizer.

We are now ready to consider the title-page of Martin's dictionary, outlining a plan which is staggering for an octavo work:

Lingua Britannica Reformata:

Or, A New English Dictionary,

Under the Following Titles, Viz.

I. UNIVERSAL; Containing a Definition and Explication of all the Words now used in the English Tongue, in every Art, Science, Faculty, or Trade.

II. ETYMOLOGICAL; Exhibiting and Explaining the true Etymon or Original of Words from their respective Mother-Tongues, . . . and their idioms, . . .

III. ORTHOGRAPHICAL; Teaching the True and Rational Method of Writing Words, according to the Usage of the most Approved Modern Authors.

IV. ORTHOEPICAL; Directing the True Pronunciation of Words by Single and Double Accents; and by Indicating the Number of Syllables in Words where they are doubtful, by a Numerical Figure.

V. DIACRITICAL; Enumerating the Various Significations of Words in a Proper Order, viz. Etymological, Common, Figurative, Poetical, Humorous, Technical &c. in a Manner not before attempted.

VI. PHILOLOGICAL; Explaining all the Words and Terms, according to the Modern Improvements in the Various Philological Sciences, viz: Grammar, Rhetoric, Logic, Metaphysics, Mythology, Theology, Ethics, &c.

VII. MATHEMATICAL; Not only Explaining all Words in Arithmetic, . . . according to the Modern Newtonian Mathesis; but the Terms of Art are illustrated by Proper Exercises, and Copper-Plate Figures.

VIII. PHILOSOPHICAL; Explaining all Words and Terms in Astronomy, Geography, Optics, . . . according to the latest Discoveries and Improvements in this Part of Literature.

To which is prefix'd An Introduction,

Containing A Physico-Grammatical Essay.

On the Propriety and Rationale of the English Tongue, deduced from a General Idea of the Nature and Necessity of Speech for Human Society; a Particular View of the Genius and Usage of the Original Mother Tongues, the Hebrew, Greek, Latin, and Teutonic; with their respective Idioms, the Italian, French, Spanish, Saxon, and German, so far as they have Relation to the English Tongue, and have contributed to its Composition.

By Benj. Martin.

London: . . . MDCCXLIX.

Martin's Preface is also a model of planning and detail. Dismissing other English dictionaries in the gross as of little use, Martin begins in the new way by outlining the "Requisites of a Genuine English Dictionary"; here he maintains the headings of his title-page but expands his views. It will have been observed incidentally that Martin called his work first *Universal* and *Etymological,* words associated with Bailey, and secondly *Orthographical* and *Orthoepical,* words suggestive of Dyche and Pardon; he thus intimates that he has all their claims to attention besides several other departments which are peculiarly his.

We shall summarize this intelligent and progressive prospectus under Martin's headings. Under *Universality* (I) Martin stipulates that a dictionary should avoid a "Redundancy of useless and obsolete Words" and include "all the Words in Use." Obsolete words may be found in special glossaries; proverbs, in Erasmus or Ray; historical accounts, in Morery and "the Antiquarians." The "numerous Families of Adjectives, Participles," etc. may be omitted, since, the word "being once well explained, it is an Affront to the Reader, not to suppose him capable of understanding the Meaning of all the Derivatives." The space secured by such eliminations may be advantageously devoted to "a more particular and accurate Explanation" of the useful words. *Etymology* (II) is "absolutely necessary to a due Understanding and Emphatical Expression," and any dictionary which lacks this department [Dyche and Pardon's] is "extremely deficient." Furthermore, the lexicographer must not "mock" the reader or "tantalize his vain Expectation" by merely noting the etymons; he must also explain their meanings.[13] In *Orthography* (III) "our Dictionaries most certainly want a Reformation." Martin has therefore omitted the final *k* on words like *logic* and has made other simplifications not to suit his personal preference but to offer "a sure Guide to the modern Orthography." Under *Orthoepy* (IV), Martin promises specific aids; he will indicate the number of syllables in difficult words, he will use both single and double accents, and he warns the reader of silent letters and other pitfalls.

In Section V we arrive at the outstanding innovation of Martin, the reform of the *Definition.* He writes earnestly on the need for such reform, explains his own method of building definitions, and even specifies sources:

A Critical and accurate Enumeration and Distinction of the several Significations of each respective Word must be allow'd by all to be indispensably the chiefest Care of every Writer of Dictionaries. And yet nothing is more certain, than that all our English Dictionaries are more notoriously deficient in this important Particular than in any other; ... This grand Defect it has been my principal Care to supply, and indeed was the greatest Motive to my undertaking this Work. And that I might acquit myself more perfectly herein I laid before my Amanuensis *Ainsworth's* Latin Dictionary, and the Royal French Dictionary; where, in the English Part, as the Authors were obliged to consider every different Sense of an English Word, ... this Task was by that Means greatly facilitated; and by a careful Collection and Addition of such others as the common Dictionaries, Glossaries, and Popular Speech supplied, 'tis presumed we have attain'd to no inconsiderable Perfection and Success in this most Essential Part of our Work.

Martin then proceeds to lay down a logical order for definitions, as follows: 1. the etymological or original significance; 2. the general and popular; 3. the figurative or metaphorical; 4. the humorous, poetical, and burlesque uses; 5. the "scientifical acceptations"; and 6. compounds and "phraseologies" (idioms). The ideas of laying the primary stress on definition and of introducing a systematic order of meanings, Martin may well have derived from Johnson's *Plan*. His own scientific nature, however, would already have inclined him to more careful analysis and more precise order; and the familiar bilingual dictionaries not only demonstrated such a system in practice but offered him a store of usable material. It will be recalled that, after discussing various phases of lexicography in his *Plan*, Johnson had wound up to a climax with the statement that "The great labour is yet to come, the labour of interpreting these words and phrases with brevity, fulness, and perspicuity." [14] Johnson then outlined the order of senses as follows:

In explaining the general and popular language, it seems necessary to sort the several senses of each word, and to exhibit first its natural and primitive signification; ... Then to give its consequential meaning, ... Then its metaphorical sense, ... Then follows the accidental ... Then the remoter or metaphorical signification; ... it will be proper to subjoin the poetical sense ... To the poetical sense may succeed the familiar; ... The familiar may be followed by the burlesque; ... And lastly, may be produced the peculiar sense, in which a word is found in any great author: ... [15]

Johnson's *Plan* presented two proposals of outstanding importance, the carefully divided and ordered definition and the citation of authorities.

While the latter was manifestly not feasible for an octavo work to be turned out in a limited time by a scientist, the former was possible and Martin anticipated Johnson in this respect.

English Philology (VI) is used loosely to include "Grammar, Rhetoric, Logic, Metaphysics, Theology, Mythology, &c." Martin here promises to "convey a clear, just, and Scientific Notion" of terms in these fields. For a more particular account he refers to treatises on the individual subjects. While the above are dismissed as stock subjects hastily and with little show of interest, Martin has been "designedly very particular and explicit in giving an accurate Definition and full Exposition of all the Words and Terms now used" in *Mathematics* (VII), with illustrative examples and figures. He explains further:

As the Newtonian Mathesis is not only *new*, but of a very sublime Nature, it is no Wonder if no Vestigia thereof can be found in any of our common Dictionaries, worth any Mathematician's Notice; and it is evident from that little you find, that the Authors had scarce any Idea of it themselves, and consequently were but ill qualified to explain it to others.

In [Natural] *Philosophy* (VIII), "the most reigning Science of the Age," "it is highly incumbent on the Compiler of an English Dictionary to see that all the Words, Terms, and Phrases, used in this important and polite Species of Learning, should be in the clearest Manner defined; . . ." Here too, "Sir *I. Newton's* Definitions and Doctrines have been solely regarded; . . ." In Section IX Martin promises to give an adequate treatment of *Fortifications, Military and Naval Affairs,* since they should be "well understood by a People whose Honour, Power, Wealth, Religion, Liberty, and Security depend so much upon them; . . ." Martin takes his stand on *Grammar* in Section X. A "bare English Grammar," he declares, probably with Dyche and Pardon's in mind, "belongs to a Spelling Book"; but "a more general and Philosophical Account of Languages, and in particular the English, should be made the Entrance to the Dictionary." Finally, as a guide to usage, he has set off words that "have found Admittance into our Tongue, and yet appear like Aliens" and others "not to be used in common Discourse, or the genteel Diction" by italic characters and obelisks respectively.[16] He concludes his capable preface with the satisfied remark:

Thus you have the Plan and general Oeconomy of the Work; and though upon the Whole, I presume, this Dictionary is by much the most perfect of its Kind; yet I am not so vain as to think it without Faults and Imperfections.

It is now time to weigh the results of all this planning. Martin may be credited first with a unified and purposeful vocabulary of about 24,500 words, obviously selected with care. It includes both ordinary and difficult words; and, despite an obvious fondness for terms from mathematics and natural philosophy, it substantially reduces the number of highly specialized and technical terms. In drawing up his word list Martin probably consulted both the *Universal Etymological English Dictionary* and the *Dictionarium Britannicum* of Bailey, but his definitions more often follow the shorter ones of the octavo work. Thus both Martin, and Dyche and Pardon are in a limited sense derivatives of Bailey; Martin, however, favors the fundamental words whereas Dyche and Pardon prefer the highly specialized and eccentric, and both Martin, and Dyche and Pardon have numerous and heavy debts elsewhere.

As would be expected, Martin is discriminating in his definitions. He sometimes merely abridges Bailey's definitions; and there is a general resemblance between their works, as shown in these parallel entries:

BAILEY, *Universal . . . Dictionary* 1745 Edition	MARTIN, 1749
Kal'endar (. . .) an Ephemeris or Almanack, to shew the Day of the Month.	*Ká lendar* (. . .) an almanack, or ephemeris.
Ká li, a Sea-Herb, the Ashes of which are used in making Crystal Glasses and Soap, called also *Glass-wort*.	*Ká li*, a sea-herb, of the ashes of which they make glass, &c.
Kan, the Name of an Officer in *Persia*, answering to *Governor* with us.	*Kan*, a Persian governor.
To *Kaw* (. . .) to cry as a Jack daw does. To *Kaw* (. . .) to fetch one's Breath with much Difficulty, to gape for Breath.	*Kaw*, 1 to cry as a Jack daw does. 2 to gape for breath, or fetch it with difficulty.
A *Kay* (. . .) a Place to land or ship off A *Key* Goods; a Wharf.	*Kay*, or *Key*, a wharf, or place to land, or ship off goods.

BAILEY, *Universal ... Dictionary* 1745 Edition	MARTIN, 1749
Keel, a Vessel for Liquors to stand and cool in. *Keel* (...) is the lowest Piece of Timber in a Ship, in the Bottom of her Hull, ...	*Keel*, 1 the piece of timber which lies lowest in the hull of a ship. 2 a vessel for liquor to stand and cool in.
Ken'nel (...) a Water-course. *Kennel* (...) a Hut for a Dog, a Fox's Hut or Hole. *Kennel of Hounds* (*Hunting Term*) a Pack or Cry of Hounds.	*Ke'nnel*, 1 a water course in the middle of a street. 2 a place to keep dogs in. 3 a fox's earth, or hole. 4 a pack, or cry, as a Kennel of hounds, *i.e.* a pack, or cry of hounds.

In his most characteristic definitions, however, Martin used consistently the new method—dividing, arranging, and numbering the various senses of the word. Here Martin received great help, which he duly acknowledged in the passage quoted above from Section V of the Preface, both from Abel Boyer's *Dictionaire* [*sic*] *Royal, François-Anglois et Anglois-François,* which had originally appeared in 1699 but was many times revised and augmented thereafter, and from Robert Ainsworth's *Thesaurus Linguae Latinae Compendiarius,* which had first appeared in 1736 and was often reissued.[17] In the second (English-French) part of Boyer, Martin found the English words analyzed in their various meanings before the French equivalents were given. Here Martin could select from copious material.

BOYER, 1727 Edition	MARTIN, 1749
Keen, Adj., (sharp, that cuts well) ... *Keen*, (sharp or subtle)... A *keen* air, ... He was very *keen* or (eager) upon the business, ... A *keen* (or pungent) Stile, ... A *keen* appetite, ...	*Keen*, 1 sharp, that cuts well. 2 sharp, or subtile. 3 cold, or serene. 4 eager, or ardent. 5 pungent, or satyrical. 6 sharp, or hungry.
Kern, Subst. (a Country Bumkin) ... *Kern*, (an Irish Foot-Soldier lightly armed with a Dart or Skene) ... A *kern*, (or vagrant Fellow) ...	*Kern*, 1 a rustic, or country-bumkin. 2 an Irish foot-soldier, lightly armed with a dart or skene. 3 a vagrant fellow.

Boyer, 1727 Edition	Martin, 1749
Kickshaw, Subst. (a French Ragoo) . . . *Kickshaw*, (or slight Business) . . .	*Kickshaw*, 1 a French ragoo. 2 a slight business.
To *Knit*, Verb Act. (to tie) . . . Ex. To *knit* a thing into a fast Knot, . . . To *knit* Friendship with one, . . . To *knit* Stockings, . . . To *knit* fast a Horse's Vein, . . . To *knit* the Brows, . . . To *knit*, Verb Neut. (to gather, as a Horse does) . . . To *knit*, (as Bees do) . . .	To *Knit*, 1 to tie or make a knot. 2 to make stockings, &c. 3 to draw up the brows. 4 to gather, as a horse does. 5 to cling together, as bees do.

Martin made similar use of the Latin-English section of Ainsworth.

Ainsworth, 1736	Martin, 1749
Labyrinthus . . . (1) A labyrinth, or maze, a place full of turnings and windings, made so that one could not get out again without a guide, or clue of thread to direct one. (2) An oration, or any thing that is difficult, or intricate, . . .	*La"byrinth* (. . .) 1 a maze, or place full of turnings and windings, made so that one could not get out again without a guide, or clue of thread to direct one. 2 any thing that is difficult, or intricate.
Langueo . . . (1) To languish, to be sick, feeble, or faint. (2) To grow cool, or droop, to sneak. (3) To fade and decay. (4) To become listless, to grow dull and heavy. (5) To be cloyed and weary.	To *Lánguish* (. . .) 1 to be sick, feeble, or faint. 2 to fade, and decay. 3 to become listless, to grow dull and heavy. 4 to consume, and pine away.
Lamentor, . . . (1) To lament, bewail, weep, or mourn for. (2) To bemoan, to take on sadly.	To *Lamé'nt* (. . .) 1 to bewail, weep, or mourn for. 2 to take on sadly.

In the science of definition Martin represents a transitional stage; he is experimenting with an admirable system, but he does not always get satisfactory results. In his definitions of the commonest words especially (e.g., *Keen* quoted above and *Keep* quoted below), certain weaknesses are evident. In many such cases Martin fails to distinguish adequately between the various senses listed; and the reader alternately charges him with oversubtlety or suspects that he is merely trying to amass as many senses as possible—a temptation incident to the divided definition. Actually, a comparison with Ainsworth and Boyer reveals that he is abridging from his source and that he has cut too severely. Martin is also unwise in placing his trust in synonyms; for commoner words he uses them excessively and, what is still more baffling, he has a habit of coupling synonyms for each sense of a word. Here an urgent need is felt for two other developments in lexicography: the illustrative quotations, which were to come soon in Johnson, and the synonymy, which was to be introduced by James Barclay in his *Complete and Universal English Dictionary* of 1774.

Notwithstanding these shortcomings, however, the distinction of senses is a notable step forward on the road to accurate definition, which, though slow to win interest and slower to be perfected, is, of course, the true goal of the lexicographer. It is curious that this important development, while perhaps suggested by Johnson's *Plan* and congenial to Martin's own scientific nature, owed so much to the pattern and the material of the Latin-English dictionaries. The importance of the role which Thomas Thomas' *Dictionarium* and other Latin-English dictionaries played in the development of the English dictionary in the seventeenth century has been stressed. In the early eighteenth century, however, as a body of precedent, a storehouse of material, and a sense of authority were built up by successive English dictionaries, there was less tendency to turn to their Latin-English prototypes. True, Bailey and others undoubtedly consulted the bilingual dictionaries on various occasions; but the English dictionary was for the most part working out its own destiny. When, however, Johnson's *Plan* and Martin's Preface called attention to the limitations of current English dictionaries and called for the ideal dictionary, recourse was had again to the practice and the material of the Latin-English dictionaries. Ironically, Ainsworth's *Thesaurus* used here is, through intermediaries, a descendant of Thomas' *Dictionarium*, which was present at the birth of the English dictionary and attended it in its earliest years. An incidental mechanical improvement not to be overlooked is the clearer and more attractive spacing of definitions on the page. As to the order of senses, while the exact sequence outlined in Martin's Preface is hard to distinguish, he has given serious thought to the matter. It is his custom to begin with the literal and then to branch out logically to the figurative and special meanings, as in the following instance:

Life, 1 the union of the soul with the body.
　　　2 the time that union lasts.
　　　3 the manner of living.
　　　4 the history of what a man has done during his life.
　　　5 mettle, sprightliness.
　　　6 noise, scolding.[18]

A few examples may be inserted here to give some notion of the evolution of the definition from Bailey to Martin and from Martin to Johnson and to show the importance of Martin's role as the transition between the old and the new methods. It may be observed, incidentally, that, while Martin originally stole Johnson's thunder in regard to the divided definition, Johnson could ultimately profit by Martin's experimentation both through its deficiencies and through its attainments. Johnson's definitions were, of course, clarified by meticulously selected quotations, here omitted for economy of space. Johnson's rare command of words, however, stood him in fine stead in distinguishing nuances of meaning so that even without his helpful quotations his definitions are much clearer than Martin's.

BAILEY Dictionarium Britannicum, 1730 Edition	MARTIN, 1749	JOHNSON, 1755
Keen, sharp, that cuts well; also cunning, subtil.	*Keen,* 1 sharp, that cuts well. 2 sharp, or subtile. 3 cold, or serene. 4 eager, or ardent. 5 pungent, or satyrical. 6 sharp, or hungry.	*Keen,* 1 Sharp; well edged; not blunt. 2 Severe; piercing. 3 Eager; vehement. 4 Acrimonious; bitter of mind.
To *Keep,* to retain, preserve, nourish, to look to, &c.	To *Keep,* 1 to take care of, or preserve. 2 to stay, or abide. 3 to last, or endure. 4 to lay up, or reserve. 5 to observe, or not break. 6 to abstain from. 7 to conceal, or hide from. 8 to nourish, or provide for. 9 to celebrate, or solemnize. 10 to continue, or to live. 11 to perform, or stand to.	To *Keep,* 1 To retain; not to lose. 2 To have in custody. 3 To preserve; not to let go. 4 To preserve in a state of security. 5 To protect; to guard. 6 To guard from flight. 7 To detain. 8 To hold for another. 9 To reserve; to conceal. 10 To tend, etc. [Johnson lists 29 meanings.]

BAILEY	MARTIN, 1749	JOHNSON, 1755
Universal . . . Dictionary, 1745 Edition		
To *Languish*, to grow faint or weak, to droop, to fall away, to consume or pine away.	To *Languish*, 1 to be sick, feeble, or faint. 2 to fade, and decay. 3 to become listless, to grow dull and heavy. 4 to consume, and pine away.	To *Languish*, 1 To grow feeble; to pine away; to lose strength. 2 To be no longer vigorous in motion; not to be vivid in appearance. 3 To sink or pine under sorrow, or any slow passion. 4 To look with softness or tenderness.

While the definitions are indisputably the most progressive feature of Martin's dictionary and that on which he spent most thought and effort, we must turn now to the other features in which he boasted improvement. Here his achievement falls short of his intentions, as is understandable in the light of his busy career, which necessitated his delegating details to his amanuensis. He made good his promise as to the cautious simplification of spelling; and he maintains considerable interest in pronunciation, the double accent and the numbering of syllables being conspicuous throughout his word list.[19] Etymology, however, is often missing. Only a few items are annotated on some pages, and words of Germanic origin are commonly neglected. In many cases, however, Martin does carry out his promise not only to cite but to explain the etymons:

> To *Adulterate* (of *adultero,* lat. of *ad* with, and *alter* another) . . .
> *Adumbrate* (of *adumbro,* lat. of *ad* of, and *umbra* a shadow) . . .
> *Advocate* (of *advocatus,* lat. of *ad* to and *voco* to call) . . .
> *Affability* (of *affabilitas,* lat. of *ad* to, and *fari* to speak) . . .
> *Aggregate* (of *aggrego,* lat. of *ad* and *grex* a herd) . . .

In his vocabulary, according to his promise, Martin includes the basic terms from the various sciences with adequate definitions and capably develops the representation and treatment of mathematical terms.[20]

Perhaps the most conspicuous innovation of this dictionary aside from the improvement in definitions is the "Physico-Grammatical Essay on the Propriety and Rationale of the English Tongue." This impressive treatise of 108 pages includes such topics as: man's physical and mental endowment for receiving and communicating ideas; alphabets ancient and modern; the history of England with specimens of the language at various periods; a study of the individual letters and of vowels and consonants; a sketch with paradigms of Hebrew, Greek, Latin, Italian, French, Spanish, Portuguese, German, Saxon, and modern English grammar; and a discourse on etymology. While material on the history of the language was available in the 1736 edition of Bailey's *Dictionarium Britannicum* and on letters, vowels, and consonants in various spelling books and grammars, Martin's treatment of these topics is much broader and more advanced than that of any predecessor. That it was also too advanced for his contemporaries may be deduced from the fact that this treatise was omitted without comment from the second edition of the dictionary.

Of special interest in an age which was so concerned with purifying and fixing the national tongues is the following astute remark from the essay on grammar:

...the pretence of fixing a standard to the purity and perfection of any language, ... is utterly vain and impertinent, because no language as depending on arbitrary use and custom, can ever be permanently the same, but will always be in a mutable and fluctuating state; and what is deem'd polite and elegant in one age, may be accounted uncouth and barbarous in another. Of this truth none I think can doubt, as we have such numerous instances of it in the fore-going part of this essay, to which perhaps two or three centuries may add as many more. And Addison, Pope, and Foster may appear to our posterity in the same light as Chaucer, Spenser, and Shakespear do to us; whose language is now grown old and obsolete; read by very few, and understood by antiquarians only.[21]

Here, besides combatting a popular concept, Martin may have had in mind Johnson's assertion in his *Plan* that "one great end of this undertaking [his dictionary] is to fix the English language." [22] Johnson's statement was, however, intended only in a limited sense [23] and expressed only a transitory hope, which he abandoned in the course of his work, as shown by the stirring passage in the Preface:

Those who have been persuaded to think well of my design, will require that it should fix our language, and put a stop to those alterations which time and chance have hitherto been suffered to make in it without opposition. With this consequence I will confess that I flattered myself for a while; but now begin to fear that I have indulged expectation which neither reason nor experience can justify. When we see men grow old and die at a certain time one after another, from century to century, we laugh at the elixir that promises to prolong life to a thousand years; and with equal justice may the lexicographer be derided, who being able to produce no example of a nation that has preserved their words and phrases from mutability, shall imagine that his dictionary can embalm his language, and secure it from corruption and decay, that it is in his power to change sublunary nature, and clear the world at once from folly, vanity, and affectation.[24]

In 1754 the second and last edition of the *Lingua Britannica Reformata* appeared. In this revision the grammatical treatise was dropped, as previously indicated; and about 2,500 items were added. The additions are described by Martin in the Preface as follows:

In this Second Edition, besides a Multitude of considerable Improvements in every Branch, there are interspersed in alphabetical Order, the following Additions:

1. The Description of each Kingdom in *Europe*, as to their Situation, Length, and Breadth, Nature of their Government, Produce, Religion, and Strength.

2. The capital Cities of each Kingdom are described, including their Latitude and Longitude, Nature of their Situation, Circumference, Distance and Bearing from each other, Number of Inhabitants, Manufactures, &c.

3. A Description of each City and Town in *Great-Britain* and *Ireland*, giving the exact Latitude and Longitude . . . the Days of their Fairs and Markets; the Distance from *London* . . . Also an Account of their Manufactures, charitable Foundations, principal Buildings, and other Curiosities; the Number of Members sent to Parliament, and the Names of Families some Towns give Titles to.

4. The Description of each County in *England* and *Wales*, giving the Number of Acres, Cities, Towns, Villages, and Hundreds contained in each; their Situation . . . to what Bishopric they belong; their chief Productions and Manufactures; Nature of the Soil; the Number of Members each sends to Parliament, with the Name of their chief Towns.

5. To each Letter in the Alphabet we have prefixed a Dissertation, shewing how the Organs of Speech are formed to pronounce it, how pronounced in other Languages, and in Conjunction with other Letters.

Actually the changes made in this edition are neither impressive nor significant. The inclusion of the geographical matter is in the nature of a concession to Dyche and Pardon and other rival dictionaries. Here Martin derives data from the same source as Dyche and Pardon, Thomas Cox's *Magna Britannia et Hibernia,* 1720-1731. Martin, however, includes Scotch and Irish shires and towns as well as English and, in contrast to Dyche and Pardon's stress on the unusual, takes a matter of fact approach. Compare, for example, the following entries, both based on Cox:

DYCHE AND PARDON, 1750 Edition

Glastenbury (S.) in Somersetshire, is almost encompassed round with rivers, by which means it is a sort of an island; the town is large, and well built, containing two parish churches, a good market weekly on Tuesdays, and two yearly fairs, when horses and fat cattle are very plentiful; the story of *Joseph* of *Arimathea's* being sent hither by the apostles to preach the gospel, about the year 31, and his actual residence at this place, with the wonders he wrought, the account of the blooming hawthorn tree upon *Christmas-day,* &c. are not proper subjects for so short an account of things and places as our room obliges us to; this town is distant from *London* 103 computed, and 121 measured miles.

MARTIN, 1754 Edition

Glastonbury [latitude and longitude] a town corporate in Somersetshire, where was formerly one of the most magnificent abbeys in the west, but it is now entirely gone to ruins. Here are two parish churches. The only manufacture is the making of stockings; it has a good market on tuesdays, and fairs on the 8th and 29th of September, which are mostly frequented for horses and fat cattle. Distant from London 120 measured miles; and 24 from Bristol.

Martin also boasts of the inclusion of countries and capital cities of Europe. This feature involves, however, comparatively few items with brief and factual accounts probably based upon Louis Morery's *Grand Dictionnaire Historique,* which made a specialty of "La Description des Empires, Royaumes, Républiques, Provinces, Villes, . . . où l'on remarque la situation, l'étendue & la qualité du Pays; la Religion, le Gouvernement, les Moeurs & les Coutumes des Peuples: . . ." [25]

The so-called "Dissertation" prefixed to each letter proves to be only a short paragraph describing the position of the letter in the alphabet, the method of forming the letter, its proper sound, and its special uses

in numbers, abbreviations, etc. Such elementary material, coming originally from the grammars, had appeared in Bailey's various dictionaries
and in Dyche and Pardon; Martin, however, by following the arrangement of Ainsworth's *Thesaurus* gives it greater prominence in his work.

With such miscellaneous additions and the occasional enlargement
of an item, Martin completed his revision. The fact that so progressive
a work had so short a career is at first surprising but is to be accounted
for, no doubt, simply by the appearance of Johnson's dictionary. Ironically enough, the very similarity to Johnson, which constitutes Martin's
main claim to attention, proved his undoing, for Johnson so obviously
surpassed Martin on their common ground that no competition was
possible.

Chapter XX

A Pocket Dictionary (1753)

LITTLE NOTICE HAS BEEN TAKEN OF THE ANONYMOUS *Pocket Dictionary* of 1753, copies of which are exceedingly rare. Wheatley merely lists the work without analysis, Kennedy records only the first and second editions, and Long overlooks it.[1] This octavo dictionary is, however, far from negligible. While it introduces no innovations, it is intelligently planned to include the most progressive features of its rivals on the market; and it is calculated for a specified audience. That it suited this audience and performed a real service is evidenced by the fact that it achieved at least four editions.

The title-page reads as follows:

A Pocket Dictionary or Complete English Expositor:
Shewing Readily The Part of Speech to which each Word belongs; its true Meaning, when not self-evident; its various Senses, if more than one, placed in proper Order; and the Language, from whence it is deriv'd, pointed out immediately after the Explication.

Also The Technical Terms are clearly explain'd; every Word is so accented, that there can be no Uncertainty as to the Pronunciation;

And The Names of the Cities and Principal Towns, their Distance from London, their Market Days, and Fairs, according to the New Style, are alphabetically interspers'd; with other useful Articles.

To render this Book complete, many modern Words are introduc'd, which are not to be found in other Dictionaries; and to make it more concise and portable, such Words are omitted, as being neither properly English, nor ever used by good Authors, would only serve to mislead and embarrass the Learner.

A Work entirely new, and design'd for the Youth of both Sexes, the Ladies and Persons in Business.

To which is prefix'd An Introduction Containing an History of the English Language, with a compendious Grammar: And a Recommendation of the Manuscript Copy, In a Letter from Dr. Bevis to the Publisher. . . . London: . . . 1753.

An odd feature is the "Account of this Work, in a Letter from Dr. *Bevis* to the Bookseller," which appears in lieu of a preface by the author. This descriptive and commendatory letter, signed "J. Bevis" and dated September 5, 1752, is plausibly attributed to John Bevis, M.D., F.R.S., 1693-1771.[2] Professing to be "quite ignorant of the author and his name," Dr. Bevis obliges the bookseller with his candid opinion after a careful perusal of the work. As he points out the main features of the *Pocket Dictionary*, the bulk of his letter will be quoted. Most significant is the final paragraph, which offers the key to the whole design of the dictionary.

Mistakes as to the meaning of words must needs have a mischievous influence on those who set themselves upon acquiring a just knowledge of a language, and rely on a dictionary for their expositor. Your author, I find, has been very scrupulously accurate in restoring the genuine signification of a great number that had been misinterpreted by former writers; at the same time avoiding a fault some have fallen into, of explaining terms by others equally difficult, or by their synonyms: and where the same word has various significations, he has been careful to give them all in their proper order, beginning with the most obvious and general, and distinguishing them by 1, 2, 3, &c; but he has judiciously suppress'd the significative and metaphorical meanings, as too apt to mislead and perplex.

He has rejected all obsolete, bad, low and despicable words; the etymologies he has likewise omitted, being of no use to those who aim at English only; he has however indicated by an initial letter from what language the word is derived when it is not of our own growth, and he takes the same method to signify of what part of speech it is. Thus the size of the volume is considerably reduc'd, without parting with any thing of consequence.

He has been very exact in spelling and accenting; points essential to a just orthography and pronunciation.

And whereas our mother tongue has within half a century been much refined and changed, whether by discharging antiquated words, coining new ones, or adopting them from abroad; our author has kept up to these alterations, and inserted a great number of technical terms, which he has so explained as to render them intelligible even to those unacquainted with the arts to which they belong.

He has introduced here and there several articles, which though they are not of a philological kind, will yet be found of importance in the concerns of life; such as the names of all towns of note in England, their distances from London, and the days of their markets, and fairs...

To conclude, each of our later English dictionaries may be allowed to have some excellencies that are peculiarly its own: but there was still wanting one formed on such a plan as might unite and concentrate them all in a small compass, a thing the great Mr. Locke long ago recommended, and which, in my humble judgment, our author has happily executed in this his work; which if made public, cannot fail of being an inestimable benefit to the youth of this kingdom, and to others who have miss'd of a literary education.[3]

From the title-page and the description by Dr. Bevis two major points stand out. First, this dictionary is intended to assist "Youth," "Ladies," and "Persons in Business"—in general, all those "who have miss'd of a literary education." The author does not, however, regard his less educated audience as license for a hasty or careless performance. On the contrary, he assumes that these people, though less privileged, are interested and intelligent; and he applies himself seriously to removing all obstacles from their path and to supplying them with the best apparatus to make word knowledge accessible.

Secondly, the work is admittedly a composite. The compiler's first step was naturally to analyze the most recent successful dictionaries— Dyche and Pardon's *New General English Dictionary* (sixth edition, 1750, or seventh edition, 1752) and Martin's *Lingua Britannica Reformata* (1749)—with a view to incorporating into his own work their special features. Here he has shown good judgment. In etymology, indeed, he reverted to earlier models, since he believed it sufficient for his purpose merely to indicate the language from which each word was derived.[4] From Dyche and Pardon, however, he transferred the stress on grammar, orthography, and pronunciation and the useful geographical feature;[5] and from Martin, the divided and numbered definition. It appears, indeed, from the fact that the same bookseller sponsored both works that, from a commercial point of view, the *Pocket Dictionary* was an offshoot of the Martin enterprise.[6]

Besides Dr. Bevis' letter the prefatory matter offers "A Concise English Grammar; with A short Historical Account of the Genius and Progress of that Language." Here the compiler again shows discrimination in adapting the history of the language available in Bailey's *Universal Etymological English Dictionary*. He accepts Bailey's plan and data but omits a few points and adds others, and for the most part rephrases his original. Such parallel passages as the following make it certain, however, that Bailey was his source:

Bailey, *Universal . . . Dictionary*, 1751 Edition	*Pocket Dictionary*, 1753
So the *British* Language being in a manner quite extinct in all other Parts of *Britain*, the *Saxon* Language became the Language of the Country, and so continued 'till near the Year 800, when the *Danes* infested *England*, and made Settlements in the *North* and *East* Parts of *Britain*, and at length, in about 200 Years, arrived at the sole Government of it; but their Government lasting only about 26 Years, made not so considerable a Change in the *English Saxon*, as the next Revolution. Then about the Year 1067, *William* Duke of *Normandy*, commonly called *William the Conqueror*, came over to *Britain*; and, having vanquished *Harold* the *Danish* King, made an entire Conquest of *Britain*: And as a Monument of their Conquest, the *Normans* endeavoured to yoke the *English* under their Tongue, as they had them under their Command, . . .	In this situation England continued till about the year 800, when it was invaded by the Danes, who after being several times repulsed, established themselves in the northern and eastern parts, where their power increasing, they at length, after a contest of two hundred years, made themselves the sole masters of England; and by this means the language became tinctured with the Danish: but as their government was of no long duration, it did not make so great an alteration in the Anglo-Saxon, as the next revolution, when the whole was again subdued by William duke of Normandy, afterwards called William the Conqueror; for the Normans, as a monument of their conquest, endeavoured to make their language as universally received as possible.

The grammatical section of the introduction also shows little verbal borrowing but adopts the Dyche and Pardon system with four parts of speech and has the same scope, topics, and general arrangement as their "Compendious English Grammar." The author here simplifies and condenses the discussion, clarifies the definitions, and inserts his own examples. He also adds a few practical hints such as the following:

As some are apt to mistake the use of *shall* and *will*, the signs of the future tense, it must be observed that when we only simply foretell, we use *shall* in the first person, and *will* in the rest; but when we promise, threaten or engage, we use *will* in the first person, and *shall* in the others.

The word list, consisting of about 18,500 items, is similarly composite. We may picture the compiler at work with Bailey's *Universal Etymological English Dictionary*, Dyche and Pardon, and Martin spread out before him and with his audience constantly in mind. From Bailey he extracts many definitions, especially of scientific terms; in such entries Martin's treatment was longer and more technical, but Bailey provided the essential data:

BAILEY, *Universal . . . Dictionary,* 1751 Edition	*Pocket Dictionary,* 1753
Ori'on (. . .) a Southern Constellation, consisting of 39 Stars.	*O'rion,* (S.) A southern constellation, consisting of 39 stars.
Or'rery, an Astronomical Machine for giving a clearer Account of the Solar System.	*O'rrery,* (S.) A curious instrument, invented to give a clear account of the solar system.
Orthog'onal (. . .) right-angled.	*Ortho'gonal,* (A.) Right-angled.
Orts (. . .) Fragments, Leavings, Mammocks.	*Orts,* (S.) Fragments, leavings.
Oscilla'tion, a swinging up and down; also a Vibration like the Pendulum of a Clock.	*Oscilla'tion,* (S.) A vibration like the pendulum of a clock.
Osteocol'la (. . .) the Glew-bone Stone; a soft Stone said to be of great Virtue for the uniting of broken Bones.	*Osteoco'lla,* (S.) A soft stone, said to be of great virtue in uniting broken bones.

From Martin comes the bulk of the definitions, especially those of ordinary words. Here the compiler chooses certain senses and sometimes varies the order but carefully retains Martin's system:

MARTIN, 1749	*Pocket Dictionary,* 1753
To *Keep,* 1 to take care of, or preserve. 2 to stay, or abide. 3 to last, or endure. 4 to lay up, or reserve. 5 to observe, or not break. 6 to abstain from. 7 to conceal, or hide from. 8 to nourish, or provide for. 9 to celebrate, or solemnize.	*Keep,* (V.) 1. To retain, 2. To nourish, or provide for, 3. To last or endure, 4. To observe, 5. To stay or abide. —

MARTIN, 1749

10 to continue, or to live. 11 to perform, or stand to.

Ke'rnel, 1 the seeds of an apple. 2 the
eatable part of nuts, almonds, &c. 3 a
fleshy, and porous substance in the body.
4 the best part of a thing.

Key, 1 an instrument to open a lock. 2
the middle stone of an arch. 3 a wharf
for landing or shipping off goods. 4 a
small piece of iron to go through the eye
of a bolt, or pin to fasten it. 5 an explication of persons or things contained
in a book. 6 (in the plural number) the
horizontal rows of small pieces of wood,
or ivory, or both, of an organ, harpsi-
chord, &c.
Key (in Music) a certain tune, . . .

Ki'ndle, 1 to set on fire, both in a proper
and figurative sense. 2 to take fire. 3 to
bring forth young, as an hare, or rabbit.

Pocket Dictionary, 1753

Ke'rnel, (S.) 1. The eatable part of nuts,
2. A porous substance under the skin.

Key, (S.) 1. An instrument to open a
lock, 2. The middle stone of an arch,
3. An iron to go through the eye of a
bolt, pin, &c. 4. An explication of persons or things in a book, 5. A wharf, 6. A
tone in musick.

Ki'ndle, (V.) 1. To set on fire, 2. To
take fire, 3. To bring forth young, especially rabbets.

Relatively few items come from Dyche and Pardon. While these
items, often dealing with mythology, are leisurely and detailed in the
original, the compiler usually takes only a brief identification for his
Pocket Dictionary.

DYCHE AND PARDON, 1750 Edition

Ops (S.) one of the names of the goddess *Cybele.*

Os (S.) in *Anatomy,* is any sort of bone,
. . .

Oscopho'ria (S.) a feast celebrated by the
Athenians the 10th day of *October,* in
honour of *Bacchus* and *Ariadne;* . . .
O'siris (S.) a famous god of the *Egyptians,* . . .

O'sprey or *O'ssifrage* (S.) a sort or kind
of an eagle, . . . It is thus called, because
it breaks the bones of animals, in order to
get at the marrow; . . .

Pocket Dictionary, 1753

Ops, (S.) One of the names of the goddess Cybele.

Os, (S.) In Anatomy, a bone.

Oscopho'ria, (S.) A feast celebrated by
the Athenians on the 10th of August, in
honour of Bacchus and Ariadne.
O'siris, (S.) A famous god of the Egyptians.

O'sprey, or *O'ssifrage,* (S.) A kind of
eagle that breaks the bones of his prey.

A more considerable debt is owed Dyche and Pardon for the numerous entries on English towns; [7] here again the compiler practices abridgment and limits himself to the essential facts presented in businesslike style.

DYCHE and PARDON, 1750 Edition

Pocket Dictionary, 1753

Ki'ngsbridge (S.) in *Devonshire*, which, although it be but a mean town, yet it has a good market weekly on Saturdays; distant from *London* 170 computed, and 202 measured miles.

Ki'ngsbridge, (S.) A mean town in Devonshire, 202 miles from London, with a market on Saturdays.

Kingscle're (S.) a pleasant town in *Hampshire*, seated in the wood-lands, was famous formerly for being the seat of the *Saxon* kings; its market is weekly on Tuesday; distant from *London* 45 computed, and 52 measured miles.

Kingscle're, (S.) A town in Hampshire, 52 miles from London, with a market on Tuesdays.

Ki'ngston upon Thames (S.) (over which it hath a large bridge) in the county of *Surrey*, is a large, well-built, pleasant, and ancient corporate-town, whose market is weekly on Saturday; the summer assizes for the county are usually held here; it was formerly noted for being the place where the *British* and *Saxon* kings were crowned; distant from *London* 10 computed, and 12 measured miles.

Ki'ngston upon Thames, (S.) A large town in Surrey, whose market is on Saturdays; distant 12 miles from London.

The second edition of the *Pocket Dictionary*, "greatly improved," appeared in 1758. There was no change in the prefatory matter, but the vocabulary was expanded in two ways. To the definitions originally carried further senses were often added; and about 6,500 new items were inserted, to make a total vocabulary of about 25,000 words. The reviser, like the original compiler, did his work well and abridged definitions from the best dictionary then available. He has, in fact, derived both the new items and the enlargement of the original items from Johnson's *Dictionary* as issued in two octavo volumes in 1756.[8] The following are definitions of items added in 1758 with their parallels in Johnson:

JOHNSON, 1756 Edition

Abandoned. part. ad.
1 Given up. *Shakesp.*
2 Forsaken.
3 Corrupted in the highest degree.

Abasement. s. The state of being brought low; depression. *Ecclesiasticus.*

Abb. s. The yarn on a weaver's warp; among clothiers. *Chambers.*

Abbreviature. s. (...)
1 A mark used for the sake of shortening.
2 A compendium or abridgement. *Taylor.*

Aberrance. s. A deviation from the right way; an errour. *Glanville.*

Abhorrent. a. (...)
1. Struck with abhorrence.
2 Contrary to, foreign, inconsistent with. *Dryden.*

Above. prep. (...)
1 Higher in place. *Dryden.*
2 More in quantity or number. *Exod.*
3 Higher in rank, power or excellence. *Psalm.*
4 Superiour to; unattainable by. *Swift.*
5 Beyond; more than. *Locke.*
6 Too proud for; too high for. *Pope.*

Above. ad.
1 Over head. *Bacon.*
2 In the regions of heaven. *Pope.*
3 Before. *Dryd.*

From above.
1 From an higher place. *Dryd.*
2 From heaven. *James.*

Pocket Dictionary, 1758 Edition

Aba'ndoned, (A.) 1. Forsaken, 2. Given up, 3. Wicked in the highest degree.

Aba'sement, (S.) A being brought low; depression.

Abb, (S.) The yarn on a weaver's warp, among clothiers.

Abbre'viature, (S.) 1. A mark used for shortening, 2. A compendium or abridgement.

Abe'rrance, (S.) An error, a deviation from the right way.

Abho'rrent, (A.) 1. Struck with abhorrence, 2. Contrary to, foreign, inconsistent with.

Above, (P.), 1. Higher in place, over head, 2. More in number or quantity, 3. Higher in rank, power, excellence, 4. Too high for, too proud for, 5. In the regions of heaven, 6. *From above,* from a higher place, from heaven.

Although the *Pocket Dictionary* was issued for a third time in 1765 and a fourth time in 1779, it was not further revised.[9]

Chapter XXI

[JOHN WESLEY'S]

The Complete English Dictionary (1753)

J OHN WESLEY's *Complete English Dictionary*, A DAINTY BOOK WITH a minute vocabulary, impresses one at first as a surprising rever- sion to a long outmoded type. It lacks all the departments which had been developed in the course of a century and a half of experimentation in lexicography; [1] and it even describes itself as a col- lection of "hard words"—a type characteristic of the early seventeenth century and long since replaced by a more flexible and inclusive concept of a dictionary. On further examination, however, it becomes apparent that this little work possesses real individuality and that its retrogressive character is purposeful.

The title-page with its simplicity and brevity contrasts oddly with the elaborately planned and formally phrased title-pages of Martin's and other contemporary dictionaries. The ironic title and the facetious expression also arouse our interest:

> The Complete English Dictionary, Explaining most of those Hard Words, Which are found in the Best English Writers.
> By a Lover of Good English and Common Sense.
> N.B. The author assures you that he thinks this is the best English Dictionary in the World.
>
> London:... 1753.

Wesley's name, as has no doubt been observed, did not appear on the title-page of this edition; nor was it added in the later known editions. There seems, however, never to have been any doubt as to his authorship of the work.[2]

The address to the reader is equally droll in manner. It accomplishes some good-natured satire and at the same time reflects the wry amusement of the preacher at being obliged to turn off a dictionary amid the multifarious tasks which devolved upon him or which he conscientiously assumed. Beneath the veneer of levity, however, lies a deep seriousness, for Wesley is here the earnest teacher; he is striving to make knowledge as attractive, easy, and accessible as possible. Indeed, as Louis B. Wright points out, "Throughout Wesley's long life, he was scarcely more concerned over the souls than over the minds of his followers in Britain and America." [3] Besides a light manner and a serious purpose, the address reveals sureness of design, for Wesley rules out various classes of words with a sternness approaching dogmatism. In order to convey the inimitable flavor of the original, we quote the address in full:

As incredible as it may appear, I must avow, that this dictionary is not published to get money, but to assist persons of common sense and no learning, to understand the best *English* authors: and that, with as little expence of either time or money, as the nature of the thing would allow.

To this end it contains, not a heap of *Greek* and *Latin* words, just tagged with *English* terminations: (for no good *English* writer, none but vain or senseless pedants, give these any place in their writings:) not a scroll of barbarous *law expressions*, which are neither *Greek*, *Latin*, nor good *English*: not a croud of *technical* terms, the meaning whereof is to be sought in books expresly wrote on the subjects to which they belong: not such *English* words as *and, of, but;* which stand so gravely in Mr. *Bailey's, Pardon's,* and *Martin's* dictionaries: but 'most of those hard words which are found in the best *English* writers.' I say, *most;* for I purposely omit not only all which are not hard, and which are not found in the best writers: not only all law-words and most technical terms, but likewise all, the meaning of which may be easily gathered from those of the same derivation. And this I have done, in order to make this dictionary both as short and as cheap as possible.

I should add no more, but that I have so often observed, the only way, according to the modern taste, for any author to procure commendation to his book is, vehemently to commend it himself. For want of this deference to the publick, several excellent tracts lately printed, but left to commend themselves by their intrinsic worth, are utterly unknown or forgotten. Whereas if a writer of tolerable sense will but bestow a few violent encomiums on his own work, especially if they are skilfully ranged in the title-page, it will pass thro' six editions in a trice; the world being too complaisant to give a gentleman the Lie, and taking it for granted, he understands his own performance best.

In compliance therefore with the taste of the age, I add, that this little dictionary is not only the shortest and the cheapest, but likewise, by many degrees, the most correct which is extant at this day. Many are the mistakes in all the other *English* dictionaries which I have yet seen. Whereas I can truly say, I know of none in this; and I conceive the reader will believe me: for if I had, I should not have left it there. Use then this help, till you find a better.

Since this dictionary is obviously a by-product of Wesley's career and ideals rather than the lineal descendant of its predecessors, it will be necessary here to trace the circumstances which led to its compilation. Wesley was himself an Oxford scholar with a genuine love of learning and literature. When he embarked on his chosen career, he devoted himself all the more ardently to the study of language and literature, for he saw daily proof of the power of the spoken and the written word. He dropped the academic manner for simple earnestness and advised his followers to do the same. Most characteristic is his letter to the Reverend Samuel Furly on the subject of "a good style":

"What is it that constitutes *a good style?*" Perspicuity and purity, propriety, strength, and easiness, joined together. Where any one of these is wanting, it is not a good style. Dr. Middleton's style wants easiness; it is *stiff* to an high degree.... "It is pedantry," says the great Lord Boyle, "to use an hard word where an easier will serve." Now, this the Doctor continually does, and that of set purpose.... *Artis est celare artem;* but his art glares in every sentence.... Here [Pope's "Elegy to Memory"] is style! How clear, how pure, proper, strong! and yet how amazingly easy! This crowns all; no stiffness, no hard words; no *apparent* art, no affectation; all is natural, and therefore consummately beautiful. Go thou and *write* likewise.

As for me, I never think of my style at all; but just set down the words that come first. Only when I transcribe anything for the press, then I think it my duty to see every phrase be clear, pure, and proper. Conciseness (which is now, as it were, natural to me) brings *quantum sufficit* of strength. If, after all, I observe any stiff expression, I throw it out, neck and shoulders.

Clearness in particular is necessary for you and me, because we are to instruct people of the lowest understanding. Therefore we, above all, if we think with the wise, yet must speak with the vulgar. We should constantly use the most common, little, easy words (so they are pure and proper) which our language affords. When I had been a member of the University about ten years, I wrote and talked much as you do now. But when I talked to plain people in the Castle or the town, I observed they gaped and stared. This quickly obliged me to alter my style and adopt the language of those I spoke to. And yet there is a dignity in this simplicity, which is not disagreeable to those of the highest rank.[4]

Wesley also exhorted his preachers to continue their studies; even when they were on the road they were required to carry books always in their saddle-bags and to read at least five hours a day.[5]

So convinced was Wesley of the importance of education for his followers that he undertook an ambitious educational program for their benefit. Not content with his labors at the Kingswood School, Wesley soon found himself in the position of literary dictator to the humbler classes.[6] For his school he had provided grammars of five languages; and he also produced in rapid succession such ambitious works as: *The Concise Ecclesiastical History, The Concise History of England, A Survey of the Wisdom of God in the Creation or a Compendium of Natural Philosophy*, and a *Collection of Moral and Sacred Poems*. The culminating achievement came in 1749-1755 with the publication of the fifty volumes of the *Christian Library: Consisting of Extracts from, and Abridgements of, the Choicest Pieces of Practical Divinity which have been published in the English Tongue*. Then, after Wesley had painstakingly extracted, summarized, and annotated for years and had supervised the printing of his compilations in cheap editions, came the grim realization that his work was still over the heads of his followers and that they needed simple reading aids. Wesley then undertook to prepare his dictionary for the express and immediate purpose of making the *Christian Library* and his other compilations comprehensible to the common people. An appreciation of these facts is the only valid approach to Wesley's dictionary.[7]

It is therefore unfair to expect too much of this little work. It was intended to be carried in the pocket and to give when consulted a brief explanation of difficult words; it was not intended to compete with current dictionaries or to offer a wealth of background or supplementary learning as they did. Hence Wheatley's criticism, for example, seems harsh and misguided:

We cannot agree with the compiler in the estimation of his book. There is no explanation of the origin of the words, and the definitions are usually neither very clear nor very correct. It is rather too bad to have a hard word explained by a harder one—as in this instance, "An abscess, an imposthume." ... The following entry is not very explicit from a Natural History point of view—"An ortolan, a very dear bird"; and the reader who came upon some allusion to the changing hue of the chameleon, would not be much enlightened by the following: "A chameleon, a kind of lizard, living on flies." [8]

The vocabulary, including only about 4600 words, is the smallest of all we have considered except that of Cawdrey, the first English lexicographer. Regularly a single form of a word only is given. Accent is indicated, but there are no annotations as to etymology or usage. Definitions are brief—in fact, they rarely exceed a line; but, although too casual from a lexicographical point of view, they are usually adequate for their modest purpose.[9] There are only a few proper names, and specialized terms are usually excluded as promised.

While Wesley shows his familiarity with current dictionaries in his address to the reader and while he probably had his favorites available for consultation, there is no conspicuous debt to any one source. In fact, so frankly does the vocabulary reflect Wesley's personal preoccupations that it seems likely that he chose the unusual procedure of drawing up his word list independently. We can discern, for example, a large group of terms connected with religion. Such definitions as the following are often quoted for their special interest:

Calvinists, they that hold absolute, unconditional Predestination.
Catholick spirit, universal love.
Conversion, a thorough change of heart and life from sin to holiness; a turning.
Deism, infidelity, denying the Bible.
The *Elect,* all that truly believe in Christ.
Enthusiasm, religious madness, fancied inspiration.
Jansenism, nearly the same as Calvinism.
A *Latitudinarian,* one that fancies all religions are saving.
Methodist, one that lives according to the method laid down in the Bible.
The *Millennium,* the thousand years during which Christ will reign upon earth.
Presbyterians, they who believe the ancient bishops and priests were of one and the same order.

Purgatory, a place where the papists fancy departed souls are purged by fire.

A *Puritan,* an old strict Church of England man.

Quietists, who place all religion in waiting quietly on God.

Socinians, men who say Christ was a mere man; Arians held him to be a little God.

A *Swaddler,* a nick-name given by the papists in Ireland to true protestants.

Another large body of words deals with anatomy and medicine; [10] here we find some specialized terms, but the majority of the items are such as might, unfortunately, be encountered in the ordinary experience of the time. In this connection, we recall Wesley's constant concern for the health of his followers and his work, *A Primitive Physick: or an Easy and Natural Method of Curing most Diseases,* published in 1747 and reissued twenty-four times within the century. Also conspicuous are musical terms, reflecting another personal interest,[11] and French words or phrases such as might conceivably be found in ordinary reading: *Alamode, Belles Lettres, Billet-Doux, Boutefeu, Carte-Blanche, Eclaircissement, Eclat, Gout, Jet d'Eau, Maugre, Valet de Chambre,* etc. A smaller group of colloquial, slang, and dialectal expressions seems out of keeping with the purpose of the dictionary. Perhaps, however, by such entries Wesley intended to fit his itinerant preachers for understanding the speech of their illiterate and rustic followers. A few representative entries may be cited:

A *Beck,* a little brook.

To *Bilk,* to cheat.

A *Buss,* a kind of fishing boat.

Chuffy, rough, clownish, surly.

Crump, hump backed.

A *Cully,* one that is apt to be made a fool of.

A *Mope,* a stupid, heavy person.

To *Scruse,* to squeeze, or press hard.

As for Wesley's "hard words," it becomes apparent that he uses this term in its literal rather than its traditional sense. He has, to be sure, a scattering of elegant expressions of Latin and Greek origin; [12] most of his words are, however, as the address led us to expect, well established in the language but above the level of a person who has had little school learning and has not been accustomed to reading. Wesley is not concerned with elegance; he is thinking only of comprehension.

The following consecutive entries will demonstrate both the nature of the vocabulary and the method of definition:

> The *Galaxy*, the milky way.
> A *Galeon*, a large ship.
> A *Galley*, a ship with oars.
> A *Gallicism*, a way of speaking peculiar to the French tongue.
> To *Gambol*, to dance, skip, frisk.
> The *Gamut*, the scale of musick.
> A *Gangrene*, the beginning of a mortification.
> A *Gantlet*, an iron glove.
> A *Garb*, a dress.
> *Garboil*, trouble, tumult, uproar.
> A *Garner*, a store-house.
> To *Garnish*, to furnish, to adorn.
> *Garrulity*, talkativeness.
> A *Garth*, a yard.
> A *Gasconade*, a bravado, cracking, boasting.
> *Gauging*, the art of finding how much any vessel contains.
> *Gaunt*, lean, thin.
> A *Gavot*, a brisk dance, or air.

The second edition of Wesley's dictionary, published in Bristol in 1764, was slightly enlarged by the following method:

> In this Edition I have added some hundreds of words, which were omitted in the former: chiefly from Mr. *Johnson's* dictionary, which I carefully looked over for that purpose. And I will now venture to affirm, that, small as it is, this dictionary is quite sufficient, for enabling any one to understand the best Writings now extant, in the English tongue.[13]

There were, however, probably fewer than three hundred additions; and the definitions were so simplified that the Johnsonian flavor was lost in the process.

While the dates and editions of this work have been badly garbled, the Reverend Richard Green, the most reliable authority, mentions two later editions. The third edition, printed by R. Hawes in London in 1777,[14] was a reprint of the second.[15] Probably no further revision occurred; but another edition "miscalled second" was printed and sold at the New Chapel on City Road in 1790.[16] It is perhaps the most eloquent proof of the practical value of this work that its users wore out their copies and left us so few to study.[17]

Chapter XXII

THE SCOTT-BAILEY

A New Universal Etymological English Dictionary (1755)

AND RETROSPECT

IN 1755, THIRTEEN YEARS AFTER THE DEATH OF NATHAN BAILEY, its main author, the largest, finest, and last of the Bailey dictionaries appeared; this folio, entitled *A New Universal Etymological English Dictionary*, came out under the nominal editorship of Joseph Nicol Scott. Both the circumstances of publication and the make-up of the work indicate, however, that this dictionary was designed as a booksellers' measure to hold the market against that redoubtable newcomer in lexicography, Samuel Johnson. Except for contributing the preface, correcting the etymology of classical and Oriental terms, and revising some medical and religious items, Scott probably did little but lend his name and prestige to the enterprise.

Joseph Nicol Scott (1703?-1769) makes a sufficiently imposing editor for title-page and advertising purposes. A public figure with an unusual range of interests, he possessed considerable learning in religion and science as well as a taste for linguistics. He had begun life as an assistant to his father, a clergyman, but had been dismissed in 1737-1738 because of an increasing tendency to Arianism. Although he continued to attract large audiences by his eloquence and striking views, he later turned to medicine, obtaining his M. D. at Edinburgh in 1744 and thereafter practicing in Norwich. Besides numerous sermons, he published in 1755 *An Essay toward a Translation of Homer's Works in Blank Verse, with Notes.*[1]

The title-page of the dictionary is here quoted almost in entirety:

A New Universal Etymological English Dictionary:
Containing not only Explanations of the Words in the English Language;

And the Different Senses in which they are used; With Authorities from the Best Writers, to support those which appear Doubtful;

But Also Their Etymologies from the Ancient and Modern Languages: And Accents directing to their Proper Pronunciation; Shewing both the Orthography and Orthoepia of the English Tongue.

Also, Full and Accurate Explanations of the Various Terms made use of in the several Arts, Sciences, Manufactures, and Trades. Illustrated with Copper-Plates.

Originally compiled by N. Bailey.

Assisted in the Mathematical Part by G. Gordon; in the Botanical by P. Miller; and in the Etymological, &c. by T. Lediard, Gent. Professor of the Modern Languages in Lower Germany.

And now Re-published with many Corrections, Additions, and Literate Improvements, by Different Hands. The Etymology of all Terms mentioned as derived from the Greek, Hebrew, Arabic, and other Asiatic Languages, being Revised and Corrected By Joseph Nicol Scott, M. D.

London:... MDCCLV.[2]

In his Preface Scott takes the point of view of a clergyman and promises a more competent, original, and inclusive treatment of religious topics than had been previously given in a general dictionary. "As *Words* are the Medium ... thro' which we come at TRUTH," he says, they are not only of "great importance in every Art and Science but perhaps nowhere of more Consequence than under *Revealed* Religion: Because here a certain BOOK is admitted for a *Rule* or *Standard* both of Faith and Worship." Accordingly this dictionary offers:

Not a mere Enquiry into the *Origin*, and *Signification* of Words; but an Enquiry so circumstanced, as to include many a useful Hint, and Remark, whether of the Historic, Poetic, Philosophic, Rhetoric, or Theologic Kind; and this not merely in Relation to the *various* Shapes and Forms, which the Christian Profession has assumed; but comprehending many Things with Reference to the *Jewish*, the *Chinese*, the *Magian*, the *Mahometan*, and other Religious Systems.

Admitting that " 'tis not unusual for Lexicographers to borrow from one another," Scott protests that "we [those responsible for the work] are not mere *Copyists* from others; ... Not taking Things upon Trust, as is too often done; but having traced them up to the *Fountain-Head*; ..." Maintaining his religious approach, Scott continues:

... a Rule which has been more especially observed in Subjects of the *highest Moment, i.e.* where any Branch of Religion, whether *Natural* or *Revealed,* is concerned; for each of which we have endeavoured to secure their respective *Rights* and *Honours;* and hope the Friends of either will find themselves alike well pleased: Not to observe, what (if duly attended to) may possibly have its Use with both, *viz.* That when describing the *Rise* or *Fall* of the most celebrated States and Empires, we have, from Sir *Isaac Newton,* and other judicious Writers, pointed out those *ancient Scriptural Prophecies,* which seem to have been *fulfilled* in these Revolutions.

Scott then pauses to refute two objections that may be raised against the work: "that in some Things we have left the *beaten* Road" and "that we have retained many of our *English* Words, that are now almost entirely out of Use." He defends the supposed radicalism in the first instance by claiming that through the study of the best sources he and his collaborators have been enabled to correct many errors in his predecessors and to set forth new truths. He defends the supposed conservatism in the second instance by arguing that obsolete terms help us to understand "our *old* Authors, who are not yet absolutely laid aside" and by asserting that in any case some of these expressions "are *too good* . . . to be lost; whether for their *Force* and *Energy* in point of Sense, or their *Felicity* with Reference to *Measure* and *Sound.*" This remark is of interest as showing the lexicographer trying in a small way to direct the flow of the language; the illustrations given are, however, few and unconvincing.[3]

Scott comments on style with perhaps a malicious glance in Johnson's direction:

As to our Style, we have chosen the plain and unadorned; as best suiting Works of this Nature; and indeed the *florid* Diction is an artifice too often used to cover a *poverty* of Thought.... Whereas our chief Ambition has been to advance the Truth; and not to amuse our Readers with *historic Romance,* and *scholastic Jargon;* ...

The Preface concludes with a specific acknowledgment of indebtedness. As most of the sources mentioned had, however, been used earlier in the compilation of the *Dictionarium Britannicum,* the most significant remarks are those concerning recent authorities especially consulted for this work—notably Johnson and the author of the *Appendix ad The-saurum H. Stephani.*

What remains is, to do Justice to some *previous* Writers, from whom we have taken (as is not unusual in Works of this Sort) many Things. And here we confess ourselves to be much indebted to *Jacob* and *Cowel*, for Law; to *Miller*, for Plants; to *Hill*, for Fossils and other Branches of Natural Philosophy; much also to *Boerhaave*, *Galen*, *Hippocrates*, *Bruno*, *Gorraeus*, *Keill*, and other Physicians, whether *ancient*, or *modern*, in Things relative to the Portraiture of *Diseases*, and Structure of the human body. In particular to the elaborate Mr. *Johnson*, for the different Acceptation of Words in *English* Writers; tho' in *Justice to ourselves*, it should be observed, that we have inserted in this Collection several Hundreds of Words, that are not to be found in him. And as to those Terms that are adopted from the *learned* Languages, we must refer to *Buxtorf*, *Golius*, *Pocock*, *Taylor's Hebrew Concordance*, *Hesychius*, and others; joined with what *personal Acquaintance* the Author of the late Essay on Homer professes to have with those Tongues, for which he stood engaged; . . .

But after all, there is another Writer who has deserved much of the *learned* World, and should not be overlooked by us, as being one whom we have had frequent Occasion to quote; we mean the Author of the *Appendix ad Thesaurum H. Stephani, Constantini, Scapulae,* &c. who has not only published, in two Folios of a most correct Edition, several Thousands of *Greek* Words, supported by their *proper Authorities;* which Authorities the preceding *Lexicographers* had omitted: but has also thrown in about 15000 Words more, which *H. Stephanus*, and the rest had absolutely overlooked; . . .[4]

The circumstances behind the publication of this work, disclosed by Philip B. Gove in a recent article,[5] are of interest as revealing from a business point of view some curious links between the Johnson and the Scott-Bailey enterprises. Gove describes the parallel advertising campaigns conducted in *Jackson's Oxford Journal* in 1755 for the Scott-Bailey (1755) and for the second edition of Johnson's dictionary (1755-1756), both of which were published serially. The advertisement for the Scott-Bailey stresses (1) multiple authorship—besides Bailey, the mathematician Gordon, the botanist Miller, the etymologist Lediard, and the versatile Scott are mentioned; (2) convenience and cheapness—the Scott-Bailey is in a single volume and costs only half as much as Johnson's two "elegantly printed" volumes; and (3) novelty—the Scott-

Bailey is illustrated with full-page copper plates.[6] What lends piquancy to the situation is the fact that the Scott-Bailey volume in the course of its serial publication was calmly incorporating the best features of Johnson while retaining the specialties of the *Dictionarium Britannicum*. Gove writes:

The introductory "Historical Account of the English Language" is "new" in the sense that it owes little to any previous edition of Bailey, but it copies, paraphrases, and reworks Johnson's "History" with the indebtedness of a servile but dully alert mind, too imitative to plan a reorganization of material that must after all cover the same ground, yet a mind active enough to draw occasionally upon its own background. To be charitable, one may say it is modelled on Johnson. The succeeding article on grammar, however, remains too close to be called anything but downright copying, with alterations. . . . The principal differences in this part of the two dictionaries can be explained as differences in length. Where Johnson requires over four columns for the verb, the other disposes of it in a little over one. Johnson's thirteen-page "Grammar of the English Tongue" is condensed in Bailey to a five-and-one-half page "Compendious Grammar." [7]

Although Gove is correct in his accusations, his indignation is perhaps misplaced. He treats plagiarism in lexicography as sternly as he would plagiarism in literature, and he takes the modern rather than the historical point of view. Actually, much as we may wish to overlook the fact, three unsavory corollaries are implied in the foregoing sketch of the development of the English dictionary: (1) in this early period lexicography progressed by plagiarism; (2) the best lexicographer was often the most discriminating plagiarist; and (3) a good dictionary was its own justification, whatever the method of compilation.

As to the word list, Gove comments truly: "A glance at any page of Bailey will reveal that line after line is rankly plagiarized from Johnson." [8] Gove further charges the compilers of the Scott-Bailey with laziness in copying, as "definitions became more and more sketchy, and the illustrative quotations almost disappeared as the work approached conclusion, . . ." [9] Even the vaunted plates, twelve in all, are, according to Gove, unwisely planned and placed, poorly explained, and inadequately connected with the definitions they were designed to elucidate.[10] Finally, in reference to the subsequent rivalry between the two dictionaries, Gove writes:

The attempt of the Bailey proprietors to enter a folio to rival Johnson's great *Dictionary* remained alive through 1772, three years after Scott's death. The dates of the new title-pages, 1764 and 1772, precede respectively by one year those of the third and fourth editions of Johnson. Perhaps the Bailey proprietors learned that new editions of Johnson were contemplated; or perhaps they discovered that copies available in the booksellers' hands were nearly exhausted. It does not matter. Although the Bailey-Scott *Dictionary* owes its principal merit largely to Johnson's involuntary contribution, it persevered in competition against the superiority of Johnson's own *Dictionary* primarily because it took the proprietors seventeen years to dispose of the sheets hopefully printed in 1755.[11]

And here the case for Johnson rests!

We have no desire to deny the superiority of Johnson's dictionary or to act as counsels for the defense of the Scott-Bailey. These dictionaries had fundamentally different purposes and attracted different readers. Johnson, apparently disappointed by the reception of his work, touched the crux of the matter when he wrote:

Having been long employed in the study and cultivation of the English language, I lately published a dictionary like those compiled by the academies of Italy and France, for the use of such as aspire to exactness of criticism or elegance of style.

But it has been since considered that works of that kind are by no means necessary to the greater number of readers, who, seldom intending to write or presuming to judge, turn over books only to amuse their leisure, and to gain degrees of knowledge suitable to lower characters, or necessary to the common business of life: these know not any other use of a dictionary than that of adjusting orthography, or explaining terms of science or words of infrequent occurrence, or remote derivation.[12]

It should be pointed out, however, that three facts receive insufficient attention in Gove's study: 1. that Johnson owed Bailey's *Dictionarium Britannicum* a considerable debt, which he duly acknowledged; 2. that the compilers of the Scott-Bailey also acknowledged their borrowing from Johnson in a manner that was then probably considered adequate; [13] and 3. that the Scott-Bailey contains much material that was not derived from and is not paralleled in Johnson. The Scott-Bailey folio is thus not simply nor merely a plagiarized work.

Turning now to the vocabularies of the rival dictionaries, we approach

with great diffidence the question of their relative size. It has been estimated above that Bailey's *Dictionarium Britannicum,* which Johnson
used as a repository for his items, contained about 48,000 words in the
1730 edition and about 60,000 in the 1736 edition.[14] Johnson was, however, primarily concerned with definition and illustration rather than
with size of vocabulary and was, of course, disposed to be exclusive
rather than inclusive. He therefore freely rejected items in the *Dictionarium Britannicum* with the result that his dictionary probably contains about 40,000 words as compared to about 65,000 in the Scott-Bailey.
Large classes of words unrepresented or sparingly represented in the
Johnson dictionary but featured in the Scott-Bailey are obsolete terms,
proper names, and such highly specialized scientific, religious, and other
terms as seemed to Johnson more suitable for treatment in an encyclopedia.[15] P. W. Long seizes the fundamental difference between the two
vocabularies when he writes:

. . . a page by page comparison [of Johnson] with Bailey reveals discrepancies
in large measure analogous to the contrast between the Oxford English
Dictionary and the Century Dictionary,—notably in the omission of scientific
terms, proper names, alien words, encyclopedic matter, etc., with corresponding fullness in the treatment of words strictly English and in good use. Thus
we find in Bailey and not in Johnson, *Aach, Aw, Abacus, abacot, Abaddon,
abandum* (law), *abaptiston, Abbasides.* But Johnson is incomparably superior
for *abandon.* Here a definite selective principle was at work, and the type of
dictionary sought after was a dictionary, not of hard words, or of elementary
words, or of all words,—but of words fitted to live.[16]

One may here comment in passing on the typographical feat of the
printers of the Scott-Bailey in compressing this huge compilation into
a single volume. The two volumes of Johnson with their readable print
and their pleasing spacing are, of course, much more agreeable to consult; but by means of minute print and crowded pages the Scott-Bailey
actually offers a larger vocabulary in a single volume. This compression
was necessarily achieved at a sacrifice. The compilers had already cut
Johnson's copious quotations to a minimum both in number and in
words, and the printers took further liberties in omitting both authorities and quotations as the work progressed and they felt increasingly
pressed for space. It should, however, be credited to the good judgment
of the compilers of the Scott-Bailey that such scanting was permitted

only in the quotations. Johnson's excellent definitions were fully appreciated, and only in exceptional instances has the Scott-Bailey dropped any of the meanings which Johnson so carefully distinguished.

The method of compiling the vocabulary of the Scott-Bailey and the nature of that vocabulary may be most clearly presented by a study of parallel sections in the various dictionaries concerned. It will be observed from the chart which follows that Johnson omits several of the words treated in the *Dictionarium Britannicum* and that he adds a few. The Scott-Bailey retains all items carried in the *Dictionarium Britannicum*, adds those contributed by Johnson, and supplies some further items—usually proper names.

Dictionarium Britannicum		JOHNSON	SCOTT-BAILEY
1730 Edition	1736 Edition	First Edition, 1755	1755
Dancette			
(heraldry)	——	omits	shortens
Danche			
(heraldry)	——	omits	——
		Dancing master	Johnson's definition
		Dancing school	Johnson's definition
Dandelion . . .			
an herb well			
known.	——	new definition	Johnson's definition
Dandeprat	——	Bailey's definition	——
To *Dandle*	——	new definition	Johnson's definition
		Dandler	Johnson's definition
Dandriff	——	definition enlarged	——
Dane Geld	——	omits	——
Dane Lage	——	omits	——
Dane Wort	——	definition enlarged	Johnson's definition
Danger	enlarged	definition shortened	shortened from 1736
Dangerium . . .			
a payment of			
money	——	omits	——
		To *Danger*	Johnson's definition
		Dangerless	Johnson's definition
Dangerous	——	similar	—— with J.'s qu
	Dangerously	similar	—— with J.'s quot.

Dictionarium Britannicum		Johnson	Scott-Bailey
1730 Edition	1736 Edition	First Edition, 1755	1755
Dangerousness	———	new definition	Johnson's definition
To *Dangle*	———	new definition	B.'s and J.'s def.
	Dangler	new definition	J.'s def. enlarged
Dangling	———	omits	———
Dank	———	new definition	Johnson's definition
Dankish	———	new definition	Johnson's definition
Dankishness	———	omits	———
	Dantele		
	(heraldry)	omits	———
			Dantzic
			Danube
		To *Dap* (angling)	Johnson's definition
Dapatical . . .			
sumptuous.	———	Bailey's definition	———
	Daphneon . . .		
	the Pleasant-		
	ness of		
	Laurel.	omits	———
Daphnephoria			
. . . a festival	———	omits	———
Daphnophagl			
. . . certain			
prophets	———	omits	———
Daphnitis . . .			
the laurel.	———	omits	———

Other sections show a much greater divergence in vocabulary than that reflected above. At the beginning of the *N* section, for instance, Johnson has 33 words up to and including the word *Nare*, while the Scott-Bailey has 76. Johnson's words are as follows:

N, To *Nab* ("to catch unexpectedly"), *Nadir*, *Naff* (a sea-bird), *Nag*, *Nail*, To *Nail*, *Nailer*, *Naked*, *Nakedly*, *Nakedness*, *Nall* (an awl), *Name*, To *Name*, *Nameless*, *Namely*, *Namer*, *Namesake*, *Nap*, To *Nap*, *Naptaking*, *Nape*, *Napery*, *Naphew* (an herb), *Naphtha*, *Nappiness*, *Napkin*, *Napless*, *Nappy*, *Narcissus*, *Narcotick*, *Nard*, *Nare*.

The Scott-Bailey also includes such unusual words as:

Nab (cant for "hat"), *Na'am* (law), Lawful *Naam*, Unlawful *Naam*, *Namium Vetitum* (law), Aera of *Nabonassar*, *Nacca* (in old deeds),

Naenia (funeral songs), *Naevus* (a mole), *Naevosity, Naevose, Nagel* (a weight for wool), *Naiades, Naiant* (heraldry), To *Nail* Cannon (military), *Nairne* (town in Scotland), *Naissant* (heraldry), *Namation* (law), *Napeae* (nymphs of the mountains), *Napellus* (botany), etc.

The policy of the Scott-Bailey in regard to definition is probably clear from the above discussion and the chart. When words treated in the *Dictionarium Britannicum* are rejected by Johnson, the Scott-Bailey retains the definitions of the *Dictionarium Britannicum;* but when words are newly defined by Johnson, the Scott-Bailey usually prefers Johnson's definition. While the Scott-Bailey rarely omits a meaning of a word, it does abridge and rearrange the definitions; and it regularly reduces the number and length of the illustrative quotations, and sometimes omits them entirely. Compare the following definitions:

Dictionarium Britannicum 1730 Edition [17]	JOHNSON, First Edition, 1755	SCOTT-BAILEY 1755
	(Note: An asterisk indicates a quotation.)	
To *Entreat* (...) to beg earnestly or beseech; to court with fair words; also to treat of, or handle a matter.	To *Entreat,* ... 1. To offer a treaty or compact.* 2. To treat; to discourse.* 3. To make a petition.*	To *Entreat,* ... 1. To offer a treaty or compact.* 2. To treat; to discourse.* 3. To make a petition; with for.*
	Entreatance, ... Petition; entreaty; solicitation.*	*Entreatance,* ... petition, entreaty.*
Entreaty, request, supplication, &c.	*Entreaty,* ... Petition; prayer; solicitation; supplication; request.*	*Entreaty,* ... petition, prayer, request.*
	Entremets, ... Small plates set between the main dishes.*	*Entremets,* ... small plates set between the main dishes.*
Entry (...) entering or coming in, a passage. *Entry* (in Law) is the taking possession of lands. *Entry* (with *Merchants*) the setting down the particulars	*Entry,* ... 1. The passage by which any one enters a house.**** 2. The act of entrance; ingress.***	*Entry* (...) 1. The act of entering or coming in.* 2. The passage by which one enters a house.*

Dictionarium Britannicum 1730 Edition	Johnson, First Edition, 1755	Scott-Bailey 1755
of trade in the books of accounts. To make an *Entry* of Goods (at the Custom-House) is the passing the bills through the hands of the proper officers. *Entry* ad communem legem . . . *Entry*, a solemn reception or ceremony performed by kings, princes or ambassadors, upon their first entering a city, or upon their return from some successful expedition, by way of triumph.	3. The act of taking possession of any estate.	3. The act of registering or setting down in writing in general.*
	4. The act of registering or setting down in writing.*	4. A solemn reception or ceremony performed by kings, princes or ambassadors, upon their first entering a city, or upon their return from some successful expedition, by way of triumph.*
	5. The act of entering publickly into any city.*	[Adds all other items on *Entry* carried in the *Dictionarium Britannicum*.]
Entry ad terminum . . . *Entry* Causa Matrimonii . . . *Entry* in casu proviso, . . . *Entry* in casu consimili, . . . *Entry* sine ascensu . . . *Entry* per le cui . . . *Entries* (with *Hunters*) . . .		
To *Enubilate* (. . .) to make clear.	To *Enubilate*, . . . To clear from clouds. *Dict.*	To *Enubilate*, . . . to make clear from clouds.
To *Enucleate* (. . .) to take out the kernel.	To *Enucleate*, . . . To solve; to clear; to disentangle. *Dict.*	To *Enucleate* . . . to solve, to disentangle.
To *Envelop* (. . .) to cover, wrap or fold up in any thing; also to surround them in, to beset; also to muffle up.	To *Envelop* . . . 1. To inwrap; to cover; to invest in some integument.	To *Envelop* (. . .) 1. To cover, wrap, or fold up in anything.
	2. To cover; to hide; to surround.****	2. To surround with, to beset; to muffle up, to hide.*
	3. To line; to cover on the inside.*	3. To line, to cover on the inside.*

Thus constituted, the Scott-Bailey dictionary was reissued in 1764 and in 1772. These later editions were, however, reprints or possibly, as Gove suggests, simply new issues of stock printed in 1755.

With the great tomes of Johnson and the Scott-Bailey before us, we have an impressive illustration of the progress of the English dictionary in the 150 years since Cawdrey's modest *Table Alphabeticall*. To be sure, it is customary for the modern scholar to condescend toward these eighteenth-century works with their feeble etymology and their often inadequate definitions and to point out that even the *Oxford English Dictionary* and the latest and largest twentieth-century unabridged dictionary fall far short of perfection. It is too often forgotten that these recent achievements are the product of joint enterprise with public support and financial backing; what is even more important, they are also the heirs of years of experimentation, much barren and much fruitful. The modern lexicographer would, we are convinced, be the first to realize and to acknowledge his indebtedness to his long line of forebears including the nameless, the odd, and the wise.

From this vantage point we may take a retrospective glance over the array of English dictionaries which had appeared by 1755.

The seventeenth-century pioneers made their way along a devious path with many excursions into tempting bypaths but with slow progress toward their goal. These early dictionaries are strongly marked by the personalities and predilections of their authors—a feature which, while constituting part of their charm, is also a measure of their imperfection. In this period we are acutely aware not only of personalities, rivalries, and recriminations but, more significantly, of the formative process itself. These early dictionary-makers are struggling to form an adequate concept of a new art; they must weigh their own purposes and responsibilities, decide on the public they wish to serve, and define the nature, scope, and limitations of their subject matter. All of these basic problems must reach at least a working solution before the lexicographer can even approach his main business, the mystery of his art—the study of the word.

The seventeenth-century dictionaries are also the meeting places and often the battle grounds for various traditions. First comes the pedagogical tradition, stemming from Richard Mulcaster's *Elementarie* (1582) and other schoolmasters and schoolbooks; according to this practical and elementary point of view, a dictionary is a list of ordinary words intended as an aid in pronunciation, in orthography, and in the comprehension of simple texts. While influential in Cawdrey, this tradition comes into conflict even in his work and is vanquished for the rest of the seventeenth century by another, which we may call "the 'hard' word tradition." The latter has varied origins: in the Latin-English dictionaries, such as Thomas Thomas' *Dictionarium* (1588?, etc.), which formed convenient models and sources for the early English dictionaries; in the wholesale influx of classical and other foreign expressions into the English tongue in the sixteenth and seventeenth centuries; in the resultant controversy over the nature and the expansion of the language; and in the general and growing admiration for elegance in speech and writing. As a result of this potent and complex tradition the vocabularies of the seventeenth-century dictionaries consisted mainly in "hard" words; *i.e.*, words mainly of Latin or Greek origin which were thought to add elegance to speech and writing but which inevitably proved to be formidable obstacles in reading for the person without a classical education. A third tradition, which we may call "the reference book tradition," runs parallel to the last. Uneducated persons would encounter difficulties not only in understanding the rapidly expanding vocabulary of the age but also in grasping the frequent allusions to classical history, literature, and mythology which were so characteristic of English literature of the period. The great storehouse for such classical history and legend was Charles Stephanus' *Dictionarium Historicum, Geographicum, Poeticum* (1553, etc.); but lists of names of famous persons and places were also commonly carried in other Latin and Latin-English dictionaries of the period. Here are involved such nice questions as the distinction between fact and fiction as well as between dictionary and encyclopedia. Lastly, from its feeble beginning in Cawdrey to its development in Blount and in the *Gazophylacium Anglicanum* appears an awareness of another body of material contributing to lexicography—etymology. Among the etymological dictionaries which form the background here, undoubtedly Stephen Skinner's *Etymologicon Linguae Anglicanae* (1671) was the most influential in the early history of the English dictionary.

These and other traditions exerted their claims on the lexicography of the seventeenth century. Their relative progress may be summarized as follows: the pedagogical tradition stressing the ordinary word soon gave way to the "hard" word tradition, which prevailed throughout the century; the entries on proper names, which formed a large body of reference material, were widely developed with little concern for distinguishing fact from fiction; and, finally, etymology attained recognition, though the slow development of linguistic science severely restricted and often invalidated work in this field.

As to the individual seventeenth-century works, we may undertake a rapid recapitulation. Cawdrey's *Table Alphabeticall* (1604), a brief list with simple definitions, included ordinary words side by side with "hard" words and made an overture to etymology. The *Table Alphabeticall* was, however, a beginning and no more. The rival works of Bullokar (1616) and Cockeram (1623), in the course of their long careers, not only abounded in "hard" words but reveled in curious facts and legends, extended the vocabulary to include legal and medical expressions, and experimented with novel divisions of the vocabulary. Blount's *Glossographia* (1656) was marked by a greater depth of scholarship and a more responsible attitude. He reduced legendary and curious items, enlarged the medical and legal vocabularies, and introduced specialized terms from numerous other departments; and he stressed etymology, though his procedure was not uniform nor his information dependable. Phillips' *New World of Words* (1658), the first folio dictionary, was characterized in its original form mainly by a great influx of proper names threatening to outweigh the "hard" word part of the vocabulary and by elaborate preliminary apparatus, including a misleading list of collaborators and a history of the language. Coles's dictionary (1676) was an unpretentious but workmanlike product combining all materials so far exploited and utilizing all departments so far established. Though small in format, minute in type, and unduly compressed in style, Coles offered a more comprehensive word list than any predecessor; to the groups previously introduced—the "hard" words, specialized terms, and proper names, he added cant and dialect. He also included brief annotations as to etymology and usage. Finally, the *Gazophylacium Anglicanum* (1689) was perhaps in part an outgrowth of Blount's stress on etymology but was more directly an evidence of the reawakened interest in the Anglo-Saxon heritage of the language. It was, in fact, a lineal descendant of the etymological dictionaries and a translation of certain parts of Skinner.

The first half of the eighteenth century solved many of the problems previously encountered, reconciled some conflicting traditions, and gradually built up a body of material and a set of recognized duties upon which later lexicographers could focus their talents. In other words, the lexicographers of the seventeenth century had pointed out the preliminary difficulties; those of the first half of the eighteenth century overcame these difficulties and left the field clear for the more rapid progress and finer works of their successors.

J. K.'s (John Kersey's?) *New English Dictionary* (1702) opened the eighteenth century with a significant contribution. He revived the school-book tradition which had lain dormant since Cawdrey and introduced the ordinary word—that is, the fundamental part of the language— into the English dictionary. *Cocker's English Dictionary* (1704), though a slavish borrower from various sources, experimented with a new arrangement in four separate vocabularies and with some new groups of words; to the conventional "hard" words and proper names the compiler added military and commercial terms. The Kersey-Phillips folio of 1706 made notable progress. A fine revision of Phillips with the elimination of legendary items, the substitution of thousands of up-to-date scientific terms from John Harris' *Lexicon Technicum* of 1704, and the blending with the traditional "hard" words of a representation of ordinary words—it was the first universal dictionary and a worthy though remote precursor of Johnson. The *Glossographia Anglicana Nova* (1707) was a derivative work, stemming mainly from Harris and Blount and thus oddly combining the new scientific vocabulary with the older "hard" words and with Blount's peculiar stress on etymology. Kersey's *Dictionarium Anglo-Britannicum* (1708) was the first abridged dictionary, the parent work being the Kersey-Phillips, and shows a competent solution of the difficulties inherent in abridgment. Kersey was, obviously, the first outstanding lexicographer: he was probably responsible for the *New English Dictionary* of 1702, which called attention at last to the forgotten common word; and he produced both the first comprehensive and well executed folio dictionary and the first abridged dictionary.

It is a tacit tribute to Kersey that there was no new dictionary for thirteen years after his *Dictionarium*. Then begins the busy career of the second outstanding lexicographer, Nathan Bailey. Using Kersey's

Dictionarium as a fine basis, Bailey expanded his vocabulary and developed etymology in the octavo *Universal Etymological English Dictionary* (1721), which because of its phenomenally long and successful career is usually considered the representative eighteenth-century dictionary. Bailey's so-called *Universal Etymological English Dictionary, Vol. II* (1727) was another octavo work, erratic and changing in nature, but roughly describable as supplementary to the original volume and preparatory to his folio *Dictionarium Britannicum* of 1730. This last volume was the second universal dictionary and offered a valuable working base for the two large and fine dictionaries which climax our period —the Johnson and the Scott-Bailey, both of 1755.

The intermediate dictionaries may be rapidly dismissed with one exception. Dyche and Pardon's *New General English Dictionary* (1735) is remembered mainly for its stress on pronunciation and grammar; its vocabulary was, however, small and curious for its day, and its definitions were verbose. Like Dyche and Pardon, the four dictionaries of 1735, 1737, 1739, and 1741, carrying a common vocabulary, derived from Bailey; they were, however, characterless. The *Pocket Dictionary* of 1753 was a more intelligent derivative volume, which succeeded in uniting in brief compass and simple form some of the distinctive features of Bailey, Dyche and Pardon, and Martin. Wesley's *Complete English Dictionary* (1753), despite its title, was the smallest since Cawdrey and showed little interest in the departments of lexicography which had been developed through the years; it was merely a practical expedient with a vocabulary and definitions especially designed to enable his simplest followers to understand his various compilations. The exceptional work in this group is Benjamin Martin's *Lingua Britannica Reformata* of 1749. This work was characterized by unusual care in planning, for in its preface the author outlined the various duties of the lexicographer. While his plan is notable for its comprehensiveness, we are most impressed by the strong emphasis on fine definition, which marks the beginning of a new epoch in English lexicography. Martin's definitions are divided into parts, setting off and arranging in logical order the various meanings of the word. Johnson had recommended this type of definition in his *Plan of a Dictionary of the English Language* (1747), and the Latin-English and other bilingual dictionaries had long been demonstrating such a type; but Benjamin Martin was the first to incorporate this technique on any appreciable scale into the English dictionary.

In closing, let us summarize the attainments of lexicography by 1755, with particular reference to the Scott-Bailey and the Johnson of that date. Progress was, we believe, registered in three ways: in the dictionary, in the lexicographer, and in the public. Turning first to the dictionary, we observe that the make-up of a vocabulary in 1755 is no longer a matter of chance or whim; it may be molded by the convictions of the lexicographer, but its material is largely predetermined. The vocabulary has evolved as a result of the accumulations and the rejections of many predecessors, as a result of constant thoughtful experimentation and constant struggle for survival on the market. The word list has expanded to notable size and many-sidedness in the Scott-Bailey and has attained notable purity and unity in Johnson. Definitions have at last been accorded their proper place as the prime concern of the dictionary-maker; and an attempt is now made to distinguish carefully, to order logically, and to phrase lucidly the various significations of a word. Etymology has received recognition as an important department; the etymologist is credited on the title-page; and the best linguistic authorities are consulted, compared, and cited. It was not the fault of the eighteenth-century lexicographer that the science of etymology was slow to develop and that he was therefore committed to much guesswork and error. Special classifications of words and levels of usage are indicated with more or less consistency, accentuation is marked, and grammar is treated both in an introductory section and throughout the word list.[18]

These are memorable attainments; they are, however, posited upon similar developments in the lexicographer and in his public. Early seventeenth-century lexicographers were dilettantes or specialists, they undertook their task in spare moments that their time might not be "worse employed," and they aimed to assist the ladies or the artisans or the foreigners. After the turn of the century, however, with Kersey, Bailey, and Martin, the function of the lexicographer comes to be regarded with increasing gravity. A scholar of depth and scope, the lexicographer now devotes his best years and abilities to his task and stands ready to serve alike Englishmen and foreigners, men and women, the educated and the would-be educated. The name of Nathan Bailey gathered honor; and Johnson, despite his ironic gibe at the lexicographer, invested the calling with lasting dignity. By the mid-century not only are more able scholars feeling the call to dictionary-making; but modern methods of organization are taking shape, and the scholarly editor now deputes routine tasks to competent subordinates while he directs the whole.

By 1755 the public has also awakened to the interest and the usefulness of lexicography. Dictionaries had long offered their services to "all those who desire to understand what they read," and the growing reading public now began to take them at their word. Impressive sales of rival works indicate many owners and at least some habitual users of the dictionary, and the constant and animated fire of reviews and controversies proves that there has also sprung up a super-race of critics of dictionaries. Johnson's work indeed precipitated an avalanche of criticism, as the public turned increasingly from its preoccupation with the academic question of a perfect English language to the more specific and practical question of the perfect English dictionary. In analyzing the deficiencies of Bailey and Johnson and attempting to define the ideal, the public made straight the way for modern lexicography.

Appendix I

MEDIEVAL AND RENAISSANCE VOCABULARIES

AND THE ENGLISH DICTIONARY

P ROBABLY ONE OF THE FIRST STEPS IN WHAT MAY BE CALLED
the evolution of a dictionary is the interlinear gloss. For the
hard words of a discourse, synonyms in simple words or
phrases are written between the lines. The synonyms may be
in the same language as the original text; or, if the text is in a foreign
language, the interlinear substitutes may be in the vernacular. If, for
example, the original is in Latin, the interlinear gloss may consist of
easier Latin words or phrases, or even English words which translate
the original. The purpose of such a gloss would be, obviously, to assist
the understanding of those not well versed in the language of the text.
Before the day of dictionaries, teachers of foreign language often thus
glossed their texts. Given a number of interlinear glosses, one might
collect from them all the hard words with their synonyms and arrange
them in alphabetical order. One would then have a composite of glosses
so arranged as to facilitate their use and of great value in the study of
new texts. One would have, in other words, a little dictionary.

The pattern thus described is found in *The Corpus Glossary*, in a
manuscript of the eighth century. This gloss consists of hard Latin words
arranged in alphabetical (AB) order and followed by easier Latin
synonyms or the equivalent in Anglo-Saxon. According to W. M.
Lindsay, the most recent editor,[1] *The Corpus Glossary* is based upon four
other vocabularies, which had been compiled from interlinear glosses.
Lindsay characterizes the Corpus compilation as "England's oldest dictionary." Very similar in method and content is the Épinal and Erfurt
Glossary, probably of the same century. Other examples of alphabetical
Latin-English glosses from the tenth, eleventh, and fifteenth centuries

are edited by Richard Paul Wülcker.[2] These bilingual glosses and vocabularies seem to anticipate the hard-word English dictionaries of the seventeenth century. But a more popular type of vocabulary, which flourished from the Anglo-Saxon period to the nineteenth century, is that in which the terms were arranged in related groups, according to subject as *Church, Pulpit, Funeral, Churchyard,* etc. It is this tradition of vocabulary-compiling which we wish to trace here.

As early as the tenth century Aelfric, Abbot of Eynsham, compiled a Latin-Anglo-Saxon vocabulary.[3] In this collection the Latin words are placed first with single Anglo-Saxon equivalents following, as *Aratrum,* suhl; *Buris,* suhlbeam; *Stiba,* suhlhandla; *Vitularius,* cealfahus; *Radii,* spacan; *Rota,* hweol. Though the compiler gives only fifteen headings in the text proper, there are in fact thirty topics or groups. The lists begin with the names of agricultural implements or tools and conclude with the names of ships and their parts. Included between are groups of words pertaining to ecclesiastical affairs, to officials in the church and state, to Roman law, to man, his kindred, the parts of the body, diseases, the house with its parts and contents, food, drink; the names of beasts, birds, herbs, trees, colors, clothes, games and amusements, weapons; heaven, earth, sun, moon, angel, and archangel.

A Latin-Anglo-Saxon vocabulary of the eleventh century [4] carries on the tradition, with an interesting modification. Though somewhat condensed and lacking topical headings, this vocabulary falls roughly into eighteen groups. The topics (supplied by the present writer) of the eleventh century collection run thus: (1) God, heaven, angels, archangels, sun, moon, earth, sea; (2) man, woman, the parts of the body; (3) terms of consanguinity, professional and trades people, artisans; (4) diseases; (5) abstract terms (*impious, just, prudent,* etc.); (6) times of year, of day, seasons, weather; (7) colors; (8) birds; (9) fishes; (10) beasts; (11) herbs; (12) trees; (13) house furnishings; (14) kitchen and cooking utensils; (15) weapons; (16) parts of the city; (17) metals and precious stones; (18) general—both abstract and concrete terms. At this point the compiler of the vocabulary seems to have tired; and he concludes with the statement: "We ne magon swa þeah ealle naman awritan ne furþor geþencan."

Two aspects of this vocabulary are noteworthy: (1) the correspondence with respect to word groups to those of the tenth-century list discussed above, and (2) the arrangement of the groups. In beginning with God and the angels, the planets, the earth and the sea, then proceeding to man in general, particular types of professional men and artisans and their occupations; to beasts, birds, fishes; then to plants, trees, and houses, the compiler suggests a logic in disposing his topics which is uncommon among the early word collectors. Furthermore, this is the sole example I have found before the sixteenth century—though there may well be others—in which the group of words pertaining to God, heaven, earth, etc. stands at the head of the list. In the period of the Renaissance, such a beginning becomes the rule rather than the exception.

The next document which shows the persistence of the tradition is a semi-Saxon vocabulary of the middle of the twelfth century.[5] Though this vocabulary is fragmentary and lacks topic-headings, a glance through the list shows that the compiler—probably a teacher, as most of these vocabularies and glosses were gathered and used by teachers—had in mind what we may now term the conventional subjects. He begins with the names of parts of the body and follows with the nomenclature of consanguinity, artisans, craftsmen, diseases, beasts, birds, fish, herbs, trees, houses, furnishings, etc. Incidentally, beginning the vocabulary with the names of parts of the body in Latin and English became the common practice in the fifteenth century.

One other text in the Anglo-Norman period, though not strictly in the tradition we are studying, deserves special mention. This is the *De Utensilibus* of the celebrated scholar, Alexander Neckham.[6] Neckham's work is of the interlinear-gloss type. He has in Latin a sort of continuous discourse, beginning oddly enough with the kitchen and its implements, articles of food and their preparation, and so on through the various subjects usual in the formal, simple vocabularies. The point of interest is that he still keeps together the words in their different classes in a continuous discourse. This method is an anticipation, as we shall see, of a practice in the seventeenth century.

There are few, if any, manuscripts of vocabularies or educational treatises between the thirteenth and the fifteenth centuries. This scarcity is due, according to Thomas Wright,[7] to the neglect into which school teaching had fallen. Whatever the cause of the dearth of matter in the fourteenth, manuscripts of grammatical treatises and of Latin-English vocabularies are common in the fifteenth century.

Three of these are printed by Wright in his *Volume of Vocabularies*. The first, entitled an *English Vocabulary*,[8] and the second, a *Nominale*, may be treated summarily. In both, the Latin headings for all distinct groups of words are very prominent; and the word list for each group is longer than in the earlier vocabularies. Both place first the names of the parts of man's body and proceed, though not in the same order, through the conventional topics of man and his activities, animals, birds, fishes, insects, herbs, trees, fruits, time, the seasons, etc.; but neither of these uses the comprehensive topics: God, the heaven, the earth, or the four elements. They do, however, place before the Latin nouns the proper qualifying adjectives, as *hic crinis, haec facies, hoc tempus*.

The third vocabulary in this fifteenth century group is, in one respect, a distinct innovation: this is a pictorial vocabulary. As to topics under which words are assembled, this collection is fairly conventional, beginning with names pertaining to the human body, then continuing with words relating to the church, names of domestic animals and wild animals, of fresh water fish and sea fish—distinctions not generally made in the earlier vocabularies. Then, too, this compiler has more about the baker, the brewer, the butler; about waters, lands, and planets. Though this vocabulary includes the conventional elements, it is somewhat more comprehensive and more careful as to classification. The unique feature is, however, the crude pictures. These sketches occupy the margins and what would have been otherwise blank spaces. Some of the drawings, such as those on the second page, seem to have no reference to the text. Others, such as the bell (756), the cock (760), the dragon (765), the flask (772), the *cloaca* (privy) (800), and the well (800) are definitely illustrative sketches, placed near the words they are designed to illustrate. Incidentally, the *cloaca* is probably the best illustration. This pictorial vocabulary was not printed until the middle of the nineteenth century; and I know of no other vocabulary or dictionary in which illustrations appear before the seventeenth century.

The traditional methods and matter in vocabulary-building are continued by three English schoolmasters: John Stanbridge, William Horman, and Robert Whittinton. Stanbridge's published works pertinent to this discussion are the *Vocabula* (1496) and the *Vulgaria* (1508), books designed to assist English boys in the study of Latin. As the principle of presentation is very similar in the two texts, we shall discuss only the earlier. Though the *Vocabula* was first published in 1496, it enjoyed greater vogue in the sixteenth century, going through six editions between 1510 and 1531.[9] In his choice of topics Stanbridge is conventional. He begins with parts of the body, treats man, his diseases, his professions and crafts, animals, birds, fish, etc. His method of presentation, however, varies. For the first few pages of his *Vocabula* he has the usual arrangement in parallel columns under general topics. Thereafter, though he retains general headings, he presents the words, metrically arranged, across the page—the Latin in large type and the English equivalents above in smaller type. The page has thus the appearance of an interlinear translation but without the links, except the association of words and the metrical arrangement, designed to assist the memory.

William Horman's *Vulgaria* (1519), though not strictly in the tradition we are tracing, is relevant to this study, as will appear later. Horman's book has been briefly described as follows:

> The book consists of some three thousand Latin sentences with English translations under them arranged in chapters on such topics as *De Pietate, De Impietate, De Animis Bonis et Malis,* etc., the whole forming a compendium of Tudor knowledge on almost every subject.[10]

This plan of organization obviously derives from the anthologies or flowers of Latin poetry or the *Polyanthea* of Mirabellius, so popular in the sixteenth century.

Robert Whittinton, a competitor of Horman and Stanbridge, published his *Vulgaria* in 1520. This work effectively combines the method of Horman with certain features of the earlier vocabularies. In illustration of grammatical principles, Whittinton employs sentences—the English above the Latin equivalent—under headings of abstract words, such as *piety* and *impiety*, *virtue* and *vice*, as in Horman. Whittinton goes farther, however, and presents in sentence form the stock subjects of the older vocabularies, such as parts of the body, diseases, terms of consanguinity, etc. Characteristic entries in his *Vulgaria* are these:

Exempla plenitudinis vel inopiae
A foole is so ful of wordes that he dassheth
out all that lyeth on his herte.
Fatuus verbis adeo turgidies est: ut omnia
animi secreta ebulliat vel effutiat. [11]

Exempla de, affinitate
My masters fader in lawe wyll be here to daye.
Socer heri vel hero affuturus est, vel aderit hodie.
This is my broders moder in lawe.
Haec est socrus fratris vel fratri.
She is daughter in lawe to myn uncle.
Illa est genera patrui vel patruo.[12]

The methods evolved by Horman and Whittinton are definitely suggestive of those employed by a more famous teacher of the seventeenth century, to be discussed below.

Texts by the schoolmasters we have just discussed had their vogue in the first half of the sixteenth century, the *Vocabula* of Stanbridge, which was nearer to the traditional vocabularies, being the most popular. In the meantime a book published on the Continent in 1549 shows that the medieval tradition in vocabularies and dictionaries persisted elsewhere in Europe, and doubtless helped to perpetuate the practice in England. We refer to a small dictionary in Latin, Flemish, and Gallic compiled by Ioannes Paludanus [13] and published in Belgium.[14] The Latin title-page states, in substance, that this is a small dictionary of ordinary things for the general use of boys and children. The words and phrases are in the conventional arrangement of parallel columns— Latin, Flemish, French—under the traditional topics. The headings begin (1) Of God and divine things, (2) Of Times, (3) Of the Names of the Twelve Months of the Year, (4) Of the Four elements and the things which are engendered of them, (5) Of Lands, of waters . . . and continue through forty-three headings, including all the conventional groupings of the early vocabularies and some subjects, such as books, the seven liberal arts, weights and measures, money, and numbers, not hitherto common.

Two observations on this book are here pertinent: (1) the tendency to all-inclusiveness, as beginning with divine affairs and the four elements and including topics on the larger aspects of the life of man and beast, and (2) the incorporation—for the first time, to my knowledge—under the title of *dictionary* [15] of topics and word lists in parallel order which had hitherto appeared in conventional vocabularies and nominales.

In England a few years after Paludanus' book, there appeared a similar text, *A Shorte Dictionarie for Yonge Begynners*, by John Withals, 1553. This is an English-Latin text similar in its choice of topics and in the order of presentation, as in its comprehensiveness, to that of the Belgian compiler. To the latter, Withals may well be indebted. His indebtedness to Elyot's Latin-English dictionary is demonstrable, in that he has reversed the order by placing the English before the Latin and borrowed numerous definitions from Elyot. Certain entries also derive from Stanbridge's *Vocabula*. And the whole text of Withals is in the tradition we are tracing, the one noteworthy change being that the English is placed before the Latin.[16] Withals also introduces under the various headings many phrases and sentences which have precedents not in the vocabularies but rather in the alphabetical dictionaries. But a glance at the *Shorte Dictionarie for Yonge Begynners* reveals at once the conventional character of the topics chosen under which to group the words, and the usual method of the early vocabularies. Here are the sky, the stars, the planets, the seasons, the four elements, with the words pertaining to each; the sea "with all that belongeth to it," including ships and fishes; man, the parts of his body and his diseases; his houses; his occupations and crafts; beasts and birds, trees and herbs, etc. And Withals, more than his predecessors, strives for logic in his arrangement of groups.

Beginning with the aether, for example, he presents things celestial, as the sky, the spheres, the stars; he mentions the twelve signs of the zodiac; he continues with the seven planets, the divisions of time, the seasons, the four elements of fire, air, water, and earth and the common words and ideas associated with each. So throughout, the author sought to suggest by arrangement a close relationship of words with groups as well as connections between groups themselves. Apparently Withals shared the belief of his time in a definite cosmic order.

This little *Dictionarie* became popular at once and was reissued at regular intervals until 1634. Through Withals the tradition carries over through the first third of the seventeenth century.[17]

Other books besides the Withals gave vogue to the conventional word lists of vocabularies in the second half of the sixteenth century. Most of the bilingual manuals used in teaching modern foreign languages devoted part of their space to such lists. Claudius Hollyband, a teacher of French in London, published two manuals: *The Frenche Littleton* (1566) [18] and *The Frenche Schoole-maister* (1573). These little books contained dialogues of daily life in London, proverbs and sentences, the Lord's Prayer, articles of faith, the ten commandments, and a vocabulary —all on parallel pages with the French before the English. The more extensive vocabulary in *The Frenche Schoole-maister* has many topics similar to those in the Withals, from which it probably drew. The conventional lists appear also in Florio's *Firste Fruites* (1578), in Italian and English, and in William Stepney's *The Spanish Schoolemaster* (1591), in Spanish and English.[19]

John Rider's *Bibliotheca Scholastica* (1589), an English-Latin dictionary, arranged alphabetically, retained at the end many of the topic headings and the customary vocabulary; and this practice was continued in the Rider-Holyoke dictionaries until the middle of the seventeenth century.

It is necessary, at this point in our survey, to give some attention to three language manuals which, though not first compiled or published in England, were destined to exert a strong influence on the English vocabulary tradition. The first one, entitled *Janua Linguarum*,[20] the Gate of Tongues, was published at Salamanca in 1611. This book was a Latin-Spanish manual prepared by William Bathe (1564-1614),[21] rector of the Irish College at Salamanca, with the assistance of Irish Jesuits on the teaching staff. In 1615, William Welde translated the Spanish into English, added an index or brief dictionary, and had the *Janua* published in London as a Latin-English manual. Two years later, Jean Barbier, retaining the English of Welde and the Latin and Spanish of the original *Janua*, added French, and published the book under the following title:

Ianua Linguarum, Quadrilinguis, or a Messe of Tongues: Latine, English, French, and Spanish Neatly Served up together, for a wholesome repast, to the worthy curiositie of the studious.... Londini ... M.DC.XVII.[22]

Bathe's book with its augmentations was very popular, nine English editions having appeared by 1645.[23] The *Janua* consisted of about 5,000 words, classified into twelve centuries, with the words fitted into 1,200 statements or sentences. Each century of sentences is concerned with some generally defined subject; and the various centuries range from the abstract topics of temperance, justice, fortitude, and other cardinal virtues to the more concrete topics of human activity, of things with and without life, and of the various arts and crafts.

Apparently the method thus described was thought of as new in 1611. It is to be noted, however, that the author introduces into his framework certain topics, such as those on human activity and the arts and crafts, which are recurrent in the vocabularies we have studied. The general plan, that of placing apt sentences under abstract topics of virtue and vice, temperance and intemperance, etc., is fairly definitely anticipated in the *Vulgaria* of Horman and the *Vulgaria* of Whittinton, not to mention the Latin *Polyantheas*, and Elyot's *Bankette of Sapience*—all current from the early sixteenth century. Bathe is, however, more systematic in his assembling of terms to be defined, more rigorous in adherence to his plan, more insistent on the teaching of morals. Incidentally, the title of his book is, so far as I know, original, and also felicitous. And this title as well as suggestions from his method were soon to be employed by a more famous educator in the seventeenth century.

The reference is to John Amos Comenius or Komensky (1592-1671), who rose to be bishop of Moravia and an educational reformer of wide renown.[24] We wish to consider briefly two of his books and their provenance: *Janua Linguarum Reserata* (1631) and *Orbis Sensualium Pictus* (1657). The title of the first was obviously suggested by that of Bathe, discussed above. Comenius is known to have received the Jesuit's book with keen interest, expecting from reports of it to find in it a system of language-teaching in consonance with his ideal. Disappointed in this book, he wrote his own text and named it, as if to satirize the title of his predecessor's book, *The Gate of Tongues Unlocked*.[25] This work was printed first at Leszna in 1631 in Latin and German and in the same year in England in English, French, and Latin; and in the course of a few years it was printed with improvements and variations in almost all the European languages. Except for the variation as to languages,[26] the content and method remained the same. The full title of the first edition suggests the scope and method of the *Janua:*

The Gate of Languages Unlocked, or the Seminary of all Languages and Sciences; that is, a compendious method of learning Latin or any other tongue, along with the elements of all the Sciences and Arts, comprehended under a hundred chapter-headings and a thousand [actually 1,058] sentences.[27]

These illustrative sentences are arranged in order of difficulty, being simple in the first part of the text and gradually increasing in complexity in the latter part.

After an introduction in which he insists that the reader give attention to things and words, Comenius proceeds (and some of the chapter-headings will convey an idea of the scope of his writings): "Concerning the Origin of the World. Concerning the Elements. Concerning the Firmament, Fire, Meteors, Waters, Earths, Stones, Metals, Trees, and Fruits, Herbs, Shrubs." These things are treated of in thirteen chapters and 141 sentences. Then we have "Concerning Animals," which, under different subdivisions, occupies the book to the nineteenth chapter inclusive. Then the headings, "Concerning Man: his Body; External Members; Internal Members; the qualities or accidents of the Body; Diseases; Ulcers and Wounds; the External Senses; the Internal Senses; Mind; the Will and the Affections," occupy the book to the twenty-ninth chapter inclusive. All the mechanic arts now follow, and are concluded in the forty-eighth chapter and 639th sentence. The rest of the book treats of the House and its parts; Marriage and the Family; Civic and State Economy; Grammar, Dialectic, Rhetoric, Arithmetic, Geometry, and all branches of knowledge; Ethics, and the twelve virtues treated in twelve chapters. Games, Death, Burial, the Providence of God and Angels, form the concluding chapters. This, as Professor Laurie remarks, is encyclopaedism. And those who have followed this discussion may now begin to see Comenius' *Janua* in perspective.

But before we venture conclusions concerning this book, we must notice briefly the *Orbis Sensualium Pictus* (1657), which, though intended to be supplementary and subsidiary to the *Janua,* is in fact a fuller application of Comenius' principles than any other text. These principles are stated by the author in his Preface thus:

The foundation of all learning consists in representing clearly to the senses sensible objects, so that they can be apprehended easily. I maintain that this is the basis of all other actions, inasmuch as we could neither act nor speak wisely unless we comprehended clearly what we wished to say or do. For it is certain that there is nothing in the Understanding which has not been previously in the Senses; and consequently, to exercise the senses carefully in discriminating the differences of natural objects is to lay the foundations of all wisdom, all eloquence, and all good and prudent action.

Here are the ideas of realism in education—of learning from Nature through the senses, of the close association of words and things, of the parallel pursuit of these, and, by the process, of reaching universal wisdom or pansophy. In the light of this Preface the words of the title-page become more intelligible: "Orbis Sensualium Pictus, . . ."[28] The World of Sensible Things drawn; that is, the Nomenclature of all Fundamental Things in the World and Actions in Life reduced to Ocular Demonstration." The text consists of 151 chapters, ranging from the Creation to the Last Judgment, including all the topics hitherto mentioned in the vocabularies and dictionaries. Each chapter is illustrated with a composite cut or engraving, each item in which is numbered. The sentences under the chapter heading bear directly upon the illustration, each sentence having an italicized and numbered word corresponding to a numbered item in the drawing. The author thus makes clear the association of the word with the thing of which it is a symbol. For example, under the caption, "The Study" (p. 120), we have the picture of a small room with a shelf of books at one end, and in the foreground a student seated at a table poring over a book—the room, the book, and the desk having numbers corresponding to the numbers in the lesson thus: "The *Study*, 1, is a place where a *Student*, 2, apart from Men, sitteth alone, addicted to his *Studies*, whilst he readeth *Books*, 3, . . ."

These illustrations with their heightened appeal to the senses constitute the fundamental difference between the *Orbis* and the *Janua*. Another difference is that the sentences in the *Orbis* are not numbered; numbers are there employed for words which refer to the pictures and for parts of the pictures themselves. There is considerable correspondence as to topics in the two texts, but the range of the *Orbis* is the greater. It has 151 chapters as against 100 for the *Janua*.

Inadequate as these descriptions are of the *Janua* and the *Orbis*, they suffice to convey a general conception of the matter and the method. We are now prepared to ask to what extent are the materials and the plan of presentation traditional; or to what degree do they represent that which is novel in thought and in the method of teaching languages? Recalling the descriptions and summaries in this survey, we see that the principle of compiling vocabularies under a series of certain well-defined topics had been active from the early Middle Ages and that in the Renaissance the range of such topics was wide enough to afford inclusiveness, as exemplified in the small dictionaries of Paludanus and of John Withals, not to mention all. Again, in the early sixteenth century the method of including in sentences the words for study and placing the sentences in parallel columns under conventional topics or headings, was, as in the *Vulgaria* of Horman, occasionally used; and in the early seventeenth century more systematically employed by William Bathe. Finally, we recall that there was at least one example of a pictorial or illustrated vocabulary. In brief, there were current before Comenius all the elements that are found in his *Janua* and his *Orbis*—the tested topics under which words were grouped, the wide range, implying universality, the use of sentences to give coherence to word lists, and the arrangement in parallel columns with the vernacular first. But no other book, so far as I know, exhibited the particular combination of these elements that is found in the manuals of the Moravian bishop and educator.

In the work of John Ray (1627-1705), the vocabulary tradition before it was elaborated by Bathe and Comenius is followed. In 1675 Ray first published his *Dictionariolum Trilingue,* a little dictionary in English, Latin, and Greek. This book was reissued at intervals through the first quarter of the eighteenth century, being entitled after the fourth edition *Nomenclator Classicus, sive Dictionariolum.*[29] It contains thirty-two chapters without illustrations but with the conventional headings: "Of Heaven," "Of the Elements and Meteors," "Of Stones and Metals," "Of Herbs," etc. Only in the range of topics does Ray's work reflect a possible influence of Comenius. Incidentally, Ray's book is probably more accurate in recording the names of plants and animals.

It remained for James Greenwood (d. 1737) to effect a consummation of the vocabulary tradition in *The London Vocabulary*, printed first about 1700 [30] and frequently thereafter during the eighteenth century. The obvious purpose of this little book was to give boys a working Latin vocabulary so that, as the author suggests, they might "enter upon the reading of Corderius, The Latin Testament, Erasmus, Aesop, Cato, Ovidii Tristia, etc." As to the method, the author states in the Preface:

I have made choice of the most Natural and Entertaining that the subject is capable of; and distributed Matters into such an Order that the Learner may at the same time and with the same Pains, with the Knowledge of the Words, understand the things themselves which they express, with their Order and Dependance upon one another. And the better to fix both upon the Memory of the young Readers, and to give them as clear an idea as possible of what they learn I have caused little Draughts and Pictures to be made of such Things as are known and distinguished by their outward Shapes, with References to the Words that mention them. . . .

The London Vocabulary consists of thirty-three chapters or topics, under each of which are grouped words immediately related to or suggested by the general topic; as under *fire*, for example, are *spark, smoke, flame, soot, a fire-brand, a live coal, a dead coal, ashes, cinders.* The subjects thus grouped have a wide range. They extend from God, heaven, the planets, through the four elements of fire, air, water, earth; through things on the earth, as man, the parts of the body, the mind, diseases, clothes, food and drink, man's activities and institutions—including agriculture, warfare, and funerals; through beasts, birds, fishes, herbs, trees; to time and the seasons, stopping short of the Judgment Day, but suggesting a principle of presentation analogous to that in the first two chapters of Genesis.

The lists of words under a general topic are arranged in parallel columns on the page, the English before the Latin; but the columns are broken at intervals by a link word or phrase, indicating the relation of small groups of words each to the other and to the general topic. Under the heading, "Of Judicial Matters," for example, the arrangement is as follows:

In Government there are

A Law 1	Lex, egis, f.
An Example	Exemplum, i, n.

In Law there are

A Judge 2	Judex, icis, m. & f.
A Counsellor 3	Consultor, oris, m.
A Witness 4	Testis, is, m. & f.

The Judge hath for Writing

A Secretary, or Scribe   Scriba, ae, f.

For speaking publicly

A cryer   Praeco, onis, m.

For executing the Sentence

A Hangman   Carnifex, icis, m.
Or Jack Ketch   5

Though the links here appear at more frequent intervals than in most chapters, they exemplify the author's attempt to give a sort of coherence to his vocabulary.

One of the most interesting features of this little book is the illustrations or the draughts and pictures referred to above. Immediately underneath each general heading and occupying about one-third of the page, is a composite cut designed to illustrate the topic. In each picture the numbers correspond to numbered words in the vocabulary which follows. To refer again to the chapter "Of Judicial Matters," the rectangular cut consists of two parts. The longer part shows a section of a courtroom with a judge ("1") seated at a desk on the dais, leafing through a law book ("2"); somewhat below and to the left is a counsellor ("3") obviously addressing the judge; and to the left of the lawyer is a witness ("4"). The second half of the picture is even more suggestive—it is a portion of a jail yard. In the background a barred window is visible; in front and below is a gallows against which leans a long ladder. Just above the ladder and astride the horizontal beam of the gallows is a villainous-looking person with long hair and a large hat, who in the Latin is called *carnifex*, in the English Jack Ketch ("5") or Hangman. Jack's business apparently is to cut the rope and free the corpse of the thief ("6"), which dangles from the beam. An impressive lesson for young schoolboys!

What with the illustrations, the selections and groupings of words, and the convenient format and cheapness of the text (one shilling), *The London Vocabulary* was an extremely popular book. It was reissued at fairly regular intervals in England from *ca.* 1700 to 1816, the year when the twenty-sixth edition [31] was published; and between 1787 and 1816 it went through at least four editions in America.

Though Greenwood states on the title-page [32] that his *Vocabulary* was "put into a New Method," and, by implication, was quite novel in the world of nomenclators and vocabularies, his statement cannot be taken seriously. Some of the immediate sources for content and method may be found in the late seventeenth century. But the tradition of which *The London Vocabulary* is a part is very old in European vocabularies, schoolbooks, and dictionaries; it goes back, indeed, at least seven hundred years.

Though it is the consummation of a long tradition, the immediate sources of the *Vocabulary* are two. For the topics or chapter headings and the vocabulary he drew largely from Ray's *Dictionariolum* or *Nomenclator*.[33] For the pictorial illustrations, the methods of reference to them, the use of phrases and sentences for links, Greenwood imitated the method of the *Orbis*, and in a few cases seems to have copied some of the pictures.

In conclusion we may observe that, as early as 1868, Thomas Wright suggested the value of these vocabularies, with their topical groupings, as illustrative of the conditions and manners of society and as a body of matter of special worth to the philologists. Wright was thinking, however, of vocabularies made before 1500. Our survey shows that similar lists continued to be made for another 150 years, and suggests that systematic study of them may be of even greater value. This survey, furthermore, supplies the historical background essential to the evaluation of the Comenius textbooks and methods, not, so far as we know, hitherto supplied by writers on education. Finally, it is worth remarking that certain features, such as the illustrations of the Comenius and the Greenwood, carry over to modern dictionaries; and there is some wonder that a tradition of so long standing did not exercise a greater influence on English lexicography.

Appendix II

THE DEVELOPMENT OF CANT LEXICOGRAPHY

IN ENGLAND, 1566-1785 *

IN THE FIRST QUARTER OF THE SEVENTEENTH CENTURY THE pioneer lexicographers of the English language—Cawdrey, Bullokar, and Cockeram—launched their dictionaries on their long careers, during which they were constantly revised and expanded; and after the middle of the century Blount and Phillips made notable advances in their dictionaries, which also underwent many revisions and expansions. Despite the variety of their materials, however, none of these lexicographers showed any interest in cant, the language of rogues and vagabonds, which had won and held great popularity in literature from early Elizabethan days. Elisha Coles in his *English Dictionary* of 1676 was the first to include any considerable body of cant. By that time, however, the development of specialized cant glossaries was well under way.

In the following discussion I intend to trace the beginnings of the cant dictionary, describe and compare some early specimens, and indicate the slow advance in lexicographical technique up to the publication in 1785 of Francis Grose's superior *Classical Dictionary of the Vulgar Tongue,* which ushered in a new period and new standards for cant lexicography. Although the works to be considered have attracted the attention of bibliographers,[1] some of them are rare and little known to students of literature. While I am primarily interested in their relation to the development of lexicography, I believe that these works are curious in themselves and that their number and popularity shed a significant light on the tastes of the reading public.

The table which follows may prove helpful as a guide to the discussion. For convenient cross reference each title is preceded by a letter

* Reprinted with permission from *Studies in Philology,* XXXVIII (July, 1941), 462-79.

symbol. Another letter symbol following the title shows the work under consideration to be derived from the earlier work represented by that symbol. Thus, item *f*, Head's *Canting Academy*, is based upon item *e*, the same author's *English Rogue*. It is not surprising that in cant lexicography, even more than in early English lexicography generally, progress has to be measured in terms of constant borrowing. Works marked with an asterisk are especially important: Harman's *Caveat* as the first to offer a cant glossary; Dekker's *Lanthorne and Candle-light* as an early popularizer and transmitter of cant; Head's *Canting Academy* as transitional; B. E.'s work as the first dictionary of cant and the contributor of much original material; the anonymous 1725 dictionary as an intelligent adaptation of B. E.'s and a more valuable dictionary; Coles's *English Dictionary* as the first general English dictionary to admit cant; Shirley's miscellany, with its many editions and imitations, as another popularizer of cant terms; and our terminus, Grose's *Classical Dictionary*. These points will be clarified and expanded below.

GLOSSARIES OF CANT	DICTIONARIES OF CANT	GENERAL ENGLISH DICTIONARIES
* a. Harman, *Caveat*, 1566?		
b. *Groundworke of Conny-Catching*, 1592 (a)		
* c. Dekker, *Lanthorne and Candle-light*, 1608-1648 (a)		Cawdrey, 1604
d. S. R., *Martin Mark-All*, 1610 (c)		No
		Bullokar, 1616
		Cockeram, 1623
		Cant
		Blount, 1656
		Phillips, 1658
e. Head, *The English Rogue*, 1665 (c)		
* f. Head, *The Canting Academy*, 1673 (e)		* g. Coles, 1676-1732 (f)
* h. Shirley, *The Triumph of Wit*, 1688-1760? (f)	* i. B. E., *A New Dictionary*, 1690-1700	j. *Ladies Dictionary*, 1694 (f)

GLOSSARIES OF CANT	DICTIONARIES OF CANT	GENERAL ENGLISH DICTIONARIES
l. Hall, *Memoirs*, 1708		k. Cocker, 1704–1724 (g)
m. Hitchin, *Regulator*, 1718		
n. Smith, *Compleat History*, 1719 (i)	* o. *A New Canting Dictionary*, 1725 (i)	
p. *Bacchus and Venus*, 1737 (o)		q. Bailey, 1737 (o)
r. Carew, *Life and Adventures*, 1745 (o)		
s. Carew, *Apology*, 1749 (o)	t. *Scoundrel's Dictionary*, 1754 (h)	u. Johnson, 1755 v. Ash, 1775 (g)
w. Parker, *A View of Society*, 1781		
	* x. Grose, *A Classical Dictionary*, 1785 (c, o, q, r)	
y. Parker, *Life's Painter*, 1789		

Thomas Harman's *Caveat or Warening, for Commen Cvrsetors vvlgarely called Vagabones*, 1566 or 1567, was the first work to carry a glossary of cant terms and may therefore be considered the first—though remote—precursor of the cant dictionary. Harman introduces his glossary contemptuously:

Here I set before the good Reader the leud, lousey language of these lewtering Luskes and lasy Lorrels where with they bye and sell the common people as they pas through the country. Whych language they terme Peddelars Frenche, a vnknowen toung onely, but to these bold, beastly, bawdy Beggers, and vaine Vacabondes, . . .[2]

In these early days the cant vocabulary cannot have been extensive, as, despite Harman's deep interest and wide acquaintance with rogues, he lists only 114 words.[3] These are arranged not in alphabetical order but by a random classification (parts of the body, clothes, money, food, etc.) and are defined for the most part by a single synonym. He follows his glossary with a sample dialogue in cant and concludes:

By this lytle ye maye holy and fully vnderstande their vntowarde talke and pelting speache, mynglede without measure; and as they haue begonne of late to deuyse some new termes for certien thinges, so wyll they in tyme alter this, and deuyse as euyll or worsse.[4]

Robert Greene's conny-catching pamphlets (1591-1592) concern what Awdeley called "the company of cousoners and shifters" rather than "the fraternitye of vacabondes." Yet the brotherhoods flourished side by side; and, as might be expected, each was quick to appropriate the other's tricks and jargon. In his various pamphlets Greene offers a wealth of material on the methods and language of coseners; but his nearest approach to a glossary is in *A Notable Discouery of Coosnage*, 1591, where he gives "A table of the words of art, vsed in the affecting *these base villanios*." [5] Here he enumerates "the eight lawes [tricks] of villanie, leading the high waie to infamie" and explains the terms used in connection with each "law" except the "cheating law," about which he is provokingly reticent:

... although no man could better then my self discouer this lawe and his tearmes, ... yet for some speciall reasons, herein I will be silent.

He cuts off his table with the following remark, indicating a sad lack of the lexicographer's heroic patience: "Cum multis aliis quae nunc pracscribere longum est." A similar table of five "lawes" and "words of art vsed in these lawes" is prefixed to *The Second ... Part of Conny-Catching*, 1592. Finally, *The Blacke Bookes Messenger*, 1592, opens with a brief table of eleven "words of Art lately deuised by Ned Browne and his associates." Between these words and those recorded by Harman there is little overlapping; [6] but both kinds of glossary reflect the growing curiosity about the secret language of the professionally dishonest.

A crude link between Harman and Greene is *The Groundworke of Conny-Catching*, 1592,[7] formerly uncritically attributed to Greene. The author, however, shows none of the latter's ingenuity and undoubtedly used the characteristic Greene title for its sales value. Indeed, the piece has no connection with conny-catching and, except for a brief account of new "sleights," is a direct plagiarism from Harman, reprinting the glossary of cant word for word as it had been compiled twenty-five years before.

Thomas Dekker's *Belman of London*, 1608, abounds in cant terms;

and his *Lanthorne and Candle-light* of the same year carries a glossary. The first chapter of the latter work is a history and description of canting, which Judges considered such "an unblushing plagiarization of Harman" that he arbitrarily omitted it from his reprint of *Lanthorne and Candle-light*.[8] Dekker has indeed added little to Harman, but he has surprisingly enlivened the old material. He introduces his discussion of cant with a fantastic sketch of the confusion of tongues arising at Babel and, assuming the manner of the philologist, analyzes the language, noting a wide use of compounds and some traces of Latin: ". . . some words . . . retaine a certaine salte, tasting of some wit and some Learning."[9]

Yet the glossary is handled with a dilettante air and makes no pretensions to inclusiveness:

I wil at this time not make you surfet on too much, but as if you were walking in a Garden, you shall openly pluck here a flower, and there another, which (as I take it) will be more delightfull then if you gathered them by handfulls.[10]

Containing only 88 words, this glossary appears to be a step backward from Harman. Dekker has, however, merely omitted terms already explained in the text; he actually deals with all those in Harman's list, though the fact is somewhat disguised by an attempt at alphabetical arrangement. In the numerous editions of *Lanthorne and Candle-light*, although the title is changed,[11] new material added, and the order of contents constantly shifted, the chapter on canting and the glossary remain the same. Like Greene, Dekker was interested in the fictional possibilities of his material rather than in the glossary, which had actually been at a standstill ever since Harman. Yet the fact that it was carried through the years indicates that it held its popularity with the reading public.

Dekker ended his glossary with a remark which was little more than a formula:

If hee [the Belman] keepe not touch, by tendring the due Summe [fulfilling the promise of a further work made in *The Belman*], he desires forbearance, and if any that is more rich in this *Canting* commodity will lend him any more, or any better, hee will pay his loue double.[12]

This challenge was disconcertingly taken by S.R.,[13] whose *Martin Mark-All, Beadle of Bridewell; His Defence and Answere to the Belman of London* (first known edition, 1610) at once exposed Dekker's plagiarism from Harman and sarcastically undertook to bring up to date and enlarge his antiquated glossary:

> I haue thought good not only to shew his errour in some places in setting downe olde wordes vsed fortie yeeres agoe before he was borne; for wordes that are vsed in these dayes... But haue enlarged his Dictionary (or Master Harmans) with such wordes as an experienced souldier that hath deerely paid for it:....[14]

Dekker's list serves as a basis, corrections being indicated by a certain sign in the margin and additions by another. The resultant glossary contains 129 entries, 10 of which profess to be modernizations and 53, additions. Among the latter may be noted some local expressions (*"Cheepmans,* Cheap-side market"; *"Gracemans,* Gratious streete market"; *"Numans,* Newgate market"; *"Whittington,* Newgate"), some compounds (*"greenmans,* fields"; *"filchman,* a cudgell"), and a few distasteful expressions.

By 1610, according to Chandler,[15] "no picaresque literature out of Spain was so rich . . . as the English." Yet in the next fifty years rogue literature showed a surprising lapse, and the advance toward a canting dictionary halted. True, many pamphlets in this field have probably been lost or overlooked; [16] and the drama remained susceptible to rogue themes and even boasted whole scenes in cant.[17] However, foreign picaresque novels in translation filled the shops and discouraged English writers, who turned to other fields. The advance of Puritanism tended to curb the native output of rogue books, and the Revolution diverted attention. It was not until after the Restoration that rogue literature and the cant glossary were simultaneously revived by Richard Head.

The break in the continuity of rogue literature and the canting tradition is significant from another point of view. Up to 1610 writers of rogue literature usually professed a reforming purpose, in which at least Awdeley and Harman were sincere. The latter's title-page proclaimed that his work was "set forth for the utilitie and profytt of his naturall Cuntrey," and the Epistle enlarged upon the assertion. As concrete evidence of his zeal in exposure, Harman even sent to the proper justices a list of rogues residing in those parts, and printed a long list of wandering "vpright men, roges, and pallyards," many of whom were later apprehended.[18] The rogues were still a formidable menace when Greene and Dekker wrote, also under the guise of reformers. Both, however, were primarily attracted by the fictional possibilities and the extraordinary popularity of the material; and it is significant that in their narratives neither supposed reformer spared realistic detail, salacious or otherwise. After the Restoration beggars were no longer a contemporary problem, and there was no excuse for discussing them on the ground of reform. Rogue literature temporarily lost ground. Then the criminal biographies came into vogue, and the field was exploited for its romantic and fictive appeal. The subject still proved popular with writers and with the public. The language of rogues holds its interest, and glossaries are frequently found, while the canting dictionary is just around the corner.

Richard Head's *English Rogue,* which appeared in 1665, contained a canting vocabulary. In Part I, Chapter V, Latroon, the hero, falls in with the "Ragged Regiment," from whom he learns the various orders, the tricks, songs, and language. In the discussion preceding the glossary Head offers a condensed version of the history and description of cant prefixed to Dekker's glossary. Head's word list is also based on Dekker's (and hence on Harman's) but is considerably enlarged, at least one-third of the words being additions. The glossary, consisting of 187 words, usually with synonym definitions, concludes with a remark in the same offhand manner as those quoted from Greene and Dekker:

This much for a taste. I think it not worth my pains to insert all those canting words which are used; it is enough that I have here divulged what words are most in use.[19]

In the continuation of *The English Rogue* by Francis Kirkman, 1671, there is another beggar episode (Part II, Chapters XIV-XV) with an explanation of the various orders but no glossary.

Of much greater interest to us is Head's *Canting Academy* of 1673.[20] This curious work has rather thin and miscellaneous contents: the oath taken by rogues, canting songs, "the vicious and remarkable lives of Mother Craftsby and Mrs. Wheedle," some "joviall paradoxes," songs and catches composed by "the choicest Wits of the Age," and some horrible "examples of Covetousness, Idleness, Gluttony, and Lechery." The last features were obvious padding, but the glossary itself is justly claimed to be "more compleat than any hath been publisht hitherto." [21]

Head is indeed the first author since Harman to have exerted himself in the preparation of his glossary:

I can assure you (the helps extant being so inconsiderable) the pains I took in the Collection of new Words is unimaginable.[22]

He is also the first since Harman to give any serious discussion of his sources as well as to take into account the constant changes in cant:

I have consulted . . . what is printed on this subject, and have slighted no help I could gather from thence, which indeed is very little; the greatest assistance I had in this discovery, was from *Newgate;* which with much difficulty I screw'd out of the sullen Rogues, . . . From these I understood, that the Mode of Canting alter'd very often, and that they were forced to change frequently those material words which chiefly discovered their mysterious practices and Villanies, least growing too common their own words should betray them. Here in this Vocabulary or little Canting Dictionary, you have all or most of the old words which are still in use, and a many new never published in print, and but very lately minted, such too which have passed the approbation of the Critical Canter.[23]

Head, then, still retains practically all of Dekker's items, omitting a few as antiquated and adding a good many of more recent coinage.

A new feature of this dictionary is the double word list, the first part translating cant into English and the second, English into cant, each comprising about three hundred expressions. The glossary of *The English Rogue* has been enlarged and better arranged, although the user of the second part may experience some difficulty. For instance, the following items listed under *A* may prove elusive: *A Groat, A Receiver of stolen goods, A fine Gentlewoman, A Door,* etc. The following definition of a word appearing for the first time in the *Academy* may be cited as illustrative of a new tendency to experiment with less concise definitions:

Kidnapper. A fellow that walketh the streets, and takes all advantages to pick up the younger sort of people, whom with lies and many fair promises he enticeth on board a ship and transports them into forreign plantations.[24]

Elisha Coles, whose *English Dictionary* appeared in 1676 and went through many editions, was the first to include cant in a general dictionary, a departure justified in his preface on the following utilitarian grounds:

'Tis no Disparagement to understand the Canting Terms: It may chance to save your Throat from being cut, or (at least) your Pocket from being pick'd.[25]

The Canting Academy was probably used as the most convenient source. Coles has most of the words in Head's list and does not go noticeably beyond it. Definitions are brief, sometimes verbatim as in Head; and a few longer definitions show similarity in phrasing.[26] The point of importance, however, is Coles's introduction into a general English dictionary of cant terms.

This policy of Coles was by no means tacitly accepted by his followers. *Cocker's English Dictionary* of 1704, which imitated Coles in other respects, included no cant. This was consistent with the aim to produce "a Work necessary for all Persons who ... would attain to Eloquence in Speaking, and Elegancy in Writing." [27] In later editions, however, the reviser grudgingly capitulated:

It is likewise asserted, That it is no Disparagement to understand the Canting Terms... because it may chance to save a Man's throat from being cut; as if these Miscreants would be kinder to any one for speaking or understanding a little of their Gibberish. I have inserted some few, but omitted a multitude.[28]

Surprisingly enough, *The Ladies Dictionary* printed for John Dunton in 1694 contains some cant terms. The author's aim, however, was to offer "a *Compleat Directory* to the *Female-Sex* in all *Relations, Companies, Conditions* and *States* of Life"; [29] and most of the cant terms selected describe different orders of women beggars. The majority are briefly treated; but a few longer explanations are taken verbatim from *The Canting Academy: Autem Morts, Kynchin Morts, Mumpers, Night-Walkers, Patricos, Shop-Lifts,* etc. The appearance of cant in this work is important as an indication of its widespread vogue; and the dependence upon Head suggests that the undated dictionary of B. E. to be discussed below was not available by 1694, as in that case Dunton or his assistant would have been more likely to consult that source.

Other compilers of general English dictionaries had little to do with cant until Nathan Bailey, whose *Universal Etymological English Dictionary* from its first edition in 1721 contained a good many cant terms so designated but appearing in the main word list. This dictionary continued with the same arrangement into the nineteenth century.[30] In 1727 appeared a so-called "second volume" of the *Universal Etymological English Dictionary*, more accurately a supplementary volume, which ran through several editions and changed its contents often to suit contemporary vogues. In the third edition of this supplementary volume, dated 1737, a separate cant vocabulary of 36 pages was introduced. In the Preface the author remarks: ". . . for the Satisfaction (but not the Imitation) of the Curious, I have Added a Collection of Words, &c. used by the Canting Tribe"; accordingly at the back of the book appears a section headed: "A Collection of the Canting Words and Terms, both ancient and modern, used by Beggars, Gypsies, Cheats, House-Breakers, Shop-Lifters, Foot-Pads, Highway-Men, &c." Though the definitions are shortened, this list is, as Burke points out,[31] based on the *New Canting Dictionary* of 1725 to be discussed below. This feature was retained in subsequent editions of the supplementary volume.

As would be expected, Johnson, always a strenuous opponent of corruption in speech, lists few cant words in his *Dictionary of the English Language*, 1755. Many of the commonest terms are missing; but Johnson found passages in Pope, Swift, and other writers to authorize his inclusion of some words (*bit, bite, bub, bunter*, etc.). In each case, besides citing his authorities, he is careful to brand the word as "low" or "vulgar."

One other general lexicographer within our period may be mentioned, John Ash, whose *New and Complete Dictionary* of 1775 was boasted to be "extensive beyond any thing that has yet been attempted of the kind in the English Language." [32] Ash includes a generous sprinkling of cant terms, the commoner ones (*doxy, fambles*, etc.) without source but the less common (*margery prater, prigs, prigstar, priket, stre*, etc.) credited specifically to Coles.[33]

To return to the main line of development, as an inevitable result of the vogue of cant in literature and of cant glossaries, came the first actual canting dictionary so called and devoted exclusively to a word list. *A New Dictionary of the Terms Ancient and Modern of the Cant-*

ing Crew by "B. E., Gent." bore no date and has been variously assigned between 1690 and 1700.[34] The title-page proclaimed the work "useful for all sorts of People (especially Foreigners) to secure their *Money* and preserve their *Lives;* besides very Diverting and Entertaining, being wholly New." We cannot grant that it is "wholly new," as some definitions echo *The Canting Academy.* B. E.'s dictionary is, however, so much more extensive that its debt to any predecessor is negligible. Some idea of the comparative size of B. E.'s dictionary and the *Academy* can be derived from the following figures: under *A,* Head lists only 4 items and B. E., 57; under *G,* Head lists 20 and B. E., 130. B. E. not only defines a far greater number of words but deals under each item with related expressions or, as the title-page puts it, "Proverbs, Phrases, Figurative Speeches, &c."

The style of definition, which began to be less concise and impersonal with Head, shows a further growth in liveliness and readability. Consider, for example, the following:

Barker, a Salesman's Servant that walks before the Shop, and cries Cloaks, Coats, or Gowns, What d'ye lack, Sir? [35]

Like Head, also, B. E. still found his actual canting material too slight to fill a book and resorted to padding in the form of the inclusion of many slang and specialized terms. Under *A* alone are such varied, non-canting terms as: *acquests* and *acquisition* (legal), *addle-pate* and *addle-plot* (slang), *adrift, aft,* and *abase* (seaman's jargon), *aim* (for *endeavor*), *alabaster* (*cosmetics*), etc.

In 1725 appeared anonymously *A New Canting Dictionary,* which was in reality an intelligent revision and plagiarization of B. E.'s dictionary. Says the author noncommittally:

With Regard to the Performance in general we shall only say, There is nothing so complete of its Kind; and we have taken no small Pains to collect all the New Words made use of by Villains of all Denominations: By perusing and retaining many of which, an Honest Man, who is obliged to travel... may secure himself from Danger; which is the principal Design of compiling this Vocabulary.[36]

Although the preface of this dictionary is much longer, several leading ideas and some of the phrasing of B. E.'s preface are retained. Longer items taken over verbatim or almost verbatim near the beginning of the alphabet are: *Adam-tiler, Ambidexter, Anglers, Bandog, Barker, Bit,* etc. Practically all definitions of words in common are similar, though the later dictionary tends to even fuller explanations and often notes additional related expressions.

The compiler of the 1725 work showed most discrimination in his omissions. The numerous non-cant terms in the earlier dictionary are now consistently excluded. An interesting case is the careful justification for the treatment of the word "Astrologers":

We think we may justly include the Generality of Pretenders to this Art and Science, among the Canters, and need not to make any Apology for so doing; For who deceives the Vulgar more, by their unintelligible Canting Jargon of Trines.[97]

The 1725 dictionary thus contains fewer items than the earlier (*e.g.,* under *A*, B. E. has 57 but the 1725 author, 34; under *G*, B. E. has 130 but the 1725 author, 96; etc.) but because of the fuller definitions and the increase in derived expressions reaches almost the same total length.

It is now necessary to consider certain works in which the glossary of cant was an incidental feature. In 1688 John Shirley exploited the popularity of cant in his miscellany, which seems insignificant enough but which had many editions and exerted an influence over many years. *The Triumph of Wit* consisted of three parts: "A Variety of excellent Poems," "The Whole Art and Mystery of Love," and "The Mystery and Art of Wheedling and Canting." In the last part the author as usual professes to expose such practices so that the reader may "shun and avoid the evil Courses they tend to," [88] although presumably the danger was slight in his day and for the audience he addresses. He discusses the origin of cant, stressing its supposed connection with the Egyptians; the various orders of rogues; the ceremonies, customs, and tricks. Despite its heading, "The Gypsies and Beggars Cant" contains no Romany; it is merely an English-cant vocabulary consisting of about 200 words and 30 longer expressions. The word list is clearly derived from the second list in *The Canting Academy.* Perhaps in acknowledgment of this fact, the sub-title calls the work, "The Newest and Most Useful ACADEMY"; and the glossary is called in some editions, "The New Canting Academy." This work with the section on cant unchanged appeared as late as 1735 (ninth edition) and in an undated edition printed in Dublin (1760-1780?).

An off-shoot of the above work is *The Scoundrel's Dictionary*, 1754, picturesquely described as "printed from a Copy taken on one of their Gang, in the late Scuffle between the Watchmen and a Party of them on Clerkenwell-Green." [39] This book, often called the rarest of the cant dictionaries because so many copies are thought to have been lost in a great fire, is merely a reprint of Part III of *The Triumph of Wit* and hence another descendant of *The Canting Academy*.[40] Whereas *The Triumph of Wit* was apparently intended for the diversion of the middle class, however, this dictionary seems to have had some contact with the beggars. At any rate it concludes with an unusual plea for charity to honest beggars.

One more miscellany should be mentioned—*Bacchus and Venus*, 1737, a curious work whose compiler made free use of the 1725 dictionary. This work opens with "A Select Collection of near 200 [actually 154] ... Songs and Catches"; these are love and drinking songs of a low order but quite unrelated to beggars. The beggars' songs follow in "A Collection of Songs in the Canting Dialect with a DICTIONARY." Both the songs in this section and the dictionary are reprinted from the 1725 volume.

Next comes a group of works connected with famous criminals and offering incidental lists of cant. *The Memoirs of the Right Villanous John Hall, the Late Famous and Notorious Robber, Penn'd from his Mouth some time before his Death*, 1708, ran through at least four editions and was recently reprinted in part.[41] The justification offered in the first edition for printing the material is amusing; there is, the author says, "as much Skill in pourtraying a Dunghil, as in describing the finest Palace, since the Excellence of Things lye in the Perform-ance." [42] After "An Interpretation of the Several Qualities of Rogues" and "A lively Representation of Newgate" comes "The Canter's Ex-positor" comprising 106 words. Most of these are familiar from earlier lists, though some are further corrupted in form. Of greater interest are the newer and often more picturesque expressions: "*Harry*, a Country-man"; "*Sword*, a Soldier"; "*Stickhams*, Gloves"; "*Tatler*, Clock or Watch"; "*Evil*, a Halter"; "*Lark*, a Boat"; etc.[43]

Next in this group is *The Regulator*, 1718, written by Charles

Hitchin, corrupt City Marshal and "receiver," to denounce his former ally but now bitterest enemy, Jonathan Wild. Fully qualified by his experience and associations to be an authority in the field, Hitchin gives "An Account of all the Flash Words now in vogue among the Thieves." [44] This list contains only about 100 words, at least half of which are familiar. Definitions are very concise. A few names of tricks are, however, explained at more length and in livelier style:

The Question Lay To knock at a Door early in the Morning and ask for the Master of the House, and if he's abed to desire the Servant not to disturb him, for you'll wait till he rises, and so you take an Opportunity of stealing something.

The Kid Lay Is when you see a Boy or a Porter with a Bundle, to desire him to go on an Errand for you, telling him you'll take Care of his goods the while; but as soon as he's out of Sight, you make off with the Booty.[45]

"Captain" Alexander Smith, an indefatigable writer on the lives and ways of disreputable men, would appear, as Seccombe says, to have been "better known as a frequenter of police-courts and taverns than in military circles." [46] His *Compleat History of the Lives and Robberies of the Most Notorious Highwaymen, Footpads, Shoplifts, & Cheats of Both Sexes* (second edition, 1714) had at least five editions and was reprinted by A. L. Hayward in 1926. The fifth edition (1719) offers not only a *Thieves' New Canting Dictionary* but a *Thieves' Grammar*, a *Thieves' Key Found Out*, and a *Thieves' Exercise*. The dictionary treats over 200 words with many derived expressions and is based on B. E.'s, from which definitions are taken verbatim. The work is more usable, however, as items are arranged in accurate alphabetical order. Of the other parts of *The Compleat History*, the *Thieves' Exercise* is a small, specialized dictionary, consisting of 30 words of command with explanations. In this work, "Young Beginners" are to be "Daily Practisd by their Superiours, till they are perfect in the Art and Mystery of Thieving." The other two sections, though very curious, have no connection with lexicography.

The name of Bampfylde-Moore Carew is associated with two works which overlap confusingly: *The Life and Adventures of Bampfylde-Moore Carew*, 1745, and *An Apology for the Life of Bampfylde-Moore Carew*, 1749. Under varying titles the exploits of Carew held their popularity for a century or more; indeed these works have been re-printed at intervals down to our own day. All but the earliest editions carried a glossary of cant introduced by the following remark:

As the Language of the Community of the *Gypsies* is very expressive, and different from all others, we think we shall do a Pleasure to the Curious by annexing a short Specimen of it.

The glossary which did duty for both works was brief, containing about 300 words with concise definitions. C. H. Wilkinson in his edition of both books under the title, *The King of the Beggars, Bampfylde-Moore Carew,* 1931, correctly describes this glossary as "an unacknowledged selection of the words given in *A New Canting Dictionary* [1725]." [47] Wilkinson does not, however, analyze changes in the make-up of the glossary in later editions. The glossary in the 1812 edition has undergone extensive enlargement and modernization; and an undated but apparently still later edition shows a third form of glossary, in which some of the original words persist but many newer cant words are added as well as a separate short "Vocabulary of Words Used by the Scottish Gipsies."

We conclude with a mention of two works by the eccentric George Parker—soldier, actor, and lecturer; friend of Johnson, Reynolds, and Goldsmith; and, in the course of his travels with provincial companies, associate of rogues and vagabonds as well. In *A View of Society and Manners in High and Low Life,* 1781, ostensibly an account of his own adventures as an itinerant, there is a wealth of material on roguery. The hero joins a group of beggars at Dunkirk, French Flanders and learns 74 varieties of rogue with special tricks of each.[48] Certain anecdotes make use of cant dialogue, but there is no dictionary.

This feature is generously supplied in *Life's Painter of Variegated Characters in Public and Private Life,* 1789. After satirizing other phases of society, Parker introduces his discussion of low life with protestations of reluctance:

With a fearful foot, I enter on the soil of the following chapter, and I do beseech my fair readers to shun it, lest, in this primrose path, they meet a snake in the grass.[49]

Chapter XV [50] contains a glossary of cant with definitions in leisurely style and anecdotes interspersed. The items (about 125) are arranged not by alphabetical or by any other recognizable order, and definitions are not consistent; some are brief, whereas others are extremely discursive. Under *Reader* (pocket-book), for instance, Parker obligingly explains both the thief's method of stealing your *reader* and the method by which you can apprehend the thief and recover the *reader*.[51] The names of many new kinds of rogues are also introduced, as for instance:

Smacking Sam. A noted fellow, who on a trial will endeavour to prove an *alibi*, by swearing through as many bibles as could be packed up as high as St. Paul's.[52]

Under *Hot* (a kind of drink) Parker tells an anecdote of "that darling of his age, doctor Goldsmith," who was taken into a "ken" one night and fell into conversation with a "crap-merchant" (hangman) with dramatic results.[53] Among the words in the glossary are some surviving from the earliest lists but a majority of new ones. It may be of interest to instance a few of the fundamental terms that have to do with parts of the body as they were called in Harman's time and as in Parker's.

	HARMAN, 1566	PARKER, 1789
head	nab	napper
eyes	glasyers	peepers or ogles
nose	smelling chete	snitch
mouth	gan	bone shop
lips	gans	lispers
teeth	crashing chetes	pegs
hands	fambles	daddles
body	quaromes	trunk
legs	stampes	gams

In order to consider both works by Parker we have gone slightly beyond the nominal date for the conclusion of our study. In 1785 Francis Grose published his *Classical Dictionary of the Vulgar Tongue*,[54] in the preparation of which he acknowledged that he had collected terms from Dekker, the *New Canting Dictionary* (1725), Bailey, the *History of Bampfylde-Moore Carew*, the Sessions Papers, "and other modern authorities." [55] The facts that he made such a comparatively extensive study and that he stated his sources make us aware that we are on the threshold of a new period. The higher standards of accuracy and lexicography introduced by Grose bring to a close the quaint period with which we have dealt.

Appendix III

BIBLIOGRAPHY AND CENSUS OF DICTIONARIES

IN AMERICAN LIBRARIES

SPECIAL ACKNOWLEDGMENT IS DUE TO ARTHUR G. KENNEDY'S *A Bibliography of Writings on the English Language from the Beginning of Printing to the end of 1922* (Cambridge and New Haven, 1927), the most comprehensive and reliable work for studies on the English language during the period covered. The following list of selected books and articles dealing with the history of English lexicography contains the most helpful of the references given by Kennedy and additional items, most of which were published since 1922.

A. REFERENCES ON THE HISTORY OF ENGLISH LEXICOGRAPHY

Bailey, John E. *et al.* "N. Bailey's Dictionaries," *Notes and Queries*, ser. v, I, 448, 514; II, 156, 258, 514-15; III, 175-76, 298, 509-11; IV, 276; VII, 447; VIII, 52-53, 178; ser. vi, III, 161, 269-70. 1874-1881.

D., J. *et al.* "Early English Dictionaries," *Notes and Queries*, ser. vi, III, 141-42, 161-63, 209-10, 269-71, 319, 376, 419, 474-75; IV, 257, 279. 1881.

Gove, Philip B. "Notes on Serialization and Competitive Publishing: Johnson's and Bailey's Dictionaries, 1755," Oxford Bibliographical Society *Proceedings and Papers*, V (Oxford, 1940), 307-22.

The author explains the circumstances under which the Scott-Bailey dictionary of 1755 was published and the manner in which it borrowed from Johnson.

Long, Percy W. "English Dictionaries before Webster," Bibliographical Society of America *Papers*, IV (1909), 25-43.

A valuable essay on special features and types of English dictionaries in the seventeenth and eighteenth centuries.

Mathews, M. M. *A Survey of English Dictionaries*. London: Oxford University Press, 1933.

This work adds little to other surveys, but the chapters on "The Historical Principle in Lexicography" and "A Review of Lexicographical Methods" are helpful.

Murray, Sir James A. H. *The Evolution of English Lexicography*. (The Romanes Lecture, 1900.) London: Oxford University Press, 1900.

P. W. Long properly characterized this work as "an entertaining lecture," "not to be taken as the serious work of the chief of the Oxford English Dictionary."

Noyes, Gertrude E. "Some Interrelations of English Dictionaries of the Seventeenth Century," *Publications of the Modern Language Association*, LIV (Dec., 1939), 990-1006.

———. "The Development of Cant Lexicography in England," *Studies in Philology*, XXXVIII (July, 1941), 462-79.

———. "John Dunton's *Ladies Dictionary*, 1694," *Philological Quarterly*, XXI (April, 1942), 129-45.

———. "Edward Cocker and *Cocker's English Dictionary*," *Notes and Queries*, CLXXXII (May 30, 1942), 298-300.

———. "The First English Dictionary, Cawdrey's *Table Alphabeticall*," *Modern Language Notes*, LVIII (Dec., 1943), 600 s.

Onions, C. T. (Editor). *An Exhibition of Books Illustrating the History of English Dictionaries held in the Bodleian Library at Oxford to celebrate the completion of the Oxford English Dictionary*. London: Oxford University Press, n. d. (Cr. 8vo, 24 pp.)

Segar, Mary. "Dictionary Making in the Early Eighteenth Century," *Review of English Studies*, VII (April, 1931), 210-13.

Skeat, W. W. (Editor). *A Bibliographical List of the Works that have been published, or are known to exist in MS., illustrative of the various Dialects of English*. London: English Dialect Society Publications, 1873-1877.

Section I (pp. 3-17) contains a list of general English dictionaries which offer materials for the study of provincial words.

Starnes, DeWitt T. "Bilingual Dictionaries of Shakespeare's Day," *Publications of the Modern Language Association*, LII (Dec., 1937), 1005-18.

———. "English Dictionaries of the Seventeenth Century," University of Texas *Studies in English*, July, 1937, pp. 15-51.

——. "*The London Vocabulary* and Its Antecedents," University of Texas *Studies in English*, 1939, pp. 114-38.

——. "Literary Features of Renaissance Dictionaries," *Studies in Philology*, XXXVII (Jan., 1940), 26-50.

Vizetelly, Frank H. "The Development of the Dictionary," *New Age*, XI (1909), 385-93, 481-88.

——. *The Development of the Dictionary of the English Language with special reference to the Funk and Wagnalls' New Standard Dictionary*. New York and London: Funk and Wagnalls, 1915.

A useful survey after the pattern of Worcester. The author notices briefly the bilingual dictionaries of Huloet, Baret, Cotgrave, and Florio, and devotes several paragraphs to Cawdrey, Bullokar, Cockeram, Blount, and Phillips with special attention to definitions. To Bailey, Johnson, Sheridan, and Webster the author gives more space. There is, however, no study of sources, interrelationships, changes effected in the various editions, etc.

Weekley, Ernest. "On Dictionaries." *Atlantic Monthly*, CXXXIII (June, 1924), 782-91.

——. "Our Early Etymologists," *Quarterly Review*, CCLVII (July, 1931), 63-72.

A discussion of John Minsheu, Stephen Skinner, and Francis Junius.

Wheatley, Henry B. "Chronological Notices of the Dictionaries of the English Language," *Transactions of the Philological Society* (1865), 218-93.

"My object in the present paper," writes Wheatley, "is to give as complete a list as possible of the English Dictionaries; but as apparently no purely English Dictionary was published until the year 1616, I have introduced an account of the bilingual and trilingual Dictionaries published previously to that date, in which the English precedes the other languages." The list extends to 1864 and is the best survey hitherto published. The author reprints title-pages, quotes some of the apt prefaces and dedications, indicates dates of editions, and concludes with a concise chronological table of dictionaries.

Wiener, Leo. "English Lexicography," *Modern Language Notes*, XI (June, 1896), 351-66.

The author criticizes the *New English Dictionary* on the grounds that it made insufficient use of the early English dictionaries, which he then describes, stressing the fields in which each specialized.

Wilkins, John. *An Essay Towards a Real Character and a Philosophical Language.* London, 1668.

At the end of Part IV of this volume is printed, with a separate title-page, "An Alphabetical Dictionary, wherein all English Words According to their Various Significations are either referred to their places in the Philosophical Tables or explained by such words as are in these tables... London... 1668."

This is a dictionary to illustrate the author's theory concerning a philosophical language, and belongs in a discussion of a universal language rather than in that of lexicography. For a study of Wilkins' experiment and a reprint of his text, see Otto Funke's "Zum Weltsprachenproblem in England im 17. Jahrhundert," *Anglistische Forschungen,* LXIX (1929). The author discusses George Dalgarno's *Ars Signorum* (1661) and Wilkins' *Essay.*

Worcester, Joseph E. *Dictionary of the English Language.* Boston, 1860.

Pp. liii-lviii, "History of English Lexicography." The author begins with a survey of early lexicographers other than English, as Suidas, John of Balbus, and Friar Calepine, and refers briefly to the *Ortus Vocabulorum* and to Huloet and Rider in the sixteenth century. There is no mention of Cawdrey; but the author devotes brief space to Bullokar, Cockeram, Blount, and slightly more to Phillips, Kersey, Bailey, Dyche, Martin, Johnson, and Richardson.

Pp. lix ff., "A Catalogue of English Dictionaries." This extends from 1499 to 1856, and includes bilingual and trilingual dictionaries when English is one of the languages.

B. A CHRONOLOGICAL LIST OF DICTIONARIES WITH THEIR EDITIONS AND LOCATIONS IN AMERICAN LIBRARIES

The following list contains all the data that we have been able to compile on the editions of the various dictionaries and on the locations of copies in American libraries. For the study of editions, Kennedy's *Bibliography,* pp. 221-29, served as a valuable groundwork. Most of the locations were kindly supplied by George A. Schwegmann, Jr., Director of the Union Catalogs of the Library of Congress. Other locations ascertained in the course of our studies and correspondence have been added. We believe our census to be complete for at least the following libraries, which have been especially checked: Library of Congress, Yale, Harvard, the University of Texas Library, the Boston Public, the

New York Public, the University of Chicago Library, the Folger, and the Huntington. Finally, we hope that our record is sufficiently complete to offer some notion of the comparative rareness of the various dictionaries and to supply convenient locations for any one who wishes to consult a particular dictionary or edition.

Cawdrey, Robert. *A Table Alphabeticall, conteyning and teaching the true writing, and understanding of hard usuall English wordes,* ... 1604. Octavo.

> Cf. Kennedy: Nos. 6160, 6161.

> *1.* 1604 Library of Congress (rotograph copy of original in Bodleian).
> *3.* 1613 Not located.
> *4.* 1617 Not located.

Bullokar, John. *An English Expositor: Teaching the Interpretation of the hardest words used in our Language.* ... 1616. Small octavo.

> Cf. Kennedy: Nos. 6162, 6163, 6168, 6173, 6177, 6185, 6188, 6190, 6194, 6209, 6222.

> *1.* 1616 Folger, Huntington, U. of Illinois.
> *2.* 1621 Furness Memorial at U. of Pennsylvania, Newberry, Yale.
> *3.* 1641 Folger, Harvard, U. of Chicago, Yale.
> *4.* 1656 Boston Public, Huntington, U. of Illinois.
> *4.* 1663 Not located.
> *4.* 1667 Harvard, Library of Congress, U. of Chicago.
> *5.* 1676 U. of Chicago.
> *6.* 1680 Library of Congress, U. of Illinois, U. of Texas.
> *7.* 1684 Harvard, U. of Michigan, Yale.
> *8.* 1688 Harvard.
> *9.* 1698 U. of Chicago, U. of Texas.
> *10.* 1707 Brown.
> *11.* 1715 Not located.
> *12.* 1719 Library of Congress, U. of Texas.
> *13.* 1726 Not located.
> *14.* 1731 Boston Public, Library of Congress, Peabody Institute, U. of Illinois, U. of Michigan, U. of Texas.

Cockeram, Henry. *The English Dictionarie; or, An Interpreter of Hard English Words.* ... 1623. Small octavo.

> Cf. Kennedy: Nos. 6164-6167, 6169-6171, 6174, 6180.

> *1.* 1623 Boston Public, Folger (Folger has 2 issues of the 1623 edition).

2. 1626 Folger, New York Public.
3. 1631 Folger, Huntington, U. of Chicago.
4. 1632 Folger, Library of Congress, Yale.
5. 1637 Huntington.
6. 1639 Huntington, New York Public.
7. 1642 Harvard, U. of Chicago.
8. 1647 Library of Congress.
9. 1650 U. of Chicago, U. of Texas, Yale.
10. 1651 Library of Congress.
10. 1655 Huntington.
11. 1658 Harvard, U. of Chicago.
12. 1670 U. of Chicago, U. of Texas.

Blount, Thomas. *Glossographia: ... Interpreting all such Hard Words, ... Also the Terms of Divinity, Law, ... With Etymologies, Definitions, and Historical Observations ...* 1656. Octavo.

Cf. Kennedy: Nos. 6172, 6179, 6182, 6186.

1. 1656 Folger, Harvard, Huntington, Library of Congress, Newberry, New York Public, Princeton, U. of Chicago, U. of Texas, Yale.
2. 1661 Boston Public, Folger, Library of Congress, U. of Chicago, U. of Illinois, U. of Iowa, U. of Texas, Yale.
3. 1670 Folger, Harvard, Library of Congress, New York Public, U. of Illinois, U. of Texas, Yale.
4. 1674 Harvard, Harvard Law, Lehigh, Massachusetts Historical Society, New York Public, Princeton, U. of Texas.
5. 1681 Brown, Folger, New York Public, U. of Chicago, U. of Illinois, U. of Michigan, U. of Oregon, Western Reserve, Yale.

Phillips, Edward. *The New World of English Words: ... Containing the Interpretations of such hard words.... All those Terms that relate to the Arts and Sciences ... The signification of Proper Names ...* 1658. Small Folio.

Cf. Kennedy: Nos. 6176, 6181, 6184, 6195.

1. 1658 Boston Public, Folger, Harvard, Library of Congress, Newberry, Princeton, U. of Illinois, U. of Michigan, U. of Texas, Yale.
2. 1662 Furness Memorial at U. of Pennsylvania, New York Public, U. of Illinois.

3. 1671 Brown, Harvard, Huntington, Library of Congress, New York Public, U. of Illinois, U. of Iowa, U. of Texas, U. of Virginia.

4. 1678 Harvard, New York Public, Princeton, U. of Chicago, U. of Illinois, U. of Michigan, U. of Minnesota, U. of Texas, Yale.

5. 1696 U. of Chicago, U. of Illinois, Yale.

5. 1700 U. of Illinois, U. of Texas.

(Later editions are listed under John Kersey, reviser, below.)

Coles, Elisha. *An English Dictionary: Explaining The difficult Terms that are used in... Arts and Sciences. Containing Many thousand of Hard Words... Together with The Etymological Derivatives* ... 1676. Octavo.

Cf. Kennedy: Nos. 6183, 6189, 6196, 6202, 6207, 6217, 6223.
(Editions not numbered)

1676 Folger, Huntington, U. of Minnesota, Yale.

1677 Boston Public, Princeton, U. of Iowa, U. of Texas.

1685 Harvard, Newberry, U. of Illinois, Yale.

1692 U. of Illinois, Yale.

1696 U. of Illinois, U. of Texas.

1701 Boston Athenaeum, Harvard, U. of Chicago, Yale.

1708 Boston Public, Brown, Harvard, U. of Michigan, U. of Texas, Yale.

1713 Boston Public, U. of Illinois, Yale.

1717 Harvard, New York Public, U. of Illinois, U. of Texas, Yale.

1724 Brown, Library of Congress, U. S. Surgeon General's Office.

1732 Library of Congress, U. of Texas.

Gazophylacium Anglicanum: Containing the Derivation of English Words. ...Proving the Dutch and Saxon to be the prime Fountains.... 1689. Octavo.

Cf. Kennedy: Nos. 6191, 6192.

1. 1689 Boston Public, Library of Congress, Newberry, U. of Chicago, U. of Illinois, U. of Michigan, U. of Minnesota, U. of Texas.

2. 1691 (Under the new title, *A New English Dictionary, Shewing the Etymological Derivation of the English Tongue* ...), New York Public, Newberry.

K., J. *A New English Dictionary: Or, a Compleat Collection Of the Most Proper and Significant Words, Commonly used in the Language,* ... 1702. Small Octavo.

Cf. Kennedy: Nos. 6197, 6204, 6236, 6248.

1. 1702 U. of Chicago.

2. 1713 Harvard, U. of Illinois, Yale.
3. 1731 New York Public.
4. 1739 Not located.
5. 1748 Boston Public.
7. 1757 Not located.
7. 1759 Brown.
8. 1772 U. of Chicago.

Cocker's English Dictionary: Interpreting The most refined and difficult words in Divinity.... To which is Added An Historico-Poetical Diction-ary....Also The Interpretation of the most usual Terms in Military Discipline. Likewise The Terms which Merchants and others make use of in Trade and Commerce;... 1704. Octavo.

Cf. Kennedy: Nos. 6198, 6205, 6216.

1. 1704 Harvard, New York Public, U. of Illinois, U. of Texas, Yale.
2. 1715 Huntington, Library of Congress, U. of Chicago, U. S. Surgeon General's Office.
3. 1724 Boston Public, Library of Congress, New York Public, Yale.

Kersey, John (Reviser). *The New World of Words....* Compiled by Edward Phillips.... Revised, Corrected, and Improved; with the Addition of near Twenty Thousand Words,... 1706. Folio.

Cf. Kennedy: Nos. 6200, 6210.

6. 1706 Harvard, Library of Congress, New York Public, Newberry, U. of Chicago, U. of Illinois, U. of Michigan, U. of Texas, U. of Virginia, Yale.
7. 1720 Brown, Clark Memorial Library at U. of California at Los Angeles, Harvard, Library of Congress, U. of Chicago, U. of Illinois, U. of Texas, Yale.

Glossographia Anglicana Nova....Interpreting Such Hard Words of what-ever Language, as are at present used in the English Tongue. ...Also, the Terms of Divinity, Law....and all other Arts and Sciences... 1707. Octavo.

Cf. Kennedy: Nos. 6201, 6208.

1. 1707 Boston Public, Harvard Law, Newberry, New York Public, Princeton, U. of Chicago, U. of Illinois, U. of Texas, Yale.

2. 1719 Clark Memorial Library at U. of California at Los Angeles, Goucher, Harvard, Library of Congress, U. of Illinois, U. of Texas, U. of Virginia, U. of Washington, Western Reserve, Yale.

Kersey, John. *Dictionarium Anglo-Britannicum: Or, A General English Dictionary,... of all sorts of difficult Words,... of all Terms relating to Arts and Sciences ...* 1708. Octavo.

Cf. Kennedy: Nos. 6203, 6206, 6213.

1. 1708 Library of Congress, New York Public, Peabody Institute, U. of Chicago, Yale.
2. 1715 New York Public, U. of Texas.
3. 1721 Boston Public, Harvard, Library of Congress, New York Public, Peabody Institute, U. of Michigan.

Bailey, Nathan. *An Universal Etymological English Dictionary: Comprehending The Derivations of the Generality of Words in the English Tongue....A Brief and clear Explication of all difficult Words ...* 1721. Octavo.

Cf. Kennedy: Nos. 6211, 6212, 6215, 6218, 6219, 6221, 6227, 6233, 6250, 6255, 6258, 6282, 6288, 6332.

1. 1721 American Philosophical Society (Philadelphia), U. of Illinois, U. of Texas, Western Reserve, Yale.
2. 1724 Boston Public, Detroit Public, Library Company of Philadelphia (Ridgway Branch), New York Public, Pasadena Public, Yale.
3. 1726 Boston Public, Library of Congress, Massachusetts Historical Society, U. of Chicago, Yale.
4. 1728 Harvard, Yale.
5. 1731 Harvard, Yale.
6. 1733 Harvard Law, New York Public, U. of Texas, Yale.
7. 1735 New York Public, U. of Illinois, U. of Pennsylvania, Yale.
8. 1737 Harvard, U. of Chicago, Yale.
9. 1740 Bowdoin, Free Library of Philadelphia, New York Public, Yale.
10. 1742 Kenyon, Yale.
11. 1745 Brown, New York Public, U. of Chicago, Yale.
12. 1747 Not located.
13. 1747 U. of Chicago, Yale.

13. 1749 Not located.
14. 1751 Boston Public, Library of Congress, New England Deposit Library at Harvard, U. of Texas.
15. 1753 Library Company of Philadelphia, Massachusetts Historical Society, New York Public, Yale.
16. 1753 Not located.
16. 1755 Drexel Institute, Huntington, Library of Congress, Lutheran Theological Seminary (Philadelphia), New York Public, Peabody Institute, U. of Chicago.
17. 1757 New York Public.
17. 1759 Boston Public, Huntington, Library of Congress, Princeton, U. of Texas, Yale.
18. 1761 Boston Public, Library of Congress, Massachusetts Historical Society, Princeton, Yale.
20. 1763 Harvard, Indiana U., U. of Chicago, Yale.
20. 1764 Boston Public, Library of Congress, Massachusetts State Library, New York Public.
21. 1766 Brown, Library of Congress, U. of Chicago, Yale.
21. 1770 Boston Public, New York Public.
21. 1775 Clements Library at U. of Michigan, College of Physicians of Philadelphia, Free Library of Philadelphia, Huntington, U. of Illinois.
22. 1770 Boston Public, Drexel Institute, Mount Holyoke, Newark Public, U. of Chicago, U. of Illinois, U. of Rochester, Yale.
23. 1773 Clements Library at U. of Michigan, Library of Congress, U. of Kansas.
24. 1776 Drexel Institute, Library of Congress, Library Company of Philadelphia (Ridgway Branch).
24. 1782 Boston Public, Harvard, Huntington, Library of Congress, New York Public, Princeton, Yale.
25. 1783 Boston Public, New York Public, U. of Virginia, Yale.
25. 1790 New York Public, U. of Chicago, U. of Texas.
26. 1789 New York Public, U. of Pennsylvania.
27. 1794 Vassar, Yale.
28. 1800 U. of Chicago.
30. 1802 Boston Public, City Library of Manchester, N. H., John Crerar Library, Library of Congress, Massachusetts Historical Society, Yale.

Bailey, Nathan. *The Universal Etymological English Dictionary.... Containing I. An additional Collection.... II. An Orthographical Dictionary,* ...1727. Octavo.

Cf. Kennedy: No. 6211. (Kennedy refers rightly to this work as "a supplementary volume" to the preceding dictionary.)

1. 1727 Boston Public, Harvard, Harvard Law, Library of Congress, Library Company of Philadelphia (Ridgway Branch), New York Public, U. of Illinois, U. of Iowa, U. of Texas.
2. 1731 U. of Illinois.
3. 1737 Boston Public, Drexel Institute, Library of Congress, Massachusetts State Library, U. of Chicago, Yale.
4. 1756 New York Public.
4. 1759 Not located.
5. 1760 Grosvenor Library, New York Public, Newberry.
5. 1775 Not located.
7. 1776 Not located.

Bailey, Nathan *et al. Dictionarium Britannicum: Or a more Compleat Universal Etymological English Dictionary than any Extant....* 1730. Folio.

Cf. Kennedy: Nos. 6220, 6226.

1. 1730 Boston Public, Harvard, Library of Congress, Massachusetts Historical Society, Minnesota Historical Society, New York Public, U. of Texas, Yale.
2. 1736 American Philosophical Society (Philadelphia), Boston Public, College of Physicians of Philadelphia, Free Library of Philadelphia (Widener Branch), Library of Congress, New York Public, Princeton, U. of Michigan, U. of Virginia, Yale.

Dyche, Thomas and Pardon, William. *A New General English Dictionary; Peculiarly calculated for the Use and Improvement Of such as are unacquainted with the Learned Languages....* 1735. Octavo.

Cf. Kennedy: Nos. 6225, 6229, 6232, 6235, 6238, 6241, 6251, 6256, 6265, 6283, 6287, 6311.

1. 1735 Boston Public.
2. 1737 Not located.
3. 1740 Not located.
4. 1744 John Carter Brown Library.
5. 1748 Massachusetts State Library, U. of Chicago, Yale.

6. 1750 Yale.
7. 1752 Not located.
7. 1753 Not located.
8. 1754 Boston Athenaeum, Harvard.
9. 1758 Not located.
10. 1759 Not located.
11. 1760 U. of Texas, Yale.
11. 1761 Library of Congress.
12. 1765 Library of Congress, New York Public, U. of Chicago.
13. 1768 Not located.
14. 1771 Boston Public.
16. 1777 Harvard, Library of Congress.
17. 1794 Harvard, Library of Congress, Yale.
18. 1781 Harvard.

Defoe, B. N. *A Compleat English Dictionary. Containing the True Meaning of all Words in the English Language: Also The Proper Names of all the Kingdoms, Towns, and Cities in the World: ... Design'd for the Use of Gentlemen, Ladies, Foreigners, Artificers, Tradesmen; and All who desire to Speak or Write English in its present Purity and Perfection.* 1735. Duodecimo.

Cf. Kennedy: No. 6224.

1. 1735. Folger, Harvard, Library of Congress, New York Public, Yale.

A New English Dictionary, Containing a Large and almost Compleat Collection of Useful English Words. ... Design'd to assist Gentlemen, Ladies, Foreigners, Artificers, Tradesmen, &c. to Speak, Read or Write English in the greatest Purity and Perfection. 1737. Duodecimo.

Cf. Kennedy: No. 6228.

1. 1737 Harvard.

Sparrow, J. *A New English Dictionary, Containing a compleat Collection of useful English Words. ... Design'd to assist Gentlemen, Ladies. ... the whole founded intirely upon a new plan, and is the best in its kind ever yet printed.* 1739. Duodecimo.

Cf. Kennedy: No. 6228.

1. 1739 Not located.

Manlove, James. *A New Dictionary of All Such English Words....As are generally made Use of, in Speaking or Writing the English Language with Accuracy and Politeness.* 1741. Duodecimo.

    Cf. Kennedy: No. 6231.

    1. 1741 Harvard.

      (N. B. The above four works carry identical contents. See text.)

Martin, Benjamin. *Lingua Britannica Reformata: Or, A New English Dictionary, Under the Following Titles, Viz. I. Universal;...II. Etymological;...III. Orthographical;...IV. Orthoepical;...V. Diacritical; ...VI. Philological;...VII. Mathematical;...VIII. Philosophical;... To which is prefix'd, An Introduction, Containing A Physico-Grammatical Essay....* 1749. Octavo.

    Cf. Kennedy: Nos. 6237, 6242.

    1. 1749 Harvard, New York Public.

    2. 1754 Boston Public, Harvard, Library of Congress, U. of Chicago, Yale.

A Pocket Dictionary or Complete English Expositor: Shewing Readily The Part of Speech...its true Meaning...its various Senses...and the Language, from whence it is deriv'd,... 1753. Octavo.

    Cf. Kennedy: No. 6239.

    1. 1753 Yale.

    2. 1758 Boston Public.

    3. 1765 U. of Chicago.

    4. 1779 U. of Illinois.

[Wesley, John.] *The Complete English Dictionary, Explaining most of those Hard Words, Which are found in the Best English Writers.* By a Lover of Good English and Common Sense.... 1753. Duodecimo.

    Cf. Kennedy: Nos. 6240, 6263.

    1. 1753 Not located.

    2. 1764 Stanford.

    3. 1777 Not located.

  "*2.*" 1790 Not located.

Scott, Joseph N. (Reviser). *A New Universal Etymological English Dictionary: Containing not only Explanations of the Words in the English Language; And the Different Senses in which they are used; With Authorities from the Best Writers, to support those which appear Doubtful....* Originally compiled by N. Bailey.... And now Re-published with many Corrections, Additions, and Literate Improvements, by Different Hands. The Etymology ... being Revised and Corrected By Joseph Nicol Scott, M.D. 1755. Folio.

Cf. Kennedy: Nos. 6243, 6260, 6273.

1. 1755 Harvard, New York Public, Yale.
2. 1764 Boston Public, Harvard, Massachusetts State Library, Yale.
3. 1772 Boston Athenaeum.

Notes

CHAPTER I

1 See Thomas Wright, *A Volume of Vocabularies* (London, 1857) for a collection of these vocabularies gathered from manuscripts ranging in date from the eighth to the fifteenth century.

2 The term *dictionary* was not used before 1500 as a part of the title of any of these bilingual wordbooks published in England. Since, however, these have the features of later books so termed, we use the word for convenience.

3 Edited by Albert Way for the Camden Society in three parts: Pt. I (A-L), 1843; Pt. II (M-R), 1853; Pt. III (S-Z), 1865. Also edited by A. L. Mayhew for the Early English Text Society (Extra Series, CII, 1908). There was no printed edition before 1843.

4 Printed for the Early English Text Society (Orig. Series, No. 75, 1881), with Introduction and Notes by Sidney J. H. Herrtage and Preface by Henry B. Wheatley.

5 Baret has also French equivalents, though the emphasis is on the English and Latin.

6 Cf. Albert Way's Introduction to his edition of the *Promptorium* for the Camden Society, pp. xx ff.; also App. I.

7 The Stratford Grammar School owned a copy of Cooper's *Thesaurus* in Shakespeare's day. There is evidence that young Shakespeare was familiar with this book.

8 From A. W. Pollard's *Fifteenth Century Prose and Verse* (London, 1903), p. 240. Pollard has modernized the spelling.

9 See Samuel Jesse McCoy's "The Language and Linguistic Interests of Sir Thomas Elyot," an unprinted doctoral dissertation (University of

North Carolina, 1933); *The Governour, passim,* and especially H. H. S. Croft's glossary to the 1883 edition; E. E. Hale's "Ideas on Rhetoric in the Sixteenth Century," *PMLA,* XVIII (1903), 424-44 (cf. p. 430); J. L. Moore's *Tudor-Stuart Views on the Growth, Status, and Destiny of the English Language (Studien zur Englischen Philologie,* Vol. XLI, 1910).

10 Cf. Ralph Lever's *The Arte of Reason, rightly termed Witcraft* (1573).

11 Richard Mulcaster (*ca.* 1530-1611) was educated at Eton, Cambridge, and Oxford. From 1561 to 1586 he was Head Master of Merchant Taylors' School. He also served twelve years (1596-1608) in the High Mastership of St. Paul's School.

The influence of the pedagogical tradition on the early dictionaries was briefly discussed by G. E. Noyes in "The First English Dictionary, Cawdrey's *Table Alphabeticall," MLN,* LVIII (Dec., 1943), 600-5.

12 *Elementarie,* ed. by E. T. Campagnac (Oxford, 1925), p. 274.

13 *Ibid.,* p. 187.

14 *Ibid.*

15 *Ibid.,* p. 189.

16 In *Wiener Beiträge zur Englischen Philologie,* LX (Vienna, 1938), xxxiii-xxxiv.

CHAPTER II

1 Of Cawdrey's *A Table Alphabeticall,* we have used the facsimile photostat of the Modern Language Association, deposited in the Library of Congress. The unique copy of the first edition is in the Bodleian.

In the arrangement of the quoted title pages here and throughout, it has been thought most helpful for purposes of comparison to indicate the main sections of the title-page (and hence of the contents of the work) rather than the purely arbitrary line divisions.

2 On Cawdrey's relation to Coote and the pedagogical tradition generally, see Miss Noyes's article in *MLN,* LVIII, 600-5.

3 Cf. "To the Reader" in *A Table Alphabeticall,* beginning with the words, "Such as by their place and calling (but especially Preachers), as have occasion to speak publiquely...are to bee admonished that they never affect any strange ynckhorne termes..." and *The Arte of Rhetorique,* ed. by G. H. Mair (Oxford, 1909), pp. 162 ff.

CHAPTER III

1 Editions of *An English Expositor* were as follows: 1st, 1616; 2nd, 1621; 3rd, 1641; 4th, 1656, 1663, 1667; 5th, 1676; 6th, 1680; 7th, 1684; 8th, 1688; 9th, 1698; 10th, 1707; 11th, 1715; 12th, 1719; 13th, 1726; 14th, 1731.

2 For a discussion of the revisions of Bullokar, Cockeram, and other seventeenth-century dictionaries, see G. E. Noyes's "Some Interrelations of English Dictionaries of the Seventeenth Century," *PMLA*, LIV (Dec., 1939), 990-1006.

3 *Ibid.*, pp. 995 ff.

4 For a discussion of Cockeram's *English Dictionarie*, see below, pp. 26-36.

5 For a list of such words, see Miss Noyes's article in *PMLA*, LIV, 995, n. 17.

6 For a discussion of these sections in Cockeram, see below, pp. 32 ff.

CHAPTER IV

1 Cf. Noyes, "Some Interrelations of English Dictionaries," *PMLA*, LIV, 991. The *English Dictionarie* was entered on the Stationers' Register for Butter on February 15, 1623, but was transferred to Weaver on July 17, 1623.

Editions of Cockeram's *Dictionarie* were as follows: 1st, 1623 (two issues); 2nd, 1626; 3rd, 1631; 4th, 1632; 5th, 1637; 6th, 1639; 7th, 1642; 8th, 1647; 9th, 1650; 10th, 1651, 1655; 11th, 1658; 12th, 1670.

2 Cf. Noyes, in *PMLA*, LIV, 991-92; Bullokar, *Gab* to *Garrulitie* (1616 ed.) and Cockeram, *Gabbing* to *Garrulity* (1623 ed.).

3 Cf. Noyes, in *PMLA*, LIV, 992-93.

4 *Ibid.*, pp. 1001-2.

5 See pp. 24 ff. above.

6 For a more detailed treatment of the new organization, see Noyes, in *PMLA*, LIV, 998 ff.

CHAPTER V

1 The *Academie*, Hoyt H. Hudson has recently shown, was based upon a manuscript copy of John Hoskins' *Directions for Speech and Style*. See Hudson's edition (Introduction) of Hoskins' book (Princeton University Press, 1935).

2 "Nay, to that pass we are now arrived, that in London many of the Tradesmen have new Dialects; The Cook asks you what Dishes you will have in your Bill of Fare; whether Olla's, Bisques, Hachies, Omelets, Bouillon's, Grilliades, Ioncades, Fricasses; with a Haugoust, Ragoust, etc.

"The Vintner will furnish you with Montefiascone, Alicante, Vornaccia, Ribolla, Tent, etc. Others with Sherbet, Agro di Cedro, Coffa, Chocolate, etc.

"The Taylor is ready to mode you into a Rochet, Mandillion, Gippon, Justacor, Capouch, Hoqueton, or a Cloke of Drap de Bery, etc.

"The Shoo-maker will make you Boots, Whole Chase, Demi-Chase, or Bottines, etc.

"The Haberdasher is ready to furnish you with a Vigone, Codebec or Castor, etc. The Semstress with a Crabbat, Toylet, etc.

"By this new world of Words, I found we were slipt into that condition which Seneca complains of in his time; When men's minds once begin to enure themselves to dislike, whatever is usual is disdained: They affect novelty in speech, they recal oreworn and uncouth words: And some there are that think it a grace, if their speech hover, and thereby hold the hearer in suspence, etc." (To the Reader.)

3 Under the general title, *Rider's Dictionarie*, Holyoke's Latin-English *Dictionarium Etymologicum* was generally published along with the English-Latin (originally called *Bibliotheca Scholastica*) of John Rider.

4 Cf. Noyes, "Some Interrelations of English Dictionaries," *PMLA*, LIV, 1004.

5 *Les Termes* was first published in 1525 with the title, *Exposiciones Terminorum Legum Anglorum*, in French and English, and continued to be reissued through the sixteenth and seventeenth centuries; cf. *STC*, Nos. 2071 ff., and Kennedy, *Bibliography of Writings on the English Language* (Cambridge and New Haven, 1927), Nos. 2938 ff.

6 Blount inadvertently enters *Adeption* twice, the second entry coming after an intervening definition. In the first entry he draws from Holyoke; in the second, from Thomas.

7 Individual estimates may vary as much as 10 per cent one way or the other. Our own estimate is, in our opinion, conservative, and at least approximately correct. By counting the number of entries on representative pages under each letter and multiplying the average by the number of pages, we have estimated the total number of entries for each letter

of the alphabet. Fortunately, the author offers a guide for estimating the Latin-derived words by placing in parentheses after each entry the Latin form. A cautious counting of the Latin forms in parentheses and a checking at regular intervals with the Latin dictionaries of Thomas and Holyoke enable one to make a fairly reliable estimate of the number of such entries.

8 Some of these are: *Adfers, Amotion, Apodictical, Assuefaction, Commination, Condite* (verb), *Consequntion, Consolate, Contristate, Cruciate, Desiderable, Desumed, Enervous, Excruciate, Exercitation, Exiguity, Expunction, Immanity, Immitted, Imprecate, Inamissible, Incogitancy, Indubitate, Inspersed, Intervenient, Jucundity, Lustrations, Mansuete, Paction, Prenotions, Propense, Radicated, Refract, Refusion, Remigration, Unbratile.*

9 Here are the words from Browne's *Vulgar Errors,* the starred ones having been designated as from *Vulgar Errors,* "Dr. B.," or "Br.": **Bombilation, *Comminuible, Conglobate, *Connascencies, Contaction, Corticated, Defecate, Dilaceration, *Dequantitated, Emication, *Exantlation, Exolution, *Exilition, Expectible, Extimulating, Illation, Imbibition, Inquinated, Latitancy, Marcour, Minaration, Permansion, Remotion, *Superfluitance, Supinity, *Tralucencies, *Torrefaction, Venefical, Verticity, *Viviparous.*

10 For an interesting account of etymology in this period and later, see Ernest Weekley's "Our Early English Etymologists," *The Quarterly Review,* CCLVII (1931), 63-72. Weekley's observations pertain to Minsheu, Skinner, and Junius.

11 Blount probably refers to Alexander Ross (1590-1654), who published *Mystagogus Poeticus, or, The Muses Interpreter* (1647).

12 The reference is to William Somner, whose *Dictionarium Saxonico-Latino-Anglicum* was first printed at Oxford in 1659; cf. Kennedy, *Bibliography,* No. 3281.

CHAPTER VI

1 Florio had used the title, *A Worlde of Wordes,* for his Italian-English dictionary (1598); but the "New World of Words" is a phrase employed by Blount in his "To the Reader," from which Phillips derives other matter. It seems reasonable to suppose that he borrowed his title from the same place.

2 Cf. Kennedy, *Bibliography,* Nos. 8581 ff.

3 In the case of the *Glossographia,* Blount had a real grievance, for there can be no doubt that Phillips ransacked this book. As to the *Nomothetes* or law dictionary, Blount was mistaken. Thomas Manley, not Phillips, was the compiler; and, though Manley owed something to Blount's *Law Dictionary,* many of the similarities of the two law lexicons are accounted for by the use of a common source, Cowell's *Interpreter.* Blount's charges here are ironical, as they are indeed throughout, since he himself, as we have seen, was mainly a compiler.

It should be noted that a little earlier Blount had attacked Phillips in a tract entitled, "Animadversions upon Sir Richard Baker's Chronicle, and Its Continuation . . ." (1672). Phillips had been the continuator, and Blount had pointed out numerous mistakes in the continuation. The complete story of Blount's relationship to Phillips must be told elsewhere.

4 *Athenae Oxonienses,* IV, 760 ff.

5 There is no evidence that Phillips ever acknowledged his indebtedness to Blount or omitted or changed to any extent the numerous terms and definitions which he had appropriated, even after Blount had publicly exposed Phillips in *A World of Errors Discovered in the New World of Words* (1673). It is true that in the 1678 edition of the *New World* Phillips silently corrected or omitted the dozen or so erratic or ridiculous definitions which Blount had listed; but the great bulk of Phillips' borrowings remained intact, unacknowledged, during his lifetime.

CHAPTER VII

1 Cf. Noyes, "Some Interrelations of English Dictionaries, *PMLA,* LIV, 1005-6.

2 For example, *C* for *Canting; Che.* for *Cheshire; E* for *Essex; Der.* for *Derbyshire; Br.* for *British; Nf.* for *Norfolk; Lan.* for *Lancashire; Li.* for *Lincolnshire; No.* for *North Country; So.* for *South Country; Sc.* for *Scotch,* etc.

3 Cf. Noyes, "The Development of Cant Lexicography in England, 1566-1785," *S. P.,* XXXVIII, 471. This article has been reprinted in Appendix II.

4 *Ibid.*

5 Compare, for example: *Dental, Dentati, Denticle, Dentrifice, Dentiloquent, Dentiscalph, Dentition; Corporal, Corporation, Corporature, Cor-*

poreal, Corporeity, Corporification, Corps, Corpulent, Corpulency, Corpuscule.

6 Editions (unnumbered): 1676, 1677, 1685, 1692, 1696, 1701, 1708, 1713, 1717, 1724, 1732.

CHAPTER VIII

1 It is not the purpose of the authors to write a history of the etymological dictionaries—the earlier ones of which are in foreign languages—but simply to take note of those which are specifically related to the general English dictionaries.

2 The title-page of Minsheu's *Ductor in Linguas* is in Latin and English. The English reads: "The Guide into the Tongues. With the agreement and consent one with another, as also their Etymologies, that is, the Reasons and Derivations of all or the most part of wordes, in these eleven languages, viz.: English, British or Welsh, Low Dutch, High Dutch, French, Italian, Spanish, Portuguese, Latine, Greek, Hebrew." Immediately after the title-page is a long list of subscribers, this being one of the first books to be published by subscription.

A second edition was printed in 1627, in nine languages, the Welsh and Portuguese having been omitted. English and Latin are given relatively large space. There are many fanciful etymologies, such as *"Stepmother,* one who steps into the place of a mother"; and also etymologies that have been confirmed by subsequent historical study. A considerable number of long items are devoted to the exposition of law terms. "Quite apart from word-lore," writes Ernest Weekley, "his work contains vast and various information for every kind of archaeologist, and I can think of few better single volumes for an intelligent Robinson Crusoe."

3 See Camden's *Britannia* (1586, 1600, etc.), Verstegan's *Restitution of Decayed Intelligence* (1605, 1628), and Davies' *Welsh-Latin Dictionary* (1632).

4 As a matter of fact, William Godwin had pointed out, as early as 1815, Skinner's debt to Phillips; but Godwin's discovery has been ignored. See his *Lives of Edward and John Phillips* (London, 1815), pp. 151 ff.

5 Ser. i, XI (1855), 122-24.

6 See, for example, in the two texts the words: *Abate, Accost, Adventure, Air, Alliance, Alman (Almain), Almner (Almoner), Amayne (Amain),*

Amort, Amulet, Appartment, Apprentice, Architrave, Armory, Averie (Avery).

7 Cf., for example: "A *Jade,* or tired horse, from the AS. Eode, he went; (*i.e.*) he went once, but can go no more; as we say in Latin *vixit* for *mortuus est:* Or from the Lat. *Cadere,* to fall down: Or from the AS. Gaad, a goad, or spur; (*i.e.*) an horse that will not go without the spur."

CHAPTER IX

1 The first objection was raised by H. B. Wheatley in "Chronological Notices of the Dictionaries of the English Language," *Transactions of the Philological Society* (London, 1865), p. 240. J. D., contributing to *Notes and Queries* in 1881 (ser. vi, III, 162, 270), agreed with Wheatley. The second objection was raised by R. O. Williams in *Our Dictionaries and Other English Language Topics* (New York, 1890), p. 18. The British Museum Catalogue makes the error of assigning the work to John Kersey, the Elder, mathematician. The *DNB* article is non-committal. P. W. Long in "English Dictionaries before Webster," Bibliographical Society of America *Papers,* IV (1909), 30, and Kennedy, *Bibliography,* No. 6197, however, tacitly credit the work to Kersey, as does the *Cambridge Bibliography of English Literature,* II, 930-31.

2 Aside from his interest in lexicography, little is known about John Kersey. Beyond describing him as "flourishing" in 1720 and the son of John Kersey, the mathematician (1616-1690?), the *DNB* article merely offers conjectures.

3 Preface, A 2r.

4 Title-page of Kersey's revision of Phillips' *New World of Words,* 1706.

5 Long, *op. cit.,* p. 30.

6 For a list of such works, see Kennedy, *Bibliography,* pp. 204-7.

7 The following words, for example, have identical or almost identical definitions: *Fumigation, Function, Fungous, Furlough, Fust, Gamut, Gardian of the Spiritualities, Gargarism, Gavelkind, Generation, Genius, Girasole, Glebe, Golden-number, Gondola, Granite, Gratulatory, Grave,* etc.

It should be recognized, however, that, despite J. K.'s dependence on Coles for his comparatively few unusual words and his use of current spelling books for general models, he is in the execution as well as in the concept of his dictionary unusually original and independent.

8 The pages are distributed as follows: men's names, 8½; women's 2½; nicknames, 1. Sample entries are: *"Abel, Hebr.* Vanity"; *"Abraham, Hebr.* The Father of a Multitude." This material was available in any of the editions of Coles and in Kersey's *Dictionarium Anglo-Britannicum* of 1708; or it could have been derived even more easily from the separate lists of proper names carried in many of the spelling books (Young's, "Cocker's," etc.).

9 Preface, A 4v.

10 *The Works of the Late Rev. and Learned Isaac Watts, D.D.* (London, 1753), IV, 681.

11 This notice was printed before the Preface in subsequent editions.

12 The known editions are: 1st, 1702; 2nd, 1713; 3rd, 1731; 4th, 1739; 5th, 1748; 7th, 1757 (Dublin) and 1759 (London); 8th, 1772. For the location of copies, see Census in App. III.

CHAPTER X

1 See Sir Ambrose Heal's *English Writing-Masters and Their Copy-Books. 1570-1800* (Cambridge, 1931), pp. 33-37, 58.

2 For bibliography, see *ibid.,* pp. 135-45.

3 *Ibid.,* p. 33.

4 Pp. 99-100.

5 *Diary,* ed. by H. B. Wheatley (London, 1926), IV, 199, 200, 243, 244 (all entries for 1664).

6 I, 247.

7 P. 57.

8 *The Bibliographer,* VI, 25-30.

9 See n. 1, above.

10 Heal, *op. cit.,* p. 35. For a list of the booksellers of the various works attributed to Cocker, see *ibid.,* p. 145. The booksellers who sponsored the dictionary were as follows: first edition, A. Back and A. Bettesworth; second, T. Norris, C. Brown, A. Bettesworth; third, T. Norris, A. Bettesworth. These facts suggest that Bettesworth and Norris were mainly responsible for the work and its revision.

11 On the authorship and make-up of *Cocker's English Dictionary,* see G. E. Noyes, "Edward Cocker and *Cocker's English Dictionary,*" *Notes and Queries,* CLXXXII (May 30, 1942), 298-300. See also subsequent comments on certain biographical issues and on *Cocker's Arithmetick* by

David Salmon (*ibid.*, p. 361), Sir Ambrose Heal (*ibid.*, CLXXXIII, 50), and G. E. Noyes (*ibid.*, p. 142).

12 Preface, A 5v.

13 Preface, A 2r-v.

14 Coles had been an innovator in admitting cant terms into the general English dictionary. See Noyes, "The Development of Cant Lexicography in England," *SP*, XXXVIII, 471-73 (cf. App. II).

15 For example, *Bedfordshire* is described under *Leighton Buzard*, and *Brecknockshire* under *Leventium*.

16 Title-page.

CHAPTER XI

1 Kersey's other works and the meagre data on his life are discussed above in connection with the *New English Dictionary* of 1702, of which he was probably the author. See pp. 69 ff.

2 See above, p. 48.

3 *English Dialect Words of the Eighteenth Century, as shown in the 'Universal Etymological Dictionary' of Nathaniel [sic] Bailey* (London, English Dialect Society Publications, 1883). Axon's large list of 211 pages is, however, misleading, as it includes not only dialect but legal and trade terms, archaic words, cant, hunting words, etc.

4 "Dialekt-Materialien aus dem 18. Jahrhundert," *Anglia*, XXIV (1901), 118-32. The Försters state that the *Dictionarium Anglo-Britannicum* derived its dialectal material from Ray, Coles, Worlidge, and others. This material, however, came directly from the Kersey-Phillips *New World of Words* of 1706, which had borrowed it from Ray and Worlidge, as indicated in the text.

5 The Kersey-Phillips apparently did not use Coles as a source for dialect material. Coles had taken most of Ray's and only a few of Worlidge's items. The Kersey-Phillips has many of Ray's terms and practically the entire vocabulary of Worlidge, both groups apparently taken directly.

6 Preface, A 2v.

CHAPTER XII

1 See above, p. 37.

2 The *Glossographia Anglicana Nova*, in fact, carries "Proposals for Re-printing the First, and for Printing a Second Volume of Dr. Harris' Lexicon Technicum" (A 4r-v). The same group of booksellers spon-

sored the original Harris, the revised Harris, and the *Glossographia Angli-cana Nova.*

3 See, for example, *Abduction, Abjudicate, Ablegation,* etc.

4 Harris also included illustrations of heraldic terms.

CHAPTER XIII

1 *Notes and Queries,* ser. xi, VI, 228.

2 "Chronological Notices of the Dictionaries of the English Language," *Trans. Phil. Soc.* (1865), p. 243.

3 On the make-up and background of the dialectal vocabulary in the *Dictionarium Anglo-Britannicum,* see above, pp. 86-87.

4 On account of its considerable vocabulary of obsolete words, the *Dictionarium Anglo-Britannicum* has been often proposed as one of the sources of the synthetic poetic language used by Thomas Chatterton. This point can, however, be more satisfactorily considered in connection with N. Bailey's *Universal Etymological English Dictionary.* See p. 104 and n. 14 of Chap. XIV.

5 Preface, A 2r.

CHAPTER XIV

1 The first edition of the *Universal Etymological English Dictionary* (1721) carries the following advertisement: "Youth Boarded and Taught the *Hebrew, Greek,* and *Latin* Languages, in a Method more Easy and Expeditious than is common; also other School-Learning by the *Author* of this *Dictionary,...*" An advertisement in the 1736 edition of the *Dictionarium Britannicum* describes Bailey as then teaching "*Latin, Greek* and *Hebrew,* Writing, Accounts and other parts of School Learning at his House in Stepney, near the Church."

2 Not included in this list is the largest dictionary bearing Bailey's name, *A New Universal Etymological English Dictionary,* which appeared in 1755 after Bailey's death under the editorship of Joseph Nicol Scott. It was based on Bailey's *Dictionarium Britannicum* but was much larger, as will be shown in our subsequent discussion of the work. It was reissued in 1764 and 1772.

The *Dictionarium Rusticum, Urbanicum & Botanicum* (called in 1704 simply *Dictionarium Rusticum & Urbanicum*) deals with husbandry, hunting, fishing, merchandising, and "all Sorts of Country

Affairs." The *Dictionarium Domesticum* gives useful information on the "Management of the Kitchin, Pantry, Larder, Dairy, Olitory, and Poultry," the apiary, the vineyard, etc. We describe these works in order to suggest the range of Bailey's interests.

3 Compare, for example, Cockeram's *English Dictionarie* and Bullokar's *English Expositor*, which offered much curious material for the entertainment of the reader. Cockeram from his earliest edition and Bullokar in his later editions presented this material in a separate section as a kind of elementary reference book.

4 In his *Reminiscences* (London, 1822, p. 145), Charles Butler writes the following often quoted passage about Pitt: "His diction was remarkably simple, but words were never chosen with greater care; he mentioned to a friend of the Reminiscent, that he had read twice, from beginning to end, *Bailey's Dictionary:*..."

5 It may be helpful to illustrate here the practices of the various lexicographers who concerned themselves with etymology. Blount studied this subject seriously enough to be impressed with his own "disability for so great an Undertaking"; he had, however, "the perusal and approbation of some very learned...Friends" and "extracted the quintessence of *Scapula, Minsheu, Cotgrave, Spelmans Glossarium, Florio, Thomasius, Dasipodius, Rider, Hexams Dutch* and Dr. *Davies Welch Dictionaries, Cowels Interpreter*, &c." (To the Reader). Blount's annotations usually take the form, "*Nutation (nutatio)*"; sometimes, "*Obeisance* (Fr.)"; and in rare instances, "*Abate* (from the Fr. *abatre, i.* to break down or destroy)." See the discussion of Blount's etymology in the text, pp. 46 ff.

   Phillips, even in the later editions, does not go beyond the form, "*Combination (Lat.)*," "*Combustible (Lat.)*," "*Concert (Fr.)*." Coles and, imitating him, the revised "Cocker's" have merely, "*Beer-sheba, h.*," "*Bellitude, l.*," "*Belomancy, g.*" Kersey likewise conserves space in his *Dictionarium Anglo-Britannicum*, writing, "*Corona (L.)*," "*Corrigible (L.)*," "*Corridor (F.)*," "*Corrigidor (Sp.).*"

6 The following item, for example, is condensed from Skinner:

> To *Fuddle*, (from the Word *Puddle*, q.d. to drown himself in a Puddle of Liquors; or from *Full*, by an interposition of the Letter *d*; and hence the *Scots* use the Word *Full* for one that is Drunk) to bib or drink till one be tipsey or drunken.

It is perhaps only fair to note, however, that a satisfactory origin for this word has not yet been found, according to Webster's *New International Dictionary* or to the *New English Dictionary*, the latter commenting:

> *Fuddle*, Of obscure origin; cf. Du. *vod* soft, slack, loose, Ger. dial. *fuddeln* to swindle.

7 Of the dictionaries published during Bailey's lifetime his *Dictionarium Britannicum* of 1736 (second ed.) is the most satisfactory from the point of view of etymology. The tremendous progress made in that work was probably due in part to the help of Thomas Lediard, special collaborator in etymology for that edition.

8 See Axon's collection, *English Dialect Words of the Eighteenth Century, as shown in the 'Universal Etymological Dictionary' of Nathaniel Bailey.* Axon includes, however, various other classes of words not generally used, as well as dialect. D. and M. Förster also pointed out in their article, "Dialekt-Materialien aus dem 18. Jahrhundert" (*Anglia*, XXIV, 118-32) that the bulk of the dialect material was derived directly from Kersey's *Dictionarium Anglo-Britannicum.*

We have gone a step farther and shown that these words had been taken earlier from the Kersey-Phillips *New World of Words.* This last work had in turn derived its list mainly from two well known sources: John Ray's *Collection of English Words Not Generally Used* (1674, etc.) and John Worlidge's *Systema Agriculturae* (1669, etc.).

9 On the slow admission of cant terms into the general English dictionary, see Noyes's "The Development of Cant Lexicography in England," *SP*, XXXVIII, 462-79 (cf. App. II). Coles was the only predecessor who had included any representative selection of cant. The later editions of "Cocker's" carried only a few of the commonest cant terms.

10 Bullokar had allowed some "olde words now growne out of use"; and Cockeram had promised to mark obsolete words with an asterisk, though he evidently soon wearied of doing so. Blount as usual had a well considered policy: "I have likewise in a great measure, shun'd the old *Saxon Words;* as finding them growing every day more obsolete than other. Besides there is an excellent Dictionary thereof shortly expected from the learned Mr. *Sumner.* Yet even such of those, as I found still in use, are not here omitted." (To the Reader). As one might expect from his literary interests, Phillips has a considerable body of old words, some so annotated and others credited to Chaucer or other older writers. Coles

with his usual tolerance increased the collection with the justification: "For, though Mr. *Blount* (as he says expressly) shunn'd them, because they grew obsolete; yet doubtless their use is very great: not onely for the unfolding those Authors that did use them, but also for giving a great deal of light to other words that are still in use." The reviser of "Cocker's" grudgingly admits a few obsolete words, though with the protest: "It is alledged by some Dictionary-makers [Coles], That old obsolete Words may be very necessary for understanding of such ancient Authors as *Chaucer, Gower,* &c., but I am of the Opinion of the Ingenious Mr. *Blount,* who... says, 'That he expressly shunned them, as altogether useless, since one in a thousand never heard of their Names, nor ever saw or read their works.'" The *Glossographia Anglicana Nova* follows Blount in policy and method, and Kersey retains a good representation of obsolete words so designated from the Kersey-Phillips *New World of Words.*

11 *The Works of Mr. Edmund Spenser,* I, cxv-cxl.

12 Pp. 3-75.

13 The ninth volume of Rowe's edition and the seventh volume of Pope's both added as afterthoughts and comprising rather miscellaneous material, contained identical brief glossaries of 175 words. Some of the booksellers of the *Universal Etymological English Dictionary* also sold Rowe's edition, and all of them sold Pope's edition.

14 The definitive study of Chatterton's poetic language has not yet been written, and we can offer here only a brief comment on the subject.

A good beginning for the study of this question is to be found in C. V. Le Grice's article in the *Gentleman's Magazine,* new ser. x, II (July, 1838), 128-33. Le Grice here quotes the important passage from the inaccessible *Miscellany* by Edward Gardner (1798): "I heard him [Chatterton] once affirm that it was very easy for a person who had studied antiquities, and with the aid of books which he could name, to copy the style of our ancient poets so exactly that the most skilful observer should not be able to detect him—no, said he, not Mr. Walpole himself. I remember his mentioning Bailey as one of the books which was to enable him to deceive the learned world." Le Grice then shows that Bailey's *Universal Etymological English Dictionary* provides a satisfactory source for all the old words in several works of Chatterton then at hand.

Through the years Kersey's *Dictionarium Anglo-Britannicum* and

Bailey's *Universal Etymological English Dictionary* have been most often suggested as Chatterton's sources. Various other works have, however, been mentioned, including special glossaries like Speght's of Chaucer and Hughes's of Spenser, Skinner's *Etymologicon Linguae Anglicanae,* Verstegan's *Restitution,* etc. In his edition of the *Poetic Works of Thomas Chatterton* (London, 1915, II, xxx-xxxiii), W. W. Skeat studies the letter written by Chatterton to William Smith in obsolete and eccentric language and finds every word satisfactorily interpreted by Kersey. (Le Grice in his article had performed the same experiment with Bailey with equal success.) Skeat concludes that Chatterton probably possessed both Kersey and Bailey, which were "almost one and the same thing; the differences are trifling and the general resemblances close."

In his recent *Life of Thomas Chatterton* (New York, 1930), pp. 171-79, E. H. W. Meyerstein reviews the earlier discussion but does not reach any clear-cut conclusion. He writes: "And indeed Chatterton may well have used both dictionaries [Kersey's and Bailey's], not to speak of the glossaries to Percy's *Reliques,* Hughes's *Spenser,* Hearne's *Robert of Gloucester,* Verstegan's *Restitution,* and, it may be, many another Old English work." In the ensuing discussion, however, Meyerstein favors Kersey: "Kersey was his paint-box, and he mixed the tints he found there with others of his own fancy."

Perhaps, as has been said, Chatterton's sources and his methods of using them cannot be exactly determined. We wish here only to suggest that Bailey was actually the most comprehensive and useful source for Chatterton's purpose. We believe Chatterton would not have studied the various works long before he observed that Bailey had taken over virtually intact the vocabulary of obsolete words in Kersey and that, as we have pointed out in the text, Bailey had also absorbed the better known glossaries of Chaucer and Spenser and made liberal use of Skinner and other linguistic authorities. Bailey was also the most timely source. The last edition of Kersey had come out in 1721; thereafter Bailey usurped the field and was still the most popular dictionary during Chatterton's schooldays in the late fifties and sixties.

15 Although proverbs were here included for the first time in a general English dictionary, they had appeared in other related early works, such as Huloet's *Abcedarium,* 1552; Withals' *Shorte Dictionarie for Yonge Begynners,* 1553; Baret's *Alvearie,* 1573; etc.

For a brief discussion of this feature, see D. T. Starnes, "Literary Features of Renaissance Dictionaries," *SP*, XXXVII (Jan., 1940), 27-31.

16 These have been collected [by John Fletcher] in *Divers Proverbs with their Explications and Illustrations Compil'd ... by Nathan Bailey, 1721* (Yale University Press, 1917).

17 The known editions run as follows: 1st, 1721; 2nd, 1724; 3rd, 1726; 4th, 1728; 5th, 1731; 6th, 1733; 7th, 1735; 8th, 1737; 9th, 1740; 10th, 1742; 11th, 1745; 12th, 1747; 13th, 1747 and 1749; 14th, 1751; 15th, 1753; 16th, 1753 and 1755; 17th, 1757 and 1759; 18th, 1761; 20th, 1763 and 1764; 21st, 1766, 1770, and 1775; 22nd, 1770; 23rd, 1773; 24th, 1776 and 1782; 25th, 1783 and 1790; 26th, 1789; 27th, 1794; 28th, 1800; 30th, 1802. Editions have also been reported for the following years: 1730, 1736, 1754, 1760, 1772; but there is probably confusion in some of these cases with other Bailey dictionaries.

18 Accent had, however, been previously indicated in the supplementary volume issued in 1727 and in the *Dictionarium Britannicum* of 1730. This feature will be further considered in connection with the discussion of the second volume in the following chapter.

This improvement was introduced without comment. Bailey's method of indicating accentuation may be illustrated by the following examples: "*Impro've, Inaugura'tion, Incapa'citate*," etc.

19 Consider, for example, such entries as the following:

Knit-Stockings, were first brought into *England* by *William Rider, An. Dom.* 1564, from *Italy.* Wove stockings first devised by *William Lee,* of *St. John's College, Camb., An Dom.* 1599.

Boston, a town in *Lincolnshire;* also the capital of *New England* in *America* (1782 ed.).

20 Note that there was another twenty-fourth edition dated 1776.

21 It may be of interest to have the exact phrasing of the Preface here for comparison with that of the preceding edition cited above in the text: "... this Dictionary has justly ever had the preference to every other performance of the same kind, on account of its extensive plan, and the perspicuity and conciseness of its definitions, which are intelligible to every one who can read the English Language, and, at the same time, are not unworthy the notice of the learned, who will always esteem them for the ingenuity and erudition displayed in the etymological part. The great

number of technical words and terms used in the various Arts and Sciences which are comprehended in this Work, render it a valuable treasure to the ordinary reader; and in this respect, the present Edition will be found greatly to excel any of the former."

22 As proof of the expansion of the word list, the editor resorts to the curious expedient of printing a list of 800 of the added words in fine print at the back of the book. The following will suffice to show the miscellaneous nature of these additions: *"Balaena, Barb, Bavaria, Beaver, Behoof, Belliferous, Besmoke, Bilateral, Binacle, Biscuit, Bizarre, Bonair, Botanomancy* (divination by herbs), *Brontology* (a discourse on thunder), *Brunette, Byzantium,"* etc.

CHAPTER XV

1 R. C. Trench, *On Some Deficiencies in our English Dictionaries* (London, 1857), p. 45.

2 In thus featuring real or imaginary contributions from the public, Bailey is adopting a familiar advertising device. Compare, for example, the stress on public contributions to the *Ladies Dictionary,* sponsored by the clever bookseller, John Dunton.

3 Blount's *Glossographia* in the 1656 and later editions contained only two woodcuts, both of which illustrated heraldic terms. The *Glossographia Anglicana Nova* of 1707 illustrated many heraldic terms; and Harris' *Lexicon Technicum* of 1704—which, though not a general English dictionary, was one of the most important influences upon early eighteenth-century lexicography—illustrated copiously both heraldic and scientific words. In the two-volume edition of 1708 and in subsequent editions, Harris further developed this feature.

4 *A Guide to the English Tongue* enjoyed an extraordinary popularity; it reached its fourteenth edition in 1729 and its forty-second in 1756, and was still being issued as late as 1788. The first part of this work presents "a Natural and Easy Method to pronounce and express both Common Words and Proper Names; in which particular Care is had to shew the Accent, for preventing Vicious Pronunciation." The second part, intended for "such as are advanced to some Ripeness of Judgment," contains "Observations on the Sounds of Letters and Diphthongs; Rules for the true Division of Syllables, and the Use of Capitals, Stops, and Marks," etc.

The original title-page of the dictionary ran: "A Dictionary of all the Words Commonly us'd in the *English* Tongue; And of the most usual Proper Names; with Accents directing to their true Pronunciation." The work is commonly referred to, however, by its subsequent title, *The Spelling Dictionary*. It was reissued in 1725 and 1731, and apparently (from an advertisement carried in the *Guide to the English Tongue* of the same year) reached a seventh edition about 1756. This work is not discussed in our study of dictionaries, as its title is a misnomer and it consists merely of lists of words without definitions. While systematically and intelligently compiled, this "dictionary" was intended for elementary use as a tool "whereby Persons of the meanest Capacity may attain to Spell and Write *English* true and correctly." (Title-page of the 1731 edition). The preface contains many fine suggestions for spelling reform and for the indication of accent. Dyche will be discussed later in connection with Dyche and Pardon's *New General English Dictionary* of 1735.

Bailey's method of marking accentuation may be illustrated by the following: "di'nner, di'ocese, dire'ct, disabi'lity, disallo'w, disappea'r, disappoi'nt," etc. From this time on, accentuation was indicated in all the Bailey dictionaries; this feature appeared in the *Dictionarium Britannicum* from its publication in 1730, was carried in the *Universal Etymological English Dictionary* from 1731 on, and was, of course, retained in later editions of the second volume.

5 The Orthographical Dictionary has a separate title-page and introduction. In the latter Bailey carefully distinguishes the purposes of the two parts of the work and explains his procedure in regard to usage as follows: "... the chief Design and Use of which [the first part] is to satisfy the Curious from what Original they [difficult words] are derived, and to inform the Unknowing in the meaning of those technical Words or Terms of Art, which so frequently occur, either in Reading or Conversation; but makes no distinction between Words of approv'd Authority, and those that are not: This Second Part consists in a Collection of common and familiar Words in the *English* Tongue, without regard to their Etymologies, &c. and the main design of it is to assist the Ignorant in the Orthography (true Spelling, Writing, &c.) and in the Orthoepia (right Pronunciation); and is design'd for the Assistance of as many of our own Country as want it, and Foreigners....

"To those Words of approv'd Authority and imitable by the Illiterate,

I have prefix'd an *Asterism* (*), and to the others an *Obelisk* (†), and some which I would not determine for or against, I have omitted to prefix any Mark at all, leaving them to be used or not, according to the Judgment of the User: But have, I think, mark'd with (*) as good and approv'd Words, enough to serve for use on any common Occasion.

"But I would not be understood to mean, that those Words to which I have prefix'd an *Obelisk*, are Words not fit to be used at all in writing about Common Concerns, for many of them may be most proper, drawn by the Pen of an accomplish'd Writer intermix'd with an agreeable Stile; but that Persons of a slender acquaintance with Literature should rather content themselves with the use of such Words, the force and significancy of which they know proper and apt to convey their Mind, than to intersperse here and there Words above the reach of their Knowledge, either improperly, or in a Stile which in the whole is low and groveling."

6 The title-page of the second edition contains the following boast: "Illustrated with above Five Hundred CUTS, giving a clearer Idea of those Figures, not so well apprehended by verbal Description."

7 On the curious vogue of the canting language at this time and on the sources and the nature of *The New Canting Dictionary*, see Noyes's "The Development of Cant Lexicography in England," *SP*, XXXVIII, 462-79 (cf. App. II).

8 Bailey died on June 27, 1742 (*Gentleman's Magazine*, XII, 387), and Cox on Feb. 3, 1754 (*ibid.*, XXIV, 95).

9 John E. Bailey and others contributed a series of notes in regard to the Bailey dictionaries to *Notes and Queries* (ser. v, I, 448, 514; II, 156, 258, 514-15; III, 175, 298; VIII, 52-53; ser. vi, III, 141, 161, 269). J. E. Bailey had apparently seen most of the editions of the second volume and describes them briefly (ser. v, III, 509-10). His description of the 1756 volume is, however, misleading, as he says that it has the same contents as the preceding edition; it has, in fact, the same sections, but the make-up of the main part is considerably altered.

We have used the editions of 1727 (Harvard), 1731 (University of Illinois), 1737 (Yale), 1756 (New York Public), and 1760 (Newberry). For other locations of copies of this rare work, see Census.

10 As these editions merely carry Bailey's Introduction from the earlier editions, the title-page is the most explicit statement as to the revision.

11 The *Monthly Review* for 1757 (ser. i, XVII, 82-83) carried a devastat-

ing review of the *Linguae Britannicae vera Pronunciatio;* the reviewer objects that the proposal of teaching pronunciation by book alone is "in its own nature impracticable" and further that "Mr. Buchanan himself [a Scotchman] does not seem a competent judge of English Pronunciation." When Buchanan's *New Pocket-Book for young Gentlemen and Ladies: or, A Spelling-Dictionary of the English Language* appeared later in the same year, the same reviewer (*ibid.*, p. 376) remarked laconically: "For an idea of Mr. Buchanan and his compilations, see . . . [previous reviews] As to his present performance, to say, that it is as well executed, and may prove altogether as useful to the public, the author, and his bookseller, as either of the former, is saying enough." Buchanan was also attacked by William Kenrick in the latter's *New Dictionary of the English Language* (1773).

A more recent authority, Alexander J. Ellis (*On Early English Pronunciation*, London, 1874, Pt. IV, pp. 1050-55), comes to the rescue of Buchanan. Ellis remarks that Kenrick "is particularly severe on his [Buchanan's] Scotticisms, and very unnecessarily abuses his method of indicating sounds. Kenrick himself is not too distinct; . . ." Ellis then performs the feat of printing the "All the world's a stage" speech in parallel columns in phonetic characters according to Buchanan's and Kenrick's systems.

Buchanan was, of course, an innovator in a difficult field. Even Johnson lacked the temerity to attempt much in this department of lexicography. The latter commented in his *Plan of a Dictionary of the English Language* (London, 1747), p. 12, on the baffling variety in the current pronunciation of vowels and proposed to show words of similar sound either by indicating pairs (e.g., *flow, woe; brow, now*) or by quoting a couplet. He later, however, abandoned this idea.

The British Museum Catalogue and the *Cambridge Bibliography of English Literature* credit several works on linguistics and grammar to Buchanan; and A. G. Kennedy's article (*MLN*, XLI, 1926, 388-91) suggested him as the author of the anonymous *British Grammar* of 1762, a point now generally conceded.

12 Much of this material was available soon afterward in the Scott-Bailey folio *New Universal Etymological English Dictionary*, which came out in the same year and appropriated the quotation feature. The Scott-Bailey, however, took only a small percentage of Johnson's quotations and reduced

each to its most pertinent words. The reviser of the supplementary volume in 1756 preferred longer and more numerous quotations.

13 In the following representative section of the vocabulary, for instance, only *Labour* and related forms carry illustrative quotations:

> *L, Labiate, Laboratory, Laboratory Tent, Laborious, Laboriously, Laboriousness, Labour, Labring, Labyrinth of Egypt, Labyrinthian, Lacca, Lachryma Christi, Fistula Lachrymalis, Laciniated, Lacker, Lacker Hat, Lactant, Lactific, Ladanum, Ladder* (several items), *Lade, Ladies* (several items), *Lag, Lagon, Lagotrophy, Laicality,* etc.

14 So we infer from J. E. Bailey's notes (see n. 9 above) and from the data in the British Museum Catalogue.

The numbering of the late editions of this work is not clear. I have described in the text the two issues of the fourth edition (1756 and 1759). According to Bailey (*N & Q,* ser. v, III, 509), there were also two issues of the fifth edition (1760 and 1775). The British Museum Catalogue describes the 1775 volume merely as "a reissue" and lists a "seventh edition" in 1776. Bailey describes the 1775 volume as carrying the same contents as the 1760.

CHAPTER XVI

1 Except for the dedication to Thomas Earl of Pembroke and Montgomery, there is no prefatory matter. The dedication is mainly eulogistic and makes no specific comments on the work.

2 Both George Gordon and Philip Miller were copious writers and acknowledged authorities on their respective subjects.

Gordon (*fl.* 1728) is remembered mainly for the following works: *Remarks on the Newtonian Philosophy,* 1719; *A Compleat Discovery of a Method for Observing the Longitude at Sea,* 1724; and *An Introduction to Geography, Astronomy, and Dialling,* 1726 (second and third editions, 1729 and 1742). He also has a connection with John Harris, author of the *Lexicon Technicum,* as he corrected the second edition of the latter's *Astronomical Dialogues between a Gentleman and a Lady: Wherein the doctrine of the sphere, uses of the globes, and the elements of astronomy and geography are explain'd,* 1729.

Miller was probably the outstanding gardener of his time (1691-1771). He was foreman of the Chelsea Garden, introduced many plants and new methods of cultivation into England, was an early convert to

Linnaeus' system, and wrote many important works on gardening. His *magnum opus* was *The Gardener's Dictionary* of 1731, which reached eight editions in his lifetime and was translated into various languages. His *Gardener's Kalendar* of 1732 also enjoyed numerous editions and translations. For further bibliography, see the *DNB* article and the British Museum Catalogue. It is sufficient for us to note here that Miller was expert not only in botany but in lexicography in his own field.

Obviously the prestige of Bailey's work would be greatly increased by the use of these eminent names, and his work would be improved by whatever actual assistance these experts found time to give it.

Subsequent analysis of the word list in the text will reveal, however, that the new entries (i.e., those which had not previously appeared in the *Universal Etymological English Dictionary* or the second volume) form an inconspicuous part of the whole and are extremely varied in nature. Many of them are merely additional forms of words already included in the octavo Baileys; such routine expansion was probably executed by Bailey himself or under his immediate supervision. The experts in botany and mathematics no doubt revised items in their fields and added others, but their contributions would appear too slight to warrant their being admitted as coauthors on the title-page unless Bailey believed this policy would make effective advertising.

3 The entry on *Gothick Building* quoted above illustrates one of the main reasons for Bailey's popularity, for here as elsewhere Bailey aptly reflects the attitudes of his time.

For other examples of encyclopedic entries, see: *Abstraction, Aesculapius, Aether, Age, Air, Alchymy,* etc.

4 In order to show the proportion and nature of such new items, we cite the following statistics. In 60 words examined from the *L* section, 10 new items appear; these are, however, brief and consist mainly of additional forms of words already present in the octavo volumes (*e.g.,* *Laborant* and *Laborious*). In a section under *M*, 10 of 72 words are new; and these offer considerable variety, including *Masculine Rhymes, Masonry,* and *Mosque,* all of which are discussed in technical fashion and at length. About 20 new items are found in the opening 200 under *K*, including many Oriental terms reflecting a current vogue. Some of these were probably taken from Lewis Morery's *Great Historical, Geographical,*

Genealogical and Poetical Dictionary (1701 edition by Jeremy Collier) and others from the anonymous *Compleat History of the Turks* (London, 1719), the third volume of which contained a dictionary, and other sources.

5 Thomas Lediard (1685-1743) is described by the *DNB* article as "a miscellaneous writer." His career was an interesting one, as he was attached at different times to the staff of the Duke of Marlborough and served apparently as a kind of foreign secretary in Hamburg. He had returned to England by 1732, where he settled in Westminster and was made Surveyor of the Westminster Bridge and Fellow of the Royal Society.

Aside from his assistance in the 1736 edition of Bailey's *Dictionarium Britannicum,* apparently his only philological work was his *Grammatica Anglicana Critica, oder Versuch zu einer vollkommen Grammatic der englischen Sprache,* published in Hamburg in 1725. This work, consisting of 270 pages of discussion of English pronunciation and orthography, was translated in part and studied by Alexander J. Ellis in his *On Early English Pronunciation,* Pt. IV, pp. 1040-49.

Other works by Lediard are amazingly varied and are discussed in the *DNB* account. However, in order to show how colorful a figure Lediard was and to suggest that he may have made contributions outside of the field of philology as well as within it, I cite the following works: *The Naval History of England,* 1735; a translation of [John Terrasson's] *Life of Sethos. Taken from the Private Memoirs of the Ancient Egyptians,* 1732 (the *Cambridge Bibliography of English Literature* describes this work as "a historical novel with a moral purpose and antiquarian interest,... an imitation of Telemachus and the Travels of Cyrus"); *Britannia. An English Opera,* 1732; a translation of J. J. Mascon's *History of the Ancient Germans,* 1737; *A Scheme... for Building a Bridge at Westminster,* 1738, etc.

6 Of the assistants mentioned in the Preface, "Dr. Martin, Professor of Botany," can be identified as John Martyn (as his name is usually spelled), 1699-1768. In early life Martyn practiced as an apothecary, lectured on botany and materia medica, and belonged to a botanical society of which Philip Miller was secretary. He was made Fellow of the Royal Society in 1724 and attended Emmanuel College, Cambridge, for several terms after 1730 but never received his medical degree, though he was

commonly called "Dr. Martyn." In 1732 he was made Professor of Botany at Cambridge; but, as the subject was not popular at the time, he was mainly occupied in later years with medical practice and writing. He made an abridgment of the *Philosophical Transactions* in five volumes, worked on a translation of Virgil with notes from natural history, wrote a *Historia plantarum rariarum*, and other longer works and papers on various topics including the aurora and the earthquake. For further details and bibliography, see the *DNB* article.

The "Rev. Mr. Collier, Rector of Langford near Sarum," was probably the Rev. Mr. Arthur Collier (1680-1732), metaphysician, who occupied the family living of Langford Magna, Wiltshire, from 1704 to his death, when the rectory devolved upon Corpus Christi College, Oxford. Collier was well known as a theological writer and disputant, and conducted a large correspondence on various questions with prominent contemporaries. He is remembered for the following major works: *Clavis Universalis*, 1713; *A Specimen of True Philosophy*, 1730; and *Logology*, 1732. The only difficulty with this identification is that Bailey refers to Collier as if he were still alive; this may, however, have been merely an oversight, and Collier would in any case have been most likely to transmit his suggestions soon after the appearance of the first edition of the *Dictionarium Britannicum* in 1730, when he was closely studying the work. The Rev. Mr. Collier and his family were well known and esteemed, and mention of his assistance would increase the prestige of Bailey's work. For further information on Collier, see Richard C. Hoare's *History of Modern Wiltshire* (London, 1822-1844), II, i, 12-14 and VI, 451-52, and Robert Benson's *Memoirs of the Life and Writings of the Rev. Arthur Collier* (London, 1837).

7 The number of words in this edition is, however, particularly difficult to estimate because of the many long entries and the continual insertion of proverbs.

8 In the 1730 edition these items had been very briefly treated, as follows:
    Little (litel, *Sax.*) small.
    To *Live* (libhan or leofan, *Sax.*) to enjoy Life.

CHAPTER XVII

1 The known editions are as follows: 1st, 1735; 2nd, 1737; 3rd, 1740; 4th, 1744; 5th, 1748; 6th, 1750; 7th, 1752 and 1753; 8th, 1754; 9th, 1758; 10th, 1759; 11th, 1760 and 1761; 12th, 1765; 13th, 1768; 14th, 1771; 16th, 1777; 17th reprinted, 1794; 18th, 1781.

2 For further details and bibliography, see the *DNB* account.

3 For a summary of editions and revisions, see Kennedy, *Bibliography,* p. 206.

4 The double accent was also used in the first edition of Dyche's spelling dictionary (discussed just below in the text) but was discarded in the later editions of that work and was not introduced into the *New General English Dictionary*. The device was, however, revived by Benjamin Martin in his *Lingua Britannica Reformata* of 1749, and will be further discussed in that connection.

5 This work was subsequently entitled *The Spelling Dictionary* and is usually referred to by that title.

6 The seventh edition, which we have not found mentioned elsewhere, is advertised in the 1756 edition of Dyche's *Guide to the English Tongue.*

7 Introduction, A 3v.

8 *Ibid.,* A 2r.

9 *Ibid.* This division of the parts of speech was, of course, not original with Dyche and Pardon but was used elsewhere, especially among logicians. Locke, for example, devotes a chapter of his *Essay concerning Human Understanding* to "Particles" (Bk. III, Ch. VII; A. C. Fraser, ed., Oxford, 1894, II, 98-100). It is, however, debatable whether Dyche and Pardon were actually simplifying grammar for their readers when they adopted this less familiar classification.

10 "A Compendious English Grammar," A 4v. It should be noted, however, that the authors make no great claims for the grammar. It is described in the Introduction (A 3v) as "intended only as a general Hint or Specimen, and not as a critical Treatise upon that Subject; yet I doubt not, but if carefully attended to, especially with the Assistance of a Master, those Persons that never learnt any Thing but English, may as correctly distinguish one Part of Speech from another, and write as good Sense, and coherently, as tho' they had employed a great deal of Time in learning in the common Methods, Latin, &c."

11 Typical definitions will be quoted in the text. The following representative section of the word list illustrates its encyclopedic character: *Megalesia* (Roman festival), *Mela* (surgeon's instrument), *Melcomb* (town), *Melford* (town), *Melilot* (herb), *Melites* (precious stone), *Mellet* (disease in horses), *Melopes* (medical term), *Melos* (medical), *Melpomene, Melters* (workers in a mint), *Melton Mowbray* (town), *Member* (Anatomy), *Membred* (Heraldry), *Membretto* (Architecture), *Memphites* (Egyptian stone), *Mendicant Friar, Mendlesham* (town), *Meni* (ancient goddess worshipped by the Jews), etc.

12 For example, the following items near the beginning of the work come from Calmet: *Ab, Abyss, Aceldama, Adar, Adultery* (in part), *Agape, Age, Ape, Apis, Areopagus, Azymos,* etc.

13 While Chambers obviously used Harris' *Lexicon Technicum* as a basis for many definitions, the items quoted above and many others taken by Dyche and Pardon had not appeared in Harris. The borrowing from Chambers is much heavier than that from Calmet. The following items from the beginning of the alphabet, for example, were based on Chambers: *Abased, Abbess, Abbey, Abbot, Abdication, Abecedarian, Abjuration, Ablactation, Ablaqueation, Ablution, Abolition, Abortion, Acroteria, Adultery* (in part), *Advowson, Adytum, Agate, Alkalization, Allantois, Allerions, Almoner, Alternate, Altimetry, Aludels, Amber Grease, Amercement, Analocism,* etc.

14 It is obvious that Defoe borrowed largely from Collier's revision of Morery (1701) for his *Dictionarium* of 1723. Dyche and Pardon probably knew both works, Morery as a popular encyclopedia and Defoe's *Dictionarium* as a recent work on religion, in which the *New General English Dictionary* shows a lively interest. The following long items near the beginning of the alphabet are found verbatim in Defoe and Morery: *Adamites, Alcoran, Anabaptists, Antichrist, Antinomians, Antitrinitarians, Baal,* etc.

The Harris items are scattered, Harris having been generally superseded as a scientific source by Chambers.

15 This revision may have occurred in the second or third edition (1737 or 1740) which we have not been able to study. The 1744 edition is available in the John Carter Brown Library.

16 For example, in the brief *K* section alone, 22 geographical items were

added in this revision. They thus constitute about one-sixth of the words in that section in the 1744 and later editions.

There are also a few items on countries, which, like those on towns, betray personal judgments. The item on England extends to five and a half columns, beginning: "the best and largest part of the island called *Great Britain,...*" There is no entry on France; but that on Germany begins: "a large, fruitful, and pleasant country of Europe,..." It is, however, amusing that, after discussing the current government, etc., Pardon describes the inhabitants by quoting Tacitus.

17 Pardon did not, however, borrow material from *Cocker's English Dictionary* or follow that work closely in policy. Whereas Pardon deals mainly with British shires and towns, *Cocker's* had included geographical terms of all kinds, both British and foreign. Also, whereas Pardon describes his items from a topographical and economic point of view as for a sight-seer, *Cocker's* stressed historical features, earldoms, etc. The reviser of *Cocker's* had, of course, used different sources. See pp. 82 ff.

18 The item on the *Kraken* is interesting as showing the long survival of such pseudo-scientific material as had appeared in the early seventeenth century dictionaries: "*Kra' ken* (S.) a most amazing large sea animal, seemingly of the crablike form; it is a very rare animal, and a full grown one has never been seen in all its parts and dimensions, but when it rises to the surface, its back or upper part emerges, which seems a mile and a half in circumference."

CHAPTER XVIII

1 This title-page is probably slightly abbreviated. We are quoting it from Wheatley's "Chronological Notices of the Dictionaries of the English Language," *Trans. Phil. Soc.* (1865), p. 248.

2 A passage quoted by Wheatley (*ibid.*) from the preface to the 1739 volume follows the original preface exactly.

3 Wheatley (*ibid.*, pp. 247-48) had not seen the 1735 and 1741 volumes but comments as follows on the 1737 and 1739 volumes: "In the British Museum copy of this work [the 1737 dictionary] is written the following note, 'This book is commonly call'd Defoe's English Dictionary'; this is a mistake, for it was republished in 1739 with the name of J. Sparrow as the author."

4 H. R. Plomer, G. H. Bushnell, and E. R. McC. Dix in their *Dictionary*

of the Printers and Booksellers . . . from 1726 to 1775 (Oxford, 1932), p. 194, make brief mention of Oliver Payne, bookseller at Horace's Head, Round Court, the Strand (the address given on the title-page of the 1737 dictionary). He is said to have been the first bookseller to print catalogues but "got into serious financial difficulties and was adjudged bankrupt in March 1738/9, . . ."

5 H. R. Plomer and his assistants in *A Dictionary of the Printers and Book-sellers . . . from 1668 to 1725* (Oxford, 1922), p. 313, mention Wilcox' long career as extending from 1721 to about 1762. They also recall the interesting fact that Benjamin Franklin, while working near by, was allowed to use Wilcox' stock as a lending library.

6 *Cambridge Bibliography of English Literature*, II, 713.

7 The British Museum Catalogue mentions J. Sparrow as translator of C A de Bonneval's *Complete History of the Wars of Italy* in 1734; and he was one of the three translators of N. A. Pluche's popular work, *Spectacle de la Nature: or Nature Delineated* (second ed., 1740).

8 The items quoted from the common vocabulary of the four dictionaries are consecutive.

9 J. K.'s *New English Dictionary* originally dealt mainly with ordinary words, but in the 1713 revision a considerable body of Biblical names was introduced. The Biblical portions were not identified, however, as they were supposed to be generally known; only the etymological significances of the names were given.

10 While geographical items had appeared in Phillips, Coles, and Bailey, they were first stressed and developed in the revised version of *Cocker's English Dictionary* (1715 and 1724). They were also given great prominence in Dyche and Pardon's *New General English Dictionary*, which appeared in 1735, the same year as the first of these four volumes.

11 In the parallel *L* sections studied, the compiler took 131 of Bailey's 408 items.

12 With this crude definition compare the type commonly found in the spelling books and sometimes used in J. K.'s *New English Dictionary*. See above, p. 73.

13 In this connection it may be of interest to quote a few other attempts of the period to define common animals. Dyche and Pardon define *Cat* as "a common domestick creature of the voracious kind, which has a natural antipathy to the vermin called mice." Martin defines both *Cat*

and *Dog* merely as "a well-known animal." Johnson's definition of *Cat* follows: "A domestick animal that catches mice, commonly reckoned by naturalists the lowest order of the leonine species."

CHAPTER XIX

1 Kennedy (*Bibliography*, pp. 441-42) has a section headed, "Efforts to Improve the Language."

Thomas Birch in his *History of the Royal Society of London* (London, 1756, I, 499, and II, 7) records the following minutes from the meetings of Dec. 7, 1664, and Jan. 18, 1664/5, respectively: "It being suggested, that there were several persons of the society, whose genius was very proper and inclined to improve the English tongue, and partly for philosophical purposes; it was voted, that there be a committee for improving the English language; and that they meet at Sir Peter Wyche's lodgings in Gray's-Inn, once or twice a month, and give an account of their proceedings to the society, when called upon.

"It was ordered, that Dr. Wilkins meet the first time (at least) with the committee for improving the English tongue; and that particularly he intimate to them the way of proceeding in that committee, according to the sense of the council, viz. chiefly to improve the philosophy of the language:..."

H. B. Wheatley in his *Early History of the Royal Society* (Hertford, 1905, pp. 38-39) states that the committee, whose chairman was Sir Peter Wyche, consisted of Dryden, Evelyn, Sprat, Sir Samuel Tuke, and Waller. Of great interest is Evelyn's letter to Sir Peter Wyche (*Diary of John Evelyn*, ed. by William Bray, London, 1906, III, 309-12), wherein Evelyn, who was unable to attend the meetings of the committee, submitted his ambitious proposals for the reform of the language.

2 Henry Morley, ed., *The Earlier Life and the Chief Earlier Works of Daniel Defoe* (London, 1889), pp. 125-26.

3 Temple Scott, ed., *The Prose Works of Jonathan Swift, D. D.* (London, 1907), XI, 14-15.

4 "Dictionary Making in the Early Eighteenth Century," *Review of English Studies*, VII (April, 1931), 210-13.

5 Johnson's comment in his "Life of Addison" (*The Works of Samuel Johnson*, New York, 1903, IX, 161) is as follows: "It is related that he [Addison] had once a design to make an English Dictionary, and

that he considered Dr. Tillotson as the writer of highest authority. There was formerly sent to me by Mr. Locker, clerk of the Leathersellers' Company, who was eminent for curiosity and literature, a collection of examples selected from Tillotson's works, as Locker said, by Addison. It came too late to be of use, so I inspected it but slightly, and remember it indistinctly. I thought the passages too short."

6 In his *Plan of a Dictionary of the English Language* (London, 1747, p. 31), Johnson mentions Pope's interest: "It has been asked, on some occasions, who shall judge the judges? And since, with regard to this design, a question may arise by what authority the authorities are selected, it is necessary to obviate it, by declaring that many of the writers whose testimonies will be alleged, were selected by Mr. Pope; of whom I may be justified in affirming, that were he still alive, solicitous as he was for the success of this work, he would not be displeased that I have undertaken it."

7 Warburton's Preface to the Pope and Warburton edition of *The Works of Shakespeare* (London, 1747), I, xxv.

8 *Plan*, p. 32.

9 George Birkbeck Hill, ed., *Boswell's Life of Johnson* (Oxford, 1887), I, 292.

10 Martin's dictionary has previously attracted little attention except for the considerable notice it receives in P. W. Long's "English Dictionaries before Webster," Bibliographical Society of America *Papers*, IV (1909), 25-43. Long comments (pp. 39-40): "Perhaps the most striking work in its innovations is a small and little-known dictionary by Benjamin Martin, published in 1749." Long then discusses some of the progressive features of Martin.

11 Here and below in our account of Martin, certain resemblances to Edward Cocker in interests and career will be apparent. Both were mathematicians, inventors, and makers of optical and other scientific instruments.

Long (*op. cit.*, pp. 36-37) comments pertinently on the variety of professions from which the early lexicographers came and the effect which this factor had upon the development of the dictionary: "Fortunately, the most varied professions have from time to time contributed to the growth of the dictionary. Thus Cockeram was a gentleman of fashion, Blount a barrister, Phillips a miscellaneous writer educated by his uncle, the poet Milton, Coles a private tutor, Cocker an arithmetician, Kersey and Bailey philologists, Dyche a schoolmaster, Martin an optician and globe maker, Johnson a *littérateur*, Scott (the reviser of Bailey) a doctor, Kenrick a lawyer, Ash a minister, Thomas Sheridan an elocutionist, John Walker an actor,—these will suffice. Only gradually and from such varied sources did precision of definition become extended over the whole body of the vocabulary, and the collection of terms along all these lines become reasonably full."

12 This and subsequent quotations in this paragraph come from the *DNB* account.

13 Martin argues his point at some length and gives several examples, including the following: "Thus to say, the Word *Abominate* is derived from the Latin *Abominatum*, is saying nothing at all; but if the Reader be told that it is derived from two Latin Words, *Ab*, from, and *Omen*, a Sign of Ill-luck by Augury; he will naturally know the true and emphatical Signification of the Verb, *to Abominate*, is, *to fly from*, or *avoid any Thing as ominous*, or *presaging some ill Event*."

14 *Plan*, p. 20.

15 *Ibid.*, pp. 22-24.

16 As examples of alien words Martin gives: "*Item, Omen, Memorandum, Module, Jet d'Eau, Alegro*, &c."; of words "not to be used in common Discourse": "Decapitate, Decease, &c."

Johnson in his *Plan* (p. 7), also proposes to print in italics words "which still continue in the state of aliens, and have made no approaches towards assimilation, ..." This was, however, one of the features of the *Plan* which were not executed in the *Dictionary*.

17 It will be recalled that Bailey used Boyer as one of the sources of the "Orthographical Dictionary," which formed part of the 1727 edition of the *Universal Etymological English Dictionary*, Vol. II. On the other hand, Boyer's dictionary in its various revisions and expansions naturally borrowed material from Bailey, as the outstanding English lexicographer.

Ainsworth was also used by Johnson, who credits him with many definitions.

18 Martin arrived at this definition by combining and arranging material from Boyer and from Bailey's *Universal Etymological English Dictionary* with a slight original contribution.

19 The double accent, it will be recalled, was a device introduced by Dyche in his *Guide to the English Tongue* (1709) and used in his spelling

Dictionary (1723). In later editions of this dictionary, however, the double accent was dropped; nor was it used in Dyche and Pardon's *New General English Dictionary* of 1735.

The purpose of the device was to indicate that a single consonant is doubled in pronunciation; examples from Martin are: "*A"nimal, Mi"croscope, Centri"fugal,*" etc. The notion of numbering syllables ("*Antipodes 4, Cycloid 3,*" etc.) was original with Martin. Both devices are used extensively, though not with complete consistency.

20 An unusual feature of Martin's dictionary is the several pages of copper plates at the end of the book, to which references are given in definitions of mathematical terms throughout the work.

21 The Foster mentioned here is probably the Reverend James Foster (1697-1753), who was widely known as a preacher and a controversialist.

22 *Plan,* p. 11.

23 Johnson speaks of "adjusting" the orthography and the pronunciation, of setting standards in the various departments of lexicography, and, above all, of determining which words are suitable to form part of the English language and which should be discarded. He is indeed the recognized English inheritor and representative of all the schemes for purifying and fixing the language from the Académie française and the Royal Society on. His contemporaries thus interpreted his mission as settling the language, as the French Academicians had tried to settle their language in their *Dictionnaire;* and Johnson apparently originally concurred to some extent in this notion. Indeed in many ways Johnson's *Dictionary* did effect lasting improvements in the language.

Johnson was, however, always reluctantly aware of the inevitable flux of the language, as attested by the following passage in the *Plan* (p. 18), which is a faint precursor of his more emphatic assertion quoted in the text from the Preface written eight years later: "Thus, my Lord, will our language be laid down, distinct in its minutest subdivisions, and resolved into its elemental principles. And who upon this survey can forbear to wish, that these fundamental atoms of our speech might obtain the firmness and immutability of the primogenial and constituent particles of matter, that they might retain their substance while they alter their appearance, and be varied and compounded, yet not destroyed. But this is a privilege which words are scarcely to expect; for, like their author, when they are not gaining strength, they are generally losing it. Though art may sometimes prolong their duration, it will rarely give them perpetuity, and their changes will be almost always informing us, that language is the work of man, of a being from whom permanence and stability cannot be derived."

24 *The Works of Samuel Johnson,* XI, 254-55.

25 Morery's dictionary, which in its revision by J. Collier had been used by preceding lexicographers, had been frequently augmented and reissued in French and English during the intervening years; and geographical items loomed large in the revision.

Most of Martin's entries are mere condensations of facts, but he presents France and Paris with a bias which is especially amusing when we consider that he was probably deriving his material from a French source. For example, the inhabitants of France are said to be "entirely devoted to their prince, though he treats them as slaves" and to be Roman Catholics, though "they seem less devoted to the Pope than any other nation of that communion." Or consider the following excerpt from the item on Paris: "*Paris,* [latitude and longitude] the capital of the kingdom of France, . . . about six leagues in circumference, and consequently stands on more ground than London; but those who have viewed both, are of another opinion; certain it is London is more populous. The houses are built of white hewn stone, and as every nobleman almost has a large palace, with courts and gardens, it must be allowed that these excel every thing of that kind in London. . . . It is an archbishop's see, and university, in which, 'tis said, there are a hundred colleges, tho' there are but fifty-four that bear that name; and of these there are but ten where exercises are performed. . . ."

CHAPTER XX

1 Wheatley ("Chronological Notices of the Dictionaries of the English Language," *Trans. Phil. Soc.,* 1865, pp. 250-51) gives the title-page and part of Dr. Bevis' recommendation. Kennedy, *Bibliography,* Nos. 6239 and 6249; Long, "English Dictionaries before Webster," Bibliographical Society of America *Papers,* IV, 25-43.

2 The *DNB* account of this Dr. Bevis makes no mention of his connection with the *Pocket Dictionary,* probably because it was only a minor occurrence in his crowded career. The British Museum Catalogue, however, attributes the letter to him; and, as he was undeniably the outstanding Dr.

J. Bevis at the time, there seems no reason to doubt his authorship of the letter.

Although Dr. Bevis studied and at various times practiced medicine as a profession, he was best known as an astronomer. He fitted out his own observatory at Stoke Newington in 1738, became a friend and assistant of Edmund Halley, made some important discoveries, and wrote various works on astronomy. He was elected Fellow of the Royal Society in 1765 and, while acting as its foreign secretary from 1766 to 1771, was also made a member of the Berlin Academy of Sciences and a correspondent of that of Paris. The *DNB* account and the British Museum Catalogue record various works; and the *Gentleman's Magazine* (XLI, 523) paid the following tribute to Dr. Bevis at his death on Nov. 6, 1771: "John Bevis, M. D. and F. R. S. in the Middle Temple, whose great abilities were well known to the learned all over Europe."

While Dr. Bevis did not reach the height of his fame until the sixties, he must have been well known at the time of the appearance of the *Pocket Dictionary* for his edition of Halley's *Astronomical Tables* (in Latin in 1749 and in English in 1752) and for his many important observations, including that of the great comet of 1744.

It is significant that the bookseller sought a recommendation of his dictionary from a scientist rather than a literary man. This is, however, in keeping with the past of the dictionary, in which literary men had played little part; with the current interest in science; and with the large scientific vocabulary, which was then considered one of the most important elements in a dictionary.

3 In a well known passage of his *Essay concerning Human Understanding* (Bk. III, Ch. XI, Sec. 25; Fraser, ed., II, 162-64) Locke gives his desiderata for an English dictionary. If this is the passage which Dr. Bevis had in mind, however, his interpretation of Locke's remarks seems to us rather free.

4 The compiler prints a list of abbreviations before his vocabulary and then merely affixes an abbreviation to his definitions, as follows: "*Keep*, [definition] *B*. [British]; Orts, [definition] *T*. [Teutonic]"; etc.

5 Definitions quoted in the text will illustrate these departments. The geographical material, it will be recalled, was added in the revised Dyche and Pardon, which the compiler undoubtedly used.

6 J. Newberry, the exclusive sponsor of the *Pocket Dictionary* in its first

three editions, was also one of the sellers of both editions of Martin's dictionary.

7 It will be recalled that such material was not available in Martin until the revised edition of 1754.

8 The abridged Johnson dictionary seems the easiest and most probable source for the revision of the *Pocket Dictionary*. Similar material was, of course, available in both the Johnson and the Scott-Bailey folios of 1755; but much more abridgment would have been necessary if either of these sources had been used. It is also observable that, where the Johnson and the Scott-Bailey dictionaries diverge, the compiler of the *Pocket Dictionary* seems to prefer Johnson's treatment. For example, the definitions quoted just following in the text from the *Pocket Dictionary* more closely resemble those quoted from Johnson than these from the Scott-Bailey:

> *Aberrance* (...) a straying, erring, or wandring out of the way, an error.
>
> *Abhorrent* (...) 1. That hates, loathes, is averse to, 2. Foreign, or opposite to, inconsistent with.

9 For the locations of these very rare volumes, see the Census.

CHAPTER XXI

1 Except for the simple indication of accent ("*Wárden, Wárdrobe, Wárrantable,*" etc.).

2 Richard Green writes in *The Works of John and Charles Wesley. A Bibliography* (London, 1896, p. 80): "Although Wesley's name does not appear on the title-page or appended to the preface, there is no doubt as to his authorship. He includes it in the lists of books 'published by J. and C. Wesley.'"

3 "John Wesley: Scholar and Critic," *South Atlantic Quarterly*, XXIX (1930), 281.

4 Letter dated July 15, 1764; John Telford, ed., *The Letters of the Rev. John Wesley, A.M.* (London, 1931), IV, 256-58.

5 T. B. Shepherd, *Methodism and the Literature of the Eighteenth Century* (London, 1940), p. 83. Chapter IV of this work (pp. 83-96) discusses the educational and literary publications of Wesley. T. W. Herbert also treats the "Instructional Writings" of Wesley in Chapter XI (pp. 112-20) of his *John Wesley as Editor and Author* (Princeton Studies in English, 1940).

6 Compare Wright, *op. cit.*, pp. 262-63: "While Pope and Johnson held in succession the dictatorship in the narrow circle of letters, Wesley preached salvation and intelligence to the teeming proletariat and lower middle-class. What Wesley said about books meant infinitely more to his followers than did Dr. Johnson's ponderous dicta. Although Wesley left no impress upon the literary development of the age, he did powerfully influence the developing literary taste of a large segment of the British and even of the American public."

7 The Reverend Luke Tyerman takes this position in his *Life and Times of the Reverend John Wesley, M.A., Founder of the Methodists* (New York, 1872, II, 182): "To rightly appreciate this curious publication [the dictionary], it must be borne in mind, that Wesley was now putting into the hands of thousands of the common people extracts from 'the best English writers,' in the numerous volumes of his 'Christian Library.' Hence the necessity he felt of giving to the same readers a compendious dictionary explaining words in that Library, which many, at least, were not likely to understand."

8 H. B. Wheatley in "John Wesley's English Dictionary," *The Bookworm. An Illustrated Treasury of Old-Time Literature* (London, 1888), I, 18.

In his "Chronological Notices of the English Dictionaries" (*Trans. Phil. Soc.*, 1865, p. 250), Wheatley contents himself with the brief condemnation: "Although called a dictionary, it is nothing more than an alphabetical list of words with explanations."

9 Among the less satisfactory definitions are the following:
Coenibites, a sort of monks.
A *Felucca,* a sort of boat.
Literature, learning.
A *Madrigal,* a song.
Pantaloons, a sort of trousers.
A *Weft,* a thing lost, and coming to the lord of the manor.

10 We cite a few sample entries from this large group:
Anodynes, remedies that ease pain.
Ataxy, irregularity.
Cachexy, an ill habit of body.
A *Calenture,* a burning fever.
A *Cataplasm,* a poultis.

Chalybeates, medicines.

Colliquative, causing profuse sweats.

Collyrium, eye-salve.

To *Couch* the eye, to depress a film that covers it.

A *Gland,* a spongy body that separates some humours from the blood.

An *Hectic,* a lingering fever.

Opthalmic, good for the eyes.

The *Tonsils,* the almonds of the ear.

11 For example, *Cadence, Gamut, Gavot, Guitar, Harmony, Lyre, Madrigal, Shawn,* etc.

12 Consider, for example, the following:

Affusion, pouring on.

Assentation, flattery.

Caliginous, dark, misty.

Capitation, a poll tax.

Immarcessible, never-fading.

Procacity, sauciness.

13 This brief note was appended to the address to the reader in the second edition.

14 Green, *op. cit.,* p. 81.

15 Wheatley, *The Bookworm,* I, 17 (see n. 8 above).

16 Green, *op. cit.,* p. 81. It will be observed that Green has elucidated the editions from a bibliographical point of view and that Wheatley has described them from a lexicographical point of view. The latter (*op. cit.,* I, 16-17), owned a copy of the first edition without a title-page and used the second and third editions in the British Museum; this copy of the third edition also had a defective title-page, lacking the date.

    The third edition of 1777 and the "second" of 1790 have been recently confirmed by contributors to *Notes and Queries,* respectively, H. Ll. Davis, CLXXXVII (Nov. 18, 1944), 238-39, and T. Murgatroyd, *ibid.* (Oct. 7, 1944), p. 172. While not bibliographical reprints, these volumes appear to have the same contents as the 1764 edition, except for such minute variants as "A Committee" (1764) and "Committee" (1790).

17 We have studied this work from the only copy that we were able to locate in this country—a copy of the second edition in the Stanford University libraries, Stanford University, California, which provided the facsimile title-page.

CHAPTER XXII

1 For further information see the *DNB* article.
2 The collaborators mentioned (Gordon, Miller, and Lediard) have been discussed above in connection with the *Dictionarium Britanicum*.

For purposes of comparison it may be of interest to subjoin here the relatively simple title of Johnson's dictionary:

A Dictionary of the English Language:
In which The Words are deduced from their Originals, and Illustrated with their Different Significations.
By Examples from the best Writers.
To Which are Prefixed, A History of the Language, and An English Grammar.
By Samuel Johnson, A.M. In Two Volumes. . . .
London, . . . MDCCLV.

3 The examples given are: *Strift* ("a hard and violent Struggle") and *Won* ("dwell").
4 The Scott-Bailey derives many articles from the *Appendix ad Thesaurum* and duly credits that work. The excessive praise of the *Appendix* in the Preface here may be attributed to the fact that the *Appendix*, published in 1745-1746, was compiled by Daniel Scott, half-brother of J. N. Scott's father. This puff was no doubt intended to recall the work to public attention.
5 Philip B. Gove, "Notes on Serialization and Competitive Publishing: Johnson's and Bailey's Dictionaries, 1755," Oxford Bibliographical Society *Proceedings and Papers*, V (1940), 307-22.
6 Gove prints the advertisements of the rival works (*ibid.*, p. 308).
7 Since Gove has stated that the Scott-Bailey derived its prefatory apparatus from Johnson, we need only point out briefly here the nature of the borrowing. The "Historical Account of the English Language" offered in the Scott-Bailey consists of a mere thread of history frequently interrupted by quotations illustrating the state of the language at various periods. Here the plan and many of the quotations are derived from Johnson; some of Johnson's quotations are, however, shortened, and in other cases Scott supplies his own illustrative passages. The "Compendious Grammar of the English Tongue" in the Scott-Bailey is also based on the parallel

feature in Johnson with considerable verbatim borrowing but with some abridgment and some rearrangement of material.

In regard to Gove's estimate of the relative length of these features in the two works, we should comment: (1) that the abridgment is sometimes desirable, since Johnson's long quotations are hardly necessary to prove his points and detract from the continuity of his historical sketch; and (2) that the abridgment cannot in any case be estimated in pages, since the Scott-Bailey uses minute print and crowds much more material on the page.

8 Gove, *op. cit.*, p. 314.

9 *Ibid.*, p. 317. This point will be considered later in connection with the typographical make-up of the work.

10 *Ibid.*, p. 318.

11 *Ibid.*, p. 322.

12 From the Preface to the first abridged edition of Johnson's *Dictionary of the English Language* (London, 1756).

13 Gove notes that Johnson is sometimes credited in the word list but says (*op. cit.*, p. 314): "This occurs too infrequently to constitute even the pretence of an acknowledgement." The blanket acknowledgment in the Preface (quoted in the text above, p. 182) is, however, unusually generous for the time.

Johnson adopts a similar policy toward Junius and Skinner, as explained in his Preface: "For the Teutonic etymologies, I am commonly indebted to Junius and Skinner, the only names which I have forborne to quote when I copied their books; not that I might appropriate their labors or usurp their honors, but that I might spare a perpetual repetition by one general acknowledgment."

14 Johnson probably consulted both editions of the *Dictionarium Britannicum*. It is true that definitions of such words as Johnson used in his word list were usually the same in the 1736 as in the 1730 edition and that the numerous proverbs and technical terms added in 1736 would have hindered rather than helped Johnson. The main advantages to him in consulting the 1736 edition lay in the improved etymology and in the conscientious attempt there made to round out families of words. To be sure Johnson had other etymological sources and was capable of filling out families of words for himself, but he would doubtless wish to have

available for consultation the latest and presumably most accurate edition of his most successful predecessor.

15 Johnson, of course, explains and defends the make-up of his vocabulary in his Preface.

16 "English Dictionaries before Webster," Bibliographical Society of America *Papers*, IV, 32.

17 The items here quoted are practically unchanged in the 1736 edition.

18 Of course, some departments of lexicography had not even appeared by 1755; most notable among these were probably synonymy and the phonetic treatment of pronunciation. Other departments urgently called for improvement. Etymology cried out for a complete revision, definitions were unequal, and grammatical annotations were needed for irregular conjugations, plurals, and comparisons. All of these improvements were, however, to be introduced in some form by the close of the century. Perhaps our most appropriate attitude toward the state of lexicography in 1755 is that of Johnson toward his dictionary as described at the end of his Preface: "In this work, when it shall be found that much is omitted, let it not be forgotten that much likewise is performed; ..."

APPENDIX I

1 *Publications of the Philological Society*, VIII (Oxford, 1921).

2 See Thomas Wright's *Anglo-Saxon and Old English Vocabularies*, second edition, edited and collated by Wülcker (London, 1884). 2 vols.

3 *Ibid.*, I, 106 ff.

4 Reproduced in Wright-Wülcker, pp. 306 ff. The MS, which follows that of Aelfric's *Grammar*, is printed from a copy of MS Cotton, Julius A II, in the British Museum. See the Wright-Wülcker text, p. 306 n.

5 Printed by Wright-Wülcker, pp. 538 ff.

6 Cf. Thomas Wright, *A Volume of Vocabularies* (London, 1857).

7 *Ibid.*, Preface.

8 Also edited by R. P. Wülcker in the second edition of Wright's work (1884), I, 635-813.

9 Printed by W. de Worde, 1510; by Pynson, 1513, 1516, 1519; and by de Worde, 1525, 1531. The *Vulgaria* was printed by de Worde in 1508, 1516, 1518, 1528? See *Short-Title Catalogue*.

10 Quoted from Beatrice White's edition of *The Vulgaria of John Stan-*

bridge and the Vulgaria of Robert Whittinton (Early English Text Society, Orig. Series, No. 187, 1932; Introduction), p. xxv. Horman's *Vulgaria* was reprinted by the Roxburghe Club, 1926. I have not seen a copy.

11 Cf. B. White, *op. cit.,* p. 76.

12 *Ibid.,* p. 55.

13 For information on Paludanus, see the *Biographie Nationale de Belgique.*

14 I have consulted in the British Museum the edition of 1549, which has these words on the title-page: "Dictionariolum Rerum Maxime Vulgarium, in Communem Puerorum Usum, ex optimis quibusque autoribus congestum, cum Flandrica & Gallica interpretatione . . . Gandani. . . . MDXLIX."

15 The dictionary of John of Garland includes many of the groups in the conventional vocabularies, but the method of presentation is similar to that of an interlinear gloss.

16 For this order Withals, of course, had a precedent in the *Promptorium Parvulorum,* the earliest English-Latin dictionary.

17 Copies I have consulted in the British Museum are dated as follows: 1556, 1568, 1574, 1581, 1586, 1599, 1602, 1608, 1616, 1634.

18 The name is taken from Littleton's *Tenures,* the popular work on English law.

19 *The Nomenclator, or Remembrancer* (London, 1585), in Latin, Greek, French, Spanish, and English, by Adrian Junius, a Dutch physician, is in the vocabulary tradition. The influence of this book is more pronounced, however, on seventeenth-century dictionaries than on vocabularies or other nomenclators.

20 The title-page of a copy of the 1611 edition in the British Museum (B. M. C. 33. f. 7) reads thus: "Ianua Linguarum sive Modus Maxime Accomodatus, Quo Patefit Aditus Ad Omnes Linguas Intelligendas . . . Salmantieae Apud Franciscum de Cea Tesa. Anno, M.D.C.XI."

21 For a detailed account of Bathe and his work, see the Reverend T. Corcoran's *Studies in the History of Classical Teaching, 1500-1700* (Dublin and Belfast, The Educational Co., Ltd., 1911). Part I of Corcoran's book treats Bathe and his method of language teaching. In Part III, Appendices, there is additional biographical information in Latin on Bathe.

22 A copy of this edition is in the Rare Book Collection, The University of Texas Library.

23 Corcoran, *op. cit.*, pp. 87 ff. For the author's exposition of Bathe's method of choosing the vocabulary and the plan of presentation, see *ibid.*, pp. 17 ff.

24 On Comenius' life, see S. S. Laurie's *John Amos Comenius, Bishop of the Moravians, His Life and Educational Works* (Syracuse, N. Y., 1882); the same author's *Studies in the History of Educational Opinion from the Renaissance* (New York, 1903); Will S. Monroe's *Comenius and the Beginnings of Educational Reform* (New York, 1900); *Biographie Universelle, Ancienne et Moderne* (Paris, n. d.); and J.-C. Brunet's *Manuel du Libraire* (Paris, 1810).

25 The title-page of the second English edition (1633) reads thus: "The Gate of Tongues Unlocked and Opened, or else A Seminarie or seed-plot of all Tongues and Sciences. That is a short way of teaching and thorowly learning within a yeere and a halfe at the farthest, the Latin, English, French, and any other tongue, together with the ground and foundation of Arts and Sciences, comprised under an hundred Titles, and 1058 Periods ... London ... 1633."

   The University of Texas Library has a copy of the *Janua*, dated 1643, in Latin and English; and also a copy, dated 1682, in Latin, English, and Greek. The plan of presentation is the same in all editions, except the variation as to the number of languages.

26 Editions appeared in England in 1631, 1633, 1637, 1639, 1643, 1662, 1670, etc. At Danzig, in 1634, the *Janua* was printed in Latin, German, Swedish; at Amsterdam, in 1661, in Latin, French, Italian, Spanish, and German; at Amsterdam, 1662, in Latin, French, and Dutch, etc., not to mention all. See Brunet, *Manuel*.

27 In the description of the text I follow Professor Laurie. I have not examined the first edition. The editions of 1639, 1643, and 1662, which I have examined, are substantially the same as to plan and content.

28 The full Latin title is "Orbis Sensualium Pictus: Hoc est Omnium Principalium in Mundo Rerum, & in cita Actionum, Pictura & Nomenclatura." See the reprint (Syracuse, N. Y., Bardeen, 1887), p. x. All page references to the *Orbis* are to this reprint unless otherwise noted.

29 According to *DNB*, editions appeared in 1675, 1685, 1689, 1706 (5th ed.), 1717, 1726, and 1735 (8th ed., Dublin).

30 A copy in the British Museum is dated, conjecturally, 1700. There is no date on the title-page. A third edition bears the date 1713. See Ken-

nedy's *Bibliography*, p. 105, No. 2851. See also Nos. 2855, 2892, 2903, 2916, 5756, 5763, 5766, 5773, 5779, 5794, 5799.

31 1713, 3rd ed.; 1723, 5th; 1745, 10th; 1782, 18th; 1785, 19th; 1797, 21st; 1807, 23rd; 1816, 26th; see Kennedy, *Bibliography*. The University of Texas Library has copies of the 13th and 18th editions.

32 I refer to the title-page of the 1749 edition of *The London Vocabulary*, which I have before me. This statement is not in the British Museum edition of *ca.* 1700. It was probably in subsequent editions, as it is in the 19th, 1785.

33 Ray has 32 chapters; Greenwood, 33. Compare the two works in the chapters on "Fire," for example, and various other topics. Greenwood rearranges.

APPENDIX II

1 Furnivall's Preface to the E. Viles and F. J. Furnivall edition of Awdeley's *Fraternitye of Vacabondes*, Harman's *Caveat*, etc. (Early English Text Society, Extra Series IX, 1869) pioneered with some helpful bibliographical notes on the earlier work concerned with cant. J. C. Hotten's *Dictionary of Modern Slang, Cant, and Vulgar Words* (1859), pp. 147-60, and J. H. Nodal's *Slang and Cant* in W. W. Skeat and Nodal's *Bibliographical List* (English Dialect Society, I, 1877) attempted bibliographies of the field, which were inevitably incomplete and misleading in many respects. Kennedy in his *Bibliography*, pp. 419-24, reworked the field but added little original comment.

W. J. Burke's *The Literature of Slang* (New York Public Library, 1939), pp. 59-97, provides by far the most extensive and accurate list of cant materials and points out several links and borrowings, which I had independently observed. In view of the size of his field, however, Burke limits himself to brief comments on individual works and sometimes makes no comment at all—notably in the case of the important transitional work, the *Canting Academy* of Head. Furthermore, not being primarily interested in dictionaries, Burke does not separate them from other cant materials, present them in strict chronological order (he arranges his items alphabetically within each century), or attempt to trace the development of cant lexicography.

Also helpful are the following: F. W. Chandler's *The Literature of Roguery* (1907), Vol. I; Frank Aydelotte's *Elizabethan Rogues and*

Vagabonds (1913), pp. 114-39; A. V. Judges' *The Elizabethan Underworld* (1930), pp. 491-521; and Eric Partridge's *Slang Today and Yesterday* (1934), pp. 37-75.

2 Furnivall and Viles, *op. cit.*, p. 82. Harman's debt to Awdeley's *Fraternitye of Vacabondes* (1561?) has been adequately treated by Furnivall, pp. i-iv. Although Awdeley had used most of the cant terms, he had furnished no glossary.

3 Only ten years later William Harrison in his *Description of England* (Book III, Chapter V) reported that the vagabonds "are now supposed, of one sex and another, to amount unto above 10,000 persons." The figure, however exaggerated, indicates that the vagabonds were recognized as an increasing and alarming menace to the rest of the population. The cant vocabulary would naturally increase with its spokesmen.

4 Furnivall and Viles, *op. cit.*, p. 87.

5 G. B. Harrison, ed. (1923), pp. 37-39.

6 In *A Notable Discouery* and *The Second Part*, the following terms used by Harman occur: *bong,* a purse; *nip,* a cutpurse; *priggar,* a horse-stealer; and *prancar,* a horse. *The Blacke Bookes Messenger* contains no terms from Harman.

7 The parts that differ from Harman's *Caveat* are reprinted by Viles and Furnivall in their edition of *The Fraternitye of Vacabondes,* etc.

8 Judges, *op. cit.*, p. 511.

9 *Lanthorne and Candle-light* (second ed., 1609), B 4v.

10 *Ibid.*, C 1r.

11 In 1612 the title was *O per se O;* in 1620, *Villanies Discovered;* in 1632, 1638, and 1648 (ninth ed.), *English Villanies.*

12 *Op. cit.*, C 3r.

13 Although this work was formerly attributed to Samuel Rowlands, Aydelotte (*op. cit.*, pp. 133-36) built up such a good case for Samuel Rid as author that his view is now widely accepted.

14 E iv.

15 Chandler, *op. cit.*, I, 205.

16 Such as those mentioned by Furnivall, *op. cit.*, pp. xxi-xxiii.

17 See Chandler, *op cit.*, I, 232-82 on roguery in the drama. Especially notable for interest in cant are the following plays: Middleton and Dekker's *The Roaring Girle* (produced, 1611); Jonson's *Gipsies Metamorphosed* (produced, 1621); Fletcher's *Beggars' Bush* (produced, 1622);

Brome's *A Joviall Crew* (produced, 1641); and Shadwell's *The Squire of Alsatia* (printed in 1688 with a very brief glossary of cant).

18 Aydelotte, *op. cit.*, p. 150.

19 Head, *English Rogue* (1665 ed., rep. 1874?), E 3r; (1667 ed.), E 3r.

20 I have not been able to locate any copy or even any description of the second edition of *The Canting Academy*, 1674. The first edition is also rare and has received no adequate analysis.

21 In the address, "To all sorts of Persons, . . ."

22 *Ibid.*

23 *Ibid.*, pp. 56-57.

24 *Ibid.*, p. 40.

25 A 3v.

26 E. g., *bulk and file, palliard, marinated,* etc.

27 Title-page (1704 ed.). As Edward Cocker, the supposed author, died in 1676 and John Hawkins, the supposed editor, died in 1692, this work was probably a booksellers' compilation.

28 "To the Reader," A 3v (1715, second ed. and 1724, third and last ed.).

29 A 2v. The dedicatory letter is signed "N. H.," but the work was probably the product of a group employed by Dunton.

30 I have seen the thirtieth edition (Glasgow, 1802), which Kennedy (*Bibliography*, p. 229) believes to be the last.

31 *Op. cit.*, p. 68.

32 "Advertisement," p. 1.

33 Burke does not consider Cocker, Dunton, or Johnson in relation to cant.

34 Among other estimates, Kennedy (*Bibliography*, p. 420) gives the date as 1690; and Burke (*op. cit.*, p. 65), by ingenious reasoning from the printers' careers, 1698. The Yale Library has a copy bearing the date 1699, the last figure being very slightly blurred.

35 B. E., *A New Dictionary*, B 4r.

36 A 6r-v.

37 *Ibid.*, B 2v.

38 A 2r.

39 Title-page.

40 Burke (*op. cit.*, p. 75) indicates the dependence of *The Scoundrel's Dictionary* on *The Triumph of Wit* but offers no comment on the sources of the latter.

41 The section called "An Interpretation of the Several Qualities of Rogues" was reprinted by Raymond Postgate in his *Murder, Piracy and Treason. A Selection of Notable English Trials* (1925), pp. 239-42.

42 A 2v.

43 Burke does not discuss Hall's glossary.

44 The glossary is reprinted by Posgate, *op. cit.*, pp. 233-38.

45 *Ibid.*, p. 235.

46 *DNB.*

47 P. ix.

48 Vol. II, Chap. I, pp. 1-181.

49 P. 122.

50 *Ibid.*, pp. 136-80.

51 *Ibid.*, pp. 151-53.

52 *Ibid.*, pp. 159-60.

53 *Ibid.*, pp. 144-47.

54 Parker appears not to have used Grose as a source, as he treats expressions that do not occur in Grose and develops in greater detail expressions dismissed briefly by Grose.

55 *Classical Dictionary* (1785 ed.), pp. iii-iv.

INDEX

Abcedarium Anglo-Latinum, 2, 256
Académie française, 147, 273
Addison, Joseph, design for a dictionary, 147-48, 270-71; mentioned, 160
Aelfric, Abbot of Eynsham, 198, 281
Aesop, 209
Ainsworth, Robert, *Thesaurus Linguae Latinae Compendiarius,* Martin's use of, 152, 155-56, 157, 163; used by Johnson, 272
Alvearie, An, 2, 242, 256
Arrowsmith, W. R., 65
Ascham, Roger, 6
Ash, John, 272; *The New and Complete Dictionary,* 214, 221
Avicenna, 21
Awdeley, John, *Fraternitye of Vacabondes,* 215, 284, 285; mentioned, 217
Axon, W. E. A., "English Dialect Words of the Eighteenth Century," 86

Bacchus and Venus, 214, 224
Bacon, Francis, Viscount St. Albans, 43, 44, 46
Bailey, Nathan, *Dictionarium Domesticum,* 99, 253, *Dictionarium Rusticum, Urbanicum, & Botanicum,* 99, 252-53; editions of Ovid's *Metamorphoses* and *Tristia,* 99, 111; trans. of Erasmus' *Colloquies,* 99; *Divers Proverbs with their Explications,* etc., 257; mentioned, 69, 89, 114, 127, 148, 163, 173, 193, 194, 260, 263, 271
—*Dictionarium Britannicum,* 117-25 and notes; importance in history of English lexicography, 117; title-page, 117-18; relation to *Universal Etymological,* both volumes, 118-20; special features, 118-20; in second edition, additions, 120-22;

other miscellaneous features, 122-25; culmination of Bailey's career, 125; and Dyche and Pardon, 131-32; and Martin, 154-58; and Johnson, 184-89 and notes; mentioned, 99, 108, 112, 146, 181, 194, 252, 254, 257, 279
—*An Universal Etymological English Dictionary,* 98-107 and notes; successor of Kersey and forerunner of Johnson, 98; professional attitude towards lexicography, 99; prominent features of title-page, 99-100; introductory history of the language, 100; size of vocabulary, 100; interest in etymology, 100-2; borrowing from *Dictionarium Anglo-Britannicum,* 102-3; other borrowings, 103; obsolete expressions, 104; proverbs, 104-6; editions and revisions, 106-7; the representative eighteenth-century dictionary, 107; and second volume, 108-16; and *Dictionarium Britannicum,* 118-20, 121, 122, 124; and four identical dictionaries, 142-43; and Martin, 151, 154-55; summary of features, 193-94; cant terms in, 221; source for Chatterton, 255-56; mentioned, 75, 86, 89, 117, 129, 131, 151, 167, 173, 251, 252, 253, 263
—*An Universal Etymological English Dictionary,* Vol. II, 108-16; erratic supplement to first volume, 108-9; miscellaneous contents, 109-10; stress on illustrations and aids to pronunciation, 110; other features, 110-12; expansion of vocabulary in second edition, 112; stress on cant in third edition, 112-14; further editions after Bailey's death, 114-16; Buchanan's revision, borrowing from Johnson, 104-16; relation to first volume, 120; mentioned, 94, 117, 118, 194, 221, 259, 263